SMALL WORLD

Seamus Deane was one of the most vital and versatile authors of our time. *Small World* presents an unmatched survey of Irish writing, and of writing about Irish issues, from 1798 to the present day. Elegant, polemical, and incisive, it addresses the political, aesthetic, and cultural dimensions of several notable literary and historical moments, and monuments, from the island's past and present. The style of Swift; the continuing influence of Edmund Burke's political thought in the USA; the echoing debates about national character; aspects of Joyce's and of Elizabeth Bowen's relation to modernism; memories of Seamus Heaney; analysis of the representation of Northern Ireland in Anna Burns's fiction – these topics constitute only a partial list of the themes addressed by a volume that should be mandatory reading for all those who care about Ireland and its history. The writings included here, from one of Irish literature's most renowned critics, have individually had a piercing impact, but they are now collectively amplified by being gathered together here for the first time between one set of covers. *Small World: Ireland, 1798–2018* is an indispensable collection from one of the most important voices in Irish literature and culture.

Seamus Deane was a founding director of the Field Day Theatre Company, editor of the annual journal *Field Day Review*, the general editor of the Penguin Joyce, a member of the Royal Irish Academy, and the author of several books, including *A Short History of Irish Literature*; *Celtic Revivals: Essays in Modern Irish Literature*; *The French Revolution and Enlightenment in England*; and *Strange Country: Modernity and Nationhood in Irish Writing since 1790*. Deane also edited the monumental *Field Day Anthology of Irish Writing* in three volumes, and wrote four books of poetry and a novel, *Reading in the Dark*, which has been translated into more than twenty languages and was shortlisted for the Booker Prize in 1996. After a lengthy career at University College Dublin, he was Professor of English and Donald and Marilyn Keough Professor of Irish Studies Emeritus at the University of Notre Dame.

SMALL WORLD

Ireland, 1798–2018

Seamus Deane

University of Notre Dame, Indiana

CAMBRIDGE
UNIVERSITY PRESS

University Printing House, Cambridge CB2 8BS, United Kingdom

One Liberty Plaza, 20th Floor, New York, NY 10006, USA

477 Williamstown Road, Port Melbourne, VIC 3207, Australia

314–321, 3rd Floor, Plot 3, Splendor Forum, Jasola District Centre, New Delhi – 110025, India

79 Anson Road, #06–04/06, Singapore 079906

Cambridge University Press is part of the University of Cambridge.

It furthers the University's mission by disseminating knowledge in the pursuit of education, learning, and research at the highest international levels of excellence.

www.cambridge.org
Information on this title: www.cambridge.org/9781108840866
DOI: 10.1017/9781108892810

First published 2021
Reprinted 2021

Printed in the United Kingdom by TJ Books Limited, Padstow Cornwall

A catalogue record for this publication is available from the British Library.

ISBN 978-1-108-84086-6 Hardback

TO CIARAN AND CORMAC

Contents

Foreword

Since the 1970s, Seamus Deane has been Ireland's most notable literary critic. Over a career spanning half a century, he has been a literary and intellectual historian, a critical essayist, gifted lecturer, anthologist, poet, novelist, theatre company board member, institution-builder, journal editor, and book publisher. He is among modern Ireland's most distinguished public intellectuals. Few twentieth-century writer-critics – William Butler Yeats, Daniel Corkery, Seán Ó Faoláin – have done as much as he has done to reshape the ways in which we comprehend modern Irish literary culture, and none of these, even Yeats, has so wide an intellectual scope of reference as Deane. Educated in Northern Ireland and at the University of Cambridge, where he studied the reception of the French Enlightenment and Revolution in early nineteenth-century English letters, he began his career by teaching Irish literature in Reed College, Oregon, and the University of California at Berkeley before then returning to Ireland, to University College, Dublin (UCD), where, reversing roles, he taught American and English literature. In mid-career in 1993, he returned again to the United States to head the newly founded Keough-Naughton Institute for Irish Studies at the University of Notre Dame, Indiana, until his retirement, teaching part of the year in the United States, part in Dublin.

In his formative disciplinary commitment to French and English intellectual history, Deane's work was from early on unusually internationalist by Irish standards. It was later deepened by extensive reading in Frankfurt School critical theory, Western Marxism, postcolonial studies, and French poststructuralism. Nevertheless, despite this uncommon critical reach, Deane's work has often been tagged in obtuse misreadings as narrowly and rebarbatively 'nationalist'. Few Irish critics or historians have in fact been more vigilantly attentive to the antinomies of cultural nationalism than Deane, so the application of the term 'nationalist' to his career is therefore a misnomer, though by no means simply an error. Raised in the 1940s and 1950s in the nationalist and republican Bogside district of the then unionist-controlled city of Derry, Deane maintained throughout the Troubles commitments of a kind sufficiently out of step with the political views that then dominated the university, literary, and media worlds of Dublin and Belfast as to make him seem unamenable to 'right thinking' and by such a measure he was deemed perforce a 'nationalist' or 'republican'. Hence, the apparent paradox that Ireland's most European-minded literary critic has also appeared throughout his career in his home country as both a presiding intellectual presence and something of an aloof or isolated déraciné.

Nevertheless, Deane's accomplishments were not, of course, achieved in isolation. He came of age professionally in a period in the late 1960s and early 1970s when Irish society was convulsed by the Troubles in the North, by American corporatization and political Europeanization in the South, and by a variety of social movements, most notably the women's movement, that eventually exerted considerable force on both parts of the island. In this context, as Irish academics of the less timorous variety were called out of their habitual professional routines, several literary critics, historians, and economists became, for a few decades at least, public intellectuals of some significance. Furthermore, Irish academia in this period produced literary criticism of a higher order than the country had witnessed since independence. Because of the under-resourced and tightly self-policed character of the Irish university system, many of this generation of literary critics spent much of their careers overseas, most working in the United Kingdom or the United States, ably connecting Irish studies to emergent cultural critical currents internationally.

Given his evident early-career brio, Deane soon found himself called upon to positions of leadership in this contentious period. He joined Brian Friel, Stephen Rea, Seamus Heaney, Tom Paulin, and David Hammond to become part of the directorial board of the Field Day Theatre Company, which Friel and Rea had founded in 1980 to produce one of Friel's landmark works, *Translations*. Thomas Kilroy, playwright and professor of English in Galway, later joined that board in 1988, the only southern-born writer to do so. As is now well known, Field Day quickly became one of the most unlikely and innovative intellectual groupings of its kind in the English-speaking world, combining a literary-intellectual theatre of note with a commitment to critical thinking and public debate. In a country where things 'literary' and 'intellectual' were generally quarantined off from each other, and where anything that resembled ambitious analytical thinking was typically treated with suspicion, the cooperation of figures like Friel and Rea, Heaney and Paulin, or Deane and Hammond, represented a new departure not only in terms of the crossing of sectarian Northern Irish community boundaries but also of literary/intellectual lines. While sceptical Irish commentators at the time tried to pinpoint where precisely Field Day stood on 'the national question', as if this were the only thing that mattered about the grouping, the declaration of intent intrinsic to the company's constitutive composition was obvious. Field Day was compositionally anti-sectarian and non-doctrinaire yet in Deane's version at least it was also unapologetically republican-minded and hostile to the notion, as firmly rooted in Ireland as in England, that the 'Celtic temperament' was inherently lyrical and imaginative rather than critical or practical, let alone political or theoretical.

Deane's early immersion in the French Enlightenment of Rousseau, Diderot, and d'Holbach, and in early nineteenth-century radical English republican writers such as Hazlitt and Shelley, had made him inherently suspicious of British and Irish romanticisms and bequeathed to him a strong appreciation of the conservative functions they could serve. For him, the achievement of Edmund Burke, as political thinker and rhetorician, equalled only by that of Rousseau in Europe, remained exemplary, and, as far as Irish writing was concerned, foundational. The liberal cultural nationalist tendencies favoured by Heaney or Friel, or the secular republicanism of Paulin or Rea, helped identify Field Day as an aspirationally civic republican group in its ambition to create not so much a new Ireland as a more robust public sphere that might eventually nurture the vision and thinking that the creation of any new Ireland would certainly require. In the Irish Republic, however, Field Day was taken by many to represent northern Irish republican pretensions to advance a third 'Irish revival' that no longer assumed Dublin as its capital nor the Abbey Theatre as its Bayreuth, while in unionist Northern Ireland the Derry-based company was viewed as an unsolicited Greek gift lodged ominously inside Londonderry's Trojan walls.

In the 1980s, Field Day won a considerable reputation as a creative and combative theatre company. The combativeness was mainly associated with Deane's pamphlets, 'Civilians and Barbarians' (1983) and 'Heroic Styles: The Tradition of an Idea' (1984) – both collected in this volume – though the edgier political tones of Heaney's 'An Open Letter' (1983) and Paulin's 'A New Look at the Language Question' (1983) caused some to worry that Deane's republicanism was beginning to warp even the more moderate-minded group members. 'Civilians and Barbarians' provoked because it suggested that the discourses of civility and savagery inherited from the Tudor and Stuart settlements continued to fashion both Irish and British understandings of the Troubles and of the Hunger Strikes more particularly. 'Heroic Styles' offered a critique of varieties of what Deane styled, in a provocative phrase, 'literary unionism', this associated with Yeats and other writers who traced their literary influences chiefly to English sources and had set their faces against modernity and what they saw as its mass-democratic vulgarities. However, in the same pamphlet Deane also diagnosed in Joyce's later works an aestheticized expression of a liberal pluralism that anticipated the post-political consumer culture Deane associated with the contemporary Irish republic and the postmodern condition generally. These were widely considered harsh estimates of both writers and appeared to ask too much of literature and the arts at a time when they were held by most commentators to be valiantly sustaining the human spirit and some precarious sense of Irish decency assailed by the vicious Northern strife. However, Deane's scholarship continued to insist on the tentacular complicities of literature and politics, exempting neither writers nor the cultivated classes generally from their contributions to the histories that conditioned a conflict they loudly abhorred. From Deane's perspective, the assumption that writers could create a serious literature by playing the role of irenic inter-communal mediators or simply by condemning violence was inadequate; something more was called for from the arts and universities. Even if it was far from obvious what that envisaged 'more' might be, some intellectual determination to search out that 'more' was precisely what Deane demanded of himself, of Field Day, and of Irish writers and critics more generally.

The publication of *The Field Day Anthology of Irish Writing*, Volumes I–III, in 1991 has passed into Irish cultural lore as both culmination and catastrophe for the Field Day project. Under Deane's general editorship, the volumes assembled Irish writing in a diversity of modes in Latin, Irish, and English over a period of some fifteen hundred years. This project reached beyond the theatre company members proper to collaboratively include other scholars and specialists not affiliated with Field Day who offered short introductory essays to sections of the *Anthology* covering periods and genres of writing from the Middle Ages to the contemporary moment. Looking back with the hindsight of thirty years, the *Anthology* project now seems in some respects very much of its time: most of the section editors were male, as were all of the Field Day Theatre Company members, and the representation of women's writings was inadequate. In other respects the *Anthology* appears to be struggling methodologically – ably or weakly depending on one's view – with the critical conundrums of its moment. On the one hand, it tried to find some way to accommodate a plurality of conflicting micro-histories to what Deane called in his introduction a 'hospitable metanarrative' capable of concatenating without suppressing its constituent parts; on the other hand, it tried to avoid making inclusivity its only governing principle in some postmodernist fashion. These were difficult ambitions to coordinate. However, on publication the volumes were dismissed from a Northern unionist perspective as just the latest version of an 'assimilationist' nationalist agenda, a belated cultural relay of the Dublin-based New Ireland Forum a decade earlier. More damagingly, many, though not all, feminists dismissed the anthology as a throwback to a time when the issue of gender equality was subordinated to the national imperative. The charge was that Deane and Field Day were so fixated on Northern Ireland that they had overlooked the struggles to liberalize and modernize the Irish Republic led by the women's movement and others since the sixties. Deane immediately conceded the project's deficiencies on this count and set about raising funding for a further two volumes of women's writings, this latter venture published as *The Field Day Anthology of Irish Writing: Irish Women's Writing and Traditions* (2002).

For all the furor that attended its early reception, the *Anthology* seems in retrospect neither culmination nor catastrophe though certainly a defining turning point for all involved. For Deane personally, the *Anthology*'s hostile reception coincided with his move from UCD to the University of Notre Dame, a move that would soon see him publish a novel, *Reading in the Dark*, which was shortlisted for the Booker Prize in 1996, and become, with financial support from Notre Dame, the general editor of the Field Day Critical Conditions series. The Field Day Company generally was changing anyway as its members went on to new stages in their careers; Seamus Heaney, for example, won the Nobel Prize for literature in 1995 and became Poet in Residence at Harvard University in 1998. What has often gone unremarked in subsequent comment on the controversies is the extent to which Volumes I–III represented an actualization of Deane's call for the creation of a more engaged national critical community responsive to its wider society, a call that had unintended consequences when the *Anthology*'s neglect of women scholars and writers also mobilized feminist literary critics to decisive collective action. The five Field Day volumes taken collectively can be said to have recalibrated conceptions of 'Irish writing' more decisively than any other equivalent contemporary enterprise of its kind managed to do. Indeed, when measured against today's more professionalized and pacified Irish university system, one where only historians and economists now seem to attract much attention as public commentators, the company's mobilizations of writers and critics during those decades seems to mark a short-lived moment of commendable public-facing literary scholarship. That Field Day had its weaknesses – especially its failure to address questions of gender and sexuality or capitalism and class as persistently as those of state violence and imperialism – cannot be denied. Yet whatever faults might be laid at its door, Field Day in its heyday must be credited for making a real attempt to stir things up intellectually and culturally in Ireland.

Deane's organizational abilities in these decades should be acknowledged, and in the years since his professional retirement no comparable figure has emerged to play some similar coordinating function. As mentioned earlier, his role in contemporary Irish culture might on these grounds alone be compared to that of Yeats during the Revival or Seán Ó Faoláin during the meridian of *The Bell* in the 1940s. Pamphlets, anthologies, small magazines, and publishing ventures have typically been essential outlets for such cultural movements and Deane, as already noted, has worked his way through many such forms. Nevertheless, he could only play such a leading role because he was by then widely acknowledged to be the most versatile critic of his generation. Key critical essays – on Burke and the French philosophes, Voltaire, Joyce, Ford Madox Ford, Conrad, J. M. Synge, Austin Clarke, Sean O'Casey, John Banville, Yeats, and others – had appeared from the late 1960s onwards. Deane's first three books were published in quick succession in the mid-1980s, each displaying different strengths: *Celtic Revivals: Essays in Modern Irish Literature, 1880–1980* (1985); *A Short History of Irish Literature* (1986); and *The French Revolution and Enlightenment in England, 1789–1832* (1988).

The French Revolution and Enlightenment in England, 1789–1832 is the last in this sequence of publications but, as the subject of Deane's doctoral dissertation, the earliest in conception. Though still little discussed in most accounts of his work, it nonetheless remains foundational to Deane's formation and to all of his subsequent critical writing. The volume offers an overview of how British writers interpreted the French Enlightenment and Revolution against the backdrop of the Terror and the rise and fall of Napoleon, these events welcomed by few and feared by many in Britain as likely to foment a second revolution in that state as the United Irish insurrection had attempted to do in Ireland. Deane's focus is on the intellectual careers of Edmund Burke, James Mackintosh, Samuel Taylor Coleridge, William Godwin, Percy Bysshe Shelley, and William Hazlitt, though there are slighter cameos also of William Wordsworth, Robert Southey, John Wilson Croker, Francis Jeffrey, Thomas Holcroft, Thomas Paine, and Joseph Priestley. The study teases out how the main figures here engaged conceptually with some of their leading French counterparts including Jean Jacques Rousseau, Montesquieu, Baron d'Holbach, La Mettrie, Helvétius, and others. It examines instances of the intricate relay of ideas of freedom and liberty as they migrated from England into the works of the eighteenth-century French philosophes and then travelled from there back to nineteenth-century England, where French writings were rejected or reabsorbed by some of the leading English writers of the apocalyptic years between Burke's late career and those that ended the first Romantic generation.

One of the book's major claims is that, despite their political and intellectual antagonisms, British writers, conservative and radical alike, came, with few exceptions, to attribute the degeneration of the French Revolution and the Napoleonic dictatorship to the defects of French national character and to assign the apparent successes of the Glorious Revolution to the assumed superiority of British national character. From this standpoint, Parisian intellectual life was volatile and irreligious, French sexual manners shocking and scandalous, and the effect of centuries of Catholicism had inclined the French in favour of the despotism that Napoleon finally embodied. Whiggish and radical Protestant England and Ireland initially welcomed the Revolution because it had seemed to signal an astonishing triumph by the French over their Catholic and absolutist inheritances. However, as the Revolution faltered, the already long-standing views of the contrasting French and English national characters were updated and refined to 'explain' developments in contemporary history. An excessive reliance on 'theory', ideology, and abstract thought, a lack of respect for the gravity of settled custom, the vanity of the intellectuals, and the venality of the owners of both the old and the new wealth were all blamed for the disaster in France. In this propaganda war, a conception of a stable and loyal British national character, the antithesis of innovative brilliance and irresponsible experiment, became one of the most effective weapons in the counter-revolutionary arsenal. As a companion piece to this counter-revolutionary conception of Britishness, there was to hand an equally useful portrait of Irish national character. Deane's work suggested that this weaponized conception of Englishness, eloquently elaborated by Burke, Coleridge, and Wordsworth, subsequently taken up by Matthew Arnold and others, and later outfitted with race theory, became one of the foundational supports for British political thought and literature for over a century to come. Ireland was inevitably affected by ideas that were current among intellectuals and writers in Britain; indeed, *Celtic Revivals* and *Strange Country* would propose that these ideas of national character, reworked in Irish conditions, would become formative to nineteenth- and twentieth-century Irish cultural life and literature also.

Celtic Revivals: Essays in Modern Irish Literature, 1890–1980 is possibly Deane's signature work. A slim volume of fourteen essays, it runs to less than two hundred pages. Its longest essay, 'Joyce and Stephen: The Provincial Intellectual', is scarcely seventeen pages; most individual pieces are little more than ten pages each. The opening chapter on 'Arnold, Burke and the Celts' looks back to the first Celtic revival in the late eighteenth and early nineteenth centuries. This revival was associated in Scotland with Macpherson's Ossian forgeries of 1760 and then taken up in Ireland with Charlotte Brooke's *Reliques of Irish Poetry* (1789), Edward Bunting's *The Ancient Music of Ireland* (1796), and the first volume of Thomas Moore's *Irish Melodies* (1808). Chapters 2 to 9, the book's core section, deal with the late nineteenth- and early twentieth-century Irish Revival, and engage with Yeats, Synge, Joyce, O'Casey, and Beckett. The final section running from Chapters 10 to 14 is the shortest of all; it gingerly assesses then leading contemporary writers Thomas Kinsella, John Montague, Derek Mahon, Brian Friel, and Seamus Heaney. The stress on writers from the northern part of the country in this final sequence caused some commentators to speculate whether Deane was quietly proposing a third 'Northern Revival' in his own day, one to which Field Day was offering itself as the directive intellectual light.

The essays in *Celtic Revivals* include many stylishly succinct and arresting insights. '*Portrait* is the first novel in the English language in which a passion for thinking is fully presented: *Ulysses* is the first novel in which the activity of thought is the central concern and the determining influence on the form' ('Joyce and Stephen: The Provincial Intellectual', 75–6).[1] '[Yeats's] abhorrence of the neutralization of death in the middle-class consciousness led him towards disciplines and interests in which the notion of death was pre-eminent and the contemplation of it a crucial activity' ('Yeats and the Idea of Revolution', 41). 'Ireland, with its dead language, its deadening politics, its illiberal legislation, is the historical correlative of the personal state of nirvana-nullity for which Beckett's people crave. Silent, ruined, given to the imaginary, dominated by the actual, it is the perfect site for a metaphysics of absence' ('Joyce and

Beckett', 130). 'People talk themselves into freedom. No longer imprisoned by sea or cottage, by age or politics, Synge's heroes and heroines chat themselves off stage, out of history, into legend' ('Synge and Heroism', 58). On Heaney's 'A Lough Neagh Sequence': 'That sibilant sensuousness, however spectacular, is not devoted entirely to description. It gives to the movement of the eel an almost ritual quality, converting the action into a mysterious rite, emphasizing the sacral by dwelling so sensually on the secular' ('Seamus Heaney: The Timorous and the Bold', 177). No single volume of essays on Irish writing since Yeats had matched such elegant expression with such intellectual dash nor so deftly probed so many senior reputations with such easy authority. A series of lightning critical forays from Burke and Arnold to Mahon and Heaney, *Celtic Revivals* delivered its assessments with a debonair aplomb that bordered on insolence.

What *Celtic Revivals* lacks is an overview, a combinatory or totalizing metanarrative. In his *Short History of Irish Literature* (1986), the introduction to *The Field Day Anthology of Irish Writing* (1991), and again in *Strange Country* (1995), Deane would strive to find that metanarrative. The last of these works is his most ambitious attempt to do so. For admirers of *Celtic Revivals, Strange Country* can seem a strange book. Gone are the earlier volume's tautly compact chapters, gone the single-author studies or author pairings ('Arnold, Burke and the Celts', 'Joyce and Beckett'), gone too any engagement with contemporary Irish literature beyond Beckett, the earlier sketches of Deane's contemporaries such as Heaney, Friel, Kinsella, and Mahon nowhere now in sight. On second look, though, *Strange Country* is not so much some wholly new departure for Deane as a complex reshuffle of earlier concerns and, bringing to harvest his labours as author of the *Short History* and general editor of the *Field Day Anthology*, a widening out of his conception of 'writing'. The chronicle mode of *A Short History of Irish Literature*, with its steady march through centuries and expected forms, is replaced, therefore, and the more exclusive focus on the great tradition of Irish 'literary' writers in *Celtic Revivals* is downgraded. As Deane's works so often do, *Strange Country* begins with Burke and the Romantic reaction against the French Enlightenment, but it ends not with contemporary Irish literature but with T. W. Moody, F. S. L. Lyons, Louis Cullen, and Irish historiographic revisionism. In this new conspectus, a political thinker like Burke can be orchestrated with a literary one like Edgeworth or an antiquarian music collector like James Hardiman; novelists like Gerald Griffin or Bram Stoker and poets like Thomas Moore or James Clarence Mangan appear alongside national political campaigners like Thomas Davis, John Mitchel, or Michael Davitt; Yeats features in counterpoint to a critic like Daniel Corkery; and mid-twentieth-century writers like Patrick Kavanagh or Flann O'Brien are discussed as unlikely aesthetic correlatives to the later twentieth-century revisionists with which *Strange Country* closes.

This sinuous narrative weave offers unpredictable prismatic perspectives: here, writers of different denominations, modes, and political persuasions throw curiously angled light on each other, the greater and lesser figures emerging into view as though glimpsed in some distorting gallery of mirrors. The competing and contested conceptions of 'Ireland' and 'Irishness' their writings produce are never gathered into a seamless 'tradition' but neither can they be cleanly separated from each other. *Strange Country* does not offer a new history of Irish writing in any conventional sense so much as a spiralling critical genealogy of the different ways in which writers have drawn on British, European, and Irish discourses to produce competing 'Irelands' amenable to their ambitions. If the expected literary geniuses no longer dominate the foreground in *Strange Country* as they had done in *Celtic Revivals*, this is because for *Strange Country* discourses make and constrain writers as much as writers make or manipulate discourses. One of *Strange Country*'s dominant arguments, taking its cue from Daniel Corkery's *Synge and Anglo-Irish Literature* (1931), is that Irish writing since Burke has relied on a rhetoric whereby Ireland appears as attractively or dangerously aberrant to an English modernity deemed normative. From a conservative Romantic perspective, Ireland might be saluted as an exceptional and enchanted place precisely because it had remained non-modern and had not therefore succumbed, though it always appeared to be about to do so, to the alienated conditions of industrialism, secularism, mass democracy, and an atomized individualism characteristic of England in particular and the Western world more generally. From a nineteenth-century liberal rationalist perspective, though, Irish conditions of mass poverty, sectarian strife, and excesses of violence, drink, emotion, or self-expression could be ascribed to this same non-modernity, the cure for which was a steady diet of reform and improvement on the English model. In either case, the aberrance of Irish reality was taken to be axiomatic and the very notion of a distinctive Irishness came to rely in time on this sense of the country's persistent strangeness to modernity. In their different ways, British and Irish writers collusively shared this sense of an estranged Ireland, some seeing in that strangeness fertile literary resource, others a rebarbative foreignness to be tamed.

For some Irish Revivalists such as Yeats, Ireland's non-modern strangeness was its most seductive quality and, by combating the Western modernity that threatened to obliterate it, Ireland could nurture both a heroic national literature and a valiant national destiny. However much they might be at odds otherwise, Yeats's vision for Ireland and that of the Irish Catholic Church converged on these grounds at least. For writers like Joyce, however, what defined Ireland was not its non-modernity but its belatedness and spiritually impoverished version of modernity, legacies of its intellectual subjection to the twin forces of British imperialism and Italian Catholicism. Viewed thus, Ireland was in a squalid condition that the writer might record with levels of formal brilliance and naturalistic exactitude so demanding as to represent in itself a contrasting heroism. For Deane, it was, surprisingly, this Joycean modernist commitment to the ordinary, the everyday, and the mundane that had proved the greater force in twentieth-century Irish writing, one far more persistent than Yeats's romanticism or heroic styles.

After the energies of the Irish revolutionary period, revivalism and high modernism had all run down, several mid-century Irish writers (Beckett, Kavanagh, Flann O'Brien in their different ways) had abjured not only the idea of a heroic Ireland – itself a notion absurdly out of sorts with the conservative and quietest Catholic Free State they knew – but also the idea of a heroic literature of either Joycean or Yeatsian kind. Emerging in the aftermath of the high tide of the Irish Revival and high modernism, and in a Europe twice devastated by catastrophic wars, this chastened generation substituted for the grandiose ambitions of their forerunners a satirical, parodic literature of failure, one that mocked or blessed a banal everyday world that literature could neither redeem nor transfigure. Between this mid-century literature, for which boredom rather than enchantment or the excitements of Yeatsian apocalypse was the keynote, and Irish revisionism, keen to fumigate Irish historiography of its own elements of romantic extravagance or revolutionary pretension, there was, Deane asserted, an elective affinity. By long and circuitous routes, writers and historians alike had come to accept that Ireland's great destiny, once thought to be for better or worse exceptional, was essentially to be unexceptional. Born into strangeness as a lamentably backward or commendably romantic colonial outlier to English modernity, twentieth-century Ireland had found that its real vocation was actually to be ordinary. Strange country, normal people.

The significance of Burke to Deane's understanding of the long reaction to the French Revolution is further emphasized in his next book, *Foreign Affections: Essays on Edmund Burke* (2005). Here, we see Burke in an eighteenth-century French, Irish, and English formation (Swift, Montesquieu, Diderot, and Hume among its central figures), face to face with the triumphant Revolution, and with his demonized other, Rousseau. Accounts follow of the repercussions of Burkean writing in Newman and Arnold, Tocqueville and Lord Acton, in all of whom we sense the menace of an emergent modernity in which Ireland is forecast to play or seen to have already played a key role. Joyce and Yeats emerge from these essays as moulding (and moulded) figures of the next generation.

Small World can be read in relation to these earlier works in two ways. In an obvious sense, the volume represents a selection of essays culled from across Deane's wider writings from the early 1980s to 2018. Like any selection, this one is partial in more senses than one, but the pieces included here afford readers a means to trace some of the contours of Deane's preoccupations from the earlier to the later stages of his career. As with his earlier studies, the assembled essays cover that by now familiar long-reach overview that stretches from eighteenth-century writers Swift, Burke, and Tone to contemporaries such as Anna Burns, an overview that Deane has made his own. Here, though, the reader can get some impression not only of the temporal span of Deane's scholarship but also of the variety of modes that his writings have taken. 'Civilians and Barbarians' and 'Heroic Styles' were first published as pamphlets and share with

'Wherever Green is Read', his most lacerating exposure of the embedded rhetoric of revisionism, the polemical verve of the combative public intellectual writing to the moment. The essays on Swift and Burke, or Joyce and Burns, or Bowen and Lavin, are scholarly appreciations, weighing in the case of Burke, for example, the uses to which he has been bent in twentieth-century American scholarship, or, in the case of Joyce, inspecting the rhetorical crescendos he deploys to achieve the famous closing intensities of his works from 'The Dead' through *Ulysses* and *Finnegans Wake*.

Some of the longest pieces collected here, 'Tone: The Great Nation and the Evil Empire' or 'The End of the World', represent the longer essay forms that have characterized the later stage of Deane's career, the decade from 2005 to 2015 during which he edited *Field Day Review*. Ostensibly at least, the Tone essay is a review of a three-volume edition of *The Writings of Theobald Wolfe Tone*, edited by T. W. Moody, R. B. McDowell, and C. J. Woods, but the piece immediately departs from any conventional review form. It opens with a gripping account of the 1795 trial and courtroom death by self-poisoning of the Anglican clergyman and United Irish agent William Jackson, who chose suicide over a traitor's execution and the disinheritance of his family that would follow. From there, it leads into a harrowing invocation of the reign of legal terror undertaken by the British authorities in the 1790s designed entirely to extinguish the United Irishmen even before any French-assisted revolution was attempted. The use of informers, spies, torture, execution, imprisonment, eviction, and exile to the Americas or the colonies, and the bait of briberies and honours by the British state to suppress an infant Irish republicanism, constituted, Deane argues, 'a new departure from English law, peculiar to Ireland': these would constitute exemplary modes of oppression and reward further refined over the next two centuries and practised successively against the United Irishmen, the Fenians, the post-Famine land agitations, and IRA members during the two 'Troubles' eras. In the narrative sequences that follow, Deane comments on the qualities of Tone's writings and personal friendships, on the uses to which his plain style and aristocratic deportment have been put, on the accomplishments and shortcomings of the editorial decisions that governed the collection of Tone's writings in the volumes under review, on Tone's departures from specific British republican intellectual traditions running from Milton and Harrington to Toland and Molesworth that had always conceived of Catholics as implacable foes to liberty, and, finally, on the way in which, despite his efforts for Irish Catholics, Tone's 'Roman suicide' would in the writings of later Catholic nationalist historians such as Thomas D'Arcy Magee always place republicanism's founding father outside of the Catholic family fold. What appears in one light a torqued or meandering piece taking its own easy way with the materials in hand becomes in another light a striking series of explorations of the various ways in which a neo-stoic Romanism, in its republican, aristocratic-patrician, and Catholic forms, and a crusading Britonism, in its Protestant and imperial versions, have left their mark on an Irish republicanism intellectually affiliated with and antagonistic to each.

The 'End of the World' chapter, which rounds off *Small World*, is an even more remarkable construction. Taking its inspiration from Walter Benjamin, the piece is subdivided into twelve sections – 'Helga', 'Lusitania', 'The Blaskets', 'Mar ná beidh ár leithéidí arís ann ...', 'A Minor Literature, A Major Language', 'Peig', 'Therapeutic Realism', 'A Therapeutic Language', 'Thomas MacDonagh', 'Daniel Corkery', 'Robin Flower', 'George Thomson'. What binds these vignettes? Or, if searching for any overarching argument is misconceived, the piece a constellated series of *essais* or tries, what emerges from these arrangements? The steamship *Helga* with which 'The End of the World' opens, best known in Irish history and song for the shelling of Liberty Hall during the Easter Rising of 1916, had earlier taken part, Deane notes, in the first Clare Island Survey of 1909–11, and after 1916 was to become a troopship that transported the Black and Tan militias to different ports of Ireland during the War of Independence, before eventually being purchased by the Irish Free State to become part of its tiny marine fleet. From botanical survey vessel to imperial gunboat and troop-carrier to Free State marine service, where she was renamed *Muirchú* (Sea Hound), the *Helga*, Deane observes, passed in the space of a decade 'out of the history of world domination and into the quiet desuetude of the Irish Free State naval service'. This overture prepares readers for another Deane-style history lesson that will, apparently, take them from the turbulence of history with its empires, revolutions, and atrocities into the conservative calms and retirements of posthistory: the Irish Free State and Republic born of that imperial turbulence somehow, like the *Helga*, also navigating a path into the latter condition. This end-of-history narrative is not absent from 'The End of the World', but neither is it the whole story.

In another of its registers, 'The End of the World' traces a history of the Blasket islanders, sea-scavengers who lived by fishing and for whom the cargoes washed ashore from British and American ships sunk by German submarines during World War I represented a rare bonanza: 'boxed chocolates, barrels of apples, flour, wine, bacon, castor oil, pocket watches, clothes, leather strips and cowhides, cotton bales, wooden planks' were all gifted by the tides to the marvelling islanders in 1915 after the sinking of the *Lusitania*. But the Blaskets, like Ireland's other western islands, were themselves successively scavenged by British surveyors, German philologists, Irish Revivalists, Gaelic scholars, American filmmakers, English classicists, and naturalists for evidence of a prehistorical, non-modern, or classical or epic past miraculously surviving aslant the outer end of Ireland's and Europe's modernity. In this sequence, the slow fade of the Irish language, the disappearance of a primitive way of island life, and the beginning of the end of human habitation on the Blaskets become occasions for various forms of commemorative or conservation exercises. Ranging from those of the Free State to the 'Cambridge school' of anthropology to the contemporary naturalism of Tim Robinson, these exercises are designed to transfer things on the threshold of their obliteration into the literary treasuries, archives, and languages of the successor worlds that will displace them.

Time itself, or the different scales of time that organize human and natural life, will ultimately emerge as Deane's 'theme' in this piece. The *Helga* and *Lusitania* have their places in the essay because each marks a moment in a larger passage of historical time that will, at the cost of two world wars, see the decline of the European empires and the ascendance of their American successor. 'The Great War had been a European affair; it became a World War with the American intervention.' 'The old balance of powers had given way to a new hegemony. Globalization and the World became the key terms of the vocabulary that began to rival, then replace, the legal idioms of the nation-state and the European balance of power.' The time of this transition from European empire to American world is also obviously the time of the making of Irish Free State and Republic, the new polity's first 'independent' century limned by the death of the one dispensation and the birth of the other. This era will be marked, too, not just by the removal of the Blasket islanders but also of the Irish Ascendancy – Elizabeth Bowen is saluted in two essays in this volume as one of the subtlest Irish recorders of the passing of British and European aristocratic *mentalités* – and by the old Ascendancy Ireland's brief replacement by Catholic Ireland, its anguished, but shy and circumspect life deftly caught in the slanted art of Mary Lavin.

Underlying all that clamour of cultural and political history with its ruckus of rising and falling great powers, nations, and classes, there lies yet another temporality: the dimension of evolutionary time, the aeons of earth and seas, things once but no longer thought to be inviolable to human time. Yet even our sense of the differential temporalities of botanical or natural life comes to us, Deane reminds himself, as a product of human scientific or cultural consciousness, as does the perception that the natural world's slow unhurried pace runs contrapuntally to the jaggedly destructive rush of our modernity and postmodernity. Post-Enlightenment history or modernity once promised much, now promises little salvific consolation, but to abjure history, whatever little hope it offers, is to surrender not just the past but also any sense of steerage towards a different future. 'The End of the World' registers the dissolution of Irish and other national histories into the global solvent of American World History, but it also intimates that time may be marking the cards of that World History too, or it might suggest that the end of human habitation on the Blaskets anticipates not just a post-Gaelic world but a post-human time unfathomable to us all.

For many people around the world, Ireland remains a country of writers, not critics. Today, the names of Wilde and Shaw, Synge and Yeats, Joyce and Beckett, Bowen and Banville, Heaney and Kinsella, Edna O'Brien and Sally Rooney, have an international resonance that few figures in the non-literary Irish arts can match and their literary works obviously reach wider readerships than critical writings can hope to do.

To say this does not diminish the accomplishments of Irish critics. Yeats devoted a long career not just to creating a distinctively new Irish literature in his poetry and plays but also to shaping and championing that new literature in his critical writings and essays. When he felt the occasion compelled him to do so, he was not shy to take up the role of public intellectual, plying his rhetorical skills, often intemperately, sometimes with wit, for good and bad causes. A generation later, other writers – the playwright, novelist, and short-story writer Daniel Corkery, and novelist and short-story writer Sean Ó Faoláin – also found themselves duty-bound to play the critic: Corkery addressed what he felt to be stubbornly recalcitrant colonial attitudes in Irish writing; Ó Faoláin chastised not only Yeats's, McQuaid's, or De Valera's Irelands for their perversities but also took his fellow writers to task for what he deemed their inverted romanticisms and circumspect timidities. A poet as well as an essayist in his early career, and the author of the oblique and intricately crafted *Reading in the Dark*, one of the finest novels of the Troubles period, Deane has brilliantly sustained a legacy, now in Ireland more than a century long, of the writer-critic and public intellectual. That novel's form – with its subjective intensities heightened by their communal dimension and then absorbed into an historical narrative – re-enacts his progression of the short essay into longer narrative analyses.

Like Yeats, Corkery, or Ó Faoláin, Deane has never been afraid to be unpopular or at odds with his times. Like these predecessors, he has been willing to challenge his country's dominant ideologies, both political and aesthetic, in so doing risking the hostility not only of the majesties of the law and guardians of the state but also that of those who prefer to consider themselves the keepers of creativity and champions of reasonable debate or dissent. That said, Deane has never allowed himself to settle comfortably into the role of critic if by critic one simply means a castigator or oppositional figure only. His enormous scholarly commitment to several centuries of Irish writing, his assimilation of so many European intellectual traditions from the Enlightenment to the present, his writings as poet and novelist, and his collaborative work as theatre company director, anthologist, and general editor of the Field Day Critical Conditions series, all testify to a career that has been a creatively civic and constructive enterprise. He has never devoted his energies only to the articulation of his own ambitions, but always to the furtherance of Irish writing in several modes.

If this foreword has stressed the critical writer over the early poet or novelist, this is because Deane has made critical writing and intellectual scholarship his premier vocation. This indeed is the point perhaps at which his career diverges most from those of the precursors earlier mentioned. For those who might have wished a follow-up novel to *Reading in the Dark,* this may be a matter of regret, but for Irish critical writing the gain has been immense. The decision to give priority to the critical work may have been a personal one or a matter of circumstance in the way careers so often are; whatever the reason, it is indicative of a conviction, one already evident in *Celtic Revivals,* that modern Irish writing, in and beyond Ireland, can be more deeply appreciated in an enriching intellectual perspective to be gained only by pressing Irish critical and creative temperaments towards new equilibria.

In 'The Essay as Form', Theodor Adorno argues that the essay as a genre neither begins with definitions or concepts nor ends with conclusions or takeaway theses but with its own completion. For Adorno, 'the law of the innermost form of the essay is heresy. By transgressing the orthodoxy of thought, something becomes visible in the object which it is orthodoxy's secret purpose to keep invisible.'[2] Heretical, sensuously cerebral, cerebrally sensuous, elliptic, elusive, enigmatic, melancholy, modest, ornate, acute, complete, and incomplete, the essays that compose *Small World* – which here can mean Ireland, our chastened and reduced globalized condition, the essay mode itself – show Deane to be an adept of the form as Adorno understood it. At his best, he may be said to have alloyed that difficult union of art and intellect for which in Field Day, his career, his books, he has assiduously striven. *Small World,* large ambition, a career or vocation that has brought much of that ambition to burnished realization.

NOTES

1. Seamus Deane, *Celtic Revivals: Essays in Modern Irish Literature, 1880–1980* (Winston-Salem, NC: Wake Forest University Press, 1985).
2. T. W. Adorno, 'The Essay as Form', trans. Bob Hullot-Kentor and Fredric Will, *New German Critique,* 32 (Spring–Summer 1984), 151–71 (at 171).

Permissions

The following essays are published with the permission of the editor(s) of the books or journals where they first appeared:

- 'Classic Swift', in C. Fox (ed.), *The Cambridge Companion to Jonathan Swift* (Cambridge University Press, 2003), 241–55.
- 'Burke in the United States', in David Dwan and Christopher J. Insole (eds.), *The Cambridge Companion to Edmund Burke* (Cambridge University Press, 2012), 221–32.
- 'The Great Nation and the Evil Empire', *Field Day Review,* 5 (2009), 207–43.
- 'Imperialism and Nationalism', in Frank Lentricchia and Thomas McLaughlin (eds.), *Critical Terms for Literary Study,* 2nd edn (University of Chicago Press, 1995), 354–68.
- 'Irish National Character, 1790–1900', in T. Dunne (ed.), *The Writer As Witness* (Cork University Press, 1987), 90–113.
- 'Civilians and Barbarians' (Derry: Field Day Pamphlets, First Series, no. 3, 1983); repr. in *Ireland's Field Day* (London: Hutchinson, 1986; Notre Dame University Press, 1987).
- 'Heroic Styles: The Tradition of an Idea' (Derry: Field Day Pamphlets, Second Series, 1984); repr. in *Ireland's Field Day* (London: Hutchinson, 1986); repr. in C. Connolly (ed.), *Theorising Ireland* (London: Macmillan, 2003), 14–26.
- '*Ulysses*: The Exhaustion of Literature and the Literature of Exhaustion', in Louis Bonnerot (ed.), *Ulysses: Cinquante ans après* (Paris: Didier, 1974), 263–74.

'Dead Ends: Joyce's Finest Moments', in Derek Attridge and Marjorie Howes (eds.), *Neo-Colonial Joyce* (Cambridge University Press, 2000), 21–36.

'Wherever Green Is Read', in M. Ní Dhonnacadha and Theo Dorgan (eds.), *Revising the Rising* (Derry: Field Day Publications, 1991), 91–105; repr. in Ciaran Brady (ed.), *Interpreting Irish History: The Debate on Historical Revisionism 1938–1994* (Dublin: Irish Academic Press, 1994 and 1999), 234–45.

'The Famous Seamus', *The New Yorker*, 20 March 2000, 54–79.

'The End of the World', *Field Day Review*, 8 (2012), 207–41.

Acknowledgements

My most specific acknowledgement is to Joe Cleary who has persuaded me to make this selection of essays, to blend some new with some very old material. Not content with providing me with the most searching and meticulous of readings, he has also written the Foreword for the book. All of this constitutes an act of generosity beyond any expectation.

The energy and commitment of Ray Ryan of Cambridge University Press have also been for me, as for so many in the field of Irish Studies, an enormous stimulus. In the most difficult of times he has been a model publisher. My heartfelt thanks to him.

Emer Nolan has not only encouraged me to put the book together, she has also advised me with great tact on what I should omit and with great forbearance has re-read and helped to reshape what I have included here.

My sons, Ciaran and Cormac, have long supported Field Day publications, podcasts, and the *Field Day Review.* I am forever in their debt.

CHAPTER 1

Swift as Classic

> In all my Writings, I have had constant Regard to this great End, not to suit and apply them to particular Occasions and Circumstances of Time, of Place, or of Person; but to calculate them for universal Nature, and Mankind in general.
>
> (*PW* 1.174)[1]

MADNESS

In the preface to *A Tale of a Tub* (1704), Swift finds a classic way to define the kind of writing that is not classic and the kind of reading that should properly accompany it. Shadowing this passage is Cicero's declaration in *De re publica* (*The Republic*) of the unchanging and everlasting law of right reason. In place of law, Swift gives us modern wit which, we are told, does not travel well. Even 'the smallest Transposal or Misapplication' can annihilate it (*PW* 1.26). Some jests are only comprehensible at Covent-Garden, some at Hyde-Park Corner. All the universal truths about modernity are sourced in its provinciality. Similarly, the intellectual position of a modern is open to parody, when it is rendered as a physical position:

> Too intense a Contemplation is not the Business of Flesh and Blood; it must by the necessary Course of Things, in a little Time, let go its Hold, and fall into Matter. Lovers, for the sake of Celestial Converse, are but another sort of Platonicks, who pretend to see Stars and Heaven in Ladies Eyes, and

> to look or think no lower; but the same Pit is provided for both; and they seem a perfect Moral to the Story of that Philosopher, who, while his Thoughts and his Eyes were fixed upon the Constellations, found himself seduced by his lower Parts into a Ditch. (*PW* 1.189–90)

Here the transposition of the sexually candid phrase 'seduced by his lower parts' from the lovers to the philosopher, and from the idea of intercourse to the idea of falling into a ditch and from that to the reference to the human fall into the pit of hell makes the declaration of the writer's faith in matter more emphatic, and yet also ridicules it. Swift is indeed saying that the most extreme religious enthusiasts have a gross conception of the spiritual which is explicable in psychological and physiological terms; they are ultimately materialists. But the reader's attention is taken not only by the object of the attack but also by the position of the person or persona who conducts the assault. He may himself be an embodiment of the very thing he assaults; thus his tone of svelte disengagement is deceitful. To establish the voice of the norm and then to make it the voice of deviancy, while attributing to it every form of awareness except self-awareness, has at the very least a confusing effect. Swift produces a similar confusion at the level of form when he makes digressions central to his undertaking, thus making a nonsense of the standard opposition between digression and main text upon which his humour depends.

Swift's suppleness of phrasing and of figuration has the dual effect of intensifying and of vaporizing the detail of his more vertiginously satiric passages. The world he creates is packed tight and it is also empty. He dislocates the reader by revealing that the momentum of the logic of an argument or of a figure, or of both, can lead or can seem to lead the author into unexpected trouble. For the whole notion of authority and control is questioned when the language seems to take on a life of its own, independent of any authorial restraint. And yet to represent that very condition is itself an ingenious exercise in authorial mastery.

One of Swift's great gifts is to find a way of telling stories in the voice and accent of monomaniacs, obsessives, and ideologues who are entirely unaware of their fixated condition. Sometimes he plays the role of mimic; sometimes, more subtly and dismayingly, that of ventriloquist. In general, the mimicry creates ironic effects, the ventriloquial efforts, sustained for longer and with stonier dedication (*Gulliver's Travels, A Modest Proposal*), create parody. Fanaticism has great allure for Swift. His scorn for it is the more effective because of his relish for it; he has an eye for the behaviour of the crazed who believe themselves to be rational and who can persuade others of this too. The fanatic begins by surrendering his intelligence and is thereafter no longer exercised by the labour of using it. His energy is instead devoted to consuming it, energy converting mass, the adrenalin of madness masking its hyperactivity as the operation of reason. Sometimes we listen to juvenile opinions repeated endlessly with stentorian force, the loudness of voice indicating both the strength of the convictions and their echoing vacuity. At other times, the madness is quieter in tone. Rather than the crazed blusterings of a religious enthusiast, we have the assured expositions of an expert, delivered with a smiling sibilance.

> And it is exactly at one Year old, that I propose to provide for them in such a Manner, as, instead of being a Charge upon their Parents, or the Parish, or wanting Food and Raiment for the rest of their Lives; they shall, on the contrary, contribute to the Feeding, and partly to the Cloathing, of many Thousands.
>
> (*PW* 12.110)

The frenzy of religious enthusiasm that had, in Swift's view, caused so much political and social strife in the seventeenth century was still a force to be reckoned with; his sojourn at Kilroot outside Belfast among the northern Presbyterians made that painfully clear to him. But in the new era of the Moderns, such frenzy had migrated into more secular forms; the good of mankind had taken over from redemption as the ostensible motive for virtuous action. Swift repeatedly assumes the persona of the 'most devoted Servant of all Modern Forms' (*PW* 1.27) seeking to accomplish 'the general Good of Mankind' (*PW* 1.77). Such a 'Modern' could be a politician, a hack writer, a religious bigot, an economist, a believer in the radical goodness or benevolence of humankind; whatever the role or profession, the Modern, by the abuse of 'feeling' or 'reason' – now beginning to separate into opposites – had become dangerously insane. Against the insanity of ideologues and sentimentalists, Swift responded in the classically satiric manner – by caricaturing them in stories that were parables or allegories or sermons although these were often written in the well-named 'realistic' mode of the Moderns – that of the 'history' or novel.

The constitutional historian Hallam, writing in 1827, argued that Swift's writings in *The Examiner* and elsewhere are the first in which a government, rather than seeking a solution in the law of libel, decided to 'retaliate with unsparing invective and calumny' against its vociferous enemies in the press.[2] Swift was indeed a remarkably effective political journalist. Yet Hallam, like many others, locates Swift in his historical circumstances and still implies that there is in his writings something fierce and repellent the explanation for which must be sought beyond history. This alternative source is Swift's psyche, to which many commentators have claimed special access.

Thus, enseamed within the long history of commentary on Swift the writer is the commentary on Swift's psychology and pathology. Madness, illness, sexual disturbance, revulsion at the human body and its functions, and a whole fleet of other guesses or claims are cited to explain what is remarkable about his work. This, we have been told for two and a half centuries, is what ultimately gives to Swift's work that intensity which distinguishes it from that of the other great satirists with whom he is often compared or associated – Juvenal, Rabelais, Pope, Dryden, Voltaire. The diseased subjectivity of the author is paraded as the cause of or simply described as misanthropy. Swift's eccentricity then becomes the basis for a dark view of human nature that has to be disavowed (on the grounds that it is a slur on humankind) or admitted (on the grounds that it is a penetrating truth discoverable only by the disturbed). The very brilliance of Swift's rhetoric is taken to be an index of a deep-seated disturbance that finds the corruptions and vices (radical or contingent) of his contemporaries so offensive. So his 'madness' restricts the range but deepens the reach of his access to certain aspects of human experience denied to the unafflicted. It is ironic indeed that Swift, who so often used madness as an emblem of the Modern's self-involvement, should himself be subject to this kind of interpretation. It is as though he had become for his readers one of his own adopted personae.

It is Swift's impersonation of the forms of modernity's assault on traditional moralities that makes him so anomalously and yet decisively a modern writer. The loss of secure authority is disturbing because it is so often exposed by the serene confidence of the first-person narrator who embodies the modern spirit by showing that its investment in personal, authentic experience is foolhardy and yet securely insecure. Swift does indeed record some of the ways in which a traditional moral discourse mutates into a modern commercial discourse and how, in the process, the claims to Christian or moral behaviour are the more aggressive as the grounds for such behaviour are abandoned. Yet his intensities are still disproportionate to such explanations. The question recurrently is, in what does this difference, or this radically disturbing element, consist? In this form, the question is never satisfactorily answered. But it has been countered by the contradictory claim that Swift displays the fundamental sanity that is always to be found in classic writers.[3] Yet the accounts of his sanity inevitably segue into assertions of the intensity with which he defended traditional commonplace beliefs; the trouble is that the descriptions of the intensity return the commentator to the issue of Swift's uniqueness and the problem of distinguishing this from extremism or imbalance. Revulsion and disgust at physical and sexual functions are the most alarming elements in this intensity, even though these are traditional features in satiric writing. F. R. Leavis finds Swift shares 'a peculiar emotional intensity' with 'the shallowest complacencies of Augustan common sense'.[4] In an essay more noticed than distinguished, George Orwell sees Swift as a commonplace and reactionary thinker, obsessed with dirt and disease, and yet redeemed by a Leavislike 'terrible intensity of vision'; this vagueness aids Orwell towards his well-known declaration 'that, if the force of belief is behind it, a world-view which only passes the test of sanity is sufficient to produce a great work of art'.[5] Edward Said takes issue with Orwell and, by implication, with Leavis, of whose essay Orwell's is a rewriting, arguing that Swift is, above all things, a self-conscious intellectual, a writer in a world of power.[6] Even with Said, there seems to be a relation, more sensed than articulated, between Swift's intensity and his sanity. The sanity is always under threat from the intensity; an ordinary and an extraordinary universe are combined within one vision that can thus appear either commonplace or uniquely uncompromising. As with the various arguments about Swift's 'style', there is little agreement on what constitutes it. He writes in various registers, but no one of them seems to predominate sufficiently to be called his 'style', even though again a conflict between the homely and the commonplace on the one hand and something remarkably and intensely fierce is widely remarked.[7]

Swift can thus combine contraries of the most compelling kind. John Wesley cites from Book IV of *Gulliver's Travels* in his 'Doctrine of Original Sin' (1757) to demonstrate the ineluctable depravity of human nature, while in *The Enquirer* (1797), the anarchist/utilitarian William Godwin sees the Houyhnhnms as emblems of human perfectibility. An Anglican priest and traditional Christian who could not tolerate any threat to the supremacy of the national Church, in England or in Ireland,[8] he was, in Sir James Mackintosh's words, 'an ecclesiastical Tory, even while he was a political Whig'.[9] The need to defend his Church in the circumstances of England and Ireland in the long crisis that stretched from the 1640s to the 1730s may explain the venomous ingenuity that he deployed to secure a position that varied from the threatened to the indefensible.[10] His Anglicanism or his 'Toryism', even if wholly traditional, makes him seem like an ideological curiosity, especially when combined with a coarseness of invective that threatens all established values.

Swift's coarseness and 'misanthropy' were often linked to one another and to his final state of madness. Sir Walter Scott claimed the grossness of Swift's writing could be explained by the author's mental 'peculiarities' and the conditions of the time; it was the combination that was 'nearly allied to the misanthropy' which preceded his final madness. Scott's attempts to understand Swift scarcely soften his ultimate condemnation of Book IV of *Gulliver's Travels*, 'this libel on human nature',[11] but they certainly form a telling contrast with the disturbed rant of Thackeray in his 'English Humorists', an essay that steeply intensified the tone of outrage that had been a recurrent feature of reaction to Swift and specifically to Book IV, at least since the comments of Lord Orrery and Patrick Delany in 1752 and 1754 respectively.

POLITENESS AND CIVIC VIRTUE

One other way of discounting Swift as an exceptionally misanthropic author is to see him as a writer in the 'selfish' or cynical tradition of those authors from La Rochefoucauld to Hobbes, from Mandeville to Helvétius, who have been routinely accused of having a narrow and gloomy view of human nature, because they give primacy to the passion of self-love. Mandeville was especially notorious during Swift's lifetime for his great work, *The Fable of the Bees: or, Private Vices, Publick Benefits* (1714 and 1729). It is not that Swift is in any sense like Mandeville, although they are sometimes paired together. Mandeville is renowned for his attack, not on virtue as such, but on the ways in which it had been traditionally understood, especially if it depended upon a denial of self-love or selfishness as a motor principle in human behaviour or on the overly sanguine and demonstrably foolish view of the benevolists like Shaftesbury who 'seems to require and expect Goodness in his Species, as we do a sweet Taste in Grapes and China Oranges, of which, if any of them are sour, we boldly pronounce that they are not come to that Perfection their Nature is capable of'.[12]

Swift is not at all given to any revision or reconsideration of the traditional Christian concepts of virtue, none of which would have denied the power of self-love, although Shaftesbury's malleability on the topic was anathema to him. The best-known Anglican synthesis of traditional and modern ethical systems is Bishop Joseph Butler's *Fifteen Sermons,* published in the same year as *Gulliver's Travels* (1726). It is milder in tone and more accommodating than Swift, but not fundamentally different in its doctrinal basis. However, Swift is extraordinary in the degree to which he is both repelled and fascinated by humankind's resourcefulness in disguising viciousness and corruption as virtue. Pride is a fundamental sin, hypocrisy the age-old disguise that it wears. Mandeville shocked his readers because he claimed that what had been taken to be the antithesis of virtue was that in which virtue consisted. His argument was the more upsetting because it further claimed that now, in a polite age, some of the old barbaric distinctions – like that between sin and virtue – could be abandoned and replaced by something more rational and enlightened, more in conformity with human nature and the human capacity to master and order a secular world – especially the world of material goods and luxury.[13] When the hunger for luxury and consumption has become a virtue, then a key Swiftian inversion has truly been realized.

Swift may not have mastered the economic discourse that was developing to describe the emergent systems of the colonial and Atlantic worlds of which Ireland formed a part.[14] But he understood enough to recognize that a form of rational analysis based on quantification was beginning to dominate in social and moral thinking and to introduce those new norms of civility and politeness that were so assiduously promoted in contemporary writing. Mandeville had given terms like 'luxury' and 'consumption' a bad name by showing their intimate connection with dirt and selfishness and the welfare of society in general.[15] These associations were redescribed by Hutcheson in a more muted, less scandalous manner; yet he retained the declaration that goodness (interpreted as the happiness or welfare of the many) was something that could be quantified and that the impulse to produce it was something that could be, indeed could not but be, strongly felt; and that to act in accord with such a feeling was to be in accord with our God-given nature. Thus an affective morality that could be quantified in its effects was now available for the polite world of commerce, where markets expanded to meet the demands of appetite and appetite had lost many of its traditional and pejorative connotations. Appetite provided the dynamic for an economy of gratification for the self and for others. This was the world of the modern economist and of the modern moralist; in short, of utilitarianism. In Swift's view it was no more than a glossy version of the self-involved fanaticisms of religious sectaries who had, just as much as the Moderns, believed in a version of the 'inner light' of personal conviction and its harmony with God's wish. Like the Moderns, these old-generation bigots believed that the authority of an opinion lay in the strength with which it was held. To Swift, this was a dangerous and ludicrous conviction; it sought and found authority within itself and demanded universal consent to this discovery. On the other hand, the emphasis upon consequence and the weakened role of intention or motive allowed for so much computational casuistry that moral judgement seemed to depend upon the ingenuity of the apologist rather than on any antecedent and traditional body of truth.

Yet it is also true that Swift used the conversational mode of address so favoured by those who wished to establish a standard of politeness in social and literary forms that would allow England to compete with

France and with an idea of ancient Rome. The dissonance between civility and savagery in Swift is a studied satiric effect, but it also implies a repudiation of the belief in the 'progress' of politeness and the triumph of prudence and moderation over factional enthusiasm celebrated by Hume in particular.[16] Hume's version of the development of English literary style from the mid seventeenth to the early eighteenth century is a case in point; it was only in Swift's era that English letters emulated the French, the 'judicious imitators' of the Ancients.[17] With Swift, however, the civil mode is often sustained in circumstances so grotesque that its imperturbability becomes a symptom of disturbance. The heroic and the tragic dimensions of human existence do not fit within this reduced and mundane world; yet their inversion into various extreme forms of debauchery is perfectly in accord with its appalling and dead carnality. Swift dissects the 'Carcass of Humane Nature' (*PW* 1.77) to divert rather than instruct. The analytic and instructive exposure becomes pornographic and shocking. It is a disturbingly modern mode of defending the Ancients. In satirizing the modern world of innovation and inversion Swift also demonstrates its displacement of the traditional world it sometimes imitates and at other times derides.

The aspiration to classic status in literature (and in other arts) was central to the long disputes between Ancients and Moderns in France and England in the seventeenth and eighteenth centuries. It seemed obvious to the 'Ancients' in this dispute that if any modern work were to prove as durable as the Greek and Latin classics, it must in some sense be an imitation of those features in the originals that had given them such lasting appeal. This was a much-contested feature of the theory of imitation. Against that, it was argued that the modern was specific to itself, and that imitation of the classics was rarely creative and almost always slavish or routine. Swift entered into this dispute with the famous defence of his mentor Sir William Temple against the redoubtable and much-superior scholar Richard Bentley in *The Battle of the Books* (1704). But he especially emphasized how absurd and dangerous it was to replace the inherited traditions of the classics with work of recent vintage. Thus he dramatizes in his satires the distinction between the local and the universal, almost always tying the local not only to a particular time and place but also to the psychic freakishness of a disturbed or deranged subjectivity or to the sociological novelty of the professional writer dependent upon patronage and/or the market to an unprecedented degree. A swarm of Grub Street hacks could scarcely be expected to produce a literature that would rival the serenity and wisdom of the ancient classics. They were doomed to a momentary notoriety rather than elected to a long-lasting fame unless, that is, their notoriety were to be so commemorated in the satire they provoked, that it would there be permanently preserved as an emblem of foolishness and pride. These hack writers, Swift (and Pope) would argue, were hopelessly marooned in the present moment precisely because they affected to ignore or dispense with the past.

IRELAND

Swift witnessed two revolutions. One was the Glorious Revolution of 1688–9 which initiated a profound reordering of the internal world of the British isles. This was an intricate process. Among its most notable events were the end of the Jacobite war in Ireland and the establishment of Protestant power after 1691; the Penal Laws passed from 1695 against the Irish Catholics to destroy them as a political, economic, and cultural force; the Union of England and Scotland to form Great Britain in 1707; the abortive attempts by Irish Protestants to assert a meaningful independence, especially in economic matters, against Great Britain; the defeats of the Jacobite cause in 1715 and in 1745, the year of Swift's death, and the destruction of Scottish Gaelic culture. The other revolution was European. It was completed by the Treaty of Utrecht which brought an end to the War of the Spanish Succession and Louis XIV's ambitions for a universal monarchy that would dominate the continent. It created the system of nation-states and inaugurated the *ancien régime,* a system that was to endure for no more than seventy-five years and was to be replaced, after another titanic struggle between Britain and France, in 1815.

Swift's work certainly belongs in this modern European world, partly because of its oblique relationship to the European Enlightenment, partly because its mixed English and Irish origins enabled him to question the new alliances between power and civility that were so fundamental to Britain's and Europe's self-images. A common feature of the commentary on Ireland and on Irish writing, then and since, has been its preoccupation with the issues of Irish peripherality and its troubled relationship to a metropolitan centre, usually London, occasionally Paris. In 1922, T. S. Eliot, continuing the Arnoldian search for the universal element in literature that would supervene over provinciality, claimed that Joyce's *Ulysses* was 'the first Irish work since that of Swift to possess absolute European significance'.[18] The remark indicates Swift's importance, as well as Eliot's ignorance of other Irish authors, including many of Swift's contemporaries. Swift was one of a gifted generation of writers whose political conception of Ireland was integral to their work or to the commentary it provoked or to both. Outrage at Ireland's ill-treatment at English hands, hatred of its provinciality and squalor, and the encouragement within it of a species of economic and political autonomy are evident in the more than sixty Irish pamphlets he wrote, particularly in the decades of the 1720s and 1730s. Of these, *The Drapier's Letters* and *A Modest Proposal* are the most widely advertised as works that have a universal moral and political appeal.

Nevertheless, it is somewhat remarkable that Swift's reputation in this regard should exceed that of contemporaries like John Toland or Francis Hutcheson, both of whom were much less confined and orthodox than he in their opinions. Toland's *Christianity Not Mysterious* (1696) had several targets, among them the exercise of political control through the creation by a priestly elite of mystery about religious matters.[19] The confessional basis of the British state, most especially as it applied to Ireland, could be said to be challenged by Toland's argument; no sect, no Church had a claim as such to total political control. But it is clear that Toland, although born as an Irish-speaking Catholic, came to detest 'Popery, Prelacy, and arbitrary power',[20] and that his attack on 'priestcraft' was more truly directed at Roman Catholicism than at Anglicanism. Nevertheless, the book was a rational Dissenter's credo; no churchman in particular could accept the deistic implications of its arguments. Toland's politics were, however, solidly Protestant and chauvinist. He had, as he said in a pamphlet of 1701, two chief aims – 'the stopping of the progress of the *French* Greatness' and keeping '*England* the head of the Protestant Interest all over the World',[21] even if this meant finding a way to accept the monarchy of William III by regarding it as a 'commonwealth'. Yet his criticisms of Anglican sectarianism and of monarchy were sufficient to make him appear radical in comparison with Swift and he signally lacked diplomacy and seemed almost to fear tact. 'There was not in his whole composition, one single grain of that useful quality which *Swift* calls *modern discretion.*'[22]

Hutcheson, who appears much less threatening politically than Toland, perhaps struck more deeply at the moral basis of Swift's and of Anglican political thought when he argued, in his *Inquiry* (1725), against the spirit of sectarianism and its link with exclusivity and despotism; the consequences were the destruction of 'national love', social harmony, and civil society itself.[23] Although the question of toleration for Catholics is thereby raised, it forms no central part of Hutcheson's project, since the search for the 'basis of moral knowledge independent of church authority and available to the ordinary reasonable and conscientious person'[24] was a specifically Protestant search. In Ireland especially, the universalist claims for such a basis were always threatened by the charge of sectarianism and would in the end succumb to it. But before that could happen, a particular conception of civil society as an instrument of moral improvement was formulated not in Ireland, but in Scotland, where Hutcheson became a famous teacher and earned the title of the father of Scottish philosophy. Thus, on the rare occasions when they were not wholly absorbed into accounts of English political and moral philosophy, Toland was assigned to Europe and Hutcheson to Scotland. Swift, while a classic of English writing, was nevertheless also and always associated with Ireland.

Or, more exactly, with two Irelands. One is the Ireland of the Protestant patriots, the other is the country of Irish nationalism, predominantly Catholic. The latter was to have its first signal success with the Catholic Emancipation Act of 1829, the act which finally brought an end to the confessional Protestant British state that emerged in 1688; the former was to end in 1800–1 with the Act of Union that created the United Kingdom of Great Britain and Ireland, and began with the publication of William Molyneux's *The Case of Ireland ... Stated* (1698).[25] It is with this latter group that Swift has been most frequently and persuasively associated. Certainly his *Drapier's Letters* and Molyneux's pamphlet have been widely regarded as the source books for the eighteenth century's Protestant nationalism, that culminated in 1782 when Henry Grattan reportedly welcomed legislative independence with the words, 'Spirit of Swift! Spirit of Molyneux! Your genius has prevailed. Ireland is now a nation.' By the end of the century, despite the 1798 Rebellion and the Union that extinguished the experiment in independence, Molyneux and Swift had been elevated from spokesmen for an exclusively Protestant patriotism to a nobler, more inclusive role: Irish minds had been opened by this pair and had been taught to 'nurture the seeds of freedom, and to vindicate those rights, which heaven has bestowed upon the human race'.[26]

This was the benign 'national' view of Swift as the first author who had been driven beyond the limits of his initial view of Ireland and the Irish to embrace a more generous, if paternalistic, vision of the moral and economic duties and imperatives involved in the Protestant interest in Ireland. It was not uncontested. In his famous *Memoirs of Captain Rock* (1824), Thomas Moore presents an alternative view of an intolerant Swift who 'for the misery and degradation of his Roman Catholic countrymen ... seems to have cared little more than his own Gulliver would for the suffering of so many disfranchised Yahoos'.[27]

The spirit of party certainly heightened Swift's view of the Irish–English relationship, especially after his career in English politics came to an end with the accession of Queen Anne. In the next five years, that relationship degenerated into a bitter and humiliating dispute. Molyneux had argued that Ireland was a separate kingdom, not a colony. Yet Swift, like many others, was sorely struck by the melancholy consequences for Ireland of the English connection – the conditions of poverty and famine, the punitive commercial relationship, the formation of the patriot 'persona' as a surrogate identity for a minority group that was parasitically dependent on the polity it attempted to resist.[28]

This was intensified by Swift's awareness of the very different relationship established in 1707 by the union between England and Scotland. A community of Dissenters, with a marked commercial tendency, had been given preferential treatment over a community of Anglicans with a record of political loyalty and much more need of every form of political, economic, religious, and cultural support. The Wood's halfpence affair led from small beginnings to a significant victory that had wide implications, some of them exaggerated in retrospect, although the exaggerations themselves became important. The political conflict generated by the Irish–English relationship has deep connections with Swift's obsessive rhetorical figurings of the autonomous body and the body that has neither identity nor control and that can, as a consequence, issue only in excrement, vapours, or be represented merely as an object of consumption or derision.[29] From Swift's early allegorization of political and sexual union in *The Story of the Injured Lady* (1707), his determination to expose the actuality of a maimed condition and the cosmetic pretence of a 'normal' one had been intermittently expressed. This has often been said to provide the evidence for his misanthropy and, more specifically, his misogyny.[30]

But in the 1720s, its expression became both more intense and more consistent. In fact, as Emer Nolan argues, by 1729, the year of *A Modest Proposal*, the 'debate between civic virtue and homo economicus' has been transmogrified:

> *The Drapier* represented an ambivalent but useful blend of the language of economics and the language of civic virtue, but now the Proposer represents their divergence ... there is no solution: this is a satire of both colonialism and of the resistance to colonialism, in the form in which it could then be articulated by protestant Ireland.[31]

The political impasse, finally exposed in and by the English–Irish colonial relationship, is figured finally as a murderous action in which the atrocity of nurturing children to be eaten is redescribed in the modern way as the production of a crop or commodity that satisfies a theory of economic behaviour. Swift's writing seems classically colonial to many precisely because of this internal disturbance; it is 'a rhetoric characterized by constant crisis, just as colonial rule itself continually creates its own crisis of authority'.[32]

Some earlier modern readings see Swift's work in general, and *Gulliver's Travels* in particular, as characteristic examples of the Enlightenment's assault on the assumptions of traditional authority. The unreliability or instability of the narrator is thus taken to be an index of the writer's awareness of a new form of sensory and intellectual relativism. That itself had a peculiarly Irish origin in the new epistemological questions raised by William Molyneux's work on optics, *Dioptrica nova* (1692), and Bishop Berkeley's *Essay towards a New Theory of Vision* (1709).[33] This at least has the merit of establishing a philosophical rather than a political connection between Swift and his compatriots that might account for or supplement the anxiety about authority and about the concession of trust to the government either of the senses or of the British state. But it is not often that Swift has been seen as a witting or unwitting contributor to the Enlightenment and its subversion of authority. It is the collapse of traditional authority, not the absurdity of its claims, that enraged him. He has left many after-images – the defender of Liberty, the creator of Irish national consciousness, the writer torn by his 'saeva indignatio' at the spectacle of injustice and corruption, the party hack, the greatest satirist of early modernity. These versions of him influenced the form of his commemoration by two of his country's greatest writers, Joyce and Yeats. In *Ulysses* (1922), he is the misanthropic dean: 'A hater of his kind ran from them to the wood of madness, his mane foaming in the moon, his eyeballs stars. Houyhnhnm, horsenostrilled.'[34]

In Yeats's play, *The Words upon the Window-pane* (1934), and in the Preface to it, which is a sustained, if shrill, meditation on Swift and on his notion, expressed as early as 1701 in *A Discourse of the Contests and Dissentions between the Nobles and the Commons in Athens and Rome,* of 'the universal bent and current of a people', Swift becomes a tragic figure whose dread of 'the historic process became . . . a dread of parentage'. He was of the traditional world that Rousseau and the French Revolution destroyed, profoundly opposed to democracy and yet that 'created the political nationality of Ireland'.[35]

Irish democracy's celebration of Swift has had many unintended ironies – one of which is that any democracy should celebrate one who so much dreaded its arrival. Eliot's strange pairing of Swift and Joyce helped to emphasize another. In 1978, Swift appeared on the Irish Republic's currency, on the ten-punt note; in 1994 he was replaced by Joyce. Now, perhaps sometime in the future of the euro currency, the Drapier might yet make another appearance on coin or paper. Even the shade of William Wood might smile at that Euro-Hibernian prospect.

NOTES

1. *The Prose Works of Jonathan Swift,* ed. Herbert Davis, 14 vols. (Oxford: Basil Blackwell, 1939–68). References are identified in the text as *PW* followed by volume and page number.
2. Henry Hallam, *The Constitutional History of England from the Accession of Henry VII to the Death of George II,* 4 vols. (Paris: Baudry, 1827), vol. III, 446–67.

3. See Ricardo Quintana, *The Mind and Art of Jonathan Swift* (London and New York: Oxford University Press, 1936), 37.
4. F. R. Leavis, 'The Irony of Swift,' in *Determinations* (London: Chatto and Windus, 1934), 72–87.
5. George Orwell, 'Politics vs. Literature: An Examination of *Gulliver's Travels*' (1950), in *The Collected Essays, Journalism and Letters,* ed. Sonia Orwell and Ian Angus, 4 vols. (London: Secker & Warburg, 1968), vol. IV, 205–23, esp. 222–3.
6. Edward Said, 'Swift as Intellectual,' in *The World, the Text, and the Critic* (Cambridge, MA: Harvard University Press, 1983), 72–89, esp. 87; see also the preceding essay, 'Swift's Tory Anarchy', 54–71.
7. See William Wotton and Francis Jeffrey, quoted in Kathleen Williams (ed.), *Swift: The Critical Heritage* (London: Routledge & Kegan Paul, 1970), 316, 324, 45. Also see Thomas De Quincey, *Works,* 15 vols. (Edinburgh: Black, 1862–3), vol. VII, 47–50.
8. See Irvin Ehrenpreis, *Swift, the Man, His Works and the Age,* vol. I (Cambridge, MA: Harvard University Press, 1962), 119–225; Louis A. Landa, *Swift and the Church of Ireland* (Oxford: Clarendon Press, 1954); Phillip Harth, *Swift and Anglican Rationalism: The Religious Background of A Tale of a Tub* (University of Chicago Press, 1961); Michael DePorte, 'Swift, God, and Power', in Christopher Fox and Brenda Tooley (eds.), *Walking Naboth's Vineyard: New Studies of Swift* (University of Notre Dame Press, 1995), 73–97; Robert Eccleshall, 'Anglican Political Thought in the Century after the Revolution of 1688', in D. George Boyce, Robert Eccleshall, and Vincent Geoghegan (eds.), *Political Thought in Ireland since the Seventeenth Century* (London and New York: Routledge, 1993), 36–72.
9. *Memoirs of the Life of the Right Honourable Sir James Mackintosh,* 2 vols. (London: Moxon, 1835), vol. I, 178.
10. See Warren Montag, *The Unthinkable Swift: The Spontaneous Philosophy of a Church of England Man* (London: Verso, 1994).
11. Williams (ed.), *Swift: The Critical Heritage,* 296, 313.
12. Bernard Mandeville, *The Fable of the Bees: or, Private Vices, Publick Benefits,* ed. F. B. Kaye, 2 vols. (Oxford University Press, 1924), vol. I, 323. Mandeville's work was published in two parts, I in 1714 and II in 1729.
13. See Albert O. Hirschmann, *The Passions and the Interests: Political Arguments for Capitalism before its Triumph* (Princeton University Press, 1977), 19.
14. See Nicholas Canny, 'Identity Formation in Ireland: The Emergence of the Anglo-Irish', in Nicholas Canny and Anthony Pagden (eds.), *Colonial Identity in the Atlantic World* (Princeton University Press, 1987), 159–212; Brendan Bradshaw and John Morrill (eds.), *The British Problem, c. 1534–1707: State Formation in the Atlantic Archipelago* (New York: St Martin's Press, 1996).
15. M. M. Goldsmith, 'Liberty, Luxury and the Pursuit of Happiness', in Anthony Pagden (ed.), *The Languages of Political Theory in Early-Modern Europe* (Cambridge University Press, 1987), 225–51.

16. Nicholas Phillipson, 'Politeness and Politics in the Reigns of Anne and the Early Hanoverians', in J. G. A. Pocock et al. (eds.), *The Varieties of British Political Thought 1500–1800* (Cambridge University Press, 1993), 211–45.
17. David Hume, *The History of England from the Invasion of Julius Caesar to the Revolution in 1688,* 6 vols. (London: T. Cadell, 1778), vol. VI, 543–5.
18. T. S. Eliot, 'The Three Provincialities', *Tyro,* 2 (1922), 11–13 (at 11).
19. *John Toland's Christianity Not Mysterious,* ed. Philip McGuinness, Alan Harrison, and Richard Kearney (Dublin: Lilliput Press, 1997).
20. See the account of his life that prefaces John Toland's *A Critical History of the Celtic Religion and Learning* (1722; London: Lackington, 1810), 40.
21. John Toland, *The Art of Governing by Partys* (London: Lintott, 1701), 145.
22. Toland, *A Critical History,* 41.
23. Francis Hutcheson, *An Inquiry into the Original of our Ideas of Beauty and Truth* (London, 1725), Treatise II, Section IV, 9–22.
24. John Rawls, *Lectures on the History of Moral Philosophy* (Cambridge MA: Harvard University Press, 2000), 8.
25. William Molyneux, *The Case of Ireland's Being Bound by Acts of Parliament in England, Stated,* ed. J. G. Simms, afterword by Denis Donoghue (Dublin: Cadenus Press, 1977).
26. Francis Plowden, *An Historical Review of the State of Ireland from the Invasion of that Country under Henry II to its Union with Great Britain on the 1st of January, 1801,* 3 vols. (London: Egerton, 1803), vol. I, 390; see also Thomas Campbell, *An Historical Sketch of the Constitution and Government of Ireland* (Dublin: Luke White, 1789), 362. For Grattan, see *The Speeches of Henry Grattan,* 2 vols. (London: Lackington, 1822), vol. I, 123.
27. Thomas Moore, *Memoirs of Captain Rock, the Celebrated Irish Chieftain, with Some Account of his Ancestors* (London: Longmans, 1824), 123–4; ed. Emer Nolan, (Dublin: Field Day, 2008), 69–70. For a general account of Swift's reception among Irish Protestants and Catholics, see Robert Mahony, 'Swift and Catholic Ireland', in Fox and Tooley (eds.), *Walking Naboth's Vineyard,* 178–99.
28. See Carole Fabricant, *Swift's Landscape* (1982; 2nd rev. edn University of Notre Dame Press, 1995); and her 'Jonathan Swift as Irish Historian', in Fox and Tooley (eds.), *Walking Naboth's Vineyard,* 40–72; Joseph McMinn, 'A Weary Patriot: Swift and the Formation of an Anglo-Irish Identity', in *Eighteenth-Century Ireland: Iris an dá chultúr,* 2 (1987), 103–13; Robert Mahony, *Jonathan Swift: The Irish Identity* (New Haven, CT: Yale University Press, 1995); Thomas O. McLoughlin, *Contesting Ireland: Irish Voices against England in the Eighteenth Century* (Dublin: Four Courts Press, 1999), 41–87; S. J. Connolly (ed.), *Political Ideas in Eighteenth-Century Ireland* (Dublin: Four Courts Press, 2000).
29. See Emer Nolan, 'Swift: The Patriot Game', *British Journal for Eighteenth-Century Studies,* 21 (1998), 39–53; and Robert Mahony, 'Protestant Dependance and Consumption in Swift's Irish Writings', in Connolly (ed.) *Political Ideas In Eighteenth-Century Ireland,* 83–104.
30. See Ellen Pollak, *The Poetics of Sexual Myth: Gender and Ideology in the Verse of Swift and Pope* (University of Chicago Press, 1985), 13–21, 163–72.

31. Nolan, 'Swift: The Patriot Game', 45, 49.
32. David Spurr, *The Rhetoric of Empire: Colonial Discourse in Journalism, Travel Writing, and Imperial Administration* (Durham, NC: Duke University Press, 1993), 11.
33. Ernst Cassirer, *The Philosophy of the Enlightenment,* trans. F. C. A. Koelln and J. C. Pettegrove (1932; Boston: Beacon Press, 1951), 108–17; David Berman, 'The Irish Counter-Enlightenment', in Richard Kearney (ed.), *The Irish Mind* (Dublin: Wolfhound Press, 1985), 119–40.
34. James Joyce, *Ulysses,* ed. Hans Walter Gabler et al. (London: Bodley Head and Penguin, 1986), 33, 109–11.
35. W. B. Yeats, *Explorations* (New York: Macmillan, 1962), 343–69. Among other Irish literary treatments of Swift are Shane Leslie, *The Skull of Swift* (1928), Paul Vincent Carroll's BBC television programme, *Farewell to Greatness* (1956), Denis Johnston's play, *The Dreaming Dust* (1940), and biography, *In Search of Swift* (1959), and Tom McIntyre's play *The Bearded Lady* (1984).

CHAPTER 2

Burke in the USA

LEO STRAUSS'S NATURAL RIGHT AND HISTORY (1953) MARKED an important stage in his evolution into America's Carl Schmitt. In its final chapter, he made the contentious claim that Burke, despite his readiness to invoke a universal natural law, was a historicist, in the sense that he regarded human rights, for instance, as the product of historical circumstances and not as deriving from abstract, universal principle. He was like Hegel in his preference for what is over what ought to be – a charge first made by Lord Acton that survives to the present day.[1] In Strauss's account, Burke unwittingly contributed to the erosion of the classical/Christian belief in a universal moral law and to the establishment in its place of the modern belief in the cultural relativity of values. This conclusion relocated Burke rather abruptly from what had seemed to be his increasingly secure position as an exemplary exponent of an anti-theoretical, pragmatic, even utilitarian approach to politics. His anti-revolutionary stance had regularly been praised as characteristically British or English, although his caution about circumstance and consequence was also often taken to be, at heart, utilitarian. These two elements formed a composite upon which his reputation rested easily for more than a century. Occasionally, tremors arising from his views on Ireland and India, or from allergic reactions to the florid complexion of his prose, or even, in Woodrow Wilson's case, to his 'brogue', or from an alleged incoherence in his political philosophy or even from the accusation that he didn't have one, shook the plinth on which he stood.[2] The Burke who had so successfully opposed 1789 to 1688, the Irishman who was more British than the English could ever be, the crypto-Catholic who had a deeper vision of Anglicanism than any Anglican since Hooker, the former supporter of rebellion who became the scourge and analyst of revolution, presented so great a paradox that for two hundred years its resolution or dissolution became a structuring feature of the commentary upon him. The fright of the French Revolution had brought out his deepest convictions in a suddenly articulated but long-implicit political theology. Even when this faded, Burke's polemic against 'theory' retained its force as the most enduring and identifiable feature of his work, adopted and adapted in the service of many causes. 'Burke's remarks on the problem of theory and practice are the most important part of his work', says Strauss.[3] Yet he appeared to yield at a critical moment to the idea that since the French Revolution was itself part of the Providential order, it should be accepted; he showed himself to be 'oblivious of the nobility of last-ditch resistance'.[4] This sudden shift in the tenor of Strauss's argument presents a Burke who promoted both a fatal resignation to what is, and who denied a presiding law of what ought to be, thereby giving to relativism an unwitting but decisively important impetus.

FOUNDING FATHER

Strauss's intervention was especially controversial in the United States where Burke had always retained a special position as the defender of a specifically Christian society against a desolating modernity. Rousseau, so identified by Burke himself, was his scandalous and dangerous rival; from Irving Babbitt's *Democracy and Leadership* (1924) to J. L. Talmon's *The Origins of Totalitarian Democracy* (1952), the battle between these avatars of the contemporary world was regularly and histrionically restaged in academic publications and in journalism as the primal scene in American political philosophy. In Talmon's work, Rousseau was the prophet whose messianic fantasy of revolutionary redemption was brought to life in the Terror and the Robespierrian dictatorship which were harbingers of the twentieth-century phenomenon of the totalitarian state. Talmon's was an incomparably coarser work than Hannah Arendt's *Origins of Totalitarianism* (1951) in which, by the author's own admission, Burke's thinking on human rights played an important role. However, his promotion of the rights of

Englishmen, as opposed to those of humankind in general, seemed to anticipate, she suggested, the state-based racism of the British imperial system. Obviously, the question of a conflict between the universal and the national dimensions of Burke's notion of rights arose out of readings of his interpretation of the French Revolution and of the accompanying ideas of national and popular sovereignty.[5] Michael Halberstam's analysis of Arendt's theory of totalitarianism discovered within it crucial features of Burke's theory of the sublime, such as terror and a psychic dislocation leading to a dissolution of subjectivity.[6] This was a more glamorous version of Walter Lippmann's earlier explanation for the atrocities of Lenin, Hitler, and Stalin, with their common root in Jacobinism – for all such figures, 'inhuman means are justified by the superhuman end: they are the agents of history or nature'.[7]

François Furet's *Penser la Révolution française* (1978), a hostile interpretation of the presiding liberal and Marxist interpretations of the Revolution, intensified the Anglophone applause for Burke. It helped to renew the double claim that he was a founding figure for a specifically Anglo-American tradition of political philosophy and that he had so effectively annihilated the intellectual claims of radical revolution (either Russian or French), that they could no longer be entertained in respectable company, although their dire consequences would have to be forever resisted. In opposing the French and supporting the American Revolution, Burke had become the great prophetic voice of the Christian West against a revolutionary, alternative, secular gospel. The Cold War struggle between capitalism and communism was presented as a rerun of that ideological battle. This analogy, pursued relentlessly until the fall of the Soviet system in 1991, then adjusted for the new war with Islam, drew much of its energy from a supposedly archetypal opposition between aggressive, doctrinal beliefs and more politically passive, but deeply seated convictions. In the United States of the fifties and sixties, there was a receptive audience for Burke's transposed call to Britain to awake from its non-dogmatic slumber to counter the missionary appeal of Jacobinism and to find a political language for the inarticulate mass of convention that was menaced by a revolutionary rhetoric in favour of all that was new and violently hostile to all that was old. Here again, Strauss's version of Burke seemed to be at odds with the views of a whole generation of commentators who had made Burke a hero of his and of their own times.

A concerted campaign to rehabilitate Burke's reputation began. Russell Kirk devoted a chapter of his influential book, *The Conservative Mind* (1953), to a polemical endorsement of Burke that was very far removed from Strauss's infinitely more educated and piercing critique. But it was Kirk's apocalyptic populism that set the tone for a discussion of Burke that was driven by hostility to the 'modern world' and by the ambition to counter modernity's presiding political heir, liberalism. In Kirk's account, the United States had to be awakened to its world role and duty as an aggressive defender of the integrity of an ancient, Christian inheritance so derided that it had almost been lost. To win the Cold War against the Soviet Union, it was necessary to win the internal battle against the liberal and communist view of the world political order. All radicals, whatever their disagreements among themselves, 'unite', according to Kirk, 'in detesting Burke's description of the state as ordained by God ... [as] the community of souls'. Burke had survived liberalism's 'hundred years of ascendancy', he 'knew history to be the unfolding of a Design', and 'never would concede that a consumption society, so near to suicide, is the end for which Providence has prepared man'.[8] This doomsday evangelism, as kitsch as can be, is yet a founding tract for the politics and aesthetics of American conservatism of the next sixty years. To effect Burke's transition from the central figure of British to that of American conservatism, the conceptual architecture of his political thought had to be altered.

As part of Kirk's continued crusade on behalf of his version of Burke, the Jesuit priests Peter J. Stanlis and Francis Canavan published, respectively, *Edmund Burke and the Natural Law* (1958; new edn 2003) and *The Political Reason of Edmund Burke* (1960). All three writers were continuing rather than initiating an attempt to reanimate American conservatism. Conservatism had begun a rebuilding programme in the aftermath of the Wall Street Crash and at the beginning of the Great Depression, with the collection of essays *Twelve Southerners: I'll Take my Stand: The South and the Agrarian Tradition* (1930). The Agrarian and the Fugitives movements took the industrialization of the South as an example of the destructive force of 'Northern' capitalism and of the peril faced by all traditional ways of community life caught up in its marauding energies. This agrestian politics reached an epitome in the work of Wendell Berry, whose opposition to the United States' recurrent wars from World War II to Iraq, highlights the isolationist and anti-imperial streak, once notable in American conservatism.[9] Burke was often, if rather casually, invoked in this literature in defence of the organic community and its 'traditional' class distinctions. Additionally, hostility to the secular state and a corresponding fetish of individualism had been central to conservative thinking in the thirties, as in the writings of an admirer of Burke such as Albert Jay Nock.[10] But Kirk and the Jesuit scholars opened up an unexpected new space for the reception of Burke as a defender of anything that could be claimed as traditional, organic, historic, communal, and, most of all, religious. This was the Irish-American Catholic space.

It was not a region, like the American South, but a virtual space, a new Catholic medieval Europe for political philosophy. It had already flashed up in Agrarianism, as an after-image of G. K. Chesterton's and Hilaire Belloc's economic theory of 'Distributism' and their medievalist ideal. In this less literary version, intellectual dominion was exercised by St Thomas Aquinas whose exposition of the natural law had long been the basis for political thought and action in the Christian world before the Enlightenment and the Revolution. Two elements had to be repositioned. One was the estimate of the presence and influence of natural law, the other was the meaning and role of prudence in his work. In this new account, Burke, being at once Irish and Catholic, Protestant and British, retained a living relationship with that old European world and with the British tradition of liberty. By drawing on these resources, he had been enabled to outface the Revolution and expose its demonic energies and potential. Yet the Revolution's gains were already so great that Burke's attack was totally darkened to a lament for a world suddenly awakened to the recognition of its imminent dissolution. The violent destruction of traditional societies in India and Ireland by the British was akin to the destruction of traditional France by the revolutionaries, although the latter were pursuing the logic of a new secular theory, while the colonizing groups were betraying the principles of an ancient,

Christian polity and thereby unwittingly colluding in a universal devastation.

This is the Romantic reading of modernity as catastrophe transposed to Cold War conditions. Burke is its sovereign authority in whom the tradition of a natural law, in its Christian, Thomist formulation – although bearing the impress of its classical precedents, as represented by Cicero – is revived at a critical moment in history. However, it was claimed, Burke's thought had been stealthily disengaged from its Christian sources by a strategy that had allowed him to remain a champion against revolution but had defamed him as a utilitarian who advocated cautious, incremental reform, thus entirely disavowing the moral nature of his political thought. It was the aim of the Irish Catholic appropriation of him in the United States to demonstrate that he was not a utilitarian (and therefore open to the charge of 'relativism' in its many guises), but a Christian thinker in the natural law tradition for whom prudence was the virtue that enabled the principles of that law to be realized in widely different sets of circumstance. In the terms of this debate, the exercise of prudence was in itself a moral action, far removed from any Benthamite calculus, but easily mistaken for it, because both reckonings acknowledged the complex variety of the actual and both derided uniform, abstract, or 'theoretic' systems. Utilitarianism was the appropriate ethical system for the materialist secular view of the world; it was, indeed, a product of this outlook. Burke's prudential view (or vision) of the world, subtler and more nuanced than the 'mechanical' estimates of utility, was founded in a metaphysical belief. Thus, practical judgement in politics was an exercise in moral thinking which Burke exemplified by his tacit or explicit allegiance to the natural law. To retrieve this dimension of Burke's thought was part of a much more general restoration.[11]

In 1993, Joseph L. Pappin III published *The Metaphysics of Edmund Burke*, a full-length argument in favour of the natural law and against utilitarianism. The second edition and third printing of Stanlis's *Edmund Burke: The Enlightenment and Revolution* (1991), which appeared in 2003, had a chapter 'Burke and the Moral Law', subtitled 'Burke's supposed utilitarianism'; it emphasized Burke's account of Ireland as ruined by the Penal Laws, an instance of a morally and politically criminal system that he had condemned on natural law, not utilitarian, principles. The 2003 edition of Stanlis's *Edmund Burke and the Natural Law* bore an Introduction by V. Bradley Lewis, who claimed that when the book was first published in 1958, 'it was with a sense that natural law thinking about ethics and politics was under siege'. But, 'by now the revival in Natural Law has happened'.[12]

Such unforgivingly eristic discourse needs a certain stylistic glamour to leaven the monotony of its address. Only William F. Buckley Jr, among American conservatives, achieved this at times – more effectively on television than in print. His journal, *National Review,* for which Russell Kirk wrote 500 articles in 20 years, helped to establish Burke's name as the password for entrance to the newly reified 'Conservative Mind' with its 'Tradition' and 'Beliefs'. Kirk's grim, hectoring tone in his 'From the Academy' column in the *National Review,* which paraded the absurdities of American higher education, needed Buckley's smiling company and his journal's circulation to make 'Burkean' a stock, laudatory epithet.[13] Willmoore Kendall, a mentor to Buckley and no admirer of Kirk, who was said to have harboured the ambition to become 'the American Burke', wrote in 1963 that modern conservatives are 'simply those who resist the revolutionary program Burke identified and opposed in the *Reflections*'.[14] In his attempt to distinguish a conservatism that would be less literary, and less intellectually arthritic than Kirk's, Kendall was one of many who took as an example, not Strauss, but another influential German émigré, the Catholic Eric Voegelin, who, like Babbitt before him, regarded modernism as a Gnostic heresy.[15]

CULTURE WARS

The events of 1968 at Berkeley and Columbia accelerated the tempo of defection from liberalism as intellectual conviction or public practice, most prominently among those Jewish academics and writers who had come to be known, not affectionately, as the New York intellectuals. Perhaps the most revered among them, Lionel Trilling, intimated in his book *Beyond Culture* (1972) how troubling, as a teacher, he found the antinomianism of a modernist literature (which had elective affinities with radical modernist political thought) that exhilarated a generation of students wholly ignorant of the dangers it posed for a liberal democracy. The culture of a (largely European) modernism menaced the politics of (a predominantly American) modernity. Trilling's rehearsal of anxious scruple seemed to many to exemplify liberalism's deadly failure to confront the Schmittian-Straussian enemy; he was altogether too fascinated by and fascinating on the subtleties of betrayal in relation to his own Jewishness, to Israel, to the United States, and to a lingering sentiment for a socialism that retained a dangerous cultural appeal when politically it had mutated into the Soviet menace. Teachers on American campuses were still praising the doctrines of the God that Failed; merely to be anxious about that was farcical. Was the enemy the Soviet Union or was it possible to be so removed from the real world as to think it was the New Criticism? Apparently so; Trilling 'stood against the New Criticism as Edmund Burke had once stood against the ideologues of the French Revolution'.[16]

The counter-parade of toughness, which presented worried distinctions in cultural matters as the sign of a fatal liberal dalliance with irrelevancy that ultimately subverted the decisiveness, even the idea, of authority, was led by Norman Podhoretz, best known as a former editor of the *Partisan Review*, a coarse and effective propagandist for whom someone like Trilling was an indulgence America could ill afford. Curiously, the assault on liberalism often took the form of an attack on the prestige it assigned to the idea of complexity; this was reconstrued as, in effect, an idiotic or sinister readiness to dissolve all certainties in the bonfires of an intellectual vanity that opposed the principles of that parental humanism which had allowed it to flourish in the first place. The reception of Jacques Derrida in the United States is perhaps the most spectacular example of this reaction to the liberalism, allegedly now transmogrified into an ideology, that had corroded the assumptions of democratic civilization and exchanged its former suavity for an apocalyptic vacuity by which higher education had been swallowed.[17] These culture wars, as they came to be called, revived the commercial-cultural idea of the Great Books of Western Culture, through a knowledge of which Tradition could be revived and the security of the state and society assured. New editions of many of these canonical authorities, financed by foundations and institutes, appeared. Burke could not but be a beneficiary. No Great

Books listing would exclude him, and no opportunity was lost to affirm that in him an Anglo-American, economically liberal, free society had an anchor. Reading for America was a serious and sustained project, even if the choice of recommended readings might be in the insecure hands of a Straussian epigone like Allan Bloom or if the ponderous, educated hero of the bewildering hour might take the comic form of one of Saul Bellow's heroes, such as Moses Herzog.[18] The point was to get back to the basics (Basic Books, Anchor Books) and renew the Western Tradition in the United States. The basics were, in that light, simple by definition.

But in another light they were not. Burke's hostility to the French intellectuals of his day was that they shoehorned complex matters to make them fit with an ideology which could never apprehend the infinite variety of human, historical circumstance and experience. Theory simplified; history, which Burke had made its antithesis, restored a sense of complexity. Stark theoretical radicalism, Irving Kristol argued, in *Reflections of a Neoconservative* (1983), belonged to the French, not the British Enlightenment which, in men like Adam Smith or Burke, had provided a secure basis for a libertarian or neo-conservative politics. Another identifying feature of radical politics was said to be a homelessness that expressed itself as or in abstraction. Burke's attack on theory was always reinforced by his complementary support for attachment, especially in the endlessly repeated citation from *Reflections* about loving 'the little platoon we belong to in society'.[19] For Jewish intellectuals in the United States, after the Second World War, this phrase had a particular attraction, since the claim to belong to such a group would counter the stereotype of the intellectual and of the Jew as someone who, precisely in not belonging to one country, thereby belongs to the world. Burke's attack on the intellectuals and on the Revolution as *une cause théoretique,* had almost criminalized rootlessness; the 'justifiable' exclusion of the intellectual from a national consciousness or consensus became a reactionary commonplace as much as the neighbouring accusation that intellectual exclusiveness is the condition for the abstraction of radical thought.

Once again, it was in Hannah Arendt's writings that the issue received a decisive political articulation. In the most Burkean of her books, *On Revolution* (1963), she contrasted the partial success of the American with the total failure of the French Revolution in producing a democratic polity. In an important modification of what she had previously said about the limitations of Burke's notion of human rights, she now claims that it is a human right to have civil rights. The tension between these two orders of right is peculiar to the political realm and the assertion that this needs to be addressed and resolved as far as possible, is made on behalf of all those who are stateless, homeless, or in a minority and yet who have a claim on the specific civil rights available in any given society to the presiding majority. This claim was developed in relation to Burke by Michael Walzer in an essay of 1984, and later in *Thick and Thin: Moral Argument at Home and Abroad* (1994) – both later echoed by Jennifer Welsh and others.[20] The reconciliation of the local, historically grounded values and their universal and abstract dimensions is foundational to liberal communitarianism. But much of its impetus originated in the specifically Jewish attempts to solve the apparent antinomies of assimilation and disassimilation, diaspora universalism and an at-homeness in the chosen double homes, 'the little platoon' of the United States and of Israel.

LIBERALS AND COMMUNITARIANS

The Burke of 'the little platoon' proved to be a creature of almost infinite adaptability. In 1976 (and again in 1986), Robert Nisbet called for a renewal of this Burkean spirit, a Tocquevillian citizenship rooted in localities as against the 'bankrupt [Jacobin] idea of *patrie*'.[21] This gave a stimulus to the communitarianism associated with Michael Sandel, Michael Walzer, and others.[22] In 1984, in another example, Richard John Neuhaus had called for the 'Christian community', which he distinguished from 'the religious new right', to enter upon 'the public square' and challenge the languages of liberalism with 'the very new-old language of Christian America'.[23] Neuhaus is one of those – Peter Viereck, Edward Banfield, Gary Wills among them – who recognize and demonstrate that what Sharon Crowley calls the 'discursive climate' in the United States is 'dominated by two powerful discourses: liberalism and Christian fundamentalism'.[24] Communitarian political philosophy supported the declaration that, in the grievous circumstances of the present, the local is the only arena for a possible politics. It was at pains to distinguish itself from a rights-based liberalism and from a polemical opposition between 'reason' and 'tradition' that was widely taken to be Burkean. Philip Selznick announced that 'Burke's reason was an anchored rationality.'[25] In him, sociology and the natural law tradition were finally introduced to one another, although the accounts of Burke's political philosophy in the ensuing debates became alarmingly perfunctory. But his reputation was such that he could then and still can be used as a brand name, little more than an organic ingredient in an advertisement for a new political health food. Selznick's real interest is organization theory, which has a considerable overlap with communitarianism.

The corporation or organization has now become the most recent version of 'the little platoon'. This new formula, according to Sheldon Wolin, 'is not pure Leninism, but Leninism clothed in the language of Burke'.[26] However, the further perfection of organization is sought in Systems Management Theory. Here again, Burke survives in a grotesque afterlife in which his name and a pseudo-Burkean language are flourished in an attempt to allow budget accounting, public administration, and 'the new science of organization' to affect a status comparable to political philosophy.[27] It's a long way from Leo Strauss.

The increasing feebleness of the name 'Burkean conservative', was forecast by David Bromwich in 1996.[28] It is appropriate that the warning came from someone who has himself at times made even Burke seem not Burkean enough and is one of the most caustic critics of the right's detention, even rendition, of Burke for its own purposes. He pleads that we learn from Burke 'the possibility of holding politics and imagination together in a single thought'.[29] The echo of Yeats in that phrase would be both appreciated and suspected by Alasdair MacIntyre, who sees in the Burkean myth of continuity in English history, both in itself and in its adaptation by Yeats, 'a prototype in and for the modern world' in that it provided for the modern state 'a much-needed mask'.[30] In MacIntyre's Catholic conservatism, there is a lingering aroma of the anarchism that had been much earlier attributed to Burke by Murray Rothbard.[31] Burke's linkages of the ethical and the political, so heavily eroded by political polemics and in part redeemed as a philosophical issue in itself by MacIntyre's work, has been further restored by the work of Bromwich and James Chandler, especially through an understanding of his impact on Wordsworth.[32] Similarly, the tacit affinities between Burke and de Tocqueville, explored with such mastery by Sheldon Wolin, have enriched our understanding of their analyses of the French Revolution and of the emergent democratic polities of the modern era.[33] Such work is especially consolatory and politically important in the face of the Disney versions of Burke that have become the soft modern equivalent in the United States of the vicious cartoons that so successfully misrepresented him in eighteenth-century Britain. We read, for instance, that the American 'Old Right' had a 'Burkean veneration of antiquity, history and tradition, a sense of the mystical charm of things that gave to otherwise mundane and quotidian commonalities of experience a special place in the imagination'.[34] The vocabulary is there, but in such examples, Burke himself has faded to a melancholy spectre of the giant figure he once had been in American political philosophy. Even now some conservative writers strive to rescue his version of 'civil society' from the radical right to restore to politics some sense of public virtue.[35]

NOTES

1. Leo Strauss, *Natural Right and History* (University of Chicago Press,1953), 319; Acton MSS at Cambridge University Library, Add. 4967.74.
2. Woodrow Wilson, 'The Interpreter of English Liberty', in *Mere Literature and Other Essays* (Boston: Houghton Mifflin, 1896), 104–60 (at 104).
3. Strauss, *Natural Right and History*, 303.
4. Ibid., 318. See Steven J. Lenzer, 'Strauss's Three Burkes: The Problem of Edmund Burke in *Natural Right and History*', *Political Theory*, 19/3 (1991), 364–90; for a hostile account of Strauss on Burke, meant to be scathing, see Claes G. Ryn, *A Common Human Ground: Universality and Particularity in a Multicultural World* (Columbia: University of Missouri Press, 2003), 58–9, 70.
5. Hannah Arendt, *The Origins of Totalitarianism* (New York: Harcourt Brace, 1951), 290–302; Cornelius Castoriades, *Fragments: Writings on Politics, Society, Psychoanalysis, and the Imagination* ed. and trans. D. A. Curtis (Stanford: Stanford University Press, 1997), 96; Peg Birmingham, *Hannah Arendt and Human Rights: The Predicament of Common Responsibility* (Bloomington: Indiana University Press, 2006), 45; Michael Hardt and Antonio Negri, *Empire* (Cambridge, MA: Harvard University Press, 2000), 104–05.

6. Michael Halberstam, *Totalitarianism and the Modern Conception of Politics* (New Haven, CT: Yale University Press, 1999), 113–16; Stephen K. White, *Edmund Burke in the USA: Burke: Modernity, Politics and Aesthetics,* (Thousand Oaks, CA: Sage, 1994), 32, 47.
7. Walter Lippmann, *Essays in The Public Philosophy* (New York: Mentor, 1955), 68.
8. Russell Kirk, *The Conservative Mind from Burke to Santayana* (Washington, DC: Regency Gateway, 2001), reprint of the 7th edn (1985), 10, 13, 11. From 1960, the title became *The Conservative Mind from Burke to Eliot.*
9. See Wendell Berry, *Citizenship Papers* (Washington, DC: Shoemaker & Hoard, 2003).
10. Albert Jay Nock, *Our Enemy, the State* (New York: W. Morrow, 1935).
11. For a recent discussion of prudence, with some specific relation to Burke, see Richard Bourke, 'Theory and Practice: The Revolution in Political Judgement', in Richard Bourke and Raymond Geuss (eds.), *Political Judgement: Essays for John Dunn* (Cambridge University Press, 2009), 73–109.
12. V. Bradley Lewis, Introduction to Peter J. Stanlis, *Edmund Burke and the Natural Law* (New Brunswick, NJ: Transaction, 2003), ix–x.
13. See Jeffrey Hart, *The Making of the American Conservative Mind: National Review and Its Times* (Wilmington, DE: ISI Books, 2006).
14. Willmoore Kendall, *The Conservative Affirmation* (Chicago: Henry Regnery, 1963), 142; see George H. Nash, 'The Place of Willmoore Kendall in American Conservatism', in John A. Murley and John E. Alvis (eds.), *Willmoore Kendall: Maverick of American Conservatives* (Lanham, MD: Lexington, 2002), 3–16.
15. See, for example, Eric Voegelin, *The New Science of Politics: An Introduction* (University of Chicago Press, 1952).
16. William M. Chace, *Lionel Trilling, Criticism and Politics* (Stanford University Press, 1980), 64.
17. See Christopher Norris, *Derrida* (London: Fontana, 1987), 142–61.
18. Allan Bloom, *The Closing of the American Mind: How Higher Education Has Failed Democracy and Impoverished the Souls of Today's Students* (New York: Simon & Schuster, 1987); Bellow wrote a Foreword to Bloom's book; *Herzog* was published in 1964.
19. *The Writings and Speeches of Edmund Burke,* ed. Paul Langford et al., 9 vols. (Oxford: Clarendon Press, 1981–2015), vol. VIII, 97.
20. See Albrecht Wellmer, 'Arendt on Revolution', in Dana Richard Villa (ed.), *The Cambridge Companion to Hannah Arendt* (Cambridge University Press, 2000), 220–41; Pierre Birnbaum, *Geography of Hope: Exile, the Enlightenment, Disassimilation* (Stanford University Press, 2008), 203–41, 374–80; Michael Walzer, 'Edmund Burke and the Theory of International Relations', *Review of International Studies,* 10 (1984), 205–18; Jennifer Welsh, 'Burke's Theory of International Order', in David Clinton (ed.), *The Realist Tradition and Contemporary International Relations* (Baton Rouge: Louisiana State University Press, 2007), 137–60.

21. Robert A. Nisbet, *Twilight of Authority* (New York: Oxford University Press,1975), 286–7; see also *The Sociological Tradition* (New York: Basic Books, 1966) and *Conservatism: Dream and Reality* (Minneapolis: University of Minnesota Press, 1986).
22. Michael J. Sandel, *Liberalism and the Limits of Justice* (Cambridge University Press, 1982); see Daniel Bell, *Communitarianism and Its Critics* (Oxford: Clarendon Press, 1993).
23. Richard John Neuhaus, *The Naked Public Square: Religion and Democracy in America* (Grand Rapids, MI: Eerdmans, 1984), 7, 19, 93.
24. Sharon Crowley, *Toward a Civil Discourse: Rhetoric and Fundamentalism* (University of Pittsburgh Press, 2006), 2. See Peter Viereck, *Conservatism Revisited: The Revolt Against Ideology* (New York: Scribners, 1949); Edward Banfield, *The Unheavenly City Revisited* (Prospect Heights, IL: Waveland Press, 1990); Gary Wills, *Under God: Religion and American Politics* (New York: Simon & Schuster, 2007).
25. Philip Selznick, *The Moral Commonwealth: Social Theory and the Promise of Community* (Berkeley: University of California Press, 1992), 40.
26. Sheldon S. Wolin, *Politics and Vision: Continuity and Innovation in Western Political Thought*, new edn (Princeton University Press, 2003), 383.
27. Akhlaque U. Haque and Anwar-ul-Haque, *Edmund Burke: Limits of Reason in Public Administration Theory* (Cleveland State University, 1994); Akhlaque U. Haque, 'Edmund Burke: The Role of Public Administration in a Constitutional Order', in Thomas D. Lynch and Todd Dickers (eds.), *Handbook of Organization Theory and Management: The Philosophical Approach* (New York: Marcel Decker, 1998), 181–202; Akhlaque U. Haque, 'Moral Conscience in Burkean Thought: Implication of Diversity and Tolerance in Public Administration', in Thomas D. Lynch and Peter L. Cruise (eds.), *Handbook of Organization Theory and Management*, 2nd edn (Boca Raton, FL: Taylor & Francis, 2006), 283–300; Thomas D. Lynch and Cynthia F. Lynch, 'Philosophy, Public Budgeting, and the Information Age', in Aman Khan and W. Bartley Hildreth (eds.), *Budget Theory in the Public Sector* (Westport, CT: Quorum, 2002, 259–305 (es. 266–7 on Burke); Michael C. Tuggle, 'Snowstorms and Saigon: Knowledge and Control', in *Confederates in the Boardroom: The New Science of Organizations* (College Station, TX: Traveller Press, 2004), 33–60.
28. David Bromwich, 'Review of James Conniff, *The Useful Cobbler: Edmund Burke and the Politics of Progress;* Stephen K. White, *Edmund Burke: Modernity, Politics, and Aesthetics*', *Political Theory*, 24/4 (1996), 739–46 (at 739).
29. David Bromwich, 'Review of Paul Langford, et al (eds.), *Writings and Speeches of Edmund Burke*, Vols. II, V, VIII', *Political Theory*, 19/4 (1991), 662–667 (at 667). See also David Bromwich, *A Choice of Inheritance: Self and Community from Edmund Burke to Robert Frost* (Cambridge, MA: Harvard University Press, 1989).
30. Alasdair MacIntyre, 'Poetry as Political Philosophy: Notes on Burke and Yeats', in *Ethics and Politics: Selected Essays*, 2 vols. (Cambridge University Press, 2006), vol. II, 159–71 (at 163).

31. Murray Rothbard, 'A Note on Burke's Vindication of Natural Society', *Journal of the History of Ideas,* 19 (1958), 113–18.
32. James K. Chandler, 'Wordsworth and Burke', *English Literary History,* 47 (1980), 741–71; David Bromwich, *Disowned by Memory: Wordsworth's Poetry of the 1790s* (University of Chicago Press, 1998). See also Bromwich's *Edmund Burke: An Intellectual Biography* (Cambridge, MA: Harvard University Press, 2014).
33. Sheldon S. Wolin, *Tocqueville Between Two Worlds: The Making of a Political and Theoretical Life* (Princeton University Press, 2001).
34. J. David Hoeveler Jr, *Watch on the Right: Conservative Intellectuals in the Reagan Era* (Madison: University of Wisconsin Press, 1991), 178.
35. See, for example, Sam Tanenhaus, *The Death of Conservatism* (New York: Random House, 2009).

CHAPTER 3

Tone: The Great Nation and the Evil Empire

On the morning of 30 April 1795, the United Irish agent William Jackson, who was also a clergyman of the Established Church, faced the chief justice, John Scott, earl of Clonmel, in the King's Bench court on Merchants' Quay in Dublin to receive the sentence of death by hanging for treason; earlier that day he had been seen vomiting from the window of the coach that brought him there from Newgate Prison. Now he was slumped against the dock, sweating profusely. He rallied for a moment and whispered to his legal counsel, 'We have deceived the senate.'[1] His hat was removed and 'a dense steam was seen to ascend from his head and temples'; his face twitched, his eyes alternately closed and glared. When ordered to stand before the court, he stood rocking from side to side, his arms crossed over his breast, and was asked to say why 'judgement of death and execution thereon should not be awarded against him, according to law'. He made no response. 'Sweat rolled down his face ... and he grasped the iron spikes, which encircled the dock, with avidity.'[2] His counsel intervened to ask for an arrest of sentence, and the windows of the courtroom were opened to relieve Jackson who, nevertheless, was in his final agony and suddenly 'sunk in the dock'. Clonmel declared: 'If the prisoner is in a state of insensibility, it is impossible that I can pronounce the judgement of the court upon him.' A Doctor Thomas Waite and a Thomas Kinsley, who identified himself as 'an apothecary and druggist', offered to examine Jackson. Kinsley was a Quaker and refused to have his opinion of Jackson's condition sworn in to the record on oath. Waite told Clonmel straight away that the prisoner was 'verging to eternity'. Indeed, within moments he was dead; his body remained in the dock in the position of its final collapse until an inquest on the following morning. Jackson was found to have swallowed a large quantity of 'metallic poison', probably arsenic, almost certainly supplied by his wife on her final visit earlier that day, when the jailer had seen him 'much agitated' and vomit 'very violently' after taking some tea.[3] And perhaps Mrs Jackson had agreed to cooperate with her husband in the shared hope that his suicide would preserve for her any chance of retaining the little money they had left from confiscation by the government – inevitable if he were to be hanged as a traitor. At any rate, after a swift inquest, Jackson was buried the following Sunday 'in all the triumph of treason'.[4]

Apart from the dramatic public suicide, Jackson's trial was significant in other respects. First, the evidence in the case so compromised Tone that he had to make a deal with the government to go into exile in America in order to avoid a charge of treason at home. It also revealed both to government and its opponents that revolutionary France had a genuine interest in the possibility of an Irish expedition. Further, it was the first in a series of trials against members of the United Irishmen in which a new departure from English law, peculiar to Ireland, was employed. Henceforth, the evidence of one witness was sufficient to convict a prisoner upon a charge of high treason (two was the minimum in England). The consequence was that a trail of informers issued from Dublin Castle, 'where they had been worked upon, by the fear of death and the hopes of compensation, to give evidence against their fellows';[5] their witness led in almost every instance to execution. This was integral to government strategy at the time: a reign of terror face-masked by the law, the summary character of the proceedings disguised in the public ritual of conformity to ancient rules.

At the heart of it all stood the friend or colleague turned informer, the state's witness. It was in this decade that he began his career, scarcely interrupted since, as the villain in Irish public imagination; infamous, a traitorous and fawning wretch in the secret organization and vengefully powerful in the 'bad eminence' of his sudden new public position; not a villain in law; au contraire, and far worse, the villain of and for the law; 'in this wicked country is the informer an object of judicial idolatry'.[6] (And the decade had an abundance of informer-villains, such as Francis Higgins, the Sham Squire, and Tone's brother-in-law, Thomas Reynolds;

Leonard McNally's even more shocking and deep-seated treachery was not revealed until his death in 1820.) When the informer came into a courtroom under guard, 'Have you not marked, when he entered, how the stormy wave of the multitude retired at his approach?'[7] asked John Philpot Curran – himself gulled all the way by McNally, who had 'entertained' Jackson and some friends within a day or two of his arrival in Dublin in 1794.

Jackson had been betrayed by his friend John Cockayne, to whom he had revealed his mission to collect information about Ireland for the French revolutionary government. It is the fact of the betrayal of friendship in his own calamitous case that gives his whispered last words to one of his assistant counsel (Curran was his chief counsel) such a melancholy resonance. They are from Thomas Otway's *Venice Preserv'd* (1682), in which the hero Pierre asks his friend Jaffeir (who has in fact betrayed him in their conspiracy against the corrupt Venetian senate) to save him from a dishonourable death on the wheel and gallows by stabbing him. The anguished Jaffeir does so and then, in remorse at his own treachery, fatally stabs himself also. Pierre exclaims: 'Now, now – thou hast indeed been faithful! This was done nobly! – We've deceived the senate.'[8]

The play was popular for about 150 years – performed every year but one of the eighteenth century in London, published in scores of editions in London and Dublin, the roles of Pierre and Jaffeir famously and repeatedly filled by David Garrick and Spranger Barry – and was generally taken to be a coded parable about Whigs or Tories or Papists conspiring against the English court or parliament. But for the most part, in popular performance and imagination, it was a play that celebrated male friendship and a male conception of honour as greater than heterosexual love and as the ground of political fidelity to the cause of justice. Equally, the part of the abandoned heroine, Belvidera, who goes mad after the final spectacular double killing on the platform of the gallows, was one of the most sought-after of all tragic roles. Her anguish was, in 'loyalist' versions of the play, taken to represent the brutal effect on human feeling of ideological fanaticism, a counter-revolutionary propagandist theme pursued with especially monotonous vigour in the 1790s. Yet there was a 'plot' by the English radical John Thelwall, as revealed by the spy Taylor at Thelwall's trial in London in 1794, 'to steal [the play] from the loyalist canon' by mounting a campaign against the current production at Covent Garden. According to Thelwall, the play had been written to damage the patriots of its day 'by representing all reformers as conspirators'. Thelwall and his friends had loudly applauded the 'republican passages' at the first night of the Covent Garden production, and the 'civic republicanism' element was further heightened in a new production at Drury Lane by Sheridan and John Philip Kemble; in the light of the Treason Trials of the previous year, the conspirators looked like 'civic martyrs'. But this production closed after only three nights, partly because of the climate engendered by an attack on the king's coach on 29 October 1795 at the state opening of parliament.[9] Still, the exchanges and speeches of Pierre and Jaffeir, or a selection from them, certainly had gained a more decisively republican timbre since Jackson's whispered last words in April. And the final gesture of giving up wife and family in the act of deceiving the corrupt and vicious senate, of refusing to allow the state to impose a criminalizing sentence carried out in public, by choosing an honourable suicide – to control one's own death even while in the jaws of the monster – bore the mark of ancient Roman stoic republican pride, which Jackson, and, three and a half years later, Tone, reasserted for posterity by the manner of their deaths.

'IF EVER I HAVE THE POWER'

> Well, for me . . . only one real sentiment exists – friendship between man and man. Pierre and Jaffeir, such a bond as theirs is what I care for most. I know *Venice Preserved* by heart.

The speaker here is the villianous Vautrin in Balzac's *Père Goriot* (1832),[10] exemplifying the later decline of the republican ideal of friendship and honour into a masquerade, as he draws the horrified Eugène de Rastignac into his debt and into his power. Vautrin's was the Paris of the July Monarchy of Louis Philippe, far from the revolutionary city of heroic virtue – although it was in the Paris of the Directory and not of Robespierre that in 1796 Tone heard the Marseillaise sung every night he went to the Comédie-Française 'and the verse "*Tremblez, Tyrans*" always received with applause' (2.42).[11] Tone remained entranced by the

Revolution and by the French, although he acknowledged in a conversation with General Clarke in March 1796 that its initial enthusiasm had subsided (2.121); for the most part he is silent about or unaware of the premonitory indications of corruption that marked the rule of the Directory that had come to power just a few months before he arrived in February 1796. Still, his 'first adventure' there was with a swindler who now appears like a characteristically shabby representative of the public sleaziness that was then rapidly colonizing the newly expanded public sphere. 'The republic of vice seemed to have succeeded the Republic of Virtue.'[12] This was not quite Tone's view; he sensed there was indeed no further appetite for revolution in Paris, after the ending of the Terror and the revolutionary tribunals which he abhorred. Nor did he want to see the Republic threatened, partly because that would further diminish the prospects of a French invasion force for Ireland. Thus, he showed no sympathy for the Babouvist conspirators, arrested on 10 May 1796. In his diary next day, he records working on the *Proclamation to the People of Ireland* for General Hoche, copies of which were to be distributed by the French army after it had landed in Ireland, and responds to the carefully overheated government announcement of the plot to massacre those in authority:

> I would show no mercy to any man, whatever might be his past merits, who would endeavour in the present position of France to subvert the existing government ... the French have at this moment an exceeding good form of government ... It might possibly be better but the advantage which might possibly result from an alteration is not such as to warrant any honest man in hazarding the consequences of another bloody revolution. (2.179)

On Bastille Day in 1796, Tone reports that Carnot told him 'he was satisfied that Babeuf's plot was the work of an Orléans [royalist] faction' (2.236). The leaders of the conspiracy, betrayed by a notorious spy, Grisel, were Babeuf and Darthé. They attempted (but failed), in keeping with their Roman stoic republican beliefs, to commit suicide in court after sentence, by stabbing themselves. They were nevertheless, after a night of great pain, hauled off to public execution on 27 May 1797. (Two years before, the martyrs of Prairial, six Jacobin members of the

'Crest' group in the Convention, had committed mass suicide, again by stabbing one another, on the way to the guillotine. For them too this was a call to action to posterity and an assertion of their freedom to die as republicans. And Robespierre of course had left himself in agony with a shattered jaw after his botched suicide in 1794.) Tone was in Cologne that day, vainly trying to fix a meeting with Hoche, seemingly unaware of the guillotining in Vendôme (outside Paris), but learning, belatedly, from a newspaper of the betrayal and arrest of a number of United Irishmen in the north of Ireland (3.75). All during his years in Paris and in French-dominated Europe, Tone lived in this liquid suspension of slow-floating information and frustration, the increasingly attenuated strains of the revolution yielding to the dark rumbling of the news from Ireland, picked up at second or third hand, the doom-laden sounds of sanctioned slaughter at home and whispered, pervasive betrayal there and in Paris too.

Spies and informers were everywhere – in Paris, in London, in Ireland. *L'or du Pitt,* Pitt's gold, spread out in a giant delta, from the north of Ireland, to Dublin, Scotland, La Vendée, into France's army and political system and into the consciousness of exiles, émigrés, and police. It became more attractive as the French currency weakened. 'Pitt is as cunning as Hell, and he has money enough, and we have nothing here but assignats' (2.120). Tone was suspicious that so many 'Americans' were to be found in Paris; even more so, he was suspicious of his own countrymen and their indiscretions or provocations. Tone lived undercover, as Citizen Smith, in a state of justified paranoia, trying to conceal his presence in France from the British authorities who believed him to be still in America. Secrecy was unavoidable, yet the boast of republicanism had always been its open, public stance. As a consequence, since he was without his wife and children (who did not get to France from America until 1797), or his closest friend, Thomas Russell, he spent a lot of time drinking a lot of wine on his own. In February 1796, after a useful meeting with the American ambassador, James Munroe, Tone marvels in his diary at 'so obscure an individual' as himself should be 'thrown into such a situation'. And goes on: 'I hope I may not ruin a noble cause by any weakness or indiscretion of mine; as to my integrity I can answer for myself. What shall I do for want of P.P. [Thomas Russell]?

I am in unspeakable difficulties for the want of his advice and consolation' (2.75). And his wife is in effect the person to whom the diary is confided; how often he wishes she could see and hear what he is recording; how much he wants to impress her and make her proud of his achievement! At the Opéra: 'I lose three fourths of the pleasure I would otherwise feel for the want of my dear love, or my friend P.P. to share it with. How they would glory in Paris just now!' (2.54).

Even in those ecstatic moments when he could delight in the democratic celebrations of the revolutionary crowds, at festivals and military displays, his unease and solitude persist. For instance, at the Victory Festival at the Champ de Mars, 29 May 1796, Tone was included with the diplomatic corps, but 'for particular reasons I chose to remain *incognito* ... the tears ran down my cheeks when Carnot presented the wreaths and the standards to the soldiers. It was a spectacle worthy of a great republic and I enjoyed it with transport. *Vive la République!*' (2.192). A couple of months later, while walking through the Tuileries gardens he by chance met an old friend, the British radical John Hartford Stone, whose brother William had been involved in the Jackson trial, and the writer Helen Maria Williams. 'I was fairly caught, for I have avoided Stone ever since my arrival; not that I know anything to his prejudice, but that I guard the incognito' (2.246). Living in such studied anonymity (or pseudonymity), Tone was greatly taken by the powerful reality, as he experienced it, of the alternative public life of the incandescent revolutionary unity in which the mixed elements of one's subjectivity could be, if only temporarily, dissolved. And the delirium of evenings at the Théâtre des Arts was heightened further by the recognition that the National Guardsmen who filled the stage were not actors but the men of the armies that had won such dazzling victories in the Netherlands and on the Rhine (2.50). '*Here*,' Tone writes, '*was no fiction*; and that is what gave it an interest which drew the tears irresistibly to my eyes' (2.52, emphasis in original). Theatre was, in his view, wisely subsidized by the government; it had become an inspirational display of music, heroic gesture, military splendour, and public enthusiasm coordinated into an official ritual. The political, pedagogical, and socially regenerative function of their theatre was one of the features that, he thought, made the contemporary French resemble the Athenians of ancient Greece (2.440).

Yet Tone had other, more frequent, occasions for tears of vexation and frustration. The delays and intricacies of his mission, straining to gain access to key figures such as Carnot, Hoche, or Delacroix via (undeservedly) suspect intermediaries such as General Clarke, sapped his patience; besieged by the anxiety that the mediocre contacts he was obliged to rely on and be nice to were putting self-interest before the cause of Ireland and, as ever, the looming fear of betrayal and the empty, imagined revenge – this was deep stress:

> Dined at Ahern's lodgings with Madgett, Sullivan, &c. Choice champagne! Got half tipsy, partly with rage and vexation at the prospect before me. Have I risqued my life, ruined my prospects, left my family and deserted my country to be baffled by a scoundrel at last? If he prove one, woe be to him! (2.156)

There was also the nagging doubt, not only about French government intentions but about his own capacity to fool himself about them; a diary entry for 18 February 1796, on foot of an encouraging conversation about which general should lead the Irish invasion force, asks: 'Am I too sanguine in believing what I so passionately wish – *that the French executive will seriously assist us*?' (2.59, emphasis in original). In similar fashion, regularly hearing of the atrocities in Ireland, often ten days or more after they happened, or of arrests of United Irish or former Catholic Committee leaders (like John Keogh), he begins to lose his natural gaiety and records the feeling:

> Well! a day will come for all this! If we cannot prevent his [Keogh's] fall, at least I hope we shall be able to revenge it; *and I for one promise if it be in twenty years from this not to forget it.* My heart is hardening hourly, and I satisfy myself now at once on points which would stagger me twelve months ago. The Irish aristocracy are putting themselves in a state of nature with the people, and let them take the consequences. They shew no mercy and they deserve none. If ever I have the power I will most heartily concur in making them a *dreadful example.* (2.149, emphasis in original)

And as the arrests of United Irishmen leaders and the assaults of the military on the civilian population continued, so the hardening of feeling continued: 'I feel my mind growing every hour more and more savage.

Measures appear to me now justified by necessity which six months ago I would have regarded with horror. There is now no medium' (3.221).

'A DOG'S LIFE'

When the French Revolution rejected historical precedent of the kind favoured by the *ancien régime* of Europe as a source of political legitimacy, it became necessary to invent or recreate an alternative in classical antiquity, particularly the republican Roman version – austere, heroic, sacrificial, suicidal. Roman or neo-Roman ideas about freedom and servitude played a comparable role before the outbreak of civil war in England in 1642.[13] But in France, at least until 1797, the Roman influence pervaded the whole public sphere, so that even the style of dress of the ancient republic was approved, indeed mandatory at times, because of its ivorian simplicity in contrast to the insolent frivolity and artificiality of monarchical fashions. Tone often comments on the 'classical' costumery of the Parisian fêtes and of actors and actresses – more often the latter. Even the opposition to this style took the form of a political fashion statement. The year before he arrived, the anti-Jacobin, royalist vigilante gangs, christened 'la jeunesse dorée', or 'Muscadins', appeared on the streets with their 'victim's style', spiked hair, long over the ears, cropped at the back to bare the neck, as for the guillotine. They rioted frequently at theatres and fêtes. Tone mentions that they 'and the *elegant women* of Paris made it a point to stay away' (unsurprisingly) from a fête at the Champ de Mars to celebrate 'the anniversary of the subversion of royalty in France' (2.307, emphasis in original). They remained a threat until the anti-royalist coup of Fructidor, 4 September 1797, which also led to the deportation of two of Tone's favoured candidates to lead the Irish invasion, Carnot and Pichegru – the latter on charges of treason. ('Such treachery', Tone writes, 'in a man of the situation, character and high reputation of Pichegru is enough to put a man out of humour with human nature', 3.148.) And in the same month General Hoche died of consumption – or possibly, according to Fouché, minister of police, he was poisoned.

Tone recognizes that he is witnessing (and is himself part of) the emergence of a new symbolic order; the old system of representation, political and aesthetic, had begun to weaken, even to disappear; what had previously 'stood for' the people, no longer did. '*Here was no fiction.*' A different form of representation was required because, in both France and Ireland, the relationship between the 'nation' and the 'people' was being reconfigured. Louis XVI was briefly rechristened 'King of the French' rather than 'King of France' in 1793; Louis Philippe in 1830 affected revolutionary credentials when assuming power specifically as 'King of the French'. However, this axiomatic, natural connection between people and nation – according to a condescending logic – had to be rediscovered and reaffirmed after enduring a long period of artificial and coercive separation. To effect this would require a sustained programme of education that would culminate in a recognition like that of Émile in Rousseau's great educational tract: 'I have decided to become what you [have] made me.'[14] That would be the revolutionary decision in which the people and the nation would become one, where the presiding idiom is one of will but the prevailing experience is one of discovery. And it is individually a discovery of identity as released in and through an indissoluble union with others.

The French had begun to exhibit the transformation they had undergone in the revolutionary drive to create this new (or 'natural', therefore not strictly new, but renewed) version of the human in their dress, decorations, and rituals. The calendar, with the *décadi* replacing Sundays (Sunday, 7 February 1796, 'I was curious to observe how this day would be kept in France', 2.43), theatre, fêtes, ballets, opera, all manifested this change; public singing in chorus and dancing (the Carmagnole, in particular), the salutation of 'citizen' replacing the titles and the old graded forms of greeting, the wearing of the *bonnet rouge*, the tricolour flag and cockade, the decorative motif of the Phrygian cap, the cult of the *sans-culottes*. Not everything was new. There were still traces in opera of the old musical tradition that Tone disliked – the French mode of professional singing, for instance, which he found did not compare with the more 'natural' Italian style that had become popular all over Europe. This echoed the famous dispute of the 1750s dominated by Rousseau and Rameau on the more melodic 'democratic' virtues of Italian as opposed to the formal, mannered court music and even language of the French. Rousseau 'won' the dispute. It was an important defeat for the cultural claims and prestige of Versailles.[15] The renewed emphasis in the 1790s on melody, and the consequent highlighting of the words of the dramatic text or song, reduced complicated harmonic and chromatic effects and increased audience participation in the great communal festive events, much enjoyed and frequently attended by Tone, fond of the melodic chorus as an instance of social unity, a political therapy for the sharpness of his solitude. He sided with the Rousseau faction in disliking the 'very heavy music by Rameau' (2.258) and greatly admiring Gluck, the most celebrated composer of Italian opera in Rousseau's day (2.256). He confesses in his diary that he goes to the opera so much (rather than the theatre) because he as yet understands music better than French (2.134). And again, 'Am I not to be pitied? ... I do lead a dog's life here. My sole resource is the Opera' (2.135).

The opera had long been more popular than the theatre in eighteenth-century France and became even more so in the revolutionary epoch. Tone celebrated the abolition of the distinction between the actors and the audience, both now agents in the great enterprise of emancipation from the strait conventions (and licensed privileges) of the past. In accord with that, he welcomed too the abolition of the distinction in uniform between officers and enlisted men; but his rapture was modified in this instance, for Tone loved dashing and elaborate military outfits. The sight of the Grenadier Guards in the garden of the Tuileries, young men conscripted in the *première réquisition* of 1793, reminded him of the Irish Volunteers as he had seen them 'in the days of my youth and innocence', and he duly supplies the details of their blue, white, and red uniforms, just as, on the next day, he describes in detail the splendid dress worn by the foreign minister Delacroix at a meeting marked by a very pleasing and encouraging ministerial courtesy and deference (2.55–6). Tone remarked how the erosion of military discipline of the Prussian sort had been replaced by an extraordinary enthusiasm, itself the new kind of discipline that he thought accounted for the astonishing French victories against conventionally trained forces (2.136, 138). Of course, he had already been involved in Ireland in some of those new forms of political organization and activity that had been developed to such a prodigious level in France – the political club, the underground conspiracy, the printing of newspapers, collections of popular songs, pamphlets, flysheets, placards – and he now witnessed the effects of the technological and political advances in the development of prints and engravings, cartoons, and even busts, of the murdered Marat, for instance, which the *jeunesse dorée* liked to destroy, and monumental sculptures, sometimes erected on the empty plinths of the dead king's statues, and paintings heroic both in scale and in subject matter. The Louvre impressed him in March 1796 with the range of its collection, the cynosure ambition that was to be so astonishingly realized under Napoleon: 'All France and Flanders have been ransacked to furnish it' (2.100). The revolutionary journée, or fête, even more than the opera or theatre, demonstrated 'the powerful effect of public spectacles, properly directed, in the course of a revolution' (2.137).

France had attained a condition that was the product of the peculiar and potent blend of the *dirigiste*, centralizing spirit of its government and the crusading, iconoclastic energies of the people at large. But the condition of Ireland was, in comparison, abysmal; 'Pat' needed a large dose of French élan if he were to be successfully remodelled for freedom. The Fête de la Jeunesse on 30 March 1796 prompted Tone to record the need to bring the Irish 'up to the enthusiasm of the French' (2.136) and, two days later, remembering the disputes he and Thomas Russell 'have had on the subject of discipline', to admit that he too would now 'make the French army our model in preference to the Prussian' (2.139). The planting of the tree of liberty, a ritual repeated thousands of times all over France and Europe – Tone attended a planting at a fête in Bonn in Vendémiaire, 22 September 1797 (3.152) – needed an enthused citizenry, the very phenomenon the English government and its lieutenant administration in Ireland were determined to eliminate by every imaginable form of coercion.

All these manifestations of a novel freedom that so impressed Tone also made him frequently disconsolate, for they reminded him of that painfully contrasting, increasingly desperate situation in Ireland. They also brought home to him his own humiliating condition of dependence on others, his writing to order of proclamations and analyses of the Irish situation that he could never be sure were either carefully or intelligently read, his endless waiting, the days when his diary records 'Blank!', or when he – most attractively to many of his later readers – registers his darker moods with a certain connoisseurship, but never with a valetudinarian relish. He regularly dismisses his own miseries with a shrug, quoting the phrase ''tis but in vain' from a popular song – which is followed in one version by the line '*For mortals to wish again*', and in another, '*For soldiers to complain*'. But the note of desperation is clearly audible at times. 'Well, here I am, and here I must remain, and I am as helpless as if I were alone, swimming for my life in the middle of the Atlantic. 'Tis terrible. However, 'Tis but in vain, &c., &c.' (2.203).

SERVITUDE

Yet these moods are not well understood simply as expressions of a 'personality'. They go to the heart of Tone's political experience and the whole concept of dependence and slavery that ramifies so widely through all republican theory. To be dependent on the wish, caprice, or undelegated authority of someone else is to lack autonomy and to be a slave. It is corrupt and corrupting, especially when sustained by violence and an endless bombardment of propaganda and threat. This is Ireland's condition and it is also Tone's. But now that he and his colleagues have moved against it for the recovery of that liberty which human dignity requires, their task is to persuade the Irish to internalize this as a demand of *right,* not just reactively to rebel against oppression. This condition of dependence has, in both subtle and gross ways, demoralized the Irish peasantry, who would have to emulate the French by theorizing their situation to effect a revolution in the very conception of autonomy and authority, not simply a rebellion against its local effects. The changes wrought in Ireland by the French Revolution were, Tone believed, already astonishing. The Dissenters, particularly in the North, were the most obvious beneficiaries, but the Catholic peasantry too had been greatly affected, he claimed. At his first meeting with him, he was asked about this by General Clarke, who was worried about the influence

> the Catholic clergy might have over the minds of the people and the apprehension lest they might warp them against France. I assured him,

> as the fact is, that it was much more likely that France should turn the people against the clergy than that the clergy should turn the people against France; that within these last few years, that is to say since the French Revolution, there had an astonishing change taken place in Ireland with regard to the influence of the priests. (2.112)

Tone's view of both the Catholic Defenders and the Protestant Dissenters and of their hopes and expectations of French help was optimistic. His First Memorial of 1796 compounds this with an overly sanguine view of the 'great majority' of the Catholic Committee as 'sincere republicans' (2.68). Still, these might also have been tactical overstatements to reassure the French – or himself. Tone believed that a great task of political education confronted him and the United Irishmen, but that it had already begun.[16]

A central function of the United Irishmen organization was the stimulation of the consciousness of the people to an awareness that the end had come for the *ancien régime* both as an idea and as a system. The downfall of the French monarchy and of the papacy marked the end of the ancient system of tyranny (3.208–10). In his *Address to the People of Ireland on the Present Important Crisis*, completed just before he set off on his final journey with the French fleet to Ireland, Tone wrote:

> Without being too much of an enthusiastic visionary, I think I may say I see a new order of things commencing in Europe ... the ancient system of tyranny must fall. In many nations it is already extinct, in others it has received its death wound ... its duration is ascertained and its days already numbered. I do not look upon the French revolution as a question subject to the ordinary calculation of politics; *it is a thing which is to be*; and as all human experience has verified that the new doctrine ever finally subverts the old, as the Mosaic law subverted idolatry, as Christianity subverted the Jewish dispensation, as the Reformation subverted popery, so, I am firmly convinced, the doctrine of republicanism will finally subvert that of monarchy and establish a system of just and rational liberty on the ruins of the thrones of the despots of Europe. (2.377, emphasis in original)

The Irish must seek independence as an ethical as well as political goal. But could that dimension be realized? Tone's official optimism faded when he addressed the problem of the effect upon the Irish of centuries of alien rule. In the same address, he says that

> we have been reduced to that lowest state of human degradation, we have almost ceased to respect ourselves; we have doubted whether the opinion of our oppressors was not just and whether we were not in fact framed for that submission to which we have been bent by the pressure of so many centuries of hard, unremitting, unrelenting tyranny. (2.376)

And, scoldingly, in the final paragraph: 'if you do not avail yourselves of the present opportunity to free your country and to make your own fortunes, you deserve to remain, as you will remain, in poverty and disgrace for ever!' (2.396). In similar but even harsher terms, he ends his address encouraging Irish sailors serving with the British fleet to rebel, with this accusation – which clearly does not refer only to the sailors: 'If all this does not rouse you, then you are indeed what your enemies have long called you – A BESOTTED PEOPLE!' (2.391).

Degradation and demoralization of the Irish by tyrannical rule were features Tone had already noticed during his sojourn in America. In a letter to Thomas Russell of October 1795, from Princeton, New Jersey, he had written:

> of all the people I have met here the Irish are incontestably the most offensive. If you meet a confirmed blackguard, you may be sure he is Irish. You will of course observe that I speak of the lower orders. They are as boorish and ignorant as the Germans, as uncivil and uncouth as the Quakers, and as they have ten times more animal spirits than both, they are much more actively troublesome. After all, I do not wonder at, nor am I angry with them. They are corrupted by their own execrable government at home ... (2.32)

The experience of servitude, according to Tone in his more pessimistic vein of thinking, could have lasted so long that servitude itself became a habit, almost a custom, certainly so ingrained that it could be confused with the natural. And the hanging implication is that along with servitude to the English power, there had also been servitude to popery and the rancid connection between the two malodorously evident in the Penal Laws and in sectarian bigotry. It was in such conditions that the animating force of the idea of the self as citizen was so menacing both to those in power and even to those to whom he wished to see power transferred. Slaves can love their enslavement and become immune to the infectious promise of emancipation.

But ultimately, the real slaves were also the real tyrants, the Anglo-Irish Protestant Ascendancy, wholly submissive to London, although given to the very occasional gesture of independence as in 1782–3, fatally weakened by 'the unjust neglect of the claims of their Catholic brethren' (2.302), but generally shameless and hardboiled in their habitual venality and violence towards those subordinated to them by the existing political order. Tone opens the full repertoire of derision and outrage in his description of this bigoted and interbred faction – as Burke too, from a different angle, regarded them:

> it is England who supports and nourishes that rotten and aristocratic faction among you ... a faction which to maintain itself by the power of England is ready to sacrifice, and daily does sacrifice, your dearest rights to her infallible lust of gold and power. (2.378)

Their lack of fellow feeling for the Catholics, their psychotic rage at the prospect of concessions to them in the franchise or in admission to professions, or at their insolence even in canvassing opinion on such issues – 'sedition, tumult, conspiracy, treason' (1.376) – were the signs of a cognitive failure that was, in its practised lockstep of tyranny and servility, the essence of provincialism. They understood perfectly that it was in their own interest to be craven towards their masters and to be ruthless towards the subjugated. They entertained no other possibility. Their horizon was closed. No generous commitment to a universal ideal was possible. The very notion of it aroused their hostility and derision. Tone adds this account of the link between the bad conscience of those who choose servility and the violence of their hatred for those who oppose it. It is, in radical enlightenment and republican discourse, a standard analysis of the tormented condition of those who deliberately violate natural basic instincts and take out their shame on those who expose them: it is to be found in Helvétius, La Mettrie, d'Holbach, and in novelists by the dozen:

> There is not a man of them that in the bottom of his soul does not feel that he is a degraded being in comparison of the men whom he brands with the

> name of incendiary and traitor. It is this stinging reflection that, among other powerful motives, is one of the most active in spurring them to revenge . . . Who can forgive the man that forces him to confess that he is a voluntary slave, and that he has sold for money everything that should be most precious to an honorable heart; that he has trafficked in the liberties of his children, and his own, and that he is hired and paid to commit a daily parricide on his country? Yet these are charges which not a man of that infamous cast can deny to himself before the sacred tribunal of his own conscience. At least the United Irishmen . . . have a grand, a sublime object in view; their enemies have not as yet ventured, in the long catalogue of accusation, to insert the charge of interested motives; while that is the case, they may be feared and abhorred, but they can never be despised, and I believe that there are few men that do not look upon contempt as the most insufferable of all evils. (3.248–9)

The triumph of Anglo-Irish servility guaranteed that Ireland would be, in every sense, a province or a colony. All its outcries, as earlier with Molyneux or Swift (or later with Flood or even now with Grattan), about its constitutional and/or commercial subordination challenged this condition briefly and shallowly. For all talk of independence that did not address the Catholic question and the need for separatism was prattle.

Thus, claims of the 'Irish nation' by the Patriot party were never more than those of a governing sect that wanted more room to manoeuvre for itself but was still politically and militarily parasitic upon England. Patriot nationalism, Whig-inflected or no, could not but be a sham. Patriots could lament, as Tone himself repeatedly did, Ireland's invisibility as a nation, but they could not, without self-contradiction, object to its servile status as a colony. The Americans had drawn what was at times a fine line between civil war and a war of independence, but they decisively drew it. The Irish Volunteers did not and could not bring themselves to do so, because a policy of separation could not be pursued without inclusion of the Catholics. There was an alternative. Ireland could forgo its colonial status in exchange for incorporation:

> For my part . . . if I were to describe a colony, I would picture a country in a situation somewhat similar to that of Ireland at present. I would describe

> a country, whose Crown was dependent on that of another country, enjoying a local legislature, but without any power entrusted to that Legislature of regulating the succession to that Crown. I would describe it as having an executive power administered by the orders of a non-resident Minister, irresponsible to the colony for his acts or his advice; I would describe it as incapable of passing the most insignificant law without the licence of the Minister of another country; I would describe it as a country unknown to foreign nations, in the quality of an independent state, and as subject to another power with regard to all the questions which concern alliances, the declaration and conduct of war, or the negociations for peace.[17]

That is Lord Castlereagh, arguing for the Irish Union, two years after Tone's death. Irish separatism, so presented, was an old colonial problem for uneasy settlers to be overcome by union, but a new solution for Tone to be realized by republican independence.

Castlereagh stole the language of the government's opponents in order to clarify further how the treaty of union, and the accusation that it was an exercise in a venality remarkable even by Anglo-Irish Protestant standards, could be dealt with by accepting that Ireland had been a colony but would now be upgraded to membership of an empire. Empire was the goal, union the method: 'It is said, Sir, that an Union will reduce Ireland to the abject situation of a colony. Is it, Sir, by making her a constituent part of the greatest and first empire in the world?' But it was to republicans that 'an Union would not act as a bribe':

> I must readily admit, that it is a measure of the most comprehensive bribery that was ever produced: It bribes the whole community of Ireland, by offering to embrace them within the pale of the British Constitution, and to communicate to them all the advantages of British commerce. It is this kind of bribe which is held out to the Protestant, to the Catholic, to the Dissenter; it is this kind of bribe which is held out to the merchant, to the manufacturer, to the landholder – indeed, I know but of one class in the community to which an Union would not act as a bribe: It is to those who call themselves the lovers of liberty and independence. That liberty, which consists in the abdication of the British Constitution, that independence, which consists in the abandonment of the British

> Connexion ... I acknowledge that these are bribes which I am not prepared to offer.[18]

That speech is in many respects a direct answer to Tone's *Argument on Behalf of the Catholics of Ireland* (1791). It uses the famous language of reconciliation between the three sects in Ireland to lead to an opposed conclusion. This in itself is not surprising; Castlereagh had once been a supporter of radical/liberal discourse, and handled it with a degree of suavity; in these few lines from his speech, apart from the more obvious stress on the word 'British', or the loaded terms 'abdication' and 'abandonment', note how often he uses words beginning with 'con-' or 'com-' that indicate union, togetherness, or completeness: *comprehensive, community* (twice), *Constitution* (twice), *commerce, communicate, consists* (twice), *Connexion.* But it is the sarcasm reserved for the 'lovers of liberty and independence' that most obviously labours to make a telling distinction between real union and its fake counterpart, between true and false sentiment.

FRIENDSHIP

The convergence of reactionary and republican language in the later decades of the eighteenth century is most evident in renewed and widespread disputes about human 'feeling' or 'feelings' and who had best claims to it or to them. Those who opposed the French Revolution and its alleged inversion of 'natural' feeling, led by Burke, claimed that the new doctrinal radicalism was characterized by a dangerous, even demonic form of abstract energy. It dissolved the actuality of all historical and traditional bonds, affections, and realities and subjected them to a fanatical repudiation in the name of historical necessity, the new age, *the thing that is to be.* But the tempo of republican language also intensified, obviously enough in the revolutionary decade, but had been rising for some time before that, with the astonishing cult of Rousseau, beginning in the sixties with his *La nouvelle Héloïse* – by which the dominant rhetoric of popular fiction was moulded for the next forty years – and especially with that novel's revitalization of the notion of a 'civil religion' that should supplant prevailing notions of national and confessional identity, reinforced in *Du contrat social* by the central republican assertion of the sovereignty of law over men and the concomitant repudiation of the mastery of the law by any faction for the sake of a private or selfish goal. 'Sincerity', 'candour', 'enthusiasm', and a whole lexicon of such interconnected words became the common currency of radical novels and political discourse – perhaps William Godwin is the most exemplary of those who gained renown in both genres with his *Political Justice* (1793) and *Caleb Williams* (1794) and, in the next generation, Mme de Staël with *Corinne* (1807) and *Considérations sur les principaux événements de la Révolution française* (1818). All of these works are buoyed by concepts of tropical sincerity or enthusiasm, yet shaken too by the tremor of deep, ineradicable betrayal or compelling renunciation.

In his *Autobiography*, written in Paris in August 1796, Tone makes a distinction between two groups of his closest friends. On the one hand, stand Thomas Russell and Thomas Addis Emmet; on the other, Whitley Stokes, George Knox, and Peter Burrowes. Between Tone and the first pair there has been, from the beginning,

> a coincidence of sentiment, a harmony of feeling on points which we all conscientiously consider as of the last importance, which binds us in the closest ties to each other. We have unvaryingly been devoted [to] the pursuit of the same object, by the same means, we have had a fellowship in our labours, a society in our dangers; our hopes, our fears, our wishes, our friends and our enemies have been the same. When all this is considered, and the talents and principles of the men taken into the account, it will not be wondered that I esteem Russell and Emmet as the first of my friends. If ever an opportunity offers, as circumstances at present seem likely to bring one forward, I think their country will ratify my choice. (2.292)

That final phrase is telling. 'Their', not 'our', country; Tone is already absenting himself, but not 'his choice'. There may be a premonition of death here; certainly the last sentence is nuanced towards heroism. The whole section is backlit by the sense of danger, as preparations and negotiations proceed for the launch of the invasion force – which began its slow uncoiling a month later.

Of the others, he remembers the loyalty of Burrowes and Knox, both of whom, despite the 'irreconcilable difference of sentiment' between them and Tone, stood by him after the Jackson trial 'when others ... shunned me, as if I had the red spots of the plague out on me' (2.292–3). Whitley Stokes's 'political opinions approach nearer to mine than those of either Knox or Burrowes'. Yet, indignant as Stokes is at Ireland's treatment at the hands of her oppressors, 'the tenderness and humanity of his nature is such that he recoils from any measures to be attempted for her emancipation which may terminate in blood. In this respect I have not the virtue to imitate him' (2.293). In what sense is Tone using the word 'virtue' here? Perhaps he is merely being humble, or ironic, perhaps the word in this context is designed to remind us that the tender virtue attributed to Stokes is not one wished for by Tone himself, although appreciated as a precious trait.

> I must observe that in the choice of my friends I have been all my life extremely fortunate. I hope I am duly sensible of the infinite value of their esteem, and I take the greatest pride in being able to say that I have preserved that esteem, even of those from whom I most materially differed on points of the last importance and on occasions of peculiar difficulty; and this too without any sacrifice of consistency or principle on either side, a circumstance which however redounds still more to their credit than to mine. (2.293)

Stokes and Knox and Burrowes can be given 'still'(!) more credit than Tone, since 'on points of the last importance' they not only differed from him but, being of more tender stuff, must have found it harder to stay friendly with him than he with them. But in republican language there is virtue and there is also *virtù*, in the sense Machiavelli used it, meaning a capacity to act politically and ethically for the sake of the community and not in deference to or for the satisfaction of one's own admirably exquisite feelings. Thus, by sympathizing with and conceding to his friends' plight, Tone is making his own 'tendresse', and the recognition of it in them, even more fastidious while retaining his political *virtù*, to use violence against a notoriously violent enemy. Still, this is a last salute to those friends. Tone hops up on his plinth to deliver it:

> If it be my lot for me to fall, I leave behind me this small testimony of my regard for them written under circumstances which I think may warrant its sincerity. (2.294)

If Sincerity as an abstraction had a loyal friend it was Serenity. Serenity, of the kind readily found in English republican writers such as Godwin, Holcroft, or Bage in the 1790s, enabled those blessed with it to face or rather outface exile or death. But exile or death were usually prefaced by betrayal and, although betrayal provoked the possessor of Serenity to unpardonably long-winded and implacably assured pronouncements, there was always a quaver audible in the voice. For betrayal of a friend was not wholly a personal matter; it was a breach of human solidarity. It was treason to humanity itself, even though the betrayed, in such narratives, often turned out to be an alleged traitor to the king or the law or the state. But then those who acted for the government in such a case were themselves open to the charge that they were traitors to the nation – usually on account of their violence or venality.

Yet treason or betrayal implies that there is something that merits loyalty in the first place. The very concept of betrayal had an inbuilt vertigo and that of friendship also had a thrilling instability. When friend and enemy can be the same person, even when a friend can unwittingly act as an enemy (by loose talk, for example, which Tone feared), and when an enemy can play almost perfectly the part of a friend, then the toxic effects of secrecy on a politics grounded in sincerity and friendship became so pervasive that it had to be accepted that this friend/enemy interchange was itself a structural feature of the politics that seemed to be so radically compromised by it. This is a point frequently made about republicanism – not only that it is a political language and not a programme but also that it is *only* that – a rhetoric that affects a great deal of swagger and dramatic gesture but that cannot deal with the actualities of power, that finds its natural antinomy in 'realism'. The charge is further expanded by the claim that republicanism, which favours consensus and discussion as against despotic or tyrannical rule or fiat, is by its own principles transformed into a talking-shop politics, whereas republicans claim that by being driven by oppression into secrecy and conspiracy its public discussive nature was deformed and its occupational hazard became, not logomachy, but paranoia.[19] Friendship was patriotism in an individual form; love for the nation was in turn a local form of human solidarity. The gradient of nobility rose with the degree of abstraction. A discourse such as this needed anchorage in the actualities of the world, otherwise its aeronautical tendencies swept it up into the stratosphere.

It is in Tone's friendship with Thomas Russell that we see an outstanding instance of *fraternité*, the heroic Jacobin version of a male bonding that is also a lived version of a public ideal of self-sacrifice and affection. It had long been a republican ideal that the obligations we have to the communal life should form the core of a true friendship. This is what makes friendship a virtue. Although it is easy to suggest that the Tone–Russell friendship is moulded in the 'romantic' model of a later generation, and that it exhibits an inescapably flawed and faked affinity between the private and the public realms, such an account would have to ignore the dynamic of self-consciousness that gave to such friendship its powerful, commemorative, neo-Roman or stoic quality. It was not that Tone and Russell (and Thomas Addis Emmet) tried to align their personal histories with the unfolding of public events – although that sometimes is the case. It is more that for them their friendship forms not just an alternative history *to* but the true history *of* their times, with its dates and places, its idyllic or its tragic moments, its exemplary idea of the sacrifice of the self to something greater, a sacrifice in which the self is not obliterated but discovered:

> my intention ... was to leave my family in America and to set off instantly for Paris, and to apply in the name of my country for the assistance of France to enable us to assert our independence ... this plan met with the warmest approbation and support from both Russell and Emmet; we shook hands and, having repeated our professions of unalterable regard and esteem for each other, we parted, and this was the last interview which I was so happy as to have with those two invaluable friends together. I remember it was in a little triangular field that this conversation took place, and Emmet remarked to us that it was in one exactly like it in Switzerland where William Tell and his two associates planned the downfal[l] of the tyranny of Austria. (2.331)

The sentiment of a passage such as this – and there are several of them in Tone's writings – is lodged in the particular, relished detail – the triangular field, the mention of William Tell. Simply because it is remembered, it has the elegiac appeal of a time gone by, a memory that delights and saddens at once, that returns 'me ravir et m'attrister', as Rousseau put it in the account of his recall of his time at Chambéry in Book III of the *Confessions.* In that pleated doubling, time past still retains its utopian promise of a future society. The friendship here celebrated by Tone is an oath of loyalty to that future; it not only will be, but already is the basis for it. Thus the time gone past has already been the opening date of the new age, the moment of separation is the new beginning, only recognized as such in retrospect – just as the Convention in Paris had declared in October 1793 that Year I of the new age had begun on 22 September 1792 when the Republic had been declared. (Thus the declaration that opened the new calendar was already in Year II.)

One can see why Pierre and Jaffeir were so readily recruited into the republican canon. They were obviously republicans *avant la lettre* and *Venice Preserv'd* its earliest melodrama. And William Tell was soon to join them as one of the best-known names among republican heroes with Schiller's play of 1804 on which in turn Rossini's opera of 1829 was based. The melodramatic element is more pronounced than the tragic in these works, for there can be no tragic ruin where virtue triumphs, even when the virtuous die.[20] Melodrama as a theatrical genre is a French revolutionary invention, although it had a long, very long, prequel in French and English fiction. Tone saw all the elements assembled at the revolutionary fêtes he attended; all that declamatory posturing and those choric crescendos presaged the later, brilliant extension of revolutionary melodrama into Italian opera. From Rousseau's *Letter on French Music* (1753), the Italian language, melodic composition, and singing styles were linked with the expression of republican sentiment; the alliance achieved its first great operatic triumph with Rossini's *Tancredi* (1813); its famous patriotic tune 'Di tanti palpiti' became so popular in Italy that it was performed often and spontaneously by crowds attending the law courts to object to Austrian injustice. (Even the wonderful trumpet call indicating the moment of freedom in Beethoven's sole opera *Fidelio,* 1814, is recognizably a gesture that belongs in the genre of French revolutionary drama.)

Republicanism had been aspiring since mid-century to the condition of an Italian music that still had to be born, although the conditions for it were assiduously pioneered by the revolutionary fête in France and by the republican apotheosis of friendship.

Tone is for the most part resolutely pragmatic, concentrating much of his attention, as he had to, on matters of political and military policy and prospects. He can sound quite Burkean on occasion: 'It is not by syllogisms that men are argued into liberty; nor by sophistry, as I trust, that they can be argued out of it. I confess I dislike abstract reasoning on practical subjects. I am buried in matter' (1.174). But what most memorably finds its sanction in the 'matter' that he supplies is the hyperbole of his feelings of hatred or of love. By hyperbole, I do not mean an exaggeration. Rather, the hyperbole, whether of friendship or of hatred, is always an indication of a failure to be adequate to reality. It is an aspiration or a stress; it can never really grasp what it reaches for. Friendship or hatred unto death is always hyperbolic, even when someone actually dies for one or the other. Suicide or martyrdom extends and enriches the hyperbolic dimension; it does not close it. It strengthens the claim that love or friendship, hatred or hostility, have an ontological status. But the claim has to remain at a high pitch of intensity if it is to survive as a living belief. Friendship is too rare and precious just to be given to a friend. What friendship is based on is something greater than any friend can be, something of which friendship is the historical, lived correlate. There are obvious similarities here with religious conviction. A Pauline eloquence and hyperbole is the mark of such friendship; it is a belief in something beyond friendship that makes love between people possible.[21] And thus what is dearest, 'the first object of his heart' has to be, not a person or persons, but a political ideal, 'the independence of his country' (3.416). In his address to the court martial which sentenced him, Tone admitted that his whole adult life had been devoted to this goal:

> For this he relinquished the dearest ties of wife & children, had suffered exile, prison & want, had braved the dangers of the sea and the fire of the enemy. Success in this life was everything, – he had failed. He attempted that in which Washington succeeded and Kosciusko failed. (3.416)

While urging the court to hasten his execution, according to the account given by an Anglican clergyman, he asked to be shot by firing squad, not hanged: 'He begged not to die on a gibbet. To him, after the failure of the great object of his heart, life had nothing to make it valuable' (3.417). Such language in these terminal conditions, attested to by an enemy, is indistinguishable from the traditional language of love. There is indeed, throughout both his *Diary* and his *Autobiography*, although more so in the first, a combat between Tone's devotion to his country and his devotion to his wife and children. The surrender of domestic to national affection is offered as proof of the power and the priority of the public weal over private sentiment. But the battle between them is a close-run thing and only Matilda Tone's complete agreement and support for him in this permits the public interest to prevail. In this, she too is a republican; but she is also a character, or an agent, in Tone's own dramatization of the conflict. The to-and-fro in the *Diary* between Tone's love for her and for Ireland produces an attractive ripple effect when we accept that the *Diary* is, as part of its rhetorical structure, imagined as addressed to her.[22] 'When I get into this track of witty and facetious soliloquy', he says, 'I know not how to leave off, for I always think I am chatting to my dearest life and love, and the light of my eyes' (2.123). This studied 'chatting', as well as the reporting of 'the most important part of the business', the mixture of formality and informality, is structural; the self-consciousness is that of someone whose subjectivity is being displayed as a historical phenomenon. It is loving so that in return it may be loved for its affectionate nature, admiring so that it may be admired for being so gifted and genial in bestowing admiration. This is an intricate and self-consciously winsome politics of republican patriotism.

> *I hope* (but I am not sure) my country is my *first object*; at least, she is *my second.* If there be one before her (*as I rather believe there is*) it is my dearest Life and Love, and the light of my eyes and the spirit of my existence ... She is my first object but would I sacrifice the interests of Ireland to her elevation? No, that I would not; and if I would, she would despise me, and if she were to despise me, I would go hang myself, like Judas ... Well, I do love my wife dearly ... she is a thousand times too good for me ... but then she is so infinitely better that it throws my great merit

> into the shade. For all that I have said of her and myself here, I will be judged by Whitley Stokes and Peter Burrowes and P.P., who are three fair men; and I have now done this day's journal ... (2.133–4, emphasis in original)

And about a year later, in April 1797, he again makes a distinction between a friend whom he 'loves dearly', like George Knox, and 'my wife and Russell, [who] make, I may say, a part of my existence' (3.45). The *Diary* enacts that incandescent relationship between himself and the two people to whom it is primarily addressed. It has as a consequence the intimacy of both an autobiography and a confession, in which the distance between the author and his specific chosen audience is always under pressure to dissolve. So the most casual asides function as something said or whispered under breath, audible only to those two whose identity is merging with his own, more than can that of the other close friends whom he loves. It is his solitude that stimulates this envisioned intimacy most vividly, as in that moment in April on his way to Cologne when he feels he 'is quite alone, without a soul to speak to that I care one farthing about or that cares one farthing about me'. Equally, when he senses the political situation slide away from him, he turns towards Matilda and begs her and his friends to assure him he is overreacting. So, in early August 1797, on board ship on the Texel in Holland, 'locked up by the wind' (3.105), enraged and frustrated by the weather delays, he writes to Matilda at some length about the possibility of their going into exile, since a peace deal between France and England that would exclude Ireland was beginning to seem more likely. There is no chance of their again bending their necks to the yoke of English tyranny; nor can he imagine Irish patriots likewise would not rather emigrate than stay; and 'if they are not capable of that exertion, they have deceived themselves exceedingly in the idea that they had the energy which makes revolutions' (3.137–8). But he is sure that there is 'among us enough of virtue and of resolution to embrace even banishment rather than slavery; we have at least the energy of despair' (3.138). Then he continues:

> My dear friends [Lewines and McNeven] and you, the dearest of my friends, and that I love a thousand times more than my existence, where is the country that with the society of those we love and esteem we could

> not be happy in? Exile I know is terrible, but so is slavery ... no situation that could be offered me would buy me to return to Ireland while she remains at the mercy of her tyrant ...
>
> Let me beg of you, all three, to answer this letter as speedily as possible and if you think me a wrongheaded enthusiast, do not scruple to tell me so, for I in some degree suspect it myself. (3.140–1)

The skills exhibited in the *Diary* in particular remind us of the fact that Tone was one of the authors of an epistolary novel, *Belmont Castle* (1790), miserably represented here by a single extract, although thankfully available in a modern edition.[23] One of the striking features of Tone's contributions to this 'parody of the sentimental novel' is his humorous and satiric attitude towards excessive, stylized heroic gesture.[24] This humour remained with him; it allows him to see the comic, bravura elements of his own habitual striking of a posture. But the novel has a curious aftereffect now on the later writings. The stagy suicides within it – that of the character Scudamore in particular – are not just echoes of young Werther; their farce now sounds as a tragic premonition of his own death. Additionally, the libertinage of the cast of characters is presented as a form of egoism. The novel as a middle-class genre inclined to exhibit libertinage as typically aristocratic, whereas sexual virtue (especially female chastity) was not only a middle-class and piously Christian trait, it was also an assertion of individual integrity and of human solidarity. This alloy is evident in Tone's representations of his love for his wife and for his country. In libertinage, there is no important distinction between lovers; but in a passion such as Tone's, one person or country only embodies perfection and remains the stable object of desire unto death.

HATRED

Tone's hatred of England, repeated in letters, pamphlets, *Autobiography*, *Diary*, in English and in French (3.165), is rooted in his belief in the baneful and corrupting effects of its dominion on Ireland, more pronounced after the conclusion of the Seven Years' War in 1763, when England's imperial control was redefined, more shamefully evident after the success of the American War of Independence had given Ireland an example, feebly echoed, and England a warning, firmly acknowledged. English global violence (Scotland, America, India) and greed, forever soldered to its propaganda on liberty, contrasted remarkably with the programme of the French Revolution, its trumpeted extension to humankind at large with the benefits of its more provincial, but still resonant, American precedent. Inevitably, the chief opponent of revolutionary France was England, the natural leader of Reaction. The release of Ireland from this monstrous global blight would be a good in itself. It would give Ireland autonomy. It would be potentially a release too for the world at large, since the loss of Ireland, a strategic possession, would cripple the marauding seaborne empire and French help might be decisive in Ireland as it had been in America. ('France would most probably assist from the pride of giving freedom to one kingdom more', 1.136.) This view of England, especially its role in harnessing continental allies, local élites, and counter-revolutionary peasants to protect its dominion, was not at all peculiar to Tone. It was a staple view of British radicals into the next generation, with Shelley, Byron, and Hazlitt perhaps the best known (all of them had a particular hatred of Castlereagh, for his role in Ireland in the Rebellion and Union years and in the foreign policy that produced the reactionary Holy Alliance in Europe).

Tone's realization of England's deathly role in Ireland is recorded in a famous passage in his *Autobiography* when, after a brief experience as a Whig pamphleteer and a subsequent spell of unemployment under the eye of the political grandee George Ponsonby, Tone, regarding himself now 'as a sort of political character', plunged into a study of the affairs of his country and

> made speedily what was to me a grand discovery, tho' I might have found it in Swift or Molyneux, that the influence of England was the radical vice of our Government, and consequently that Ireland would never be either free, prosperous or happy until she was independent, and that independence was unattainable while the connexion with England existed. In forming this theory, which has ever since unvaryingly directed my political conduct, to which I have sacrificed everything, and am ready to sacrifice my life if necessary . . . (2.284)

Later, in early July 1791, on finding that the United Irish Committee would not accept a resolution that would include the Catholics in a motion for parliamentary reform, Tone reacted by forming his 'theory' (by which he means a policy or programme):

> To subvert the tyranny of our execrable government, to break the connexion with England, the never failing source of all our political evils, and to assert the independence of my country – these were my objects. To unite the whole people of Ireland, to abolish the memory of all past dissensions, and to substitute the common name of Irishman in place of the denominations of Protestant, Catholic and Dissenter – these were my means. (2.301)

But he saw the difficulties, the Anglicans chief among them: 'The Protestants I despaired of from the outset . . . ' All of this is well known. The most notable aspect of this overquoted passage, and of Tone's pamphlet writing and memoranda in general, is the conventionality of the language. The allusion to the fourth of Swift's *Drapier's Letters* in the phrase 'the whole people of Ireland' (not at all original to Swift but canonized by his readers) is the most effective move in the passage, because on this occasion, and significantly, even shockingly, Tone includes the Catholics in it. Otherwise, 'tyranny of our execrable government',[25] 'assert the independence of [my] country',[26] 'never failing source', and even 'the common name of Irishman' (which echoes Defoe's 'An Englishman's the common name for all'), are worn locutions in a recognizable eighteenth-century republican accent. The explosive element, partly muffled by the recycled language, is the double policy – independence *and* the end of confessional identity. Singly, these are scandalous; but conjoined, especially as he argues they *necessarily* are, they reconfigure the Irish political landscape, simply in virtue of having been written as the axioms of a new logic that the French Revolution had introduced and that had now become the logic of world history. Tone's general position makes forgoing confessional identity a political act that in itself constitutes a departure from the British system, which maintains privilege, sows division, and stimulates chauvinist feeling by assiduously nursing it, most especially and maliciously in Ireland. Yet the surrender of confessional identity is in effect the demand that the English

Revolution of a century earlier admit (in contrast to the French Revolution) its sectarian and provincial basis at the very moment when Protestantism was being refashioned from being the religion of the British nation to the religion of the Empire – available at the dawn of the new century to the Irish through the Union. This changed the numbers game entirely, so that the overwhelming Irish Catholic majority in Ireland (expanding at an alarming rate) would be instantly transformed into an insignificant minority in a Protestant world-system. (This is central to Castlereagh's argument for Union.) The democratic implications of all three revolutions of 1688, 1776, and 1789 – English, American, and French – meant that numbers mattered more than ever in securing legitimacy. Tone never tired of citing the figure of three million for the disenfranchised Catholic majority and generally of citing how few Protestants there were and how much of everything they owned or controlled.

Within the British system – although rhetorically it had to be located 'outside' it, as the ultimate foreign element – the Enemy was Roman Catholicism. Hatred for Catholicism and love of liberty were a single seam in British national character or history, one regarded as entailing the other. Catholicism had a criminal, British liberty a heroic history. Tone's programme did not just challenge this politico-religious formation, moulded by centuries of suasion and propaganda. It actually transposed the positions of Catholicism and England in its schematic. England assumed the position of the Enemy of Ireland, of human advancement. Revolutionary France now assumed the role of Liberty, the world-historical cause that Ireland, with French help, could join by achieving independence through emancipation (or at least enfranchisement) of the Catholics and by liberation of the Protestants from their anti-Catholicism, the most virulent form of their slavery.

It is reasonable to hate an institution, community, or system because it has a record of persecution and oppression, but to hate it by instinct is even better, the mark of a gratifyingly spontaneous personal alert system; if others have the same instinct, then it can be regarded as a definitively human and national trait. So anti-Catholicism can be historically and ontologically grounded in human experience and in human nature. Tone dramatizes the development of his hatred of England across a similar polemical range. Its growth fascinates him. The hyperbolic note is again crucial, as the crisis of individual hatred transmutes into anathema of the great enemy at a moment of historical crisis. Burke has a similar structure of hyperbole in his hatred for various groups or individuals – Jacobins, regicides, Anglo-Irish Ascendancy, atheists, Rousseau. The rhetoric of such feeling actually depends on its power to persuade us that no excess of condemnation is possible given the radically evil nature of the target; instinctive recoil from it is the source and the consequence of the polemical attack. The wince of disgust both precedes, as an instinct, and succeeds, as an argued or catalogued culmination, the assault. Like Hazlitt, the politicized citizen needs to be 'a good hater' – that is, in Jon Cook's words, 'not just being good at hating but hating for the good'.[27]

Tone's reasons for hating are clear. England exiled him, imprisoned and executed his friends: 'Judge of my feeling as an individual when Emmet and Russell are in prison and in imminent peril of a violent and ignominious death! What revenge can satisfy me for the loss of the two men I most esteem on earth?' (3.221). It massacred Irish Catholics in the previous century like game, so members of the Catholic Committee are, Tone avers, as 'Irishmen and as Catholics doubly bound to detest the tyranny and domination of England, which has so often deluged their country with their best blood' (2.68). It is doing it again now, it is opposing the French-led emancipation of the world, it is dishonourably involved in international intrigue – the list is long, yet the most grievous part is that England has always been so: 'England will desolate what she cannot subdue. It is a most infernal policy, but no new one for her to adopt' (3.246–7). Finally, the inversion takes place. Reasoning is not abandoned, it is confirmed by instinct. Yet the confirmation provided by the historical record is, in effect, redundant. For the instinct was prior. Writing his *Autobiography* in August–September 1796, he can say: 'My object was to secure the independence of my country under any form of government, to which I was led by a hatred of England so deeply rooted in my nature that it was rather an instinct than a principle' (2.304). In November 1796, he writes in his *Diary* of the proposed razing of Bristol in a French invasion: 'And I will never blame the French for any degree of misery which they may inflict on the people of England . . . The truth is I *hate* the very name of England; I hated her before my exile; I hate her since, and I will hate her always!' (2.399, emphasis in original).

Is this Tone's dramatic/melodramatic version of his own development or is it an unwittingly dramatic exposure of Tone being overwhelmed by events and feelings? The elements are incrementally there at one level: a steady hardening of the heart; increasing resolve and courage in facing the monster from which no quarter can be expected and to which, in return, no quarter will be given; all-out vengeance. But there are two perspectives on this; one, already cited, the perspective of 'instinct', which is both originating and conclusive; the second, is the perspective of the noble cause, which has the defiance of failure as well as the 'energy of despair' at its core. He writes to Matilda in July 1797:

> Dear Love, I know not what may be the issue of this great enterprise in which we are embarked; if we fail, we fail in a great cause; we are not embarked to conquer a sugar island or a cotton-factory, but to emancipate a nation, and to change the destiny of Europe ... (3.112)

It was also in July 1797 that the British decided to withdraw from Haiti (Saint-Domingue), the French 'sugar island' which Toussaint L'Ouverture had defended so successfully against French royalism and fierce British imperial assaults in a revolutionary triumph that Tone clearly underestimated or of which he knew too little.

DEATH OF A PAGAN

Politically, Tone had by this time travelled far indeed, but socially he still spoke in an idiom that seems increasingly quaint. A business contract was being negotiated as a gentleman's agreement; the only stable currency for him was that of honour, trust, faith, and feelings that only needed to be consulted for the decisive answer to be given. Right to the end, his petitions were cast in this form. His only request to the court martial 'was that the mode of his death might not degrade the honour of a soldier' (3.423); 'he trusted that men susceptible of the nice feelings of a soldier's honour would not refuse his request' (3.390). But the response was, of course, that he would be hanged 'in the most public manner for the sake of a striking example' (3.391). And before that, his arrest at Buncrana, his transfer in chains to Derry, his four-day journey from there to Dublin, after being 'taken *through the city of Derry* with his legs ironed under his horse's belly . . . and dressed in his uniform as chef de brigade' (as described in John Mitchel's well-known letter of 1845 to Thomas Davis, 3.363, emphasis in original), provides the image of proud honour brutally dishonoured, for which the closing ignominy was to be the public execution. But Tone, like Jackson, 'deceived the senate'.

Seán Ó'Faoláin, introducing an edition of the *Autobiography* in 1937, said, somewhat fatuously, of Tone: 'His personality, the man himself, is a definition of Irish Republicanism. It is the only sensible definition that exists.'[28] It is, nevertheless, interesting that the creed had by then become a function of the personality, a crossover that was always potentially there, in the editorial construction of Tone's texts, in the *Autobiography*'s plain and programmatic appeal, and in the gravitational pull of the disconsolately dispersed *Diary*, the first literary work in Ireland in which we witness what Mark Phillips calls 'the historicization of daily life',[29] not perhaps emulated until Mitchel's *Jail Journal* (1854). In addition, Ó'Faoláin's observations remind us that it is an *Irish* republicanism that he presides over from the grave at Bodenstown. Before Tone there were republicans who were Irish, but there were no Irish republicans before him.

John Toland (1670–1722), perhaps the first republican who was Irish, sought emancipation for Jews and Dissenters, in the aftermath of the English Revolution and during a titanic war with France. His plea was meant both to confirm and to widen the Protestant ideology of Liberty which English republicanism burnished to a high gloss to reflect, dimly at times, figures such as Aristotle, Cicero, Machiavelli, Livy, Sallust, Moses, Lycurgus, Cato, and Brutus. Tone and the United Irishmen recognized themselves as belonging to that tradition. But the situation in Ireland, especially after the French Revolution, brought that Protestant ideology to a republican reappraisal that it could not survive. Thus, with Tone taking the lead, it too sought emancipation for a disenfranchised community – the enemy community of Popish believers. In this campaign, the emancipation of the Catholics became central to the inquiry into the relationship between

England and Ireland and a switch from the English claim of Protestant Liberty for French universal *Liberté.* This was, in Irish circumstances in the 1790s, in keeping with the logic of republicanism, although intolerable to the practitioners of 'priestcraft'. In comparison to Toland's emancipatory campaigns, those of the United Irishmen are not part of a philosophical critique of religion (although that is implied), nor (at first) of an effort to stimulate a gradual evolution of the principles of 1688, but are instead a revolutionary attempt to replace 1688 with 1789, to replace religious furies and theories of limited toleration – with all the discretionary power that word assumes – with a rights-based form of separatist democracy. Castlereagh's one-time secretary Alexander Knox, who believed (or at least wrote) that the Irish Catholics had been granted 'everything but dominion' by the Irish parliament in 1793, wondered at those like Fox and Grattan who could not see that a reform movement, a kind of civil rights campaign, had always had hidden within it a deeper and more sinister purpose: 'Are we to suppose that these good natured politicians [Grattan and Fox] were caught, in the simplicity of their hearts, by that verbal bait of Reform with which the United Irishmen have covered their barbed hook of revolutionary Democracy?'[30] The inevitable answer is a yes, and the familiar conclusion is that Reform should not be conceded at all, since this is to get the hook in one's mouth. But the not very well-hidden principle in Knox is that it is as much a right as a power of government to persecute as to reform. In *Vindication of the Catholics of Ireland* (1793) the question of toleration was addressed by Tone, as spokesman for the Catholics, in terms that were later to be applied to the concept of liberty. But essentially, it is the same question: 'With regard to toleration, persecution may be negative as well as positive. The deprivation of political rights, because of the exercise of any religion, is for so much a persecution of that religion' (1.387). In 1792, Tone wrote but did not publish a reply to a pamphlet that defended Catholic exclusion: 'The whole of this argument depends on this: that it is impossible for the two sects to coexist in a state other than that of tyrant and slave, and that all alteration is subversion' (1.181). This is at the heart of his objection to the system's principle;

its operation only expresses its inner flaw. A system that is based on an unflinching Protestant bigotry will be undermined by Protestant bigotry; if the 1688 revolution is to become operative in Ireland, it must extend and refine its initial terms of settlement. Toland had asked this of it for the Dissenters. Tone asked it for the Catholics. Liberty is not dependent on confessional allegiance:

> The Protestant religion is not the essence of our constitution, for that was ascertained before the other had existence. The indefeasible liberty of the subject, and of that, the animating soul and spirit, the elective franchise, is co-existent with the constitution; it is a vital and inseparable part of it; it is the substance of liberty – religion but the accident. Freedom may be found where Protestantism is not; but shew me where it exists without the elective franchise. I say, in disfranchising the Catholics, the *Parliament* which did so were guilty of a subversion of the constitution, and not the descendants of those Catholics who now, after a patient suffering of one hundred years, come humbly to demand a remnant of a remnant of their birth right. (1.181, emphasis in original)

It may be that Tone believed in the need for separation from England as early as 1791, although he denied this in the letter of 1793 *To the Editor of Faulkner's Dublin Journal,* which was not published, in response to a speech by Lord Fitzgibbon in the Irish House of Lords – which *was* published by the *Journal* – in which he was charged with being 'an advocate for separation'. He can at this stage feel Fitzgibbon's breath on the back of his neck; therefore he denied being treasonably in favour of separation (1.454–5). In his speech, Fitzgibbon had quoted from a letter sent by Tone to Thomas Russell in 1791, in which he had said:

> My unalterable opinion is that the Bane of Irish prosperity in [sic] the influence of England. I believe that influence will ever be exerted while the connexion between the Countries continues. Nevertheless, as I know that opinion is, *for the present,* too hardy, tho' a very little time may establish it universally, I have not made it part of the resolutions [for the Committee of the United Irishmen]. (1.104, emphasis in original)

Tone's experience of exile in America seems to have confirmed his conviction that separation should be United Irish policy. That, along with full admission of the Catholics (and aided by the French to effect these aims and destroy thereby the British Empire), was the fully opened programme.

In *An Argument on Behalf of the Catholics of Ireland* (1791), Tone does not, of course, advocate separation. The primary goal is to end Catholic slavery and Protestant tyranny; thence will come union and 'Ireland is free, independent and happy' (1.128). It was his combination of this vision, along with the separation from England and from the discursive as well as the geographical empire it commanded, that gave distinction to his contribution to the republican tradition. The structure of his thought is recognizably that of Toland – indeed recognizably that of republicanism in general – but with the key polarized terms of dominion and enslavement transposed: France for England, *Liberté* and *Fraternité* for Liberty, Roman Catholics for Jews. He recognized that when exclusion is a principle of the state, then any form of inclusion, however wise it might be in a given set of circumstances, can be construed as a threat to the whole system. The purity of this position was always anathema to Burke, who regarded it as an early version of a peculiarly modern fanaticism.

Even before Catholic emancipation was finally achieved in 1829, Francis Jeffrey, the editor of the powerful Whig journal the *Edinburgh Review*, was warning of 'an independent state' being formed in Ireland with 'foreign assistance'. It could be that 'by the help of a French army and an American fleet ... an Irish Catholic republic [could be] installed with due ceremony in Dublin'. This could happen, he forecast, unless Ireland was 'delivered from the domination of an Orange faction' by the British government's withholding of support from that 'miserable' group.[31] Tone had not been seeking an Irish *Catholic* republic, although the new form of Protestant Orange tyranny and government support for it had already appeared in the anti-Catholic pogroms in Armagh in 1796. The sectarian policy that had manacled Ireland in the name of liberty had not been weakened but adjusted to stifle revolutionary republicanism, whatever its origins in England or in France.

Yet for all his efforts on behalf of the Irish Catholics, Tone alienated himself from a particularly powerful cohort of them when he made the error of deceiving the senate and dying a republican death:

> Truth compels us to say he died the death of a Pagan; but it was a Pagan of the noblest and finest type of Grecian and Roman times. Had it occurred in ancient days, beyond the Christian era, it would have been a death, every way admirable; as it was, that fatal final act must always stand between Wolfe Tone and the Christian people for whom he suffered, sternly forbidding them to invoke him in their prayers, or to uphold him an example for the young men of their country.[32]

NOTES

1. William Henry Curran, *The Life of John Philpot Curran*, 2 vols. (Edinburgh: Archibald and Alison, 1822), vol. I, 275–84.
2. Candid Observer, *Biographical Anecdotes of the Founders of the Late Irish Rebellion* (London: John Crenan, 1799), 3.
3. Thomas Mac Nevin, *The Lives and Trials of Archibald Hamilton Rowan, The Rev. William Jackson, etc.* (Dublin: J. Duffy, 1846), 280.
4. Candid Observer, *Biographical Anecdotes*, 15.
5. Curran's own words; Curran, *Life*, vol. I, 321.
6. Ibid., 322.
7. Ibid.
8. Thomas Otway, *Venice Preserv'd*, ed. Malcolm Kelsall (Lincoln: University of Nebraska Press, 1969), 95.
9. See John Barrell, *Imagining the King's Death: Figurative Treason, Fantasies of Regicide, 1793–1796* (Oxford University Press, 2000), 567.
10. Honoré de Balzac, *Old Goriot*, trans. Marion Ayton Crawford (London: Penguin, 2002), 183.
11. References to the following volumes in the text are in the form of an arabic numeral to indicate the volume number, followed by a period and arabic numeral to indicate the page number. *The Writings of Theobald Wolfe Tone, 1763–98*, ed. T. W. Moody, R. B. McDowell, and C. J. Woods, vol. 1: *Tone's Career in Ireland to June 1795*; vol. 2: *America, France and Bantry Bay, August 1795 to December 1796*; vol. 3: *France, the Rhine, Lough Swilly and Death of Tone, January 1797 to November 1798* (Oxford: Clarendon Press, 1998).
12. Colin Jones, *The Great Nation: France from Louis XV to Napoleon* (London: Random House, 2002), 508.
13. Quentin Skinner, 'Classical Liberty and the Coming of the English Civil War', in Martin van Gelderen and Quentin Skinner (eds.), *Republicanism:*

A Shared European Heritage, 2 vols. (Cambridge University Press, 2002), vol. II, 14.

14. Jean-Jacques Rousseau, *Émile*, trans. Barbara Foxley (London: Dent, 1993), 522.
15. John T. Scott, 'Rousseau and the Melodious Language of Freedom', *Journal of Politics*, 59/3 (August, 1997), 803–29.
16. Kevin Whelan, *The Tree of Liberty: Radicalism, Catholicism and the Construction of Irish Identity, 1760–1830* (Cork: Cork University Press/Field Day, 1996); Thomas Bartlett, 'The Burden of the Present: Theobald Wolfe Tone, Republican and Separatist', in David Dickson, Dáire Keogh, and Kevin Whelan (eds.), *The United Irishmen: Republicanism, Radicalism and Rebellion* (Dublin: Lilliput Press, 1993), 1–15; Ian McBride, 'The Harp without the Crown: Nationalism and Republicanism in the 1790s', in S. J. Connolly (ed.), *Political Ideas in Eighteenth-Century Ireland* (Dublin: Four Courts Press, 2000), 159–84.
17. *The Speech of the Right Honourable Lord Viscount Castlereagh upon Delivering to the House of Commons of Ireland His Excellency the Lord Lieutenant's Message on the Subject of an Incorporating Union with Great Britain* (Dublin: J.Milliken, 1800), 13–14.
18. Ibid., 37.
19. Robert Hariman, *Political Style: The Artistry of Power* (University of Chicago Press, 1995), 47, 96.
20. See Peter Brooks, *The Melodramatic Imagination: Balzac, Henry James, Melodrama and the Mode of Excess* (New Haven, CT: Yale University Press, 1976), 19–21; Lynn Hunt, *The Family Romance of the French Revolution* (Berkeley: University of California Press, 1993), 181–91.
21. See Jacques Derrida, *Politics of Friendship*, trans. George Collins (London: Verso, 1997), 75–170.
22. Cf. Declan Kiberd, 'Republican Self-fashioning: The Journal of Wolfe Tone', in *Irish Classics* (London: Granta, 2000), 221–42.
23. *Theobald Wolfe Tone and divers hands, Belmont Castle; or, Suffering Sensibility*, ed. Marion Deane (Dublin: Lilliput Press, 1998).
24. Marion Deane, Introduction to *Belmont Castle*, 24.
25. For example, *A Letter from Earl Stanhope, to the Right Honourable Edmund Burke: Containing a Short Answer to His Late Speech on the French Revolution* (London, 1790), 12: 'Events are NOT to be attributed to the form of their [revolutionaries'] new Constitution . . . they are to be ascribed solely to their old wretched and execrable Government, which had been, for ages, the cause of the People's oppression, of their indigence, misery, and consequent despair. It was that execrable and wicked Government that provoked the violent insurrections that have happened in France.'
26. As in James L. Granger, *A Biographical History of England*, 4 vols. (London: J. Rivington & Sons, 1779), vol. I, 58, where, under 'Class VII. Men of the Sword', William Wallace, 'at the head of a few fugitives and desperadoes dared to assert the independence of his country, and took every opportunity of attacking the English'.
27. William Hazlitt, *Selected Writings*, ed. Jon Cook (Oxford University Press, 1991), 12–13.

28. *Autobiography of Theobald Wolfe Tone*, ed. and abridged Seán Ó'Faoláin (London: Thomas Nelson, 1937), xix.
29. Mark Salber Phillips, *Society and Sentiment: Genres of Historical Writing in Britain, 1740–1820* (Princeton University Press, 2000), 310.
30. Alexander Knox, *Essays on the Political Circumstances of Ireland, Written during the Administration of Earl Camden* (London: Plymsell, 1799), 163. For the comment on Catholic dominion, see 187.
31. Francis Jeffrey, *Contributions to the Edinburgh Review*, 4 vols.-in-one (New York: Appleton, 1844), 613–14.
32. Thomas D'Arcy Magee, *A Popular History of Ireland*, 2 vols. (New York, 1863), vol. II, 313.

CHAPTER 4

Imperialism and Nationalism

THE MANY FORMS OF IMPERIALISM HAVE IN COMMON AN expansionist economic system – capitalist or communist – that claims to have its roots in a universal human nature. They also boast of possessing a wondrous cultural system that is either the inevitable consequence of the triumph of that economic system or one of the preconditions of its emergence. As a system, imperialism is distinct from colonialism by virtue of its more coherent organizational form and its more fully articulated characterization of itself as a missionary project to the world at large. To disguise its essentially rapacious nature, colonialism has been represented in literary, historical, and political discourses as a species of adventure tale, dominated by an ethic of personal heroism that is embedded in a specific national-religious formation. Imperialism transmogrified economic rapacity into a consolidated crusade for civilization and development, with all its attendant bureaucracies, technologies, and controls.[1] In all its forms, it is immensely flexible in its internal structures, global in its homogenizing ambitions and range. It is also – with the exception in modern times of the Japanese and Ottoman Empires – a peculiarly Western form of domination, extending from the sixteenth century to the present day. Portuguese, Spanish, Dutch, Russian/Soviet, French, British, and American empires have succeeded or overlapped with one another in a series of military-ideological rivalries ever since the development of European science and technology made the prospect of world dominance an achievable reality.

Imperialism was and is successful for a wide variety of reasons. As Alfred W. Crosby has explained in *Ecological Imperialism* (1986), the migration of fifty million Europeans between 1820 and 1930 to the 'neo-

Europes' of the world – that is the temperate zones, north and south – led to the propagation and spread of what he calls 'the portmanteau biota',[2] the collective name he gives to the Europeans and all the organisms they brought with them in their unprecedented exodus. Yet the European success was not exclusively biological or ecological. It was achieved over nature, but a nature inhabited by peoples whose defeat, expropriation, enslavement, or extermination had to be justified in a series of theoretical formulations that relied on categories paraded as fundamental and universal. Among these were the categories of history and of race. In the nineteenth century, the period in which European imperialism attained its fullest expansion, geographically and ideologically, a Hegelian philosophy of history was invoked to demonstrate that the task of completing human history had been passed on to the European nations. All others had fulfilled their historical destinies and now belonged to the past. Present and future were the temporal territories of white Europeans. This version of historical destiny was blended with later neo-Darwinian concepts of evolution in a mutually reinforcing alliance. History as a concept was enfolded with race; racial evolution and historical destiny were envisaged as ineluctable forces that marched together in the name of Progress towards the triumph of 'civilization'. Progress itself was identified with technological advance, which in turn produced modernization and development. Where these agencies were introduced, empire was performing its world-historical obligation to its destiny. Colonialism was the early, amateur form of imperialism. In its ramshackle, personal way it had inaugurated the rise of empire; but it was insufficiently global in its vision. By the late nineteenth century, most especially in the era of the 'scramble for Africa' that succeeded the Berlin Conference of 1885, empire, or the New Imperialism as it came to be called, had assumed to itself the mantle of 'responsibility' for the globe.

Joseph Conrad's novels have long been regarded as among the most memorable representations of the passage from colonialism to imperialism, especially because they register the coordination between this particular transition and the modernist experience of the dissolution of the individual self into a nullity, a condition of ghostliness. Despite or perhaps because of the Eurocentric bias of Conrad's fiction, works such as *Heart of Darkness* (1899) or *Lord Jim* (1900) question the assumption that the spectacle of a European individual imposing his will upon a whole non-European people could be represented as a moral triumph for him or for European civilization. Instead, the tragic distortions involved in such an enterprise make a nonsense of the ethical and cultural system that sanctioned such 'heroism' as a form of duty. In novels such as *The Secret Agent* (1907), *Under Western Eyes* (1911), and *Nostromo* (1902), the political systems represented – British, Russian, American – are so systemic in their operation that the belief in the autonomous individual subject has to be surrendered. In effect, imperialism's success as an impersonal system reveals the illusory status of the bourgeois-humanist 'subject' and, in so doing, manifests the historical nature both of that construct and of its own expansion. In Conrad, the revelation of the criminal nature of imperialism and the destruction of the idea of the self are intimately related experiences. The arrival of imperialism put an end to 'the project of exoticism',[3] the hope that the Romantic version of the individual self might find, in some remote part of the globe, an escape from the alienating conditions of modernity. Conrad's fiction, especially *Nostromo,* had anticipated the weakening of the European rhetoric of destiny and world civilization and its exposure as a disguise for the realities of political and economic power. But it had also reproduced it. The emergence of a Westernized Sulaco from the original country of Costaguana in that work is an emblematic instance of the new means by which self-determination would itself, as a political principle, become incorporated into a new imperialism. Conrad subverts and reproduces imperialism.[4] In a similar manner, so too does nationalism.

Conrad's work also creates and subverts one of the canonical oppositions of postcolonial and postmodernist discourse – that between Self and Other, between a cultural formation that is finely and intricately articulated and one that is inchoate and amorphous. The tragic form of this opposition in Conrad derives from the conviction that the definition of the Self is produced in and through the appalling recognition of the Other's delinquent and savage formlessness. By now, that tragic dimension has been lost and has been replaced by a ludic pleasure in the capacity of discourse to shuttle between forms of determinacy and indeterminacy that are grounded in the nature of language and produced by it rather than in the experience of catastrophe. The catastrophe was, of course, experienced by those peoples – or, in the given terms of imperialism, by those races – subjected to violence and exploitation. It was, on that account, a mediated experience for Europe, at least until the Nazi extermination of Jews and others during the Second World War. In the light of that particular holocaust, Europe has undergone a series of crises about the possibility of representing such horror, the morality of attempting to do so, the complicity with it that any rendering of apocalypse as discourse might involve. There has been no comparable anxiety about the representation of imperialism's crimes. Instead, the West has discovered in postcoloniality a form of discourse that is irrepressibly given to misrepresentation of the Other. Such misrepresentation has been accorded an ontological status. The claim that representation is always misrepresentation can lead to a depoliticized celebration of heterogeneity that ignores or subdues the cultural power and political purposes of racial stereotypes, caricatures, and other, subtler, rhetorical strategies.

But this view can be contested by the reminder that postmodern theory does not merely celebrate plurality but also disturbs and disperses the sediments of prejudice and assumptions that operate in texts. Culture, when it is propagated as a canonical system, always asserts its 'monogenealogy', repressing its internal differences and hybrid origins, proclaiming itself xenophobically, ethnocentrically, in clamant and mystificatory ways as unitary. Part of the postmodern/deconstructionist project is to expose these repressions and disestablish the standard texts as sites on which such assertions, ideologically closed within an established system of representation, can be made. Is deconstruction, then, the historical companion of decolonization? Even if language is thought of as identical with power, or thought of as the effect of power, is any space left for the production of representations of and by those who do not wield it? To make a fetish of difference, of otherness, may be an emancipatory gesture in itself. But equally, the determination of what is 'difference' or 'otherness' might itself be a ruse of power. An established structure of representation cannot produce an alternative to itself, no matter how severely it is put under question. The alternative is already established within and by those structures. So postmodern and deconstruction theories, although they do take their historical bearings from the process of decolonization, may be no more than contemporary forms of a Western liberalism that can pride itself on its openness but cannot escape from being Western. Even in their most radical formulations, they still see the world under Western eyes.

Nevertheless, even if it is granted that the West has imperially constructed the world in its own image, that image itself is, obviously, a construction. One way of recognizing the power of imperialism is by acknowledging how effectively it naturalizes its own history, how it claims precedence for its own culture by identifying that culture with nature. But, then, this also reveals something about representation itself, namely that it is a process in which the relationship between a representation and that which is represented inevitably involves what Adorno and Horkheimer called the 'organized control of mimesis'.[5] Repression, both in the political and psychological sense, is central to it. That which is foreign to an established structure of representation, its other, is demonized and thereby laid open to extinction. As in anti-Semitism, the Jews are 'declared guilty of something which they . . . were the first to overcome: the lure of base instincts, reversion to animality and to the ground, the service of images. Because they invented the concept of kosher meat, they are persecuted as swine.'[6] Such an analysis led to an outright attack on the European Enlightenment as such, with its faith in reason and its central practice of abstraction. 'The distance between subject and object, a presupposition of abstraction, is grounded in the distance from the thing itself which the master achieved through the mastered.'[7] Further, the abstraction of reason led to the liquidation of the sensory, sensuous world of the primitive (or natural); this too fed into imperial theory since the occupants of colonized territories were taken to be immersed in such a world and therefore incapable of, or at least insufficiently evolved towards, the rational condition of the European. This division between the rational and other nonrational categories (myth, magic, superstition, rituals involving the body, animality, and such) has undergone many inversions, with the consequence that the totalitarian impulse in Enlightenment rationality and the totalitarianism of fascist Germany have been read as disastrous attempts to repress those mimetic forms that so-called primitive societies have continued to nourish. In the imperial-colonial encounter between Europe and non-Europe, the role of the repressed primitive in modernism was illuminated and the possibility of the West escaping from its own imposed systems of rational domination became possible. The world of the other would re-educate the West into a re-immersion in the concrete, the specific, the heterogeneous and thus emancipate it from the practices of abstraction that had made it destructive both of itself and of the world.[8]

This attack from the left on Western rationality and its degeneration into the 'culture industry'[9] and pervasive commodification is, of course, an extension of the Marxist critique of capitalism. But it was preceded, in the era of high modernism (*c.*1880–1930), by an even more influential right-wing critique, most memorably embodied in the English-speaking world in the work of poets like T. S. Eliot, Ezra Pound, and W. B. Yeats and in the novels of D. H. Lawrence, Wyndham Lewis, Ford Madox Ford, and many others. In effect, this critique was founded on the belief that the experience of the individual subject in the modern world was one of fragmentation and anxiety; that such an experience had itself been produced by a loss of the coherent unity of the civilized world and its canonical achievements (most of them in literature) along with its replacement by a culture of excess, of kaleidoscopic variety offered to an undiscriminating and uneducated, even ineducable, public. In a strange sense, it was the sensory overload of such a culture that indicated its barbaric state. In other words, rather than suffering from abstraction only, the modern world also suffered from abstraction's 'other' – immersion in the inchoate and the sensory. London is the capital of the imperial crisis. It is the metropolitan world, surfeited with the spoils of success and excess, from which an escape into an authentically national tradition must be made. This project has a particular resonance in the Irish poet Yeats because it consorts so happily with his programme of cultural nationalism for Ireland. But the whole modernist project depends upon a tensed relationship between the metropolitan and the national, between the universal and the local, between heterogeneity and specific national (and personal) identity. In trying to rescue the stability of the individual self from modernist dispersals, it attempts to relocate that version of the self in a rearticulated version of the cultural and the national. The three poets I have mentioned here are all well known for the forbidding range of arcane and esoteric reference which they deploy in their work. The whole world culture is ransacked by them for representative images that are deliberately displaced and relocated in the foreign environment of modernity. This procedure is akin to that of the great American collectors of the nineteenth and early twentieth centuries who scoured the world – particularly the European world – in a mania for 'culture' and its artefacts and who then relocated those artefacts in collections that eventually became the core of America's great museums. The museum and its commercial cousin, the supermarket, are two of the most characteristic institutions of postmodernism; but they were initially two of the most characteristic images and emblems of modernism. Access to the products of the whole world, incapacity to absorb these effectively into a canonical version of the specific tradition of the 'West', the rewriting of excess as fragmentation – these are the ills of modernism and part of the inheritance of imperialism for culture.

Nevertheless, strategies of Western representation have been and continue to be awesomely effective in affirming the propriety and order of the West in contrast to the chaos and disorder of all that is non-Western. Imperialism deploys a number of specific binary distinctions to effect a coherence between what it takes to be natural and what it takes to be cultural.[10] Darwinism and humanism, the processes of natural selection and survival and the operation of Western, enlightened humanist ideals are so conjoined that imperialism is regarded as the agency that effects a suture between them. One of the paradoxes of this enterprise is that the various imperial powers have promoted the idea of a universal civilization that has the power and duty to overcome barbarity, backwardness, and savagery in highly specific national terms. Thus the British Empire produces a complicated discourse of chivalric, gentlemanly behaviour towards inferior races as an extension of and substitute for its christianizing mission throughout the world; the French Empire relies more on the discourse of 'culture': the reactivation of the French Revolutionary mission to humankind as a conferral of the benefits of French culture to peoples otherwise not inferior; the American empire combines the discourses of moral and material improvement. In all cases, a version of national identity and destiny is translated into a civilizing mission for humanity at large.[11] These rhetorics are not merely rationales for domination, they are narcissistic repetitions, part of what Derrida calls the 'fundamental culpability'[12] of writing through which the subject subordinates the world by idealizing itself. Specific instances of such narcissism and idealization are readily visible in travel writing, most especially in those European visions of tracts of territory that seem to desire to be made over in the image of the traveller's homeland. Such 'promontory views' of the foreign landscape are endemic in the writings of the nineteenth-century explorers of 'Darkest Africa'.[13]

The sense of a common European destiny that shaped and rationalized the continent's various imperial enterprises and ambitions (including Belgian, Dutch, German, and Italian as well as the British and the French) was disrupted by the First World War. Nevertheless, by 1918, the French and British empires were stronger than ever in the Middle East; the old Austro-Hungarian, the Russian, and the Ottoman empires were at the point of collapse. In the Arab world, Turkey emerged as the most remarkable example of the modernized and secular nation-state, gravitating towards Europe and away from its imperial and Arab past.[14] This was one of the earliest examples of twentieth-century colonial nationalism, defining itself as the alternative to an earlier imperialism, although the Turkish example was a complex one since it had itself been both an imperial and a subject nation. Nevertheless, some of the constituent ingredients of the after-image of imperialism were present in Turkey – the drive towards a European-style modernization, secularity, a form of national solidarity based on ethnic identity, a controlling bourgeois Westernized elite, and a repudiation of much that was held to be 'traditional' in favour of 'modernity'. A later and more famous example, the achievement of Algerian independence from France in 1962 after eight years of war, has become exemplary because of the historically important debates it generated and the reputations of those involved in them, particularly Frantz Fanon (1966; 1967), Albert Camus (1958), and Pierre Bourdieu (1958; 1963). Fanon called for decolonization through violent revolution as the only way to effect a psychic transformation in peoples traumatized by imperialism. Camus argued, in his *Chroniques Algériennes* (1958), for a liberal and democratic *Algérie française.* Bourdieu concentrated on 'the breakdown of social structures caused by the colonial situation and the influx of European civilization' during the war and after independence had been achieved.[15] All of these writers shared, amidst many differences, the recognition that the attritional relationship between modernizing imperialism and traditional attitudes and habits would not end but would enter a new phase in the aftermath of a successful revolution. Algeria had been Europeanized but could never be, nor wish to be, European. But in what sense could it remain Algerian? Could Algerian nationalism absorb the experience of imperialism and emerge the richer thereby, or would it suffer the double impoverishment of neither realizing its own ambitions for the future nor overcoming or profiting from its past?

Nationalism's opposition to imperialism is, in some perspectives, nothing more than a continuation of imperialism by other means. It secedes from imperialism in its earlier form in order to rejoin it more enthusiastically in its later form. In effect, most critiques of nationalism claim that, as an ideology, it merely reproduces the very discourses by which it had been subjected. It asserts its presence and identity through precisely those categories that had denied them – through race, essence, destiny, language, history – merely adapting these categories to its own purposes. It also accepts the requirements of 'civilization' – modernization, development, and class and gender divisions, which are integral to the system from which it ostensibly seeks to liberate itself. In brief, in the name of emancipation for itself, it joins with the global system of late capitalism and the multinational companies, becoming economically subservient while endlessly asserting cultural independence.

Whatever the merits or demerits of this description of nationalism in relation to imperialism, it allows us to focus more closely on the role of 'culture' within such ideologies and systems. Precisely because culture has been given or has gained within both a comparative degree of autonomy, it is more susceptible to forms of analysis predicated on the assumption that there, in culture, features of these systems, not otherwise sanctioned or even visible, will be made manifest. This is itself an intricate and insecure assumption but it is sufficiently widespread, in a variety of forms and emphases, to demand scrutiny. It is particularly important to recognize the relationship between nationalism and culture, generally known as 'cultural nationalism', in order to adjudicate on nationalism's historical role in combating imperialism or in ultimate compliance with it. As Aijaz Ahmad puts it:

> Theoretical debates as well as global historical accounts are rendered all the more opaque when the category of 'nationalism' is yoked together with the category of 'culture' to produce the composite category of 'cultural nationalism.' Unlike the political category of the state, the regulatory and coercive category of law, institutional mechanisms such as political parties or class organizations like trade unions, 'culture' generally and the literary/aesthetic realm in particular are situated at a great remove from the economy and are therefore, among all the superstructures, the most easily available for idealization and theoretical slippage.[16]

Culture is, indeed, an amorphous term, especially when it is routinely and with every appearance of benignity locked in with its comparably ill-defined cousin 'tradition' in the ideological cell of nationalism. The subsequent isolation is deceptively pure, for it breeds all sorts of promiscuous fantasies that are as formless as the natal pairing might lead us to expect. The consequence is that such enclosed and hermetic national formations actually become caricatures of the unawakened communal consciousness they replace. An intellectual proletariat, with bourgeois pretensions, that claims it has achieved national consciousness is substituted for a non-intellectual sub-proletariat that once was the national consciousness. In such a situation, many forms of reaction are justified on the grounds that they are 'national'. External domination has been introjected to the point that a nation, so construed, may be said to have learned nothing from oppression but oppression itself.

The separation of culture from power that is so often found in cultural nationalism is itself a legacy of the fact that educated native intelligentsia in colonial systems were themselves kept away from the exercise of real control. Instead they were assigned the role of bureaucratic functionaries. But the diagnoses of nationalism as 'the pathology of modern developmental history'[17] derive for the most part from the examination of European nationalisms that, in the aftermath of the French Revolution, transformed the dynastic polities of Europe into a number of nation-states. Yet nationalism was not, in its origins, a European phenomenon at all. The first great nationalist revolutions took place in the late eighteenth and early nineteenth centuries in South America, partly in response to the American Revolution and partly as a consequence of the crumbling of the Spanish colonial structure there. By 1825, Spanish America had achieved independence. This was quickly succeeded by an influx of North European capital into the continent, so that the complex processes whereby South American elites reimagined themselves as national communities and European capital reinvented South America as a 'new' space for development produced a situation in which cultural independence and economic subservience were paradigmatically combined into an image of nationalist liberation nestled within economic, imperial domination.[18] The later developments of European nationalism in the nineteenth century were structurally similar to the South American revolutions in that they too were led by bourgeois elites, they too declared a cultural-national independence, and they too were flawed as emancipatory movements for the people by the fact that their proletariats were not released from economic impoverishment by independence.

European nationalism did, however, have an alternative in Marxist socialism. Because of this, it was in Europe first that imperialism found, in socialism, its true international or transnational other. This, in turn, has led many thinkers on the left to equate nationalism with various forms of reaction, to see it as a barrier to socialism because of its emphasis on the particularities of territory, language, and race and its consequent failure to transcend these fervent localisms for a broader vision of human community in which the primacy of liberation from an unjust economic system would be recognized. It is also significant that the New Imperialism of the late nineteenth century drew heavily on nineteenth-century nationalism for ideological resource and sustenance. Imperial countries, such as Britain and France, took the lead in producing for themselves nationalist ideologies, replete with newly created versions of tradition, antiquity, national essence, literary tradition and the like, all of which were exported to their empires through various educational agencies – such as the British Council – that had as their aim the replication throughout the world of the homegrown national ethos. In this form, nationalism and imperialism were not adversarial movements at all. They were interlinked elements within a system that was culturally distinct in its British or French manifestations, but identical in its economic ideology – capitalism. In addition, the various totalitarian movements in twentieth-century Europe – and in Japan – had such clear and damaging associations with nationalism and with that post–World War I 'breakdown of classes and their transformation into masses'[19] that the pathological critique of nationalism was inevitable.

Yet it has been applied with little discrimination to nationalist resurgences and revolutions in the imperial domains themselves. This is in part to be explained by the resistance of such movements to modernization as a process destructive of their integrity as separate cultures and their apparently retrograde refusal to join in the global community. Of course it is also the case that such refusal could be defended and even glamorized as a dismissal of the desolate alienation of the developed world and an admirable adherence to 'traditional' values. Such disputes about nationalism were often as internally crucial to imperializing countries themselves as they were to those territories in subjection to them. Nationalism was thus susceptible to many varieties of use and assault. The protean nature of the term is inevitable given nationalism's complex history as an ideology that both liberates and immures, that conspires with imperialism and resists it, that is imported into Europe in one form and re-exported from Europe in another, that is culturally literate in inverse proportion to its economic illiteracy, that is, as a political formation, historically defunct, transitional, or an inescapable reality for the foreseeable future.

Since nationalism and imperialism are so intimate and conflictual, it may help to look at an exemplary instance of their dialectical relationship to each other as it manifested itself at the very heart of the British Empire – in Ireland. Ireland is especially useful because its national independence movement was, from the beginning, closely involved with the production and recovery of a national literature and the question of a revival of the national language. In the process, Ireland also produced some of the masterpieces of literary modernism, thereby clarifying in a previously unprecedented manner the nature of the relationships between imperialism, nationalism, and modernism.

Two authors dominate the history of Irish cultural nationalism – W. B. Yeats and James Joyce. They had many famous contemporaries – Oscar Wilde, George Bernard Shaw, George Moore, John Millington Synge. But it is Yeats and Joyce who, between them, most potently rehearse the positions available at a foundational moment for a nation that was not only part of an empire but was also constitutionally bound up in that empire's central political formation – the United Kingdom of Great Britain and Ireland, an entity that had come into being in the year 1800–1. In that year, Ireland, long a disputed colony of the British state, was finally incorporated into it. As such, it became integral to the imperial power and yet remained a problematic element within it.

In the course of the nineteenth century, Ireland underwent two kinds of experience that between them summarized the condition of a country under imperialism. It was modernized and Anglicized; it was also devastated by famine and repression to such a degree that its population was halved and its old Gaelic culture, already in retreat since the seventeenth century, was rendered almost extinct. In addition, the Protestant/Catholic religious divisions, introduced by English invasion in earlier centuries, were coincident with complicity with British power on the one hand and resentment of it on the other. It was a bourgeois intelligentsia, predominantly Protestant in its early developments, that attempted to resolve the sectarian problem as a means towards resolving or modifying the political relationship between the two islands. To that end, it reinvented an idea of Ireland as an antique nation that had known in pre-Christian and in early Christian times a unity that English colonialism had shattered and had since then known only a disunity that the same colonialism had fostered. The characteristics assigned to the Irish by their conquerors – rebelliousness, backwardness, barbarism, fecklessness – were all features of that racial propaganda that gained such a pseudo-scientific status in the nineteenth century. In response, Irish nationalists converted the racial ideology into one that reinforced their claim to independence and reformulated the British version of irremediable Irish difference. The Irish became Celts or Gaels, the British Anglo-Saxons, and each racial grouping was depicted as inalterably opposed to one another in the drama of world-historical conflict. The Celt was given to culture – imaginative intensity, poetry, story, mysticism; the Saxon was given to power – empire, pragmatic politics, commercial greed.

Here we see at once the problem raised earlier. Given such a form of cultural nationalism, how could such a racially based concept of culture ever be reconciled with an equally racial theory of power? Clearly, culture so conceived could only envisage power in terms of a refusal of the global modernization of the Empire, rendering this refusal as an Irish or Celtic virtue that ratified the reversal of the old tradition/modernity contrast. Ireland would become a nation by recovering its traditions and refusing both modernization and modernity. The irony is that such a refusal, variously formulated by many writers, was itself one of the critical features of modernity. Tradition, once conceptualized in this fashion, was already lost; modernity, once refused and dismissed, was already in place. Nationalism could not abolish imperialism; it could only redraft for its own purposes the double narrative that was at the heart of the imperialist enterprise – the narrative of a world civilization and that of a national civilization, one enfolding the other. The Celtic version of Irish nationalism had its own world-civilization narrative, the discourse of culture as a peculiarly Celtic 'country', as a territory rescued from the dominance of an impoverishing modernity.

In Yeats and Joyce these paradoxes and anomalies are fundamental to the development of their very different discourses. Yeats's poetry and plays, along with his various prose writings, attempt to resituate in and through Ireland and through his version of the Irish national character and destiny a reconstituted ideal of the heroic individual at bay in the modern world. Such an individual belongs to a specifically invoked cultural form – Irish national culture, the culture of the occult and occluded orders of theosophy, Anglo-Irish 'aristocratic' culture. All of these have suffered marginalization at the hands of an imperial modernity. Now, in the words of one of his most famous poems, 'The Second Coming is at hand'; the modern world is free-falling into violence and disintegration and the alternative and opposite world of tradition, ceremony, and the mage is emerging to take its place and usher in another era in world history. Ireland is the site for such an emergence. In claiming this role, Yeats reverses the relationship between Ireland and England, but, since this is a role that has yet to be, that is in a future guaranteed by nothing more than his own quixotic version of national and world history, the reversal is phantasmal. The inevitability of a vertically hierarchical distinction between Britain and Ireland is preserved. Edward Said regards this position as characteristic of one, early phase of nationalist resistance, what he calls the 'nativist phenomenon'.[20]

It is certainly the case that the alternating centrifugal and centripetal movements in Yeats's writing, the disinterring from the past of traditional stable sociopolitical formations and their reinterment in modernity are symptomatic of his ambivalent position between oppositions that cannot be resolved but at least can be exploited. The velocity with which he conducts his constant migrations from world arena to local place, from a specific historical event to its vertical symbolic role in what Walter Benjamin calls 'Messianic time, a simultaneity of past and future in an instantaneous present',[21] is so great at times that the reader can only perceive the passage as a blur of apocalypse, destruction, and creation identical with one another. Yeats's cultural nationalism is created out of a series of marginalized discourses that almost vengefully become, in their combination, a central discourse. But then that central discourse is itself marginalized as the actual Irish Revolution begins with the Rising of 1916 and proceeds to what Yeats deems to be a very pallid and bourgeois version of the nation-state, Catholic rather than Celtic, seeking a compromise with the modernity it had (or he had) initially spurned. In this, Yeats exemplifies the experience of disillusion and disenchantment often repeated in later postcolonial countries. For, although cultural nationalism is one of the foundational moments of a nation-state under imperialism, once the nation-state has emerged it forsakes culture as an originating energy and commodifies it as the logo of its subsequent identity.[22]

Joyce was free of the Yeatsian nostalgia for the heroic individual in whom the nation's essence was embodied and through whom its destiny was articulated. This was the vocabulary of a belated romantic, although it should be said that colonial belatedness was recognized by Joyce as one of the inescapable heritages of imperialism. The time lag between the metropolitan centre and its outlying provinces always ensured within those territories a certain outmodedness that stimulated their desire to keep up, to be in the fashion, and at the same time allowed them to pride themselves on remaining more faithful to the traditional values than the centre itself. This had been one of the thematic preoccupations of Irish drama since the eighteenth century. It was renewed in the drama of Shaw and Wilde in the nineteenth century. But it was in Joyce's fiction that it underwent a thorough transformation.

Joyce's work introduces modernism to postmodernism. The Ireland of which he writes is a place, previously marginalized, that is now assigned a central position in world literature, history, and myth. This is not done without irony. But for the present purpose, only two main points need be made. First, Joyce finds a means of producing a modern narrative of the dissolving self; second, he finds a means of producing a modern narrative of the system or systems in which that apprehension of the self is being eroded. In *Ulysses* (1922) and *Finnegans Wake* (1939), his day- and night-fictions respectively, everything is subject to dissolution, including language itself; yet it is also the case that everything in these works is subject to enormously powerful forms of consolidation and organization. The story of Dublin or of Ireland is the story of the world, the story of humankind, a generic parable. At the same time, it is, through all its repetitions, also a story of repression, breakdown, disenchantment. It is the Fall and it is Redemption, not in serial but in dialectical relation to one another. World civilization and a national culture are brought into an allegorical relation to one another. The story of the nation is the story of the Empire and vice versa. Power relations are reversed. This Irish discourse demonstrates the Babel out of which English emerged and to which it will return. It refuses privilege to all established order and grants primacy to its originating confusion. From Joyce, especially the Joyce of the *Wake*, it is but a short step to postmodernist celebration of difference, otherness, and the refusal of the grand imperial narratives that effect their ideological aims by erasure or diminution of these primary conditions of heterogeneity.

Yet the *Wake* is indeed, like *Ulysses*, a great narrative. It exploits the miscellaneous for the sake of an ultimate ordering. So too, in Yeats, the lament for the disintegration of traditional society is part of a historical vision in which that sorrow and loss have a function and significance. These are both nationalist writers who have imperial ambitions and who recognize that this apparent anomaly, which is also a dialectic, is historically inescapable. The fact that they both write in English is also inescapable for them, but has its anomalous force too. The Irish Literary Revival was contemporaneous with the movement for the revival of the Irish language. Yeats's friend, the dramatist J. M. Synge, refashioned English through the Irish language in his plays, thereby reproducing in drama what the Irish people had done in history. Yet for all the extravagant assaults on and extensions of the English language carried out by the most renowned Irish writers, they wrote in the imperial language, English. There is a naive view that in doing so they made English their own language. There is the more complex view that a minor literature, written in a minor language like Irish-English, involves a true liberation from a major language. The major language is already established; the minor language is in a state of becoming.

> All becoming is minoritarian. Women, regardless of their numbers, are a minority, definable as a state or a subset; but they create only by making possible a becoming over which they do not have ownership, into which they themselves must enter; this is a becoming – woman affecting all of humankind, men and women both. The same goes for minor languages; they are not simply sublanguages, idiolects or dialects, but potential agents of the major language's entering into a becoming-minoritarian of all its dimensions and elements. We should distinguish between minor languages, the major language, and the becoming-minor of the major language.[23]

In Irish writing of the Revival period, English entered into the state of becoming minor, a state since repeated for it in Indian, African, West Indian, Australian, and other literatures where English was subject to such liberation from its majoritarian status. There is a certain attraction to this argument, but it may be no more than an ingenious attempt to deny what is true of Irish and all other writing that has emerged from former colonies, English, French, or other, namely that their reception and acceptance depends upon the metropolitan cultures against which they are in some ways directed but towards which equally they are aimed.

Joyce was one of the earliest in a long list of modern writers who have either chosen or suffered exile. Their distance from and disaffection with their home territories have almost always been understood as a paradigmatic refusal of the writer to surrender his or her radical freedom to the demands of an oppressive state or system. There is, indeed, a great deal of truth in this. The exile of the modernist writer was taken to be analogous to the loss of home, of somewhere to belong to; it was certainly a painful condition. But in the postmodernist era this has been significantly re-read. Exile is (in certain circumstances) only the loss of one possible home; it can lead from belonging nowhere to becoming at home everywhere, a migrant condition that owes something to the old Enlightenment ideal of the Citizen of the World, but also owes much to the contemporary belief that there is an essential virtue and gain in escaping from the singularity of one culture into the multiplicity of all, or of all that are available. In such a turn we witness the rejection of nationalism brought to an apparently liberating extreme and the hostility to the world system of imperialism and capitalism achieving a new definition. Voiced within such postmodernist acclaim is a profoundly political or politicized version of culture and power.

Still, there is also an equally strong tendency towards depoliticization within this acclaim. The reception of Joyce, especially of *Finnegans Wake*, makes this plain. Joyce is celebrated to the degree that he is (mis)understood as an anti-nationalist writer and therefore as both a modernist and an internationalist. In short, through a curious reading of his work, first by unfashionable second-rate critics then by fashionable second-rate critics, Joyce is depoliticized as an Irish writer involved in his country's anti-imperialist struggle and ostensibly repoliticized as a cult figure first of the modernist then of the postcolonial world. The writers of South American 'magic narrative' have suffered the same fate, albeit with a remarkable equanimity. But the Ireland of Joyce and the South America of Garcia Marquez, Vargas Llosa and others are still disputed and colonized territories, are still economically and politically marginalized while being granted a canonical or semi-canonical place in culture. This bespeaks no emancipation from an oppressive situation; it merely indicates how competently the imperial world, now rechristened the First World, can incorporate cultural material from the Third World and process it for worldwide consumption – just as it does with raw material for industrial and commercial purposes. Within postmodern and postcolonial celebrations of difference, within their anxious interrogations of migrancy, hybridity, and a number of other concepts of the interstitial that refuse to be hijacked within or into a larger global conceptual system,[24] there is a fading consciousness of the unshaken, even extended, global power of capitalist imperialism. The question of culture and power – their alliances, their separations, their phantom divorces, their separate upbringings – remains unanswered and increasingly unasked. It is arguable that postcolonialism has taken the harm out of nationalism by celebrating its inexhaustible capacity for minoritarian difference and that nationalism, by its endless plying of culture as a sufficient counter-agency to power, has found in postcolonialism the future that it deserves.

NOTES

1. Hannah Arendt, *The Burden of Our Time* (London: Secker & Warburg, 1951), 185–221.
2. Alfred W. Crosby, *Ecological Imperialism: The Biological Expansion of Europe 900–1900* (Cambridge University Press, 1986), 270.
3. Chris Bongie, *Exotic Memories: Literature, Colonialism and the Fin de Siècle* (Stanford University Press, 1991), 270.
4. Edward Said, *Culture and Imperialism* (London: Chatto & Windus, 1993), xix.
5. Theodor Adorno and Max Horkheimer, *Dialectic of Enlightenment* (1944; New York: Continuum, 1972), 180.
6. Ibid., 186.
7. Ibid., 13.
8. Fredric Jameson, *The Political Unconscious: Narrative as a Socially Symbolic Act* (Ithaca, NY: Cornell University Press, 1981), 227–30; Michael Taussig, *Mimesis and Alterity: A Particular History of the Senses* (New York: Columbia University Press, 1993), 254–5.
9. Adorno and Horkheimer, *Dialectic,* 121.
10. Edward Said, *Orientalism* (Harmondsworth: Penguin, 1985), 227.
11. David Spurr, *The Rhetoric of Empire: Colonial Discourse in Journalism, Travel Writing and Imperial Administration* (Durham, NC: Duke University Press, 1993), 109–24.
12. Jacques Derrida, *Of Grammatology,* trans. Gayatry C. Spivak (Baltimore, MD: Johns Hopkins University Press, 1976), 165–6.
13. Mary Louise Pratt, *Imperial Eyes: Travel Writing and Transculturation* (London: Routledge, 1992), 201–27.
14. Albert Hourani, *A History of the Arab Peoples* (Cambridge, MA: Belknap Press at Harvard University Press, 1991), 318–19.
15. Derek Robbins, *Bourdieu and Culture* (London: Sage, 1991), 14.
16. Aijaz Ahmad, *In Theory: Nations, Classes, Literatures* (London: Verso, 1992), 7–8.
17. Tom Nairn, *The Break-up of Britain* (London: New Left Books, 1977), 359.
18. Pratt, *Imperial Eyes,* 112–14.
19. Arendt, *Burden of Our Time,* 321.
20. Said, *Culture and Imperialism,* 228.
21. Walter Benjamin, *Illuminations: Essays and Reflections,* ed. Hannah Arendt, trans. Harry Zohn (1969; London: Collins, 1973), 265; Benedict Anderson,

Imagined Communities: Reflections on the Origin and Spread of Nationalism (London: Verso, 1983), 22–6.

22. David Lloyd, *Anomalous States: Irish Writing and the Postcolonial Moment* (Durham, NC: Duke University Press, 1993), 71–2.
23. Gilles Deleuze and Félix Guattari, *Kafka: Towards a Minor Literature,* trans. Dana Pollen (1975; Minneapolis: University of Minnesota Press, 1992), 106.
24. Homi Bhabha, *The Location of Culture* (London: Routledge, 1994), 236–56.

CHAPTER 5

Irish National Character 1790–1900

THE AIM OF THIS ESSAY IS TO TRACE THE HISTORY OF AN IDEA through a series of mutations over a span of about one hundred years. Much of the material is taken from literary sources because it is in these that the potent force of the idea of a national character is most frequently and most memorably realized and it is in the nineteenth century that it becomes a stereotype. The caricaturing of national types was an important instrument of propaganda warfare during and after the French Revolution; the brilliant and savage tradition of Rowlandson and Gillray was carried on through the century, becoming more and more closely bound up with the development of the popular (finally the yellow) press.[1] L. P. Curtis and R. N. Lebow have already analysed its nature and function in relation to English and Irish affairs.[2] My interest is to observe some of the ways in which it registered itself in literature of the time and to trace therein the contribution made by the idea of an Irish national character to political attitudes and ideologies.

Although there had been, since medieval times, contrasting versions of British and of Irish national character, they did not achieve their ultimate definition until the eighteenth century. As part of the British response to the Glorious Revolution of 1688, a number of writers – Dryden, Sir William Temple, Defoe, Addison, Steele, Pope, and Horace Walpole most prominent among them – constructed a version of the English literary tradition and of the English national character which had, as one of its primary purposes, the attribution to the island kingdom of a unique historical destiny which distinguished it from its continental contemporaries.[3] As England distinguished itself from the continent (particularly France) in the early decades of the century, so Ireland learned to distinguish itself from England in the later decades. Although this summarizes the process in a crude shorthand, it does call attention to the swiftness of the interchange and to the fact that the idea of an Irish national character took shape in response to the earlier and aggressive English (or British) definition.

English historical writing in the eighteenth century was remarkably free of the preoccupation with national character which is so pervasive in the country's literature. The idea of a philosophic history, the chief use of which was 'to discover the constant and universal principles of human nature',[4] survived at least into the French Revolutionary decade. This characteristically enlightened vision was, nevertheless, closely allied with the current of Anglomania in France, impelled by Voltaire and Montesquieu and by the view that the dramatic events of seventeenth-century England provided the historian with an incomparable opportunity for narrative reflection.[5] The writing of history and the writing of literature were not then so widely separated as they were later to become. But literature, burdened by the need to formulate a specifically English aesthetic to counteract the cultural hegemony of France, sought for and found a symbol in which the English genius for the conciliation of liberty with order could be represented. That symbol was the English garden, the predominant literary trope of the age. From Sir William Temple' s essay 'Upon the Gardens of Epicurus; or, Of Gardening, in the Year 1685' to Addison's long allegorical discourse in *The Tatler* of 20 April 1710 and the *Spectator* papers of 21 and 25 June 1712, the features of the ideal English landscape garden are established, as both a political and aesthetic ideal. Temple described what he called the 'Chinese' garden, although he unwittingly used the Japanese word 'sharawadgi' to identify its chief characteristic – 'studied disorder'. He thereby inaugurated that vogue for the new landscape garden which was to oust the fashion for the symmetrical gardens of Italy and France (particularly those of Versailles).

The English garden is a protest against despotic order, geometrical regularity, and uniformity. Along with the later and associated development of the 'gothic' taste in architecture, it is seen to be, like the British constitution itself, a 'natural' institution in which the general principle of order is combined with the most eccentric individualism. This was a new and influential gloss on the theme of 'ars celare artem'. With its open vistas, its picturesqueness, and its asymmetry, it rebuked the artificial restrictions of Versailles and its imitations at Schönbrunn, Peterhof, Herrenhausen, and elsewhere. Pope's garden at Twickenham and William Kent's Rousham and Stowe and, finally, the great achievements of Capability Brown and Humphry Repton, led to the adaptation throughout the continent of the *jardin anglais* and the accompanying philosophy of the picturesque. The studied disorder of the so-called Chinese garden was repeatedly associated with the English character as a typical emanation of its peculiar genius.[6] The publication in 1757 of Edmund Burke's second book, *A Philosophical Inquiry into the Origin of Our Ideas of the Sublime and Beautiful,* transformed several decades of aesthetic speculation by asserting a dualism between its two key terms and by ceding to the Beautiful all that was ordered and symmetrical and to the Sublime all that was wild, grand, or magnificent. Shadowing his discussion, especially in relation to landscape, is the distinction between the formal garden, the *jardin anglais,* and the wild nature of 'mountain gloom and mountain glory'. The link between national character and the English garden became extended to the open (and preferably 'wild') landscape. Insofar as this is an aesthetic issue, it has clear and well-known reverberations.[7] But the aesthetic aspect is never entirely detached from the political in the treatises and discussions of the period. The central term, politically speaking, is freedom; but Burke's success in giving the whole question of aesthetics a psychological emphasis enforced the relationship between feelings of awe, terror, and reverence and the idea of freedom. Burke's 1790 version of the British national character existed as an aesthetic formulation over forty years earlier.

However, between 1760 and 1765, Burke wrote his unfinished *Tracts on the Popery Laws* in which he repudiated the slanders on the Irish national character perpetrated by English historians like Clarendon and Temple (the father of Sir William Temple). The Irish were not by nature a 'turbulent people'; they had been made so by 'the most unparalleled oppression'.[8] Yet Burke was not thereby rejecting the idea of a national character as such. It would have been difficult for a Whig and a disciple of Montesquieu to do so. Burke's knowledge of and admiration for Montesquieu is well known.[9] *De l'esprit des lois* (1748) had attempted to clarify the influence of physical and political conditions on the development of national character and had also given a famous, laudatory and inaccurate description of the British constitution as a model of liberty. But its technical inaccuracy in this respect was much less important than the emphasis upon *les mœurs*, upon custom, habit, and precedent, upon the character of a people and the link between these and its chosen form of government. Montesquieu was laying the basis for a political sociology; his dependence on the idea of national character was later reproduced both in Burke and in Mme de Staël. Thus, Burke's growing apprehension of the particular and traditional characteristics of any given nation's character was sharpened by French Enlightenment and English Whig traditions, a new sociology and a new national aesthetic. Some of the long-term implications of this development had repercussions in both Britain and Ireland.

In his various crusades and causes – for the integrity of parliament against the influence of the King's Friends, India against the rapacity of Hastings and the East India Company, America against the policy of George III, Ireland against the bigotry of the Ascendancy, and the France of the *ancien régime* against the Jacobins – one consistent theme may be discerned. It is that the integrity of an established culture should not be violated by the intrusion of an external force hostile to or contradictory of its habits and customs. All factions within a state threatened to disturb traditional modes of behaviour and with that, traditional modes of feeling; these, because they were traditional, represented some of the deepest and most natural aspirations of mankind. His theme achieves its highest definition after 1790, with the publication of the *Reflections on the Revolution in France*, in which he makes his most memorable and polemical contrast between the national character of the British and that of the French. In doing so, he asserts, more openly than anyone before him, that the connection between British national character and the British constitution is a normative one and that deviations from it, like the French, are radically unnatural and dangerous. The British differ from the French in that

(1) They cherish and nurture their 'natural affections'.
(2) They preserve these out of a sense of natural awe and reverence for constituted authority which ultimately derives from God.

(3) They have little time for speculators, theorists, and intellectuals and certainly never allow such men – especially as they are deists or infidels – into power.
(4) They are bonded together by habit, custom, and precedent and therefore suspect simplicity of organization and uniformity of practice. They are exponents, in short, of studied irregularity – sharawadgi – and in being so reveal the conformity of the 'gothic' British constitution to national character.
(5) They are morally and sexually conservative and stable. In favouring the family as a natural unit, they distinguish themselves from the French who have recently sponsored groups like the philosophic cabal and the Parisian mob against the French Royal Family.

This is a brilliant redaction of Temple, Addison, Montesquieu, and a whole host of minor writers who had been helping to formulate via the idea of national character a specific national destiny. Burke transforms the idea into a counter-revolutionary notion, even exploiting the fact that it had its origins in the revolution of 1688. But he goes further by making a respect for antiquity, complexity, and asymmetry an essential feature of the traditional nation, while the countering features of the revolutionary culture were seen to be novelty, simplicity, and an overweening respect for mechanical regularity. The standard attacks of the early century upon despotism were now transferred to radicalism. The intimate alliance between this new ideology and the aesthetics of the landscape garden, the Sublime, and the numinous presence in wild nature, the sentimental appeal of the ancient edifice and of the ruin, is perfectly visible in the rich texture of Burke's rhetoric.[10]

This highly politicized version of the British national character was achieved at a time of heightened national consciousness in Ireland. The first Celtic revival, effectively launched by the Ossian forgeries in 1758 and more respectably if less popularly supported by the work of Evan Evans (*Specimens of the Poetry of the Antient Welsh Bards*, 1764), Thomas Percy (*Reliques of Ancient English Poetry*, 1765), Sylvester O'Halloran, Charles Vallancey, Charles O'Conor, Sir Laurence Parsons, and many other Irish scholars, had benefited from the new appreciation of the Sublime and its projected landscape of lonely and mountainous places, and from the perceptible shift – which they helped to accelerate – from the pejorative associations of the idea of the primitive and barbaric to the benign connotations of the spontaneous and original. Vigour and freshness of feeling, a rural traditionalism, a rediscovered antiquity, a religious feeling which was doctrinally vague but emotionally powerful, an almost complete freedom from either intellectual theory or sexual promiscuity – these were not only traditional or 'Celtic' virtues, they were also indisputably non-revolutionary characteristics. The new primitivism was not French, nor was it radical. It was British, but not wholly so. In Ireland, the emergence of the differentiation between British and Irish national character, although begun in the last decades of the eighteenth century, did not fully emerge until after the Union. But the hostility of both conceptions of national character to doctrinaire revolution is at first more important than any subsequent differences between them. Irish national character was at first an idea without a sufficient history, most especially without an origin. The various attempts by people like Vallancey and, in the next century, Sir William Betham, to provide one are absurd historical fictions with a serious purpose – the ratification of a specific Irish character and destiny, a Carthaginian rather than a Roman or British nation.[11] The origin tended to be exotic because, for purposes of reconciliation, it had to be distant. Nothing specifically Gaelic or British, Catholic or Protestant, would do. Antiquarianism was consistently a more political avocation for countries with an unsettled history than for those that had already achieved an enduring political system.

The amateurishness of the scholarship of the early revival should not disguise the reality of its achievement. The new alliance between Irish poetry and Irish music, anticipated in works like Joseph Cooper Walker's *Historical Memoirs of the Irish Bards* (1786), Charlotte Brooke's *Reliques of Irish Poetry* (1789) and, in 1796, Bunting's first series of the *General Collection of Ancient Irish Music* (1796), found its fullest expression in Moore's *Irish Melodies,* published in ten numbers between 1807 and 1834. Moore made the connection with national character explicit in a well-known letter to Sir John Stephenson, his collaborator:

> But we are come, I hope, to a better period of both politics and music; and how much they are connected, in Ireland at least, appears too plainly in

> the tone of sorrow and depression which characterises most of our early songs ... The poet who would follow the various sentiments which they express, must feel and understand that rapid fluctuation of spirits, the unaccountable mixture of gloom and levity, which composes the character of my countrymen, and has deeply tinged their music.[12]

It may be that, as Hazlitt said, 'Mr Moore converts the wild harp of Erin into a musical snuffbox.'[13] But it is the very synthetic and artificial element in his work, the determined emasculation of the Gaelic originals, which enabled him to mobilize the political power of their appeal. By 'refining' Gaelic music, he made it fashionable and made the idea of a Celtic cultural difference an acceptable literary and eventually an acceptable political idea to both Irish and English. Moore's songs, like the 'vulgar ballads' which James Hardiman complained at for having 'displaced the native lyrics so effectually',[14] were crucial in the awakening of the notion that Ireland had a unique character, a unique destiny, and a glorious past, all of which differentiated it from Britain. He was as amateurish in scholarship as his eighteenth-century predecessors but in an age which was more affected by James Macpherson's Ossian than by Evan Evans's scholarship, amateurishness was no bar to success. It was, in fact, a prerequisite. All those rediscovered countries of the eighteenth century – the gothic, the medieval, and the classical as well as the Celtic – were the product of a new aesthetic and political dispensation in Europe.

The local Irish background to the writings of Burke's last seven years is, therefore, important in helping us to see how influential his version of a traditionalist British national character could become in this context. However, it is incomplete unless we also take into account two other issues. The first of these is Burke's view of the role played in the Irish situation by the Protestant Ascendancy and its response to the increasing demands of the Irish Catholics for admission to political life, demands increasingly favoured by an English government anxious to placate them in the dangerous revolutionary decade. Burke's attack on the Ascendancy becomes increasingly violent as a comparison between his letters to Sir Hercules Langrishe of 1792 and 1795 shows. In that of 1792, two points are central to our consideration here. The first is that the

Ascendancy is not an aristocracy in the accepted sense of the word – or at least, not in the sense which Burke assigned to it.

> We know that the government of Ireland (the same as the British) is not in its constitution wholly aristocratical ... If it had been inveterately aristocratical, exclusions might be more patiently submitted to. The lot of one plebeian would be the lot of all ... But our constitution has a plebeian member, which forms an essential integrant part of it. A plebeian oligarchy is a monster: and no people, not absolutely domestic or predial slaves, will long endure it. The Protestants of Ireland are not alone sufficiently the people to form a democracy; and they are too numerous to answer the ends and purposes of an aristocracy. Admiration, that first source of obedience, can be only the claim or the imposture of the few. I hold it to be absolutely impossible for two millions of plebeians ... to become so far in love with six or seven hundred thousand of their fellow-citizens ... as to see with satisfaction, or even with patience, an exclusive power vested in them, by which constitutionally they become the absolute masters; and by the manners derived from their circumstances, must be capable of exercising upon them, daily and hourly, an insulting and vexatious superiority.

The second point is that, in this state of exclusion, the Catholics are not even virtually represented.

> Virtual representation is that in which there is a communion of interests, and a sympathy in feelings and desires, between those who act in the name of any description of people, and the people in whose name they act, though the trustees are not actually chosen by them.

Without that, the existing state of affairs, claims Burke, cannot but 'produce alienation on the one side, and pride and insolence on the other'.[15] Ireland, therefore, has no homogeneity of interest between the governed and the governors; the governors are not a true aristocracy; the mass of the people are excluded from the benefits of the constitution. The system is formally British, but in spirit not so. The reason for this violation of the spirit or, as Montesquieu would have said, the *principe* of the British system is that the Irish Protestants constitute a faction within the state. By 1795, he can declare to Langrishe, in a famous condemnation which embraces all that he fought against throughout his career:

> I think I can hardly overrate the malignancy of the principles of Protestant Ascendancy, as they affect Ireland; or of Indianism as they affect these countries, and as they affect Asia; or of Jacobinism, as they affect all Europe and the state of human society itself ... Whatever tends to persuade the people, that the *few* ... are of opinion that their interest is not compatible with that of the many, is a great point gained to Jacobinism.[16]

The lack of connection between the Ascendancy and the people, the failure to adapt the British system of government to the character of the Irish, and the very dubious status of the Ascendancy itself were to remain a matter of concern in Anglo-Irish writing from Burke to Yeats.[17]

It is in the early nineteenth century that the idea of national character becomes a crucial cultural category and the subject of intense dispute in Europe at large as well as in Ireland. Part of the reason for this is the reaction to and the attempted analyses of the French Revolution and the Napoleonic regime. In Ireland, there was, in addition, the changed circumstances which obtained after 1798 and the Union. Having lost her briefly won political identity, Ireland produced writers who were correspondingly more anxious to assert the existence of a cultural coherence which would provide an alternative to or compensation for that loss. In England, writers as opposed as Coleridge and Hazlitt were inclined to assign the failure of the Revolution or, in Hazlitt's case, the defeat of Napoleon, to the fatal weakness of the French national character which they thought to be at root attracted to despotism and authoritarianism. In this respect, it was, of course, the antithesis of the English national character with its ineluctable bias towards liberty and a mixed constitution.[18] A more interesting analysis and proposed remedy was provided by Mme de Staël whose novels and critical writings are largely preoccupied with the search for a reconciliation between the forces of contemporary nationalism and of the older eighteenth-century and Enlightenment ideal of cosmopolitanism. She pursues this reconciliation in terms partly derived from Montesquieu, but they are also indebted to the newer rhetoric of national character. German profundity and solemnity are seen as a counterbalance to French gaiety and elegance; the Protestant North of Europe is recruited to harmonize its virtues with those of the Catholic South; prudence seeks its reciprocal virtue in spontaneity and enthusiasm. Mme de Staël is indeed the earliest exponent of the theme of reconciliation between the Enlightenment and the Revolution. Nationalism and cosmopolitanism are interpreted by her as the motive principles of the age and their mutual interdependence is her favourite theme.[19] In Ireland, the same preoccupation is evinced in the novels of Maria Edgeworth and, in muted form, in later novelists, although in them the terms of the debate are more localized and tend to dwell on the desired merging of factions – Ascendancy and peasantry, Protestant and Catholic – and, equally, tend also to a final disillusion with the possibility of their final compatibility. But Edgeworth in particular is, like de Staël, confident that the starting point of her great project should be the idea of a national character, something which she regards as an indisputable sociological fact. This conviction is by no means unique to her, although she is probably the most optimistic of all those who commented upon the national character, being convinced, at least for a time, that it was capable of 'improvement'. The belief that the Irish national character was degraded beyond the point of recovery was more likely to be found in the writings of English literary men, although the fear that this was the case is a pronounced feature of much Irish writing too, especially among those who regarded Daniel O'Connell with disfavour and who felt that his demagogic crusades had had a deleterious effect on the character of the peasantry. First, though, it will help to set much of this Irish writing in perspective if we look at some of the evidence adduced by English writers on the Irish national character. The perspective is not false since so much Irish writing – especially Irish fiction – of the early nineteenth century was written with an eye to the English audience and took many of its assumptions from that audience's beliefs about the Irish character.

In *The Morning Post* of January 1800 – the same month that *Castle Rackrent* appeared – Coleridge followed up on Burke's 1795 attack on the Protestant Ascendancy:

> The Irish national character we have ever contemplated with a melancholy pleasure, as a compound of strength and vivacity: an amalgam of the

> qualities of the two rival nations, England and France. Ireland itself is placed in the most enlightened part of the world, the sister of, perhaps, the most enlightened kingdom in it . . . What indignation, then, must not every good mind feel against that parricidal faction, which has contrived, as it were, to mock a miracle of God, and make a Goshen of darkness in a land surrounded by dawning or noon-day light![20]

Fourteen years later, Coleridge had changed his mind about the Ascendancy. By then it had become for him a necessary bastion of British rule in an Ireland which could not conceivably be separated from Britain, largely because it was in Britain's interest that the Union should be maintained. Interestingly, he miscalls the Ascendancy the 'Orange Confederacy' and on another occasion describes the Orangemen as having begun as Defenders. Essentially, Coleridge sees the Irish situation through the eyes of one whose mind was dominated by the fear of Jacobinism and he was ready to attack any group which seemed to be in any way sympathetic to or supportive of that cause. Therefore the United Irishmen become the focus of the attack he launched on Mr Justice Fletcher's 'Charge' to the Grand Jury of Wexford at the Summer Assizes in 1814. In six newspaper articles (or 'Letters'), signed by 'An Irish Protestant', Coleridge gives an exaggerated account of the advance of Jacobinism among a people of Ireland, 'at once the most numerous, and with few exceptions ... the least civilised of Christian Europe'.[21] Coleridge's importance here has little to do with his versions of Irish history, but with his recurrent emphases on the conditions and circumstances which had led to the degradation of the Irish character and the near-impossibility of rescuing it by any programme of legislative or social reform.

In a similar vein, Carlyle wrote of the Irish national character in his essay 'Chartism' (1839):

> The Irish national character is degraded, disordered; till this recover itself, nothing is yet recovered. Immethodic, headlong, violent, mendacious: what can you make of the wretched Irishman? Such a people works no longer on Nature and reality; works now on Phantasm, Simulation, Nonentity; the result it arrives at is naturally not a thing but no-thing, – defect even of potatoes. Scarcity, futility, confusion, distraction must be

> perennial there. Such a people circulates not order but disorder through every vein of it; – and the cure, if it is to be a cure, must begin at the heart: not in his condition only but in himself must the Patient be all changed. Poor Ireland![22]

The last sentence here seems to indicate that Carlyle believed that character was independent of conditions and that both must be changed. However, it is difficult to elicit from his writings any determinate views on this issue. By 1850, in 'Downing Street', one of his *Latter-Day Pamphlets*, the Irish question has become part of the English question as the famine hordes descend upon England – 'The Irish Giant, named of Despair . . . advancing upon London itself, laying waste all English cities, towns and villages'.[23] What troubles Carlyle most is that this apocalypse, visited upon England because of its misrule in Ireland, will lead to a social upheaval in England if the Irish take work at substandard wages and thus increase English unemployment and unrest.

It is possible to find among English writers some who would not only chastise this view of the Irish national character's wildness and turbulence, but who would throw doubt on the validity of the idea of a national character as such. John Stuart Mill had done this in relation to the English view of the French national character in the first number of *The Westminster Review* in 1824 and his comments on Ireland tended in the same direction thereafter. Most outspoken of all was the famous wit and reviewer for the *Edinburgh Review*, Sydney Smith, whose *Peter Plymley's Letters* (1807–8) supplied a tonic alternative to the current hysteria and propaganda on both France and Ireland. On the latter he wrote:

> Before you refer the turbulence of the Irish to incurable defects in their character, tell me if you have treated them as friends and equals? . . . Nothing of all this. What then? Why, you have confiscated the territorial surface of the country twice over; you have massacred and exported her inhabitants: you have deprived four-fifths of them of every civil privilege; you have at every period made her commerce and her manufactures slavishly subordinate to your own: and yet, the hatred which the Irish bear to you is the result of an original turbulence of character, and of a primitive, obdurate wildness, utterly incapable of civilization.[24]

Like Burke, forty years earlier, and Coleridge in 1800, Smith recommended the conciliation of the Irish Catholics by admitting them to full rights under the British constitution, even if this had to be done at the expense of and in face of what he called the 'Orange tyranny'. But Smith was writing against the tide. National character, either of itself or as the product of oppressive conditions, was increasingly identified as the unchanging and unchangeable element in the Irish problem. Although Matthew Arnold was later – especially in the years 1878–82 – to remodel the Irish character as Celtic temperament and to explain the failure of English rule in Ireland as the result of an incompatibility between it and the Murdstonian British middle classes – the nature of the diagnosis was unchanged.[25] Nor was it an English diagnosis only. No group believed it more readily than the Irish writers and no body of literature is more preoccupied with national character than that produced in Ireland in the first half of the nineteenth century.

But they softened the vision of national character by attaching it to the first Celtic revival's romantic note. The word 'romantic' has had some strange effects when brought into contact with the notion of representation, especially in fiction. Generally, to cast a romantic hue upon the matter represented is, in effect, to misrepresent it by lending it an aura or attraction not essentially its own. The Irish novelists of the early nineteenth century recognized and exploited the fact that they were writing for an audience which would regard the ordinary circumstances of Irish life with incredulity. But this also imposed a heavy burden. The actuality of Irish life was regularly viewed as a romantic representation. In such circumstances, it was difficult to write realistic fiction. In the Preface to *Castle Rackrent,* Maria Edgeworth addresses herself, apologetically, 'to those who are totally unacquainted with Ireland' and admits that for them, 'the following Memoirs will perhaps be scarcely intelligible, or, probably they may appear perfectly incredible'.[26]

William Carleton says of his account of the Famine in *The Black Prophet* (1847) that he has understated rather than overstated the case. Again he looks to his foreign audience:

> the reader – especially if he be English or Scotch – may rest assured that the author has not at all coloured beyond the truth. The pictures and

> scenes represented here ... not only have escaped contradiction, they defy it.[27]

Even in works which are not (consciously) fictional, the same theme recurs. W. Stuart Trench prefaced his well-known sketches in *Realities of Irish Life* (1868) – written by this industrious land agent to give the English public an idea of some of the problems faced by an improving landlord in Ireland and to persuade it that 'Ireland is not altogether unmanageable' – with the avowal that

> it has been my lot to live surrounded by a kind of poetic turbulence and almost romantic violence which I believe could scarcely belong to real life in any other country in the world.[28]

The incredulity of the audience for Irish fiction and memoirs, insofar as they are distinguishable – the life presented by Jonah Barrington is perhaps even more remarkable than that presented by Edgeworth in *Castle Rackrent* – is one of the standard features in the literature of Irish romanticism. The English audience lives in the everyday world; the Irish writer and the Irish culture belong to a surreal world. The artist, as mediator between these two, even as apologist for one to the other, is beset by a plight which is a political as well as an imaginative one. A favoured explanation for the difference between the two worlds is the national character of each. Although this by no means excludes consideration of other factors – political, social, economic – it does always manage to provide that surplus labour which more pragmatic analyses cannot generate. Interestingly, though, the hostile use of the unfavourable view of the Irish national character gives emphasis to the untrustworthiness of Irish witness to historical fact, especially when the evidence is unfavourable to the British. This is the other side of the 'romantic' coin. Romantic misrepresentation may be passed off as something which can be expected of a poet or novelist, but it is a more serious matter when historical evidence is at issue. Thomas de Quincey provides a startling example of the political implications of misrepresentation and its putative roots in the national character in his *Autobiographic Sketches*. Three chapters of this work were devoted to de Quincey's visit to Ireland at the time of the Union. He wrote down his memories of this and of the stories he heard then about the rebellion of 1798 somewhere between 1832 and 1833. In 1853 he added a long footnote to the earlier published account he had given twenty years before of the character and behaviour of Castlereagh and of the brutal behaviour of British troops in Mayo in 1798. That account had been given him by the then Protestant bishop, Dr Stock. In the demurring footnote of 1853, de Quincey declares:

> I myself had seen reason to believe, indeed sometimes I knew for certain, that, in the *personalities* of Irish politics, from Grattan downwards, a spirit of fiery misrepresentation prevailed, which made it hopeless to seek for anything resembling truth.

Dr Stock was, it appears, a liar. De Quincey goes on:

> I shrink from the bishop's malicious portraiture of our soldiers, sometimes of their officers, as composing a licentious army, without discipline, without humanity, without even steady courage. Has any man a right to ask our toleration for pictures so romantic as these?[29]

Thus, by the de Quincey law of re-, not to say de-traction, the Irish were by nature subject to 'fiery misrepresentation' which led to the production of 'romantic' pictures. There was, therefore, a perfect safety device for the English audience. Ireland could be as romantic as it pleased in fiction or in fact; that was acceptable. But when the extremity of Irish conditions was attributed to English misrule, that was 'misrepresentation' and was not acceptable, although it was very much to be expected from so unreliably romantic a race. This placed the Irish writer in an impossible position in relation to his audience. He could – like Maginn, Sylvester O'Mahony, Lover, Lever, and many others – portray Ireland as 'a humorist's arcadia';[30] or he could – like the Banims, Griffin, Carleton, and Maria Edgeworth – portray conditions which were in dire need of improvement for a race that would, as a result, be perfectly normal. But he could not safely attribute the evils of his country to English misrule. That would be 'misrepresentation' of the de Quincey species.

Any survey of the fiction of the period from 1800 to 1850 shows how difficult it is clearly to separate it from the subgenres of travel literature, written by foreigners, and of folk or folksy reminiscences and reports, written by natives. From Arthur Young's early *A Tour in Ireland* (1780), through Eyre Evans Crowe's *Today in Ireland* (1825), Cesar Otway's *Sketches in Ireland* (1827), the Banims' *Tales of the O'Hara Family* (1825–6), and of course Crofton Croker's *Fairy Legends and Traditions of the South of Ireland* (1825), we discover a strange admixture of antiquarianism, sociology, and fiction, most of it concerned to cast some light on the linkages between Irish national character and Irish conditions. History, geography, climate are frequently brought into consideration but the senior category in all these accounts and appraisals is the national character. It is both cause of and caused by the other factors. It is both a product of history and an abiding metaphysical essence. Most important of all, perhaps, is the often-tendered opinion that the uniqueness of Irish conditions is finally attributable to the uniqueness of the national character. This can be meant either as compliment or insult; its most enduring assumption, that of uniqueness, is perhaps more important than the particular uses to which any individual writer subjected it.

Moreover, just as the English literary commentators on the Irish national character were preoccupied with its degradation, so the Irish writers were preoccupied with its redemption. The novelists were preeminent in this respect and received most of the praise, in the latter part of the century, for having achieved it. National character, it was believed, exhibited itself most strongly and visibly in the Irish peasantry. To rescue them from the degradation they had suffered at the hands of English misrepresentation was, in retrospect, one of the most memorable achievements of the Irish novelists. In 1882, Alexander M. Sullivan, one of the notorious 'Bantry Gang', looked back on the changes which had taken place in the representation of Irish peasant life since the days of the Famine:

> The Irish peasant of forty years ago – his home, his habits, manner, dress; his wit and humour, his tender feeling, his angry passions, his inveterate prejudices – all these have been portrayed with more or less of exaggeration a hundred times. Caricature has done its worst with the subject; but justice has sometimes touched the theme. One of the changes most pleasing in our time is the fact that in England the clumsy 'stage Irishman' of former days is no longer rapturously declared to be the very acme of truthful delineation. The Irish are keenly sensitive to ridicule

> or derision; and to see the national character travestied in miserable novel or brutal farce – the Irish peasant as a compound of idiot and buffoon – for the merriment of the master race, was an exasperation more fruitful of hatred between the peoples than the fiercest invective of those 'agitators' whom it has been the fashion to credit with the exclusive manufacture of Irish sedition.
>
> Banim and Griffin, Mrs. Hall and Carleton, have left pictures of Irish life and character which on the whole cannot be surpassed for fidelity and effectiveness.[31]

Yet when we look at the manner in which the Irish peasant or, indeed, the national character in general was redeemed by the novelists we find that the prescription is very similar to that recommended by Mme de Staël and by all those who wished to discover some means of reconciling European romantic nationalism with the European Enlightenment. In effect, this meant that two stereotypes would recur; one would be the standard version of an old, relatively untutored 'wildness'; the other an equally standard representation of civility brought to the point of anaemia or dullness. The old, disreputable wildness belonged to the past. To take three representative samples, in *Castle Rackrent, The Collegians,* and *Traits and Stories of the Irish Peasantry,* the wildness is associated with a group which is part of a dying culture. In Edgeworth's novel it is the Ascendancy class of the Rackrents; in Griffin's it is the class of the 'half-sirs', the Cregans; in Carleton's stories, it is the peasantry of his native Tyrone. Retrospect is important in these works. It allows us to witness the disappearance of a class while retaining our affection for it. The historical features which lend disenchantment to the nostalgic view are, respectively, the Union, Catholic Emancipation, and the degradation of the peasantry which Carleton (now in his reactionary phase) believed O'Connell had brought about by turning a truthful race into a conniving, dishonest band. In each case an alternative to this wildness is proposed. Instead of the Rackrents, 'The best that can happen will be the introduction of British manufacturers in their places.'[32] So too, in *Ennui* (1809) and *The Absentee* (1812), Edgeworth recommends Irish landlords to forgo their second-rate life of absenteeism in England and return to their estates in Ireland, bringing utilitarian common sense to their dilapidated and romantic homes. Even more clearly, in *Ormond* (1817), the eponymous hero is faced with a choice between three modes of life – that of his Rackrentish uncle Ulick O'Shane, a corrupt politician; that of Ulick's brother, Corny O'Shane, king of the Black islands, trapped in his Jacobite-Gaelic time-lock; and that of the Annaly family, representing all that is steady, thrifty, and respectable in English civilization. Her dream of order relied for its foundation upon an alliance of the wild Irish aristocratic type (Catholic or Protestant) with the pragmatic English spirit. The consequence of its realization would be, in her view, the improvement of the condition of the people and the winning of their devotion. But Edgeworth's dream soon faded in the face of actual circumstance. She wrote nothing of consequence after 1817 and, in 1834, in answer to her brother's query on her long silence, answered:

> It is impossible to draw Ireland as she now is in the book of fiction – realities are too strong, party passions too violent, to bear to see, or care to look at their faces in a looking glass. The people would only break the glass, and curse the fool who held the mirror up to nature – distorted nature in a fever.[33]

Ireland marked out the limits of her idea of mimesis. History had passed beyond the range of representation in fiction. It is a telling moment.

Part of what it tells is embodied in Griffin's famous novel. *The Collegians* promotes the replacement of the reckless and violent world of the Squireen Cregans, epitomized in Hardress, with the sober respectabilities of the Catholic middle class, epitomized in Kyrle Daly. That replacement can only be achieved, in the terms of this novel, by marriage between the noble inheritor of the Ascendancy tradition, Ann Chute, and young Kyrle. It is the first of many Irish dreams of the noble and the bourgeois man in alliance against disreputable, violent, hard-drinking rapscallion life. Like Edgeworth, Griffin too is conscious of the English reader, for he has his eye on the respectability Emancipation will confer on the Catholic bourgeois and wishes to present them in as winsome a light as possible. Even more than she, he is entirely given to the idea of national characteristics. 'National' is, in fact, one of his stock epithets. Mr Daly 'had a national predilection for Irish history'; Lowry Looby had 'the national talent for adroit flattery'; Dr Leake has 'a national turn of character' and Mr Cregan 'possessed all the national warmth of temperament and liveliness of feeling'.[34] Like most of the 'romantic' Irish novels of this period, Griffin's is as anxious to offer a political solution to the 'wildness' of the national character by tempering it with the sobriety of the new Catholic middle-class dispensation as it is ready to exploit those wild elements in catering to the taste of the incredulous English reader. His attempted balance between these elements is entirely lost in the Boucicault stage adaptation *The Colleen Bawn* (1860) and in Benedict's operetta, *The Lily of Killarney* (1862).

It is hardly necessary to say that William Carleton was, more than any other writer, the beneficiary and the victim of the age's obsession with the Irish national character. Not only did the Irish peasantry achieve an undisputed prominence in literature with his *Traits and Stories* but they also gained it in the eyes of an Irish as well as an English audience. The new energy in the Irish publishing trade helped him to survive as a writer for his own people as well as for the English audience which received him as warmly as he could have wished. Dr Barbara Hayley has analysed in detail all of the issues which Carleton touches upon in his famous 'General Introduction' to the 1842 edition of the *Traits and Stories* – national character, language, the treatment of the Irish personality in literature and especially in literature written by Irishmen, the importance of a 'national literature' and the impulse given to it both by himself and magazines like the *Dublin University Magazine*.[35] But Carleton was also the victim of the circumstances he describes. For all its virtues, his writing was marred by a series of stylistic ruptures which repeated revisions could not heal. Most of these were caused by his uncertainty about how best to represent on the page the varieties and vagaries of Irish peasant speech; how to present himself as narrator; how to pass from dialect to standard speech in a smooth transition. As with so many Irish writers, the problem of representation was almost insuperable. A direct representation (if such a thing exists) of what he knew was constantly parried by a consciousness of what he ought to present to his audience. Moreover, he had the alertness to recognize that he, like the recorders of folk tales, customs, and habits, was actually altering, even destroying the very thing he recorded by the very act of writing it down. Therefore, in him the perils of nostalgia are particularly acute. The Tyrone of his childhood is a much more threatened culture than that of Edgeworth's Rackrents or the prosperous decade of Griffin's eighteenth-century background in *The Collegians*, for it has no alternative political programme of redemption comparable to theirs. The best Carleton can offer, in the 1830 Preface to the First Series of his stories, is the hope,

> – his heart's desire and anxious wish – that his own dear, native mountain people may, through the influence of education, by the leadings of purer knowledge, and by the fosterings of a paternal government, become the pride, the strength, and support of the British empire, instead of, as now, forming its weakness and reproach.[36]

Yet Carleton's one theme – Irish national character, as evinced in the Irish peasantry – finds its only appropriate form in the tale and, in the larger frame of the novel, tends towards those melodramatic exploitations which he, among others, had been so eager to replace. He, like his portrait of the Irish national character, degenerated into caricature and a considerable degree of incoherence after mid-century. *The Squanders of Castle Squander* (1852) and the fatally popular *Willy Reilly and his Dear Colleen Bawn* (an early version in 1850–1, a later one in 1855) are sufficient indications of his decline.

Yet it may be argued that Carleton's touching trust in the power of education was not entirely misplaced in an era which had seen the setting up of the National Schools and the first attempt to provide a university education for Catholics. The necessity of education was a constant theme in the writings of Thomas Davis, even though he wished to direct the Irish people away from Westminster and the Empire towards a new conception of themselves and their nationality. 'The Library of Ireland', one of his best-known articles for *The Nation*, is a typical example of his variation upon the already worn opposition between utilitarian England and romantic Ireland. Even in its threadbare state in the 1840s, this opposition was used over and over again to dress up the national character in its implacable appearances upon every literary occasion.

> Westminster ceased to be the city towards which the Irish bowed and made pilgrimage. An organisation, centring in Dublin, connected the People;

> and oratory full of Gaelic passion and popular idiom galvanised them. Thus there has been, from 1842 – when Repeal agitation became serious – an incessant progress in Literature and Nationality. A Press, Irish in subjects, style and purpose, has been formed – a National Poetry has grown up – the National Schools have prepared their students for the more earnest study of National politics and history . . .
>
> Yet the power of British utilitarian literature continues. The wealthy classes are slowly getting an admirable and costly National Literature from Petrie, and O'Donovan, and Ferguson, and Lefanu, and the *University Magazine*. The poorer are left to the newspaper, and the meeting, and an occasional serial of very moderate merits. That class, now becoming the rulers of Ireland, who have taste for the higher studies, but whose means are small, have only a few scattered works within their reach, and some of them, not content to use these exclusively, are driven to foreign studies and exposed to alien influence . . .
>
> To give to the country a National Library, exact enough for the wisest, high enough for the purest, and cheap enough for all readers, appears the object of 'The Library of Ireland'.[37]

Although this may be regarded as a characteristic specimen of what Yeats was later to call 'the school-boy thought' of Young Ireland, it is a useful reminder of the centrality given by two intellectual movements – that of Young Ireland in the forties and that associated with the *Dublin University Magazine* in the thirties – to the idea of national character and the need to provide it with a wider and deeper cultural base. In this context, Carleton's work can be more clearly seen, for the two movements, which appeared to have a single cultural aim, were seriously divided in politics – one nationalist, the other unionist – and catered, as Davis mentions, to different classes. If national character were to be educated, if the romantic wildness could be subdued into enlightened rationality, to what end would it be directed? All seemed to agree that the end would not be utilitarian, but that did not necessarily mean that it would be Irish in the political sense the nationalists gave the term. The great exponent of the marriage between cultural nationalism and unionism was Sir Samuel Ferguson. We may see Carleton more clearly if we regard him as a figure caught between the revivalist politics of

Ferguson and Davis, each equipped with a theory of education and each confident of the transformation it could have in practice upon the national character.

Ferguson's importance is acknowledged but it has never been estimated with sufficient care. He extends the eighteenth-century antiquarian revival, not merely by the production of his influential translations from the Gaelic, but by the provision of a new context for their reception. The famous credo of 1840, published in the *Dublin University Magazine*, is his version of Davis's 'Library of Ireland', founded on the claim that Ireland can be taught to recover a lost cultural unity through

> the disinterring and bringing back to light of intellectual day, the already recorded *facts*, by which the people of Ireland will be able to live back, in the land they live in, with as ample and as interesting a field of retrospective enjoyment as any of the nations around us.[38]

But this new programme envisions a very specific form of reconciliation. Ferguson, horrified by the demagoguery of O'Connell and hostile to the spectacle of the populist and emergent Catholic nation, sought a relationship between Catholic and Protestant which would reveal to the former their true identity and to the latter their true role. The fire and passion of the Celtic and Catholic heritage could be absorbed into the modern, civil, and civic forms of the Protestant tradition, once the Catholic had been freed from the 'spiritual thraldom' of his religion and the Protestant from the 'civil degradation' he had undergone at the hands of the British government. In other words, Ferguson wants to provide a Protestant intellectual and political leadership to a Catholic and Gaelic people before that people is transmogrified into a mob (by O'Connell and the priests) and before the Protestant Ascendancy is reduced to a dying caste, a foreign garrison in its own country. In his remarkable essay of 1833, also in the *Dublin University Magazine*, entitled 'A Dialogue between the Head and Heart of an Irish Protestant', he acknowledges the Protestant rationale for refusing sympathy to the Catholic claims. But there is also the heart's claim:

> I love this land better than any other, I cannot believe it a hostile country. I love the people of it, in spite of themselves, and cannot feel towards them as enemies.[39]

Ferguson, therefore, sees the alliance between Romantic Ireland and Enlightenment Ireland in Catholic and Protestant terms. Further, he sees it as the only alliance which can effectively put a halt to the degradation of the national character by a populist nationalism which would sharpen sectarian strife and a provincial, philistine culture. This attitude is of a piece with the counter-revolutionary movements in Europe, all of which were, in their neo-Burkean fashion, attempting to recreate the notion that there was a natural and traditional fellowship between the old aristocratic leadership and the people. Ferguson is also influenced by Mme de Staël's crusade for a merger between the Nordic Protestant spirit and the Southern Catholic one. Most of all, Ferguson is important for the manner in which he anticipates the form which this debate is to take in Irish writing thereafter. He successfully separates the Protestant ideal from the utilitarian ethos with which it was to be so often identified later (e.g. by Matthew Arnold) and he distinguishes between Gaelic civilization and Catholic nationalism with a decisiveness that neither Standish O'Grady nor Yeats was to equal. In brief, he begins the rewriting of the idea of Irish national character. Rather than belonging exclusively or pre-eminently to the peasantry, it now becomes the future product of a new mutuality between Catholic and Protestant, peasantry and Ascendancy. Ferguson counters Burke's attack on the Ascendancy by restoring it to the centre of traditional Irish culture and refuses entirely any imputation of a similarity between it and Jacobinism or any such foreign body in the ancestral system.

It is in the light of Ferguson's ideal that we can observe more sympathetically the dark passages in the writings of Standish O'Grady. O'Grady's long and furious lament for the failure of the Irish landlord class to assume the political and intellectual leadership of the Irish people is not simply a characteristic specimen of late nineteenth-century neofeudalism. It is a lament for the lost opportunity in Ireland of creating a new and heroic dispensation which would not be marred by the vulgarities of the commercial, industrial, and liberal-democratic world of nineteenth-century Britain.[40] But O'Grady's historical writings and pamphlets, like Yeats's essays and poems, carried on the debate about national character and about the alliance between the Ascendancy and the people in an intellectual climate profoundly different from that of the thirties and forties. Since Renan and Arnold, Irish national character had begun to define its Celtic difference more and more at the expense of the British national character. British national character was now identified with the British middle classes, and their philistine, utilitarian, and allegedly shallow liberalism or cosmopolitanism was now coming under attack from all quarters. The Irish, now the Celtic, character was the beneficiary of most of these attacks. For, by the eighties of the nineteenth century, it was customary to find that egalitarian societies, based on the principles of liberal democracy, were criticized as manifesting, in mass form, all the symptoms of decadence. The adversarial position, increasingly adopted in literary and scientific circles, promoted the idea that spiritual health could be restored to British, indeed Western, culture by the emergence of a new aristocracy operating within a hierarchical social structure. The history of this complicated repudiation of mass democratic society is far beyond our horizon here, but its bearing upon the transformation of the idea of national character and of the uses to which this idea was put is immediately obvious in the writings of men as diverse as Shaw, Yeats, Pearse, and Synge. It is in fact an integral part of the story of Irish nationalism's resurgence at the turn of the century.

One way of approaching the issue is to look at the treatment of the theme of national degeneration, as observed above in Coleridge, Carlyle, and others when writing on the Irish problem, when its range is widened to include the degeneration of the species as a whole or, with faint modesty, the degeneration of the white races. The traditionalist Romantic advocacy of the need for a spiritual leadership or intellectual 'clerisy' (to use Coleridge's term) was drastically altered by the impact of Darwinism. The theory of evolution, treated by many as a doctrine, added a new dimension to the conception of the clerisy or, as it came to be called, of the elite. The most influential formulations of this new development were achieved in the writings of Darwin's cousin, Francis (later Sir Francis) Galton, whose book *Hereditary Genius* (1869) proclaimed the need to produce a 'highly gifted race of men'. Although it was 1883 before Galton coined the word 'eugenics' for 'the breeding of human beings who were hereditarily endowed with noble qualities', the notion of selective breeding was already widely canvassed by then. With that came the intensification of the attacks on modern degeneration and the necessity to recover from it. E. Ray Lankester's *Degeneration* (1880), Lombroso's *Man of Genius* (translated 1888), and Max Nordau's *Entartung* (1892–3), translated as *Degeneration* in February 1895, with its publication timed to coincide with the trial of Oscar Wilde for 'degenerate' offences, had profound consequences in literature, especially at first on the literary criticism of men like Alfred Orage and Havelock Ellis.[41] Ellis in particular refashioned the old oppositions found in Mme de Staël, between the Nordic and the Celtic spirit. His essay of 1906, 'The Celtic Spirit in Literature', should be read in sequence with Arnold's 1867 lecture, 'The Study of Celtic Literature', the 1893 translation of Renan's book *The Poetry of the Celtic Races,* and Yeats's 1897 essay 'The Celtic Element in Literature' to reveal the increasingly racial and pseudo-scientific basis upon which the idea of Irish national character rested by the turn of the century. But it is of course in Shaw that Irish literature registers the impact of evolutionary theory on the notion of national character, British and Irish, and provides us with the definitive left-wing theory of the authoritarian elite formed by a process of natural selection by the Life Force.

The apparently scientific approach of the evolutionist school of writers would seem to make any rapprochement between it and the fashionable new pseudo-science of the eighties unlikely. But evolutionism found an ally, however uncomfortable, in occultism. That word too was coined in the eighties, 1881 to be exact, by A. P. Sinnett, author of *Esoteric Buddhism,* but less well remembered than Madame Blavatsky, whose disordered tomes *Isis Unveiled* (1877), *The Secret Doctrine* (1887), as well as the more lucid *Outline of Theosophy* (1891) became magic books for Yeats and the various occult circles in which he moved. Occultism announced the existence of a world totally opposed to all that egalitarian mass democracies represented. It dismissed utilitarian rationality, secularism, commercialism, and liberalism with contempt. On joining the Order of the Golden Dawn in 1890, Yeats became a member of a secret society which believed in a secret doctrine, orally transmitted through the ages in cryptic and symbolic forms. Through magic, he became a believer in the essential link between the wisdom of the people and the inner cadre of the spiritual aristocrats. This was Ferguson and

O'Grady in form but with the substance of their thought radically transformed. Yeats kept it within the limits of recognizability by making Ireland and the national character of the Irish people, the peasantry, as well as that of the Ascendancy, the essential Celtic preserve for this ancient, non-utilitarian, and non-British wisdom. As he set out on his astonishing intellectual journey through nineteenth-century literature, he recognized the need to counter the old opposition between parochial and cosmopolitan by invoking the new esoteric version of Irish national character. In doing so, he brings a strange history to an unexpected conclusion:

> I would have Ireland recreate the ancient arts . . . arts like these. I think indeed I first learned to hope for them myself in Young Ireland Societies, or in reading the essays of Davis. An Englishman, with his belief in Progress, with his instinctive preference for the cosmopolitan literature of the last century, may think arts like these parochial, but they are the arts we have begun the making of.[42]

Ancient Ireland had finally arrived in Irish literature as the ultimate rediscovery of modern Ireland. The people and the Ascendancy were now, as possessors of the national character, in a new alliance to rescue the degenerate modern world from the secular-commercial triumphs of the British national character against which they had both struggled to define and distinguish themselves since the eighteenth century.

NOTES

1. See Dorothy George, *English Political Caricature 1793–1832: A Study of Opinion and Propaganda*, 2 vols. (Oxford University Press, 1959); Draper Hill, *Fashionable Contrasts: Caricatures by James Gillray* (London: Hennessy and Ingalls, 1966); Ronald Paulson, *Rowlandson: A New Interpretation* (New York: Oxford University Press, 1972); Edgell Rickwood ed., *Radical Squibs and Loyal Ripostes: Satirical Pamphlets of the Regency Period, 1819–1821, Illustrated by George Cruikshank and Others* (London: Adams and Dart, 1971).
2. Richard N. Lebow, *White Britain and Black Ireland: The Influence of Stereotypes on Colonial Policy* (Philadelphia, PA: Institute for the Study of Human Issues, 1976); L. Perry Curtis, *Apes and Angels: The Irishman in Victorian Caricature* (Washington, DC: Smithsonian Institution Press, 1972).

3. See René Wellek, *The Rise of English Literary History* (Chapel Hill: University of North Carolina Press, 1941), 24–35.
4. David Hume, *Essays Moral, Political and Literary* ed. T. H . Green and T. H. Grose, 2 vols. (London: Longmans, Green, 1875), vol. II, 68.
5. See L. L. Bongie, *David Hume: Prophet of the Counter-Revolution* (Oxford: Clarendon Press, 1965), 5–8.
6. For a fuller account, see Ciaran Murray, 'Intellectual Origins of the English Landscape Garden', unpublished PhD thesis, University College, Dublin (1985); B. Sprague Allen, *Tides in English Taste, 1619–1800,* 2 vols. (Cambridge, MA: Harvard University Press, 1937); Derek Clifford, *A History of Garden Design* (London: Faber and Faber, 1962); Christopher Hussey, *English Gardens and Landscapes 1700–1750* (London: Country Life, 1967); E. Hyams, *The English Garden* (London: Thames & Hudson, 1966); Osvald Siren, *China and the Gardens of Europe of the Eighteenth Century* (London: Ronald Press, 1949).
7. The standard work is still S. H. Monk, *The Sublime* (New York: Modern Language Association, 1935).
8. *The Works of The Right Honourable Edmund Burke,* 8 vols. (London: Bohn, 1877–8), vol. VI, 45.
9. See especially C. P. Courtney, *Montesquieu and Burke* (London: Blackwell, 1963).
10. See J. T. Boulton, *The Language of Politics in the Age of Wilkes and Burke* (London: Routledge & Kegan Paul, 1963).
11. See Norman Vance, 'Celts, Carthaginians and Constitutions: Anglo-Irish Literary Relations, 1780–1820', *Irish Historical Studies,* 22 (1980), 216–30. Betham's best-known works are *The Gael and the Cymbri* (1834) and *Etruria-Celtica* (1842); see also Jeanne Sheehy, *The Rediscovery of Ireland's Past: The Celtic Revival, 1830–1930* (London: Thames & Hudson, 1980).
12. *The Letters of Thomas Moore,* ed. W. S. Dowden, 2 vols. (Oxford University Press, 1964), vol. I, 116.
13. *The Complete Works of William Hazlitt,* ed. P. P. Howe, 21 vols. (London: J. M. Dent, 1910–34), vol. VII, 154.
14. James Hardiman, *Irish Minstrelsy: or, Bardic Remains of Ireland with English Poetical Translations,* 2 vols. (London: Joseph Robins, 1831), vol. I, v.
15. Burke, *Works,* vol. III, 304–5. See also Seamus Deane, 'Edmund Burke and the Ideology of Irish Liberalism', in R. Kearney (ed.), *The Irish Mind* (Dublin: Wolfhound Press, 1985), 141–56.
16. Burke, *Works,* vol. XI, 58.
17. See W. J. McCormack, *Ascendancy and Tradition in Anglo-Irish Literary History from 1789 to 1939* (Oxford University Press, 1985).
18. See Hazlitt, *Complete Works,* vol. X, 99, 166; vol. XIII, 56.
19. See especially *De la littérature considérée dans ses rapports avec les institutions sociales,* ed. P. van Tieghem, 2 vols. (Geneva: Librairie Droz; Paris: M. J. Minard, 1959).

20. *The Collected Works of Samuel Taylor Coleridge,* vol. III (in 3 vols.): *Essays on His Times,* ed. David V. Erdman (London: Routledge; Princeton, NJ: Princeton University Press, 1978), vol. I, 120.
21. Ibid., vol. II, 413.
22. *The Works of Thomas Carlyle,* 30 vols. (London: Chapman & Hall, 1898–9), vol. XXIX, 137.
23. Ibid., vol. XX, 194.
24. See Gerald Bullett, *Sydney Smith: A Biography and a Selection* (London: Michael Joseph, 1951), 224.
25. See Seamus Deane, *Celtic Revivals: Essays in Modern Irish Literature, 1880–1980* (London: Faber and Faber, 1985), 17–28.
26. Maria Edgeworth, *Castle Rackrent,* ed. George Watson (Oxford University Press, 1964), 4.
27. William Carleton, *The Black Prophet,* Introduction by Timothy Webb (Shannon: Irish University Press, 1972), vii–viii.
28. W. Stuart Trench, *Realities of Irish Life,* 2nd edn (London: Longmans, Green, 1869), vii.
29. *The Collected Writings of Thomas De Quincey,* ed. D. Masson, 14 vols. (Edinburgh: Black, 1889–90), vol. XIV, 285n.
30. The phrase is Yeats's, quoted in Thomas Flanagan, *The Irish Novelists, 1800–1850* (New York: Columbia University Press, 1959), 174.
31. Alexander M. Sullivan, *New Ireland: Political Sketches and Personal Reminiscences of Thirty Years of Irish Public Life* (Glasgow: Cameron & Ferguson, 1884), 3.
32. Edgeworth, *Castle Rackrent,* 97.
33. Augustus J.C. Hare, *The Life and Letters of Maria Edgeworth,* 2 vols. (London: Edward Arnold, 1894), vol. II, 550.
34. Gerald Griffin, *The Collegians* (London and Dublin: Talbot Press, 1942), 20, 31, 81, 173.
35. Barbara Hayley, *Carleton's Traits and Stories and the 19th Century Anglo-Irish Tradition* (Gerrards Cross: Colin Smythe, 1983), 357–63.
36. Ibid., 24.
37. Thomas Davis, *Prose Writings; Essays on Ireland* (London: Walter Scott, 1889), xiii.
38. M. C. Ferguson, *Sir Samuel Ferguson in the Ireland of His Day,* 2 vols. (Edinburgh and London: Blackwood and Sons, 1896), vol. I, 47.
39. *Dublin University Magazine,* 2 (1833), 588.
40. See especially Standish O'Grady, *Toryism and Tory Democracy* (London: Chapman & Hall, 1886) and *Selected Essays and Passages* (Dublin: Talbot Press, 1918).
41. For an interesting sketch of this literature, see Tom Gibbons, *Rooms in the Darwin Hotel* (Perth: University of Western Australia, 1973).
42. W. B. Yeats, 'Ireland and the Arts' (1901) in *Essays and Introductions* (London: Macmillan, 1961), 206.

CHAPTER 6

Civilians and Barbarians

THOSE WHO LIVE UNDER THE LAW ARE CIVILIANS; THOSE WHO live beyond it are barbarians. 'Law makes men free in the political arena, just as reason makes men free in the universe as a whole.'[1] Barbarians, therefore, are slaves, since they live in a world from which the operation of arbitrary individual will has not been eliminated. Law compels men to be free. In this paradox is to be found the nucleus of modern European theories of freedom, from Locke to Rousseau and beyond. But it was a common conception long before it received its articulation as an integral element in a comprehensive political philosophy. Nicholas Canny has provided us with an analysis of the background to Edmund Spenser's *View of the Present State of Ireland* (1596) which demonstrates the prevalence of the notion that the Irish must be compelled to be free by a sustained policy of war followed by good government. John Davies, for instance, is quoted as saying in his *Discovery of the True Causes why Ireland was Never Entirely Subdued* (1612) that

> the husbandman must first break the land before it be made capable of good seed: and when it is thoroughly broken and manured, if he do not forthwith cast good seed into it, it will grow wild again, and bear nothing but weeds. So a barbarous country must be first broken by war before it will be capable of good government; and when it is fully subdued and conquered, if it be not well planted and governed after the conquest, it will eftsoons return to the former barbarism.[2]

To become free and prosperous the Irish were evidently going to have to become English. Spenser had objected to the Irish habit of abusing the English system of common law by presenting false evidence or producing unfair verdicts because their loyalty was to their system of clan kinship and not to English law. Thus he suggested that the Irish septs be dissolved, that the Irish be moved into the towns, mingled with the settlers, educated in English, in grammar and in science,

> whereby they will in short time grow up to that civil conversation that both the children will loathe the former rudeness in which they were bred, and also their parents will, even by the ensample of their young children, perceive the foulness of their own brutish behaviour compared to theirs, for learning hath that wonderful power of itself that it can soften and temper the most stern and savage nature.[3]

The failure of this policy in succeeding centuries led Coleridge to contemplate with some horror the rise in Ireland of a new species of patriotism in the guise of the United Irishmen as a 'delusive and pernicious sublimation of local predilection and clannish pride, into a sentiment and principle of nationality'.[4] Writing in 1814, Coleridge gives a brief account of the failure of English policy in Ireland since the days of Henry II up to the achievement of legislative independence in 1782 and thence to the Union and the United Irishmen. In his reading of the story, he echoes Spenser's complaint that the English government policy was never sufficiently sustained; that it was concessive only under pressure and that it was now faced with a species of local patriotism which, though far removed from the real thing, was nevertheless extremely dangerous. The danger arose from three sources. First, many supporters of Irish patriotism believed that

> they were labouring as the pioneers of civilization; and that political zealotry was calculated to act on Protestantism and Papistry, with all their Irish accretions, as an alkali on water and oil; and though caustic and corrosive in its own nature, unite the two incongruous natures into a milky and cleansing quality, that would remove from the moral countenance of Ireland all the anger-spots and efflorescences produced by intestine heats.[5]

Second, there was the Irish predilection for foreign connections, through the Church, with its clergy educated abroad, and through the Catholic gentry's preference for foreign military service. Third, were all those circumstances

> which makes the population of Ireland, at once the most numerous, and with few exceptions, the least civilized of Christian Europe, with fewer gradations and modes of interdependence; with less descending influence of opinions and manners from the gentry of the country; but above all, *with a more confirmed habit of obeying powers not constituted or acknowledged by the laws and Government, and of course with as much greater devotion as conscience is mightier than law.*[6]

Although Coleridge characteristically failed to complete his account of the Irish situation on the eve of Waterloo, his journalistic writings on the topic retain many of the features of his seventeenth-century predecessors. Most pronounced among these are the assumption that the strife in Ireland is the consequence of a battle between English civilization, based on laws, and Irish barbarism, based on local kinship loyalties and sentiments; that the added complication of religion helps to intensify that Irish barbarism by fostering ignorance and sloth, disrespect for English law and respect for papal decrees in its stead, conspiracy and rebellion by cherishing foreign connections hostile to England. The one marked difference Coleridge notices in 1814 is the claim by the United Irishmen that their patriotism will subdue religious differences by substituting the common name of Irishman for that of Catholic or Dissenter. He did, therefore, see the significance of what Tone represented but he feared that the development of what he called 'local patriotism' among what he had described in 1800 as 'the vindictive turbulence of a wild and barbarous race, brutalised by the oppression of centuries'[7] would turn into a Jacobin rebellion, leading to the separation of the two islands. That would never do.

The wisdom of English commentators on Irish affairs has always been vitiated by the assumption that there is some undeniable relationship between civilization, the common law, and Protestantism. Ireland has remained a permanent rebuke to this assumption, and has been subjected to vilification on that account. The assumption has remained unquestioned. But Ireland has not been alone in this matter. The English interpretation of the French Revolution was governed for the first thirty years of the nineteenth century by the belief that the French had failed to do in 1789 what the English had done in 1688 because, being Catholics (lapsed or otherwise), and therefore acclimatized to despotism and the operations of arbitrary rule, they were unfit for liberty. This argument has been produced over and over again, *mutatis mutandis*, to deny freedom to colonial peoples. It seems a little odd to see it used by one colonial power against another. Those who, like Hazlitt, would have liked to see the Revolution, led by Napoleon, overthrow Legitimacy, did not have to look far to discover why the French failed to support their great Emperor.

> Perhaps a reformation in religion ought always to precede a revolution in the government. Catholics may make good subjects, but bad rebels. They are so used to the trammels of authority, that they do not immediately know how to do without them; or, like manumitted slaves, only feel assured of their liberty in committing some Saturnalian license. A revolution, to give it stability and soundness, should first be conducted down to a Protestant ground.[8]

Commentators of a far more virulent Francophobia than Hazlitt's produced scores of essays and pamphlets in which the new French revolutionary philosophy was described as 'barbarous' and its supporters as every species of wretch and miscreant. In 1793, Horace Walpole, having exhausted his considerable powers of invective, decided that the French deserved nothing more than their own name.

> But I have no words that can reach the criminality of such *inferno-human* beings – but must compose a term that aims at conveying my idea of them – for the future it will be sufficient to call them the *French*.[9]

More than twenty years later, Robert Southey, the friend of Coleridge and Wordsworth, and one-time radical, announced in the course of a defence of the English alliance between Church and state:

> If a breach be made in our sanctuary, it will be by the combined forces of Popery, Dissent, and Unbelief, fighting under a political flag.[10]

The threat to the English sanctuary was, in short, nationalism of the French revolutionary sort. The dispute between barbarism and civilization had by now undergone a transformation. Races like the French and the Irish, in their resistance to the English idea of liberty, had now become criminalized – '*inferno-human* beings'. As evangelicalism in England rose through the social system from the Methodists to the Anglicans, the specifically Protestant resistance to the characteristic sins of these races became more pronounced. In the case of the French, the sin was lasciviousness; in the case of the Irish, it was drunkenness. Neither was 'manly'; both were symptoms of a deep corruption; the corruption was itself a failure in self-discipline and respect for law, moral or positive. The profile of the frigidly sober English Victorian disciplinarian emerged against the political background of the old quarrels between France and England, Ireland and England, civilization (with all its discontents) and barbarism (with all its 'lewde libertie').[11]

The complicated history of the various temperance movements in Irish history and their connections with nationalist and anti-nationalist ideologies reveals the deep disquiet felt among many sects and classes about the social manifestations of Irish 'barbarism'.[12] When the movements were led by Protestant evangelicals, their aim was to extirpate the disease by introducing preventive legislation. The various licensing acts of the nineteenth century are their monument and Ian Paisley's recent defence (February, 1983) of the Northern Irish Sabbath as a tourist attraction their most recent echo. When led by Catholic Churchmen, like Father Mathew in Ireland or Cardinal Manning among the Irish in England, their aim was to promote abstinence, not by law, but by conscience. This distinction shows a curious reversal of the conventional Protestant/Catholic attitudes. In Ireland, the Protestant has tended to turn to law and the state even in matters of social and moral attitude, because Protestantism and the state have been for so long in a defensive alliance with one another. The Catholic, on the other hand, has turned to conscience and the Church (increasingly the same thing in the modern period), seeking from the Church rather than the state legitimization for social and moral issues. The temperance movement in the nineteenth century was one of the signs of the Catholic Church's increasing authority in areas which, before the Famine, had not been open to its discipline. However temperance was only one of a series of social movements which had increased civility and respectability among the masses of the people as its aim.

The attachment of the stigma of criminality to drinking, especially among the poor, was a symptom of the increasingly coercive function of law as an instrument for extending efficiency and order in a society where waste and disorder were rampant. The various state-run enterprises in nineteenth-century Ireland – in health, through the dispensary system; in education, through the national schools; in cartography through the Ordnance Survey; in policing, through the establishment, by 1836, of a nationally controlled paramilitary force; in law, through the system of Resident Magistrates – had a highly Spenserian aim in view: the civilization of the wild natives.[13] All of these schemes were, in effect, pieces of preventive legislation. A whole range of conditions – like the condition of being drunk, or illiterate, or from somewhere unheard of or unknown, or vagrant, or disaffected – was now realized as being beyond (not exactly against) the law. As with certain laws in England, like the Vagrancy Act of 1824, an imputed intention or reputation was, *in itself*, criminal. Section 4 of that Act criminalized 'every suspected person or reputed thief' who frequented the dockland areas of industrial England.[14] Such legislation need a developed police force for its implementation. In Ireland, the police force was far more advanced than in England. The legislation was far more draconian and politically directed. Because of the recurrent agrarian unrest and the political disturbances, Insurrection Acts, Arms Acts, and Peace Preservation Acts stand 'like monuments to misrule in the years between the Act of Union and the Famine'.[15]

Thus, in the nineteenth century, a new state-controlled system of education, police, preventive law, health, prison, workhouse, ordnance maps, emerged to provide that sustained governmental policy which the seventeenth-century colonizers had sought from Whitehall. In Ireland, the coercive legislation was especially prominent but its aim, while more blatant, was no different. This was to suppress a condition of mind. After all, in 1867, the Manchester martyrs were hanged on the same evidence as had led to the pardon and release of an innocent bystander, Maguire. 'The implied attitude in the home secretary's discrimination was that Maguire had shown no animosity to the authority of the queen and deserved to live, while the rest took pride in their Irish attitudes and deserved to die.'[16] That condition of mind was not necessarily Irish. It was the condition of *homo criminalis*, the criminal type, that theoretical construct of the great age of scientific criminology, the detective novel, and high industrial capitalism. The Irish mind, or certain conditions thereof, was, to the English mind, in most conditions thereof, ineluctably criminal because of the very simple fact that it tended to show remarkably consistent disrespect for English law and, therefore (!), for the Law as such. The stereotypes of the Irish person – the quaint Paddy or the simian terrorist – arise quite naturally from the conviction that there are criminal types, politically as well as socially identifiable to the police and to all decent citizens. Conrad's *The Secret Agent* (1907), with its expert conflation of Fenian and Russian anarchist stereotypes, is the most memorable of all anti-revolutionary and anti-terrorist fictions, with the outrage at its heart being the attempt to blow up Greenwich Mean Time itself with a bomb unwittingly carried by an idiot. Spenserian barbarism, transmuted into professional anarchism (or, as we would say, international terrorism), has now the organized police force and organized time and space as its civilized enemy.

This brings us to the doorstep of our own time. The language of politics in Ireland and England, especially when the subject is Northern Ireland, is still dominated by the putative division between barbarism and civilization. Civilization still defines itself as a system of law; and it defines barbarism (which, by the nature of the distinction, cannot be capable of defining itself) as a chaos of arbitrary wills, an Hobbesian state of nature. But it is a distinction which operates within a modern state-system which prides itself on the transparency of the whole population to the concentrated stare of bureaucratic (including police and military) control. In Ireland, this new situation (dating from the early nineteenth century) has enormously increased the ideological rift between the competing discourses of the civilian and the barbarian. For the romantic nationalism, born in that utilitarian century, gave to certain aspects of 'barbarism' a privileged status. In literature, for instance, 'barbarism' became 'primitivism' and represented a vigour lost to the sophisticated art of the civilized world. On the other hand, the same nationalism insisted on the high degree of civilization it had attained socially, although in some of the temperance debates both O'Connell and Davis give us a version of Irish life which seems to have been modelled on some of the more saccharine passages in Dickens. The essential issues have, however, been 'displaced' into literature in such a manner that their reality has been further attenuated in the minds of the Irish people. The writer as barbarian, the audience as civilian – that is an easily accepted exercise in role-playing. But the romanticization of writing involved in this is not nearly so important as the humiliating conquest of the audience. For such an audience is tamed; it has learned to be submissive to the massive system of controls which the modern political machine operates. Among those systems of control is the image of the writer as licensed barbarian – a sort of wild Irish native performing in an English court. But, beyond that, there is the much more concentrated manipulation of the civilian audience's reaction to the other kind of outsider – the criminal type and, above all, the *politically* criminal type, your friendly neighbourhood terrorist.

This stereotype has all the classic faults of the barbarian as seen from the view of the English civilian. First he is Irish; next Catholic; and, if not Catholic, then an extreme Protestant, a Dissenter of the old, troublesome Calvinistic or Ranter type; in addition he is from a working-class background and is unemployed /unemployable; therefore he draws money from the benevolent state which he intends to subvert and by which he is oppressed as he was also educated and fed free milk by it. He is from an area of dirt and desolation, not to be equalled in Western Europe, a blot on the fair face of the United Kingdom. He drinks a lot for, since the Fenians, it has been a standard piece of English lore that all Irish guerrilla groups meet in pubs when they are not blowing them up. Sometimes, they manage to do both. Finally, and worst of all, he is sometimes a she. Locked in a poverty trap, lost in a mist of sentiment and nostalgia, exploiting the safeguards of laws they despise, faithful to codes other than those of the English rite, they are the perfect reproduction, with some nineteenth-century romantic tints, of Spenser's wild Irish. Most important of all, they are not only barbarians, they are criminals. Their opponents, who wear uniforms, and live in barracks, and drive armoured cars, operate checkpoints, etc. etc., kill with impunity, because they represent, they embody the Law. The terrorist embodies its denial. The brutal exploitation of events by both sides demonstrates over and over again the endlessness of the battle for supremacy of one kind of discourse, one set of political attitudes over another.

This is plain enough. But complications set in – as in an illness – when modes of discourse other than the political become involved. The moral mode, much favoured of course by the Churches, although not ignored in the least by either governments, armies, or the media, has a distorting effect on the political realities involved. For it is based (however hypocritically) on the notion of an immutable Natural Law, or Moral Code, the peremptory force of which applies more directly to the terrorist than to the soldier of the state. There is an interesting political distinction between the appeals made by clergy to terrorists and those made to the forces of Law and Order. The first are made to individuals, loners, to come in out of the moral cold, to cease disgracing the cause they ostensibly represent; the second are made to a corporate body, not to the individual. The 'barbarians' are always 'men and women', or specific, even named, individuals. They enjoy the privilege of individuality precisely because they will not be granted the status of a corporate force within civil society. The ground of the appeal, however, is that of the universal condition of mankind, redeemed and unredeemed, saved and damned, or, if you like, civilian and barbarian. The moral and religious idiom, which claims this universality, has in fact been incorporated into the political idiom which appears to be more local in its range. The moral idiom therefore is no more than a reinforcement of the political while appearing to be independent of it. The systematic nature of political and moral idioms, the organic coherence conferred upon them by the prevalence of political interests, makes the distinction between them suspect. Nothing demonstrated this more than the Peace Movement, one of the most successful of all political exploitations of a moral code which was in fact a political code. Hardly anyone remembers that the incident which sparked the movement off began with the killing of an IRA man, who was driving a car, by a British soldier – who was himself in no danger. The charismatic movement in Catholicism and the evangelical movement in Protestantism combined to display, in front of the cameras, the longing for peace by a population disturbed by the guerrillas within their ranks – not by the army, or the police, or the unemployment, housing conditions, and so forth. As farces go, it was one of the most successful of modern times.

But it was an important success. For it changed nothing. Therefore it was a success for the state. It merely confirmed and spread the demonizing mythology. Later, the dirty protest at the Maze was to supply it with the most horrific imagery of degradation, although the conspiracy between the degraded and the degraders became so close at that time that the filthy nakedness of the prisoners and the space-suited automatism of the disinfecting jailers seemed to be an agreed contrast in their respective images of what they represented – vulnerable Irish squalor, impervious, impersonal English decontamination. That changed nothing either. Nor did the Hunger Strikes, although for a time it seemed as if they might change everything. The point of crisis was passed without anyone seeming to know why the explosion did not come. Perhaps the truth is that both sides had played out their self-appointed roles to such a literal end, that there was nothing left but the sense of exhaustion. Political languages fade more slowly than literary languages but when they do, they herald a deep structural alteration in the attitudes which sustain a crisis. Of all the blighting distinctions which govern our responses and limit our imaginations at the moment, none is more potent than this four-hundred-year-old distinction between barbarians and civilians. We may ask, with Bishop Berkeley in *The Querist*,

Whether the natural phlegm of this island needs any additional stupefier?

NOTES

1. John Locke, *Two Treatises of Government*, ed. and intro. Peter Laslett (Cambridge University Press, 1960), 111.
2. Nicholas Canny, 'Edmund Spenser and the Development of an Anglo-Irish Identity', *Yearbook of English Studies*, 13 (1983), 1–19 (at 15).
3. Ibid., 6.
4. *The Collected Works of Samuel Taylor Coleridge*, vol. III (in 3 vols.): *Essays on His Times*, ed. David V. Erdman (London: Routledge; Princeton, NJ: Princeton University Press, 1978), vol. II, 411.
5. Ibid., 412–13.
6. Ibid., 413 (my emphasis in the last lines).
7. Ibid., vol. I, 106.
8. *The Complete Works of William Hazlitt*, ed. P. P. Howe, 21 vols. (London: J. M. Dent, 1910–34), vol. XIII (*The Life of Napoleon Buonaparte*, written 1828–30), 56.
9. *The Correspondence of Horace Walpole*, ed. W. S. Lewis, 48 vols. (New Haven, CT: Yale University Press, 1961), vol. XXXI, 377.
10. Robert Southey, *Sir Thomas More: or, Colloquies on the Progress and Prospects of Society*, 2 vols. (London: John Murray, 1829), vol. II, 43.

11. A phrase from Spenser's *View of the Present State of Ireland.*
12. See Elizabeth Malcolm, 'Temperance and Irish Nationalism', in F. S. L. Lyons and R. A. J. Hawkins (eds.), *Ireland under the Union* (Oxford University Press, 1980), 69–114.
13. See Oliver MacDonagh, *Ireland, the Union and its Aftermath* (London: Allen & Unwin, 1977), chapter 2.
14. I am indebted to an unpublished article by Barry McAuley of the Faculty of Law at UCD for this information and some of these ideas. The article is titled, 'The Grammar of Western Criminal Justice'.
15. George Dangerfield, *The Damnable Question: A Study in Anglo-Irish Relations* (Boston: Little, Brown, 1977), 9.
16. Malcolm Brown, *The Politics of Irish Literature* (Seattle: University of Washington Press, 1972), 209.

CHAPTER 7

Heroic Styles: The Tradition of an Idea

IT IS POSSIBLE TO WRITE ABOUT LITERATURE WITHOUT ADVERTING in any substantial way to history. Equally, it is possible to write history without any serious reference to literature. Yet both literature and history are discourses which are widely recognized to be closely related to one another because they are both subject to various linguistic protocols which, in gross or in subtle ways, determine the structure and meaning of what is written. We have many names for these protocols. Some are very general indeed – Romanticism, Victorianism, Modernism. Some are more specific – Idealist, Radical, Liberal. Literature can be written as History, History as Literature. It would be foolhardy to choose one among the many competing variations and say that it is true on some specifically historical or literary basis. Such choices are always moral and/or aesthetic. They always have an ideological implication.

Similarly, both discourses are surrounded – some would say stifled – by what is now called metacommentary. History as an activity is interrogated by the philosophy of history; literature as an activity is scrutinized by literary criticism which, at times, manages to be the philosophy of literature. In Ireland, however, the two discourses have been kept apart, even though they have, between them, created the interpretations of past and present by which we live. It is always possible to see in retrospect the features which identify writers of a particular period, no matter how disparate their interests. The link between Yeats, Spengler, and Toynbee is obvious by now. They all speak the language of a particular historical 'family'. The same is true of Joyce and Lukács. What I propose in this pamphlet is that there have been for us two dominant ways of reading both our literature and our history. One is 'Romantic', a mode of reading which takes pleasure in the notion that Ireland is a culture enriched by the ambiguity of its relationship to an anachronistic and a modernized present. The other is a mode of reading which denies the glamour of this ambiguity and seeks to escape from it into a pluralism of the present. The authors who represent these modes most powerfully are Yeats and Joyce respectively. The problem which is rendered insoluble by them is that of the North. In a basic sense, the crisis we are passing through is stylistic. That is to say, it is a crisis of language – the ways in which we write it and the ways in which we read it.

The idea of a tradition is one with which we are familiar in Irish writing. In a culture like ours, 'tradition' is not easily taken to be an established reality. We are conscious that it is an invention, a narrative which ingeniously finds a way of connecting a selected series of historical figures or themes in such a way that the pattern or plot revealed to us becomes a conditioning factor in our reading of literary works – such as *The Tower* or *Finnegans Wake*. However, the paradox into which we are inevitably led has a disquieting effect, for then we recognize that a Yeatsian or a Joycean idea of tradition is something simultaneously established for us in their texts and as a precondition of being able to read them. A poem like 'Ancestral Houses' owes its force to the vitality with which it offers a version of Ascendancy history as true in itself. The truth of this historical reconstruction of the Ascendancy is not cancelled by our simply saying No, it was not like that. For its ultimate validity is not historical, but mythical. In this case, the mythical element is given prominence by the meditation on the fate of an originary energy when it becomes so effective that it transforms nature into civilization and is then transformed itself by civilization into decadence. This poem, then, appears to have a story to tell and, along with that, an interpretation of the story's meaning. It operates on the narrative and on the conceptual planes and at the intersection of these it emerges, for many readers, as a poem about the tragic nature of human existence itself. Yeats's life, through the mediations of history and myth, becomes an embodiment of essential existence.

The trouble with such a reading is the assumption that this or any other literary work can arrive at a moment in which it takes leave of history or myth (which are liable to idiosyncratic interpretation) and becomes meaningful only as an aspect of the 'human condition'. This is, of course, a characteristic determination of humanist readings of literature which hold to the ideological conviction that literature, in its highest forms, is non-ideological. It would be perfectly appropriate, within this particular frame, to take a poem by Pearse – say, 'The Rebel' – and to read it in the light of a story – the Republican tradition from Tone, the Celtic tradition from Cuchulainn, the Christian tradition from Colmcille – and then reread the story as an expression of the moral supremacy of martyrdom over oppression. But as a poem, it would be regarded as inferior to that of Yeats. Yeats, stimulated by the moribund state of the Ascendancy tradition, resolves, on the level of literature, a crisis which, for him, cannot be resolved socially or politically. In Pearse's case, the poem is no more than an adjunct to political action. The revolutionary tradition he represents is not broken by oppression but renewed by it. His symbols survive outside the poem, in the Cuchulainn statue, in the reconstituted GPO, in the military behaviour and rhetoric of the IRA. Yeats's symbols have disappeared, the destruction of Coole Park being the most notable, although even in their disappearance one can discover reinforcement for the tragic condition embodied in the poem. The unavoidable fact about both poems is that they continue to belong to history and to myth; they are part of the symbolic procedures which characterize their culture. Yet, to the extent that we prefer one as literature to the other, we find ourselves inclined to dispossess it of history, to concede to it an autonomy which is finally defensible only on the grounds of style.

The consideration of style is a thorny problem. In Irish writing, it is particularly so. When the language is English, Irish writing is dominated by the notion of vitality restored, of the centre energized by the periphery, the urban by the rural, the cosmopolitan by the provincial, the decadent by the natural. This is one of the liberating effects of nationalism, a means of restoring dignity and power to what had been humiliated and suppressed. This is the idea which underlies all our formulations of tradition. Its development is confined to two variations. The first we may call the variation of adherence, the second of separation. In the first, the restoration of native energy to the English language is seen as a specifically Irish contribution to a shared heritage. Standard English, as a form of language or as a form of literature, is rescued from its exclusiveness by being compelled to incorporate into itself what had previously been regarded as a delinquent dialect. It is the Irish contribution, in literary terms, to the treasury of English verse and prose. Cultural nationalism is thus transformed into a species of literary unionism: Sir Samuel Ferguson is the most explicit supporter of this variation, although, from Edgeworth to Yeats, it remains a tacit assumption. The story of the spiritual heroics of a fading class – the Ascendancy – in the face of a transformed Catholic 'nation' – was rewritten in a variety of ways in literature – as the story of the pagan Fianna replaced by a pallid Christianity, of young love replaced by old age (Deirdre, Oisin), of aristocracy supplanted by mob-democracy. The fertility of these rewritings is all the more remarkable in that they were recruitments by the fading class of the myths of renovation which belonged to their opponents. Irish culture became the new property of those who were losing their grip on Irish land. The effect of these rewritings was to transfer the blame for the drastic condition of the country from the Ascendancy to the Catholic middle classes or to their English counterparts. It was in essence a strategic retreat from political to cultural supremacy. From Lecky to Yeats and forward to F. S. L. Lyons we witness the conversion of Irish history into a tragic theatre in which the great Anglo-Irish protagonists – Swift, Burke, Parnell – are destroyed in their heroic attempts to unite culture of intellect with the emotion of multitude, or, in political terms, constitutional politics with the forces of revolution. The triumph of the forces of revolution is glossed in all cases as the success of a philistine modernism over a rich and integrated organic culture. Yeats's promiscuity in his courtship of heroic figures – Cuchulainn, John O'Leary, Parnell, the 1916 leaders, Synge, Mussolini, Kevin O'Higgins, General O'Duffy – is an understandable form of anxiety in one who sought to find in a single figure the capacity to give reality to a spiritual leadership for which (as he consistently admitted) the conditions had already disappeared. Such figures could only operate as symbols. Their significance lay in their disdain for the provincial, squalid aspects of a mob culture which is the Yeatsian version of the other face of Irish nationalism. It could provide him culturally with a language of renovation, but it provided neither art nor civilization. That had come, politically, from the connection between England and Ireland.

All the important Irish Protestant writers of the nineteenth century had, as the ideological centre of their work, a commitment to a minority or subversive attitude which was much less revolutionary than it appeared to be. Edgeworth's critique of landlordism was counterbalanced by her sponsorship of utilitarianism and 'British manufacturers';[1] Maturin and Le Fanu took the sting out of gothicism by allying it with an ethic of aristocratic loneliness; Shaw and Wilde denied the subversive force of their proto-socialism by expressing it as cosmopolitan wit, the recourse of the social or intellectual dandy who makes such a fetish of taking nothing seriously that he ceases to be taken seriously himself. Finally, Yeats's preoccupation with the occult, and Synge's with the lost language of Ireland are both minority positions which have, as part of their project, the revival of worn social forms, not their overthrow. The disaffection inherent in these positions is typical of the Anglo-Irish criticism of the failure of English civilization in Ireland, but it is articulated for an English audience which learned to regard all these adversarial positions as essentially picturesque manifestations of the Irish sensibility. In the same way, the Irish mode of English was regarded as picturesque too and when both language and ideology are rendered harmless by this view of them, the writer is liable to become a popular success. Somerville and Ross showed how to take the middle-class seriousness out of Edgeworth's world and make it endearingly quaint. But all nineteenth-century Irish writing exploits the connection between the picturesque and the popular. In its comic vein, it produces *The Shaughraun* and *Experiences of an Irish R.M.*; in its gothic vein, *Melmoth the Wanderer, Uncle Silas,* and *Dracula*; in its mandarin vein, the plays of Wilde and the poetry of the young Yeats. The division between that which is picturesque and that which is useful did not pass unobserved by Yeats. He made the great realignment of the minority stance with the pursuit of perfection in art. He gave the picturesque something more than respectability. He gave it the mysteriousness of the esoteric and in doing so committed Irish writing to the idea of an art which, while belonging to 'high' culture, would not have, on the one hand, the asphyxiating decadence of its English or French counterparts and, on the other hand, would have within it the energies of a community which had not yet been reduced to a public. An idea of art opposed to the idea of utility, an idea of an audience opposed to the idea of popularity, an idea of the peripheral becoming the central culture – in these three ideas Yeats provided Irish writing with a programme for action. But whatever its connection with Irish nationalism, it was not, finally, a programme of separation from the English tradition. His continued adherence to it led him to define the central Irish attitude as one of self-hatred. In his extraordinary 'A General Introduction for my Work' (1937), he wrote:

> The 'Irishry' have preserved their ancient 'deposit' through wars which, during the sixteenth and seventeenth centuries, became wars of extermination; no people, Lecky said ... have undergone greater persecution, nor did that persecution altogether cease up to our own day. No people hate as we do in whom that past is always alive ... Then I remind myself that though mine is the first English marriage I know of in the direct line, all my family names are English, and that I owe my soul to Shakespeare, to Spenser and to Blake, perhaps to William Morris, and to the English language in which I think, speak, and write, that everything I love has come to me through English; my hatred tortures me with love, my love with hate ... This is Irish hatred and solitude, the hatred of human life that made Swift write *Gulliver* and the epitaph upon his tomb; that can still make us wag between extremes and doubt our sanity.

The pathology of literary unionism has never been better defined.

The second variation in the development of the idea of vitality restored is embodied most perfectly in Joyce. His work is dominated by the idea of separation as a means to the revival of suppressed energies. The separation he envisages is as complete as one could wish. The English literary and political imperium, the Roman Catholic and Irish nationalist claims, the oppressions of conventional language and of conventional narrative – all of these are overthrown, but the freedom which results is haunted by his fearful obsession with treachery and betrayal. In him, as in many twentieth-century writers, the natural ground of vitality is identified as the libidinal. The sexual forms of oppression are inscribed in all his works but, with that, there is also the ambition to see the connection between sexuality and history. His work is notoriously preoccupied with paralysis, inertia, the disabling effects of society upon the individual who, like Bloom, lives within its frame, or, like Stephen, attempts to live beyond it. In *Portrait* the separation of the aesthetic ambition of Stephen from the political, the sexual, and the religious zones of experience is clear. It is, of course, a separation which includes them, but as oppressed forces which were themselves once oppressive. His comment on Wilde is pertinent:

> Here we touch the pulse of Wilde's art – sin. He deceived himself into believing that he was the bearer of good news of neo-paganism to an enslaved people ... But if some truth adheres ... to his restless thought ... at its very base is the truth inherent in the soul of Catholicism: that man cannot reach the divine heart except through that sense of separation and loss called sin.[2]

In Joyce himself the sin is treachery, sexual or political infidelity. The betrayed figure is the alien artist. The 'divine heart' is the maternal figure, mother, Mother Ireland, Mother Church, or Mother Eve. But the betrayed are also the betrayers and the source of the treachery is in the Irish condition itself. In his Trieste lecture of 1907, 'Ireland, Island of Saints and Sages', he notes that Ireland was betrayed by her own people and by the Vatican on the crucial occasions of Henry II's invasion and the Act of Union.

> From my point of view, these two facts must be thoroughly explained before the country in which they occurred has the most rudimentary right to persuade one of her sons to change his position from that of an unprejudiced observer to that of a convicted nationalist.[3]

Finally, in his account of the Maamtrasna murders of 1882 in 'Ireland at the Bar' (published in *Il Piccolo della Sera,* Trieste, 1907), Joyce, anticipating the use which he would make throughout *Finnegans Wake* of the figure of the Irish-speaking Myles Joyce, judicially murdered by the sentence of an English-speaking court, comments:

> The figure of this dumbfounded old man, a remnant of a civilization not ours, deaf and dumb before his judge, is a symbol of the Irish nation at the bar of public opinion.[4]

This, along with the well-known passage from *Portrait* in which Stephen feels the humiliation of being alien to the English language in the course of his conversation with the Newman-Catholic Dean of Studies, identifies Joyce's sense of separation from both Irish and English civilization. Betrayed into alienation, he turns to art to enable him to overcome the treacheries which have victimized him.

In one sense, Joyce's writing is founded on the belief in the capacity of art to restore a lost vitality. So the figures we remember are embodiments of this 'vitalism', particularly Molly Bloom and Anna Livia Plurabelle. The fact that they were women is important too, since it clearly indicates some sort of resolution, on the level of femaleness, of what had remained implacably unresolvable on the male level, whether that be of Stephen and Bloom or of Shem and Shaun. This vitalism announces itself also in the protean language of these books, in their endless transactions between history and fiction, macro- and microcosm. But along with this, there is in Joyce a recognition of a world which is 'void' (a favourite word of his), even though it is also full of correspondence, objects, people. His registration of the detail of Dublin life takes 'realism' to the point of parody, takes the sequence of items which form a plot into the series of items which form an inventory. The clean and clinical detail of *Dubliners* is akin to what he speaks of in his essay on Blake, where he describes Michelangelo's influence on the poet as evinced in

> . . . the importance of the pure, clean line that evokes and creates the figure on the background of the uncreated void.[5]

His vitalism is insufficient to the task of overcoming this void. The inexhaustibility of his texts is a symptom of a social emptiness, of a world in which the subject, although one of culture's 'sons', is also 'an unprejudiced observer' whose view of any communal relationship – familial, political, religious – is darkened by the conviction that it is necessarily treacherous. The disenchantment with community in Joyce is not simply the denial by him or by a 'rational' Ulysses-like hero of myths, like nationalism or Catholicism. It is the disenchantment with privacy, especially with the heroic and privileged privacy of the individual consciousness, which is, in the end, the more disturbing discovery. The literary correlative of this is the replacement of the univocal, heroic, Yeatsian style with a polyglot mixture of styles (in *Ulysses*) and of languages (in *Finnegans Wake*). Yeats's various recuperations of 'aristocratic' and 'community' forms – though occult or occluded energies, from the 'Celtic' myths to the Japanese Noh play, from a 'national' theatre to the Blueshirt marching songs – are rebuked by Joyce's consumer-world, where the principle of connection is paratactic merely and the heroic artistic spirit is replaced by the trans-individual consciousness.

Yeats was indeed our last romantic in literature as was Pearse in politics. They were men who asserted a coincidence between the destiny of the community and their own and believed that this coincidence had an historical repercussion. This was the basis for their belief in a 'spiritual aristocracy' which worked its potent influence in a plebeian world. Their determination to restore vitality to this lost society provided their culture with a millennial conviction which has not yet died. Whatever we may think of their ideas of tradition, we still adhere to the tradition of the idea that art and revolution are definitively associated in their production of an individual style which is also the signature of the community's deepest self. The fascination with style has its roots in a tradition of opposition to official discourse, but, as we have seen, it leads to that vacillation between the extremes of picturesque caricature and tragic heroism which marks Irish literature and politics in the period since the Union. Since Swift, no major and few minor Irish writers have escaped this fate. Even Joyce, who repudiated the conditioning which made it inevitable, is subject to it. There is a profoundly insulting association in the secondary literature surrounding him that he is eccentric because of his Irishness but serious because of his ability to separate himself from it. In such judgements, we see the ghost of a rancid colonialism. But it is important to recognize that this ghost haunts the works themselves. The battle between style as the expression of communal history governed by a single imagination (as applicable to O'Connell, Parnell, or De Valera as to Yeats or Synge) and Joycean stylism, in which the atomization of community is registered in a multitude of equivalent, competing styles, is in short a battle between Romantic and contemporary Ireland. The terms of the dispute are outmoded but they linger on. The most obvious reason for this is the continuation of the Northern 'problem', where 'unionism' and 'nationalism' still compete for supremacy in relation to ideas of identity racially defined as either 'Irish' or 'British' in communities which are deformed by believing themselves to be the historic inheritors of those identities and the traditions presumed to go with them.

The narratives we have glanced at in the works of Joyce, Pearse, and Yeats are all based on the ideological conviction that a community exists which must be recovered and restored. These communities – of the family in Joyce, of the Ascendancy in Yeats, of the revolutionary brotherhood in Pearse – underwent their restoration in literature which is self-consciously adversarial. Moreover, these narratives continue to send out their siren signals even though the crises they were designed to describe and overcome have long since disappeared. The signals have been at last picked up in Northern Ireland – for so long apparently immune to them – and are now being rebroadcast.

Both communities in the North pride themselves on being the lone and true inheritors of their respective traditions. Their vision of themselves is posited on this conviction of fidelity, even though this is slightly flawed by the simultaneous recognition that the fidelity might also be a product of isolation and provincialism. The Protestant self-image is closely bound up with the idea of liberty and with the image of the garrison. This is well known, but within that there are the only slightly less well-known support images, of the elite people (sponsored both by Protestantism and by the exclusive Whig idea of liberty as a racial phenomenon) and of the lost tribe, adrift in the desert of the worldly and demonic. In opposition, the Catholic self-image is expressed in terms of the oppressed, the disowned, the aristocrat forced into the slum, the besieger who attempts to break down the wall of prejudice which calls itself liberty. The stereotypes are easily recognized and their origins in history well documented. Both communities cherish a millennial faith in the triumph of their own conceptions of right. For the Catholic, that means the disintegration of the state, for the Protestant that means its final preservation. Certain social concepts, like employment or housing, have an almost totemistic significance in the reading both communities give to the British capitalist formation in which they are both enclosed. Discrimination in these areas against Catholics is, for the Protestant, a variant of the garrison or siege mentality, of keeping them out. Instead of Derry's walls, we now have the shipyards or Shorts. The besiegers live in the perpetual ghetto of the permanently ominous, yet still permanently unsuccessful, environ. Within that, no less within a ghetto, lie the besieged.

The spectacle is obviously pathological although, for all that, no less intimate with the social and political realities of the situation. The North has all the appearances of an abnormal, aberrant society: Yet it makes plainly manifest 'normal' injustices which are taken for granted elsewhere. The religious divide is not a disguised rendering of political and social divisions. It is, at one and the same time, an expression of them and, on a more intense level, a justification for them. No one denies the existence of serious injustices in the North. But there religion is given as the reason for them. This is true and false. It is true in that religion was introduced in the plantations and afterwards as a sectarian force. Whether the Bible followed the sword, or the sword the Bible, is irrelevant. They came, in effect, together. The very rationalizations produced to legitimize the conquest, also help to legitimize those injustices which still derive from it as well as those which are independent of it. The communities have become stereotyped into their roles of oppressor and victim to such an extent that the notion of a Protestant or a Catholic sensibility is now assumed to be a fact of nature rather than a product of these very special and ferocious conditions.

In such a situation, nothing is more likely to perpetuate and even galvanize these stereotypes than the dream of a community's attaining, through a species of spiritual-military heroics, its longed-for destiny. Each begins to seek, in such a climate, a leadership which will definitively embody the univocal style which is the expression of its inner essence or nature. But in such a confrontation, style is no less than a declaration of war. It is the annunciation of essence in a person, in a mode of behaviour, in a set of beliefs. Paisley, for example, is the most remarkable incarnation of the communal spirit of unionism. In him, violence, a trumpery evangelicalism, anti-popery, and a craven adulation of the 'British' way of life are soldered together in a populist return to the first principles of 'Ulsterness'. No other leader has the telluric power of this man. On the Catholic side, John Hume acts as the minority's agent of rational demystification and the IRA as its agency of millennial revenge. The cultural machinery of Romantic Ireland has so wholly taken over in the North that we have already seen in the last fifteen years the following characteristic paradigms repeated: a literary efflorescence, ambiguously allied to the Troubles; political theologies of 'armed struggle' and 'defence of the union'; the collapse of 'constitutionalism' in the face of British 'betrayal'; the emergence of an ancestral myth of origin, as in the work of Ian Adamson; hunger strikes which achieve world prominence and give to the republican cause the rebel dignity it sought; the burning of Big Houses, attacks on barracks, a 'decent' British Army with some notorious berserk units – the Paras, the UDR. We have had all this before. What makes it different now is the widespread and probably justified conviction that this rerun is the last. That lends an air of desperation and boredom to the scene. Again, there is that recognizable vacillation between the picturesque and the tragic, between seeing the 'Northerner' in his full and overblown self-caricature and seeing in him the working out of a tragic destiny. The repetition of historical and literary paradigms is not necessarily farcical but there is an unavoidable tendency towards farce in a situation in which an acknowledged tragic conflict is also read as an anachronistic-aberrant-picturesque one. This reading conspires with the 'modern' interpretation of the North as a place undergoing in microcosm the international phenomenon of the battle of extremes between the terrorist and the rule of law, to restate the problem as a particularly unfortunate combination of both – a 'modern' problem deriving from an 'anachronistic' base.

But this is also the standard view of modern Irish writing, and one of the apparently inexplicable features of the Irish Revival. The appearance of what we may call an 'advanced' or 'modernist' literature in a 'backward' country, is not quite as freakish as it seems. Throughout the last two hundred years there has been a widely recognized contrast between the 'modern' aspects of Irish social and political structures – the eighteenth-century parliament, the state-sponsored schemes of the nineteenth century, the advanced industrialism of the Belfast region – and the 'antique' aspects of the nation. The contrast was remarkable because the state and the nation were so entirely at odds with one another. In Yeats's programme for unity of culture, there is a similar blend of the modern Anglo-Irish intellectual tradition and the old Gaelic civilization. Joyce, in his 'Ireland, Island of Saints and Sages', remarked that

> the Irish nation's insistence on developing its own culture by itself is not so much the demand of a young nation that wants to make good in the European concert as the demand of a very old nation to renew under new forms the glories of a past civilization.[6]

There is, therefore, nothing mysterious about the re-emergence in literature of the contrast which was built into the colonial structure of the country. But to desire, in the present conditions in the North, the final triumph of state over nation, nation over state, modernism over backwardness, authenticity over domination, or any other comparable liquidation of the standard oppositions, is to desire the utter defeat of the other community. The acceptance of a particular style of Catholic or Protestant attitudes or behaviour, married to a dream of a final restoration of vitality to a decayed cause or community, is a contribution to the possibility of civil war. It is impossible to do without ideas of a tradition. But it is necessary to disengage from the traditions of the ideas which the literary revival and the accompanying political revolution sponsored so successfully. This is not to say that we should learn to suspect Yeats and respect Joyce. For Yeats, although he did surrender to the appeal of violence, also conceded the tragic destiny this involved. Joyce, although he attempted to free himself from set political positions, did finally create, in *Finnegans Wake,* a characteristically modern way of dealing with heterogeneous and intractable material and experience. The pluralism of his styles and languages, the absorbent nature of his controlling myths and systems, finally gives a certain harmony to varied experience. But, it could be argued, it is the harmony of indifference, one in which everything is a version of something else, where sameness rules over diversity, where contradiction is finally and disquietingly written out. In achieving this in literature, Joyce anticipated the capacity of modern society to integrate almost all antagonistic elements by transforming them into fashions, fads – styles, in short. Yet it is true that in this regard, Joyce is, if you like, our most astonishingly 'modernist' author and Yeats is his 'anachronistic' counterpart. The great twins of the Revival play out in posterity the roles assigned to them and to their readers by their inherited history. The weight of that inheritance is considerable. To carry it much further some adjustment must be made. It might be a beginning to reflect further on the tradition of the idea which these two writers embody and on the dangerous applicability it has to the situation in the North.

The danger takes a variety of forms. A literature predicated on an abstract idea of essence – Irishness or Ulsterness – will inevitably degenerate into whimsy and provincialism. Even when the literature itself avoids this limitation, the commentary on it reimposes the limitation again. Much that has been written about Joyce demonstrates this. A recent book, Hugh Kenner's *A Colder Eye*, exploits the whimsical Irishness of the writers in a particularly inane and offensive manner. The point is not simply that the Irish are different. It is that they are absurdly different because of the disabling, if fascinating, separation between their notion of reality and that of everybody else. T. S. Eliot, in a 1919 review of Yeats, wrote:

> The difference between his world and ours is so complete as to seem almost a physiological variety, different nerves and senses. It is, therefore, allowable to imagine that the difference is not only personal but national.[7]

This sort of manoeuvre has been repeated over and over again in the commentaries on Irish writing and it reappears in commentaries on Irish politics. The Irish, in the political commentary, are seen as eluding what Eliot called a 'relation to the comprehensible'. This is propaganda disguised as mystification. The sad fact is that the Irish tend to believe it. Yet the variations of adherence (i.e. politically speaking, unionism) and of separation (politically speaking, republicanism) and all the modifications to which they are subject in Irish writing are not whimsical evasions of reality. Our reality has been and is dominated by these variations and their stylistic responses. Although the Irish political crisis is, in many respects, a monotonous one, it has always been deeply engaged in the fortunes of Irish writing at every level, from the production of work to its publication and reception. The oppressiveness of the tradition we inherit has its source in our own readiness to accept the mystique of Irishness as an inalienable feature of our writing and, indeed, of much else in our culture. That mystique is itself an alienating force. To accept it is to become involved in the spiritual heroics of a Yeats or a Pearse, to believe in the incarnation of the nation in the individual. To reject it is to make a fetish of exile, alienation, and dislocation in the manner of Joyce or Beckett. Between these hot and cold rhetorics there is little room for choice. Yet the polarization they identify is an inescapable and understandable feature of the social and political realities we inhabit. They are by no means extravagant examples of Irish linguistic energy exercised in a world foreign to every onlooker. They inhabit the highly recognizable world of modern colonialism.

Even so, both Joyce and Yeats are troubled by the mystique to an extent that, in contemporary conditions, we cannot afford. The dissolution of that mystique is an urgent necessity if any lasting solution to the North is to be found. One step towards that dissolution would be the revision of our prevailing idea of what it is that constitutes the Irish reality. In literature that could take the form of a definition, in the form of a comprehensive anthology, of what writing in this country has been for the last 300–500 years and, through that, an exposure of the fact that the myth of Irishness, the notion of Irish unreality, the notions surrounding Irish eloquence, are all political themes upon which the literature has battened to an extreme degree since the nineteenth century when the idea of national character was invented. The Irish national character apologetically portrayed by the Banims, Griffin, Carleton, Mrs Hall, and a host of others has been received as the verdict passed by history upon the Celtic personality. That stereotyping has caused a long colonial concussion. It is about time we put aside the idea of essence – that hungry Hegelian ghost looking for a stereotype to live in. As Irishness or as Northernness he stimulates the provincial unhappiness we create and fly from, becoming virtuoso metropolitans to the exact degree that we have created an idea of Ireland as provincialism incarnate. These are worn oppositions. They used to be the parentheses in which the Irish destiny was isolated. That is no longer the case. Everything, including our politics and our literature, has to be rewritten – i.e. reread. That will enable new writing, new politics, unblemished by Irishness, but securely Irish.

NOTES

1. The phrase is from the penultimate sentence of *Castle Rackrent* (1800):

    > It is a problem difficult of solution to determine, whether an Union will hasten or retard the amelioration of this country. The few gentlemen of education who now reside in this country will resort to England: they are few, but they are in nothing inferior to men of the same rank in Great Britain. The best that can happen will be the introduction of British manufacturers in their places.

    On Maria Edgeworth's reluctance to accept fully the idea of an Irish Catholic gentleman, see the comments by Stephen Gwynn in *Irish Literature and Drama in the English Language: A Short History* (London: Thomas Nelson, 1936), 54–6.
2. James Joyce, *The Critical Writings*, ed. E. Mason and R. Ellmann (New York: Oxford University Press, 1964), 204–5.
3. Ibid., 162–3.
4. Ibid., 198. On his use of this incident in *Finnegans Wake*, see John Garvin, *James Joyce's Disunited Kingdom and the Irish Dimension* (Dublin: Gill and Macmillan, 1976), 163–9.
5. Joyce, *Critical Writings*, 221.
6. Ibid., 157.
7. T. S. Eliot, 'A Foreign Mind', *Athenaeum*, 4 July 1919, 552–3.

CHAPTER 8

Ulysses: The Exhaustion of Literature and the Literature of Exhaustion

IN THE ROMANTIC, THE FIRST PART OF HERMANN BROCH'S TRILOGY *The Sleepwalkers* (*Die Schlafwandler*), Eduard von Bertrand, the man who has escaped from the neurosis of militarist convention so widespread in his society, tells Joachim von Pasenow, on the occasion of the death in a duel of Joachim's brother, that modes of feeling always suffer from a time lag:

> Well, the most persistent things in us are, let us say, our so-called feelings. We carry an indestructible fund of conservatism about with us. I mean our feelings, or rather conventions of feeling, for actually they aren't living feelings, but atavisms.[1]

An epigraph chosen by André Gide for a chapter of *Les Faux-monnayeurs* brings, along with the quotation from Broch, the world of Stephen Dedalus into sudden view:

> There is no trace in Poussin's letters of any feeling of obligation towards his parents.[2]

Unlike Poussin's, Stephen's world is ruled, as Bertrand say, 'by the inertia of feeling'. It devolves in his case upon his parents, particularly his mother, and it is the consequent romanticization of the sorrow he feels he should feel, and the 'agenbite of inwit' that afflicts him when he finds he cannot so feel, that characterizes his own and his culture's inertia.

Again Bertrand speaks to the point:

> All the obsolete forms are full of inertia, and one has to be very tired oneself to give oneself over to a dead and romantic convention of feeling. One has to be in despair and see no way out before one can do that . . .[3]

In *Ulysses*, Stephen is the anachronistic artist hero, typified by inertia and by his search for a principle of energy which would rescue him from the atavistic feelings which he cannot control by any one or any number of the multiple and traditional methods available to him. He would have agreed with Gide's declaration that 'No work of art is possible without the help of the devil.' But his problem is that the devil of his own subjective feelings cannot escape from the God of tradition. It merely enters into a conspiracy with Him and becomes a victim of that conspiracy's complicated manoeuvres. *Ulysses* is saturated with Stephen's defeat in this respect. Bloom is one of the instruments by which it is brought to pass and to be seen to happen. Molly's is the triumph with which it has to be contrasted. Putting it in another way, Stephen attempts to recover tradition for the sake of moral consolation; self-consciousness attempts to exhaust by its endless strategies the anguish of the conscience; history is called in to place in perspective the idiosyncrasies of the private life; God tries to appease the devil.

Failure is inevitable when experience is met on such terms. Stephen's feeling is atavistic, inert; his thought is solitary, mobile. But his feeling determines the form of his thought and robs it of freedom, even though we are conscious that his thought is attempting to dictate the form of the feeling. The novel is centred on the dispute between the two as it takes place, insolubly, in Stephen and in minor fashion in Bloom. Only Molly escapes their fates because she simply does not know the restriction of the categories of feeling and thought which cause them such dismay. Stephen feels guilt and thinks of freedom; but when he thinks of freedom he feels consolation in his ability to map out the determined area of his guilt, its psychology, history, psychopathology in all its forms, parental and filial guilts in their theological, literary, political, and biological aspects. But he cannot escape from the patterns of heredity because heredity itself, especially when acknowledged with Stephen's fullness, is an inescapable pattern. Bloom the Jew, the father and also the son of an apostate, knows this too. Apostasy and heresy are only forms of faith; they constitute no escape from it. Instead they only emphasize its inescapable hold. In parodying belief, they belong to it and *Ulysses*, in parodying the form of the traditional novel, belongs to the most hallowed of all its story-telling forms, the epic.

In an epic, each adventure calls for an adjustment of tone or voice, so that, in the end. we have a number of intercalatory speech patterns which are bound in all their complication to a single place, or hero or narrative of varied events. As in *Finnegans Wake* we hear a variety of voices, each speaking in the dialect of its own area of consciousness but each speaking within the boundaries of a single language. The epic allows for this diversity of local variants arising out of a mythic simplicity. Thomas Mann's epic *Joseph und seine Brüder* has been described by the author in similar terms:

> the entire opus is fundamentally a work of speech in whose polyphony sounds of the primitive Orient mingle with the most modern, with the accents of fictive scientific method, and that it takes pleasure in changing its linguistic masks as often as its hero changes his God-masks ...[4]

The major difference between *Ulysses* and *Joseph* is that Mann tries to reconstitute the epic form as a new possibility for the traditional novel, while Joyce disintegrates it to demonstrate the possibilities of the traditional form adapted as parody for the new novel. Mann burdens the social novel in epic robes in order to teach it how to move with the contemplative dignity of a great art form, Goethean and comprehensive in its mastery of all the Nietzschean forces of the personality, characterized by an 'equanimity that must be wrested from a nervous temperament tending towards despair'.[5] Joyce uses the mock-epic form as a means by which the elephantine weight of documentary realism can be both extended (into history and culture) and parodied (into encyclopaedic comedy). *Finnegans Wake* is, more than *Ulysses*, the ultimate achievement of such an attitude. And if Joseph and Stephen are again compared in a political light, the shadows they throw are not those of other fictional characters but of F. D. Roosevelt and Parnell respectively. Each offered a New Deal for fiction, but the terms were almost comically different. Joyce's seem to have been since then the more acceptable; they amount in effect to the agreement that traditional literature is exhausted and that future literature must make of this exhaustion either a theme, or an organizing principle, or a point of departure.

The radical fact about *Ulysses* cannot, however, be described in formal terms alone. The formal involves the moral and, it must be admitted, merely formal virtuosity also involves a certain moral callowness from which Joyce never allows Stephen to be free (just as he himself is never entirely free of it in his letters). Sometimes indeed, in Stephen's case, we feel that he is callow enough to think of moral rigour as identical with the callousness he displays, for instance, towards his mother, and that this is seen in contrast to the real callowness of Mulligan's remark on her being 'beastly dead'. What is implicit in *Ulysses* and *Portrait* and evident in *Dubliners* and *Exiles* is that Joyce finally sees all conventional moral discriminations as null and void and that he expresses this formally and therefore profoundly by showing the modes of communication appropriate to such discriminations and refined to that end in the traditional novel, as equally null and void. Stephen may be worried about his conduct towards his mother but we are more concerned whether or not it is a sufficient excuse to allow us to accept his largely factitious broodings on that and related subjects. Stephen is destroyed for us because he apparently suffers from a moral compunction which does not easily consort with his artistic credo of moral freedom. Neither the compunction nor the freedom is in the end real; the novel exploits each to destroy both.

The only person in the novel free of such compunction is Molly, and she is also the only one who rejects traditional family allegiances for the pleasures of the body. But Bloom and Stephen are pruriently fascinated by the fact that they cannot separate biological fate from moral responsibility. Molly can and does. Her 'yes' is amoral; the monologue in which it occurs is aggressively 'formless' – i.e. without conventional form in itself, but part of a total formal design in the novel. Amorality and the dismissal of formal coherence, in the traditional sense, go together as inevitably in the end as moral anxiety and the desired recovery of traditional form had done in the preceding chapters. The morally sensitive are elegists for the old order. They are also anachronisms once the order has gone. It is in this context that we can perhaps most profitably view the hallowed question of Joycean realism and its meaning for the novel. It is right to say, as Harry Levin long ago did, that there will always be a hiatus between the naturalistic texture and the symbolistic structure of his work.[6]

But the question remains – Is this hiatus a flaw in the work or a function of its meaning? As I have so far argued, it would be one of the work's formal necessities by means of which we witness not Joyce's but Stephen's failure to accommodate the two major aspects of his experience one to the other. But we can be more exact than this. The realism of *Ulysses* is the chief means by which Stephen's conception of himself as heroic artist is destroyed. The first agent of this demolition is Stephen himself, so strident is his self-assertion; the second, working by comic subversion and contrast, is Bloom; and the third is Molly. Conscience does not precisely make a coward of Stephen but it is part of his belief that to have a conscience is in itself cowardly. Two things above all distinguish him – his conscience and his self-consciousness. The self-consciousness is of himself as artist, disdainful, paring his fingernails; his conscience evokes an image of himself as a failed son of his Dedalus father, his dead mother, his Church, his country. This is Stephen's language for the dispute between intellect and feeling, the one advanced, the other retarded, which the novel dramatizes by the analogous devices of realistic and symbolic method. Symbolic thinking, like that to which Stephen is prone, is indulged for the sake of appeasing his conscience by seeing his personal situation in the context of a number of cultural and historical situations – seeing himself, in other words, as a type of the son doomed by his father to death and doomed also to anguishing his mother. Realism, used in reference to the inclusion of the physical world, presents for us Stephen's artistic problem, the epistemological one of the relation of the self-consciousness to the actual world 'out there'. The two preoccupations dovetail into one another in the notion of parenthood. For Stephen perceives the world in terms of parenthood, of a parent mind giving birth to its offspring the universe, or, more reluctantly, the converse of this. The world has for him a core of reality that breeds in him awareness; or he has a core of awareness that breeds in it reality. Either way, 'breed' is the significant verb. One is father to the other.

The whole Telemachiad is a search for a new epistemology, a new way of knowing how we know the world. Its climax is of course the Proteus episode in which Stephen conducts his experiment on Sandymount strand, wondering if the world is there independent of his perception of it and concluding that it is. Or, it could be argued, concluding that it is impossible to resolve the question since one is always in bondage to one's perceptions and can therefore know nothing independently of them. Stephen is in fact incapable of coming to a conclusion, although he has great resource in producing images of himself that have a false air of finality, although with their shifting pronouns they sustain ambiguity and irony rather than grant clarification.

> me sits there with his augur's rod of ash . . .
>
> He turned his face over a shoulder, rere regardant.[7]

But his quest is hopelessly complicated by the inertia of feeling that afflicts him. He cannot escape his parenthood and the guilts that go with it. He cannot even clearly distinguish the guilts. For his conscience-stricken feeling identifies his guilt with his mother and via her with Ireland, Catholicism, Mariolatry, the mystery of birth, and revulsion at the notion of copulation:

> Wombed in darkness I was too, made not begotten. By them, the man with my voice and my eyes and a ghostwoman with ashes on her breath. They clasped and sundered, did the coupler's will.[8]

These are the pressures from which he must free himself to become an artist, and he envisages his situation as artist in paternal terms – those fathers and sons, God and Christ, Dedalus and Icarus, Shakespeare and Hamlet, Simon and Stephen. In each case, the son is a version of the consciousness of the father, perhaps even the father's self-consciousness. Stephen involves himself in a whole theology of art, drawing on the theology of the Trinity as his source. With regard to the maternal aspect of his experience, he draws on notions of the Holy Family and the various mock versions of it which he meets. The connecting tissue between these two aspects of his experience is his epistemology. But he cannot fashion an epistemology that will satisfactorily superimpose one upon the other, since to do so would demand that he invade the realm of his thought with his feeling, which leads to the agenbite of inwit, a paralysed conscience, or dominate the realm of his feeling with his thought, which leads to callousness, the proud *non serviam* of the *Portrait,* and this in itself leads viciously again to an afflicted conscience. The maternal principle is the world and the paternal principle is the mind which perceives it or creates it in perceiving it. The problem is to take account of both.

Speaking in terms of literary devices, the novel, as has been said before, uses realism and symbolism as the agencies which respectively deal with these separated realms of experience. But again, one becomes aware of a hiatus between them, a hiatus of which Stephen is aware and the existence of which is a sign of his failure. The antinomies of his existence cannot be resolved; but the attempt to resolve them has its heroic aspect. Stephen is trapped. He is undergoing a revolution of the intellect but a mere rebellion of the feelings. He rejects his family and his culture because the claims they make upon him are so overwhelming that he is given no freedom as an artist. Yet to have that freedom, he must overcome those claims. He cannot. So he can only aspire to be an artist, knowing that his conception of art does not coincide with his capacity to feel in accord with that notion. His art must be rooted in Ireland and in his personal experience; simultaneously if it is so rooted, it ceases to be art. Obviously, Joyce was able to resolve some of his own tensions in this regard by showing Stephen's inability to become anything but their victim. The telegram he remembers in the Proteus episode encapsulates his dilemma:

> Mother dying come home father.[9]

Ultimately, on reading this episode, one has to recognize that the pungency of the physical world of Sandymount strand is not simply to be accredited to Stephen's sensitivity to the physical world. More accurately it is provoked by the capacity of that sensitivity to respond to his capacity for remorse. The problem of perception is for him intractable, not per se, but because he is upset about his mother's death and his own role in it. This is his true 'ineluctable modality' – the modality of his feelings and their relationship to the heredity he cannot escape but which he must, Icarus-like, transcend. Everything we meet with in that Proteus episode – the moon, tides, menstrual cycles, afterbirth, midwife, copulation, drowning, death, sexual desire – all are related to the fact of motherhood and fatherhood, and the relationship is rendered linguistically by the grids of epistemology, history, heresy, theology, literature, Dublin slang, and so forth. We are left with the sense of multifarious life and manic obsession coexisting within one anguished and heroic consciousness.

But then, of course, there is Bloom. Once he enters, Stephen's anguish and heroism begin to be gradually diminished. Bloom is futile and 'homely'. But he merely highlights how futile Stephen in his esoteric flights can also be. He is a comic Joseph to Molly the harlot-virgin, who, like Mary, is seeded by a man other than her husband, Blazes being the mock version of the Holy Ghost. The trinitarian theology of Stephen's thought is enclosed by the comic aspect of the Holy Family when seen in the context of Bloom and Molly, especially when we realize that Stephen is their surrogate or symbolic son, as was Christ to the original Family. We see Stephen in a new light here, an unwitting victim of his own analogies. Further, they play together a kind of see-saw game throughout. Bloom's perception of the natural world rises now and again to a formulation; Stephen's formulations descend now and again to the natural world. Each is dictated to by the culture in which he is born, but where Stephen finds himself doomed to be Irish, Bloom finds he is doomed to be a Jew; each is Christian, one through apostasy the other through heresy. Each believes that experience can be significantly rendered, but where Stephen is able to do this in a multiplicity of ways, none of them finally satisfactory, Bloom cannot do it in any single way, an equally unsatisfactory fate. The one aspect of parenthood by which each feels betrayed is the sexual aspect, and for each this aspect is intimately related to the question of religious belief. Stephen's mother and Bloom's father both died in such a way as to forever solder parenthood and belief together in the minds of their respective sons. The novel brings them gradually more and more together only to finally drive them more completely apart and to do so by the consummate irony of lodging between them the barrier of the empirical world they share. The very encyclopaedic character of the world as it is exhibited in the mock-epic realism of the Ithaca episode is a mark of its meaninglessness. They have in common the world they perceive and know, which is to say they have nothing in common, since they can make no sense of it by any kind of half-understood scientific law or symbolic pattern. The world is not finally subject to form. That is an attribute of the mind and its method of consolation. But it is not an attribute of the world. The world simply is.

It can be described but not known. The epic of artistic heroism becomes the mock epic of accumulated facts.

The ambition to bring Bloom and Stephen together in a new father and son relationship, achieving on the level of feeling the aspiration of the intellect, receives its nemesis in Ithaca and achieves its anti-climax in Circe. For in Circe, the Night-Town sequence is merely phantasmagoric. The novel executes an extreme in self-parody by rendering the meeting of Stephen and Bloom which had been so long prepared as a hallucinatory experience which, going through the declension of Eumaeus, finally ends in the ludicrous mockery of Ithaca's reported communication. By parody, the novel exhausts its own possibility of resolution. Then, amazingly, out of that exhaustion, it creates a new resolution – Molly's monologue – which gains a new access of energy for the whole work by its specifically non-literary character. The preceding sections are all heavily flavoured by literary allusion and sometimes controlled by literary ventriloquism. Shakespeare and Marie Corelli are equally subject to this playful mastery. But the undifferentiated nature of Molly's consciousness and its preoccupation with sexuality comes as a refreshing recovery from the self-conscious literature, the polyphonic voices, the symbolic structures which have just been reduced so comically, and perhaps laboriously too, to the exhaustion of the Ithaca chapter. Molly's monologue is not 'literature' in that sense of the word; it is literature in the new sense which emerges when the old concept of it has been seen to be exhausted. The exhaustion of literature gives way to the literature of exhaustion. One rises from the other's collapse. The collapse is itself the book's theme. The rise is the theme's resolution. And the resolution is, in its frank sexuality, in its ignorant joy, an affront to the embrocaded tradition of thought which Stephen and Bloom together have come to represent.

What Molly accepts, is accepted unthinkingly. She does not reflect, she merely remembers and anticipates. Instead of parenthood, tradition, art, scientific law, she has her body and her memories. Her response to the present moment is what the French new novelists would call 'ludique' – no moral judgements are involved, merely the re-enjoyment of experience as it was and is, the acceptance, if you like, of the gratuitous as the only available form and the joy of submitting to that without regret, without judgement. The sexual act which has in all its ramifications so troubled Stephen and Bloom that it has rendered their sense of identity problematic, is for her the supremely valuable experience. Nor is it inevitably linked for her with the responsibilities of parenthood. She has lost a child, she is aware that Bloom has brought Stephen, the possible substitute, into the house, and yet she suffers none of that anguish of emotional inertia which has so typified the others all through. There is nothing elegiac in Molly's experience. She is not linked emotionally to something for which the present cannot account or compensate. The death of their child is remembered and dismissed and blended with Stephen and dismissed:

> O I'm not going to think myself into the glooms about that any more I wonder why he wouldnt stay the night I felt all the time it was somebody strange he brought in instead of roving around the city meeting God knows who nightwalkers and pickpockets his poor mother wouldnt like that if she was alive ruining himself for life perhaps still its a lovely hour so silent I used to love coming home after dances . . .[10]

We witness in fact Stephen and Bloom being caught up in a consciousness which is, formally speaking, undifferentiated, and morally speaking, indiscriminate. Molly's introversion, her concentration on and greed for all the detail of her experience is so intense that no single attitude emerges which one could call typical of her personality. She is in fact impersonal; and Bloom and Stephen are two subjective versions (or results) of the fact which she represents or embodies – the fact of sexuality, copulation, birth. This is the pagan fact which the vast Christian symbolism of Stephen's thought cannot accept and which Bloom, for all his physical involvements, manages to avoid – leaving it to someone else to perform for him. Each of these male protagonists considers himself as a version of a son or of a father. Their roles are not symbolic: they become symbolic, not only to us, but, more seriously, to themselves. Each is thereby condemned to own experience vicariously, through someone else; in doing so they merely exhibit the futility of a particular kind of moral and literary stance in dealing with what is most immediate to them. *Ulysses* is an epic of incompetence, their incompetence, transmitted to us by the awesome virtuosity of their techniques of evasion. The brilliance of the work's execution is in accord with its morality. One remembers Henry James accepting that there is a point where both do after all converge:

> There is one point at which the moral sense and the artistic sense lie very near together; that is in the light of the very obvious truth that the deepest quality of a work of art will always be the quality of the mind of the producer. In proportion as that intelligence is fine will the novel, the picture, the statue partake of the substance of beauty and truth. To be constituted of such elements is, to my vision, to have purpose enough.[11]

It is at this point of convergence that Molly's monologue occurs. I am suggesting that this is an important moment in European fiction because in it the standard figure of the heroic artist, the sensitive young man loose in a coarsened world is destroyed. He no longer can remain the cultural trope he had become. In destroying Stephen's position, Joyce defined it; in defining it, he showed the conventional limitations by which it was bound; in showing these he also demonstrated the standard formal procedures associated with these conventions; he parodied those procedures to the point of total mockery and then renewed the possibilities for the novel form which had so frequently assumed those conventions and procedures as part of its heritage, by introducing the Penelope section. There the exhaustion of traditional attitudes is itself the point of a new departure. Inertia of feeling leading to romantic anguish created a standard profile for the European novelistic hero; here it is abandoned for a new source of energy; and that source is precisely in the notion that the dwindling of one tradition is the initial subject matter of another. At the centre of this paradox is Stephen, the romantic artist par excellence, there to be condemned in the kind of terms in which Gide once condemned Strauss's Salomé, for his endless, proliferating, and systematic conceptions of himself:

> indiscretion of means and monotony of effects, tiresome insistency, flagrant insincerity; uninterrupted mobilisation of all the possible resources. Likewise Hugo, likewise Wagner when metaphors come into his head to express an idea, he will not choose, will not spare us a single

> one. Fundamental inartistry in all this. Systematic amplification etc. A flaw that is not even interesting to examine. One might better condemn the work as whole and wait for the bayonets, because art like this is the real enemy.[12]

Bloom is the first and commonsense opponent of Stephen; but he cannot overcome the power of the young man's attraction since he, Bloom, suffers from the same inertia of feeling himself. Only Molly, free of this inertia, is able to give the full perspective in which Stephen is to be viewed. Only the resistance built up retroactively throughout the novel by her monologue allows us to resist the homeopathic introduction of Stephen's artistic disease. The modernity of the work depends on the degree to which we recognize Stephen as its anachronistic protagonist. The quality of the work has to be considered on the grounds of its merging of the formally complicated and the emotionally inert as functions of one another; yet the novel itself, by dramatizing this, creates another area of experience, vivified by our perception of the desolate nature of Stephen's. In this way, the novel avails of the volume of the epic form, showing it to be from one point of view a mere encyclopaedic accumulation and from another point of view showing us how by perceiving that fact we transcend it – but always at the expense of Stephen. Seized by guilt, he attempts to rationalize it; plagued by feeling, he tries to quarantine it within the boundaries of a self-made system of correspondences, rationally beautiful, beautifully rational, but inert. Broch may have the last word on this, as he had the first. In *The Realist,* the last volume of the trilogy, we read this; it might be a description of Stephen's fate in *Ulysses*:

> Every system of value springs from irrational impulses and to transform those irrational, ethically invalid contacts with the world into something absolutely rational becomes the aim of every super-personal system of values – an essential and radical task of 'formation'. And every system of value comes to grief in this endeavour. For the only method that the rational can follow is that of approximation, an encircling method that seeks to reach the irrational by describing smaller and smaller arcs around it, yet never in fact reaches it, whether the irrational appears as an irrationality of one's inner feelings, an unconsciousness of what is actually being lived and

> experienced, or as an irrationality of world conditions and of the infinitely complex nature of the universe – all that the rational man can do is to atomize it. And when people say that 'a man without feelings is no man at all' they say so out of some perception of the truth that no system of values can exist without an irreducible residue of the irrational which preserves the rational itself from a literally suicidal autonomy, from a 'super rationality' that is if anything, still more objectionable, still more 'evil' and 'sinful' from the standpoint of the value system, than the irrational ... when reason becomes autonomous ... it inaugurates the system's disintegration and ultimate collapse.[13]

Yet out of this collapse emerges the Penelope chapter; and out of the interchange between the two emerges the greatness of *Ulysses.*

NOTES

1. Hermann Broch, *The Sleepwalkers*, trans. Willa and Edwin Muir (London: Martin Secker, 1932), 7.
2. André Gide, *Les Faux-monnayeurs* (Paris: Nouvelle Revue Française, 1925), Part One, 11.
3. Broch, *The Sleepwalkers*, 53.
4. Thomas Mann, *Joseph and His Brothers*, trans. H. T. Lowe-Porter (New York: Knopf, 1970), Foreword, x.
5. Ibid., viii.
6. Harry Levin, *James Joyce: A Critical Introduction*, 2nd edn (London: Faber and Faber, 1960), 181.
7. James Joyce, *Ulysses* (London: Bodley Head, 1960), 60, 64.
8. Ibid., 46.
9. Ibid., 52.
10. Ibid., 727.
11. Henry James, 'The Art of Fiction', in *Selected Literary Criticism*, ed. Morris Shapira (Harmondsworth: Penguin, 1967), 96.
12. *André Gide Reader*, ed. David Littlejohn (New York: Knopf, 1971), 344.
13. Broch, *Sleepwalkers*, 626–7.

CHAPTER 9

Dead Ends: Joyce's Finest Moments

MANY READERS SHARE THE RECOGNITION THAT THE HIGHLY specified world of *Dubliners* threatens, in subtle and disturbing ways, to fade into ghostliness. The twilit, half-lit, street-lit, candle-lit, gas-lit, firelit settings are inhabited by shadows and silhouettes that remind us both of the insubstantial nature of these lives and also of their latent and repressed possibilities. These people are shades who have never lived, vicarious inhabitants of a universe ruled by others. Highly individuated, they are nevertheless exemplary types of a general condition in which individuality is dissolved. The city of Dublin – not just the place but also the cultural system that constitutes it – exercises an almost dogmatic authority over the people who inhabit it, yet what individuality they have best expresses itself in collusion with that authority. Determined by or derived from sources and resources they do not control, Dubliners have acclimatized themselves to a servitude they affect to resist. Their 'identity' may be second-hand, but they are sufficiently meek to be glad of it. Like the sightseers of 'After the Race', the cheer they raise is that of 'the gratefully oppressed' (35),[1] one cheer for the systems of autocracy, timocracy, or plutocracy (but never democracy) by which they are ruled.

The monotonous grammar of these stories accentuates the sense of infantile repetitiveness that is the abiding feature of Dublin's condition, although the repetition involved also reminds us that immense psychic as well as rhetorical energy has to be expended on the production of stasis. One of the most obvious effects of Joyce's elaborate stylizations is to convert or pervert stories of imagined adventure, escape, heroism, or fame into studies in a cultural pathology, often by making the central figure a plaster-cast version of a great original. First there was Parnell, then there was Edward VII; there was Nietzsche, then Mr. James Duffy. Repetition is most woundingly effective when it takes the form of the echo, the epigone, the parody. This extends beyond persons to wider ranges of reference: there was the Eucharist, then there was sherry and biscuits; there was the sacred, now there is the secular. Even where there is revival, of the Fenian-Phoenix or of the Celtic Twilight sort, it too repeats itself in a fall into bathos or into the diminuendo of bad verse or even of that falling faintly, faintly falling snow in 'The Dead'.

Joyce often indicates how radical and yet elusive the state of being 'gratefully oppressed' can be by the strategic repetition of words that gain weight inexorably as they feed on their surrounding contexts and associations. In 'After the Race', we are told that Jimmy Doyle, while at Trinity College, 'had money and he was popular; and he divided his time curiously between musical and motoring circles' (36). On this day of the race, as he tries to guess and answer what the Frenchmen in the front of the car are saying, Jimmy is confused by the humming of Villona, the Hungarian pianist who is very poor, and by the noise of the motor car belonging to Ségouin, who appears to be very rich. He 'was reputed to own some of the biggest hotels in France' (36); 'he had managed to give the impression that it was by a favour of friendship the mite of Irish money was to be included in the capital of that concern' (37); he 'had the unmistakable air of wealth' (38). Rapid motion, notoriety, and the possession of money, we are informed, are 'three good reasons for Jimmy's excitement' (37). After Ségouin had introduced Jimmy to one of the competitors, who had rewarded Jimmy's 'confused murmur of compliment' with a smile, Jimmy found it 'pleasant after that honour to return to the profane world of spectators amid nudges and significant looks' (37). The world of the actor (continental) is sacred, that of the spectator (Irish) profane. Confusion makes the connection between them impossible to clarify. To be seen with continentals, to be permitted the opportunity to invest in Ségouin's proposed motor establishment in Paris, to be smiled upon is sufficient reward in the hazy world of Jimmy's Dublin that 'hung its pale globes of light above them in a haze of summer evening', and whose submissive people 'collected on the footpath to pay homage to the snorting motor' (38).

Later, at dinner, Jimmy's two interests, music and motoring, the source of confusion by day, first dominate a discussion in which Jimmy is out of his depth; drink further blurs his capacity to see what is going on. Earlier, Jimmy had been introduced to the French competitor at 'the control', meaning the place from which the race had been conducted and overseen. Only a few lines later Jimmy thinks, 'he really had a great sum under his control' (37). Unlike Ségouin's reputation for having money, this money is 'real'; but it is not under Jimmy's control. Amid all the confusion, we are to see that the investment is, like the card game, a gamble Jimmy has lost, despite the fact that he is 'the inheritor of solid instincts' and is 'conscious of the labour latent in money' (37). It has disappeared in that vaporous world of paper IOUs, of Ségouin's apparent wealth, of hazy light and alcoholic fume, perhaps even of prearranged deceit.[2] As with the money, so with the politics. His father, once an 'advanced nationalist', has become so successful a butcher that he has modified his politics in order to become the 'merchant prince' (36) who has won contracts for supplying the police with meat. At the dinner, Ségouin leads the conversation from motoring and music – including ridicule of the pseudo-romantic revival of old English music, an ironic glance at the role and function of so-called cultural revival – into politics. It is then the 'buried zeal' of his nationalist father is wakened to life within Jimmy to the point that he 'aroused the torpid Routh at last' (39) – the Englishman who is later to scoop the winnings at cards – and the same transformation occurs. The little local difficulty of Irish–English politics is dissolved by Ségouin, who proposes a toast to 'Humanity' and 'threw open a window significantly'. In the next sentence we learn that 'That night the city wore the mask of a capital' (39). The city, the money, the mask of disguise and deceit are all related in a manner too complex for Jimmy to control. The bland cosmopolitan world has duped him into believing in humanity, in glamour and style; it has taken his money with his political opinions. What really matters in this world is not the friendship that Jimmy or his father might feel for Villona and the others; it is, precisely, the control of capital which Jimmy is surrendering to these 'jovial fellows' (41).

What we see here is the Joycean method of counterposing that which is undeniably real (money, again related to food and feeding) to something which is undeniably fake and then, rather than ratifying the 'real', showing that it can be swallowed up in the illusory world, surrendered to it, by those who are, like the Dubliners, hungry for illusion, grateful to be oppressed by something 'magical' that somehow dissolves or seems to dissolve the squalor of the actual. Two kinds of capital are involved here, capital investment and a capital city that allows itself, is indeed grateful, to surrender control over its own capital (both the money and the city), bewitched by the glamour of a fake culture of Humanity, having surrendered its own 'advanced nationalism' in a haze of incomprehension. Jimmy cannot decipher the world he has entered; to motoring, music, alcohol, crowds, hazy lights, foreign languages, and glamour he pays his 'confused murmur of compliment' and a considerable part of his inheritance. Still, he does get that smile from one of the real competitors in the race which involves so many races.

Every story has some account of or reference to eating or drinking, the cost involved, the difficulty of getting the money for either, especially for those who overindulge in drink. Yet the (usually squalid) details of these rituals, emphasized for a rancorously secular effect, actually provoke a recognition of their insufficiency. They belong to a world that has committed the sin of simony (the first sin, so-called, in the volume), has exchanged spiritual for material values and yet is still haunted by the after-image of the spiritual. In 'A Painful Case', Mr. Duffy, in his usual eating-house in George's Street, catches sight of the newspaper report of Mrs. Sinico's death as he is about to put a morsel of corned beef and cabbage in his mouth. His first reading takes place there, in the full squalor of a 'secular' setting (108). The second reading has a faint aura of the sacred. It takes place in his bedroom 'by the failing light of his window', and he reads 'moving his lips as a priest does when he reads the prayers Secreto' (109). The two readings are separated by Duffy's return walk home which includes the section from Parkgate to Chapelizod, where he and Mrs. Sinico had finally parted four years before. Here, Duffy slackens his pace, and 'His stick struck the ground less emphatically and his breath, issuing irregularly, almost with a sighing sound, condensed in the wintry air' (109).

As at several other points in the story, Joyce takes a moment in which gross physical detail indicates spiritual and emotional stupefaction and etherealizes it into one where the detail is cleansed of its grossness to indicate a spectral emotional or spiritual apprehension. After the second reading, particularly 'After the light failed'[3] again, Duffy flees to the pub at Chapelizod and drinks his hot punch as a group of working men down their pints, spit on the floor, and drag the sawdust over the spit with their heavy work boots. This moment is designed to remind us of Mr. Duffy's earlier political affiliation, when he had 'assisted at the meetings of an Irish Socialist Party' (106) which he had abandoned in despair at the coarse materialism of his comrades. Here is the counterexample to the previous instance of etherealizing. Mr. Duffy neither sees nor hears the men and their conversation about money and a gentleman's estate in County Kildare. But all the detail reinforces the contrasts between the physical and the refined, the worker and the intellectual, respectability and scandal, egoism and love, that the story is elaborating. Subsequently, in the last four paragraphs, the system of repetition that had marked the routine and obsessive nature of Duffy's life intensifies to the point where the goods train from Kingsbridge station, like the slow train from Kingstown that killed Mrs. Sinico – in six lines we have the repetitions of 'winding out', 'winding through', 'winding along', 'obstinately and laboriously', 'the laborious drone' – is finally 'reiterating the syllables of her name' (113). In those final paragraphs Duffy again feels 'her hand touch his'; once realizes 'he sentenced her to death'; once that 'he sentenced her to ignominy, a death of shame'; twice sees himself as 'outcast from life's feast' and 'gnawed the rectitude of his life' (113), the ritual of eating now transposed into an entirely different register from that of the corned beef and cabbage meal in George's Street. But his pseudo-Nietzschean solitude reasserts itself. The noise fades and Mrs. Sinico with it. The last paragraph is composed of eight anaphoric sentences, each beginning 'He . . .' Routine has been re-established. The closed, repetitive structure of Mr. Duffy's inhuman life has resumed. There is no other in his world, no responsibility for the other. This is a style that excludes ethics, by the intensification of repetitive rhythms that betoken morbid self-obsession. It is the opposite of an ethical condition, the fleeting prospect of which disappears as the serried ranks of final sentences close up in their neat, neurotic repetitions.

It may be that Mr. Duffy considers himself to be a good Nietzschean in ultimately defending his solitary integrity against the decadent feelings of a Mrs. Sinico whose behaviour is very much like that of the despicable herd. It hardly matters whether he has molded himself upon a well- or ill-judged version of Nietzsche's thought as it is expounded in *Thus Spake Zarathustra* or *The Gay Science.* The point is that it is a derived identity, based on alienation from himself and from others. Mr. Duffy is not someone deprived of modernity; he embodies it. His provincialism and alienation are integral to it, not its opposite.

Jimmy Doyle's condition is similar. He has been expensively educated to admire all that is not provincial, all that bespeaks money, development, cosmopolitanism, Humanity. This is not only in its derivativeness and complicated slavishness a colonial condition; it is also, because of its profound alienation from its own past and its seduction by the siren appeal of transnational capital, a modern condition. For Joyce, the matter is both simple and involved. To be colonial is to be modern. It is possible to be modern without being colonial, but not to be colonial without being modern. Ireland exemplifies this latter condition and presents it in such a manner that the 'traditional' and the 'modern' elements seem to be in conflict with one another, like two competing chronologies. But in fact there is little of the traditional in Joyce's Ireland. Everything that has or had deep roots in the country's experience has become decayed or has been tarted up, like the Gaelic kitsch of Mrs. Kearney's world (in 'A Mother'), or the Catholicism-for-business-men that Father Purdon supplies in 'Grace'. Modernity wears the mask of capital because capital comprises both underdevelopment and development, not as opposites, but as contiguous conditions. With the entry of modernity in this form, nationalist politics is sidelined as a provincial matter, and a cosmopolitan liberalism, armed with the doctrine of Humanity, is substituted for it.

This encourages the separation of the private from the public life. But 'A Painful Case' makes it clear that the so-called separation is really a desertion. Mr. Duffy gives us the benefit of his considered opinion on these matters. He is much given to quoting himself. He has 'a little sheaf of papers held together by a brass pin' ready for the inscription of his best efforts, although 'the headline of an advertisement for Bile Beans' (103) is pasted on to the first of these, a wicked exercise in irony, we are to understand, by one who wishes to see banality counterpoint his searing insights, among which are the following:

> No social revolution . . . would be likely to strike Dublin for some centuries. (107)
>
> We cannot give ourselves . . . : we are our own. (107)
>
> Every bond . . . is a bond to sorrow. (108)
>
> Love between man and man is impossible because there must not be sexual intercourse and friendship between man and woman is impossible because there must be sexual intercourse. (108)

The denial of the possibility of human intimacy and of social revolution is central. Duffy can no more be a socialist than he can be a lover; both socialism and love are snares that would violate the integrity of his 'heroic' solitude. They would also, of course, introduce an ethical element that is otherwise entirely absent from an authoritarian and sexless narcissism. Love or socialism would deprive Duffy of the pathological alienation that has him in the habit of writing of himself in the third person and in the past tense, of living 'at a little distance from his body, regarding his own acts with doubtful side-glances' (104). He is a third person, derived from a first person; his practice is the one Joyce famously adopted for Stephen Dedalus in *A Portrait of the Artist as a Young Man*, and Stephen's final possession of the first-person pronoun at the close of that novel is all the more dramatic when we remember the hinterland that contains Mr. James Duffy and his ilk, all condemned to a third personhood from which no escape is possible.

Duffy betrays the possibility of sexual love or of social brotherhood; one is a version of the other. In stories like 'Grace' and, most memorably, in 'Ivy Day in the Committee Room', betrayal assumes other forms, well known and much discussed. Here I want to confine my attention to one feature of the 'Ivy Day' – its system of naming or, rather, of misnaming and nicknaming. The key names are those of Parnell and Edward VII, the two kings, one uncrowned and Irish, the other crowned and English, both of them associated with sexual scandal for which Parnell was destroyed and for which, a decade later, Edward earns a celebratory address from the citizens of Dublin. From the outset, the story famously arranges its chiaroscuro effects, from the cinders spread over the dome of coals and the shadow of old Jack giving way to his illumined face, the cigarette lit by Mr. O'Connor which catches the gloss of the ivy leaf in his lapel, the candles lit from the fire, the candlestick used by Henchy to light Father Keon's exit, to the fire that heats the porter and pops the corks of the bottles in mock-salutes. Neither do the cardboard that old Jack uses to tend the fire, nor the pasteboard cards bearing the name of 'Mr. Richard J. Tierney, P.L.G.' (116) that O'Connor uses to light his cigarettes fail to remind us of the inferior quality of the world and the people surrounding this dozy fire, people whose political commitment and wealth are measured in bottles of porter.

But a listing of the sequences of namings also adds to the effect: 'Old Jack' opens the story; thereafter he is referred to as 'Jack' (five times), once as 'the old caretaker' but repeatedly (thirty-eight times) as 'the old man'. Mr. Tierney, the nationalist candidate, is first given his full formal name on the pasteboard card; thereafter he will become 'Tricky Dicky Tierney' (twice: 119, 120), 'the little shoeboy', 'mean little tinker', 'Mean little shoeboy of hell', 'Tricky Dicky' (120), 'that little shoeboy', 'little hop-o'-my-thumb' (124). After the drink arrives, we hear that 'he's not so bad after all', 'as good as his word', 'not a bad sort', that he 'means well . . . in his own tinpot way' (126), and then Henchy reports himself as saying that Tierney is '*a respectable man*', '*a big rate-payer*', '*a prominent and respected citizen*', and '*a Poor Law Guardian*' (128). It is 'the old man', Jack, who refers to his son as 'the drunken bowsy' (117) and to Colgan (not *Mr.* Colgan, since he is the labour candidate), before he is named, as 'the other tinker'; whereupon Mr. Hynes, who repeats the phrase as a question ('What other tinker?'), refers to Colgan as 'a working-man', 'a good honest bricklayer', 'a plain honest man', and then refers three times to the generic type of 'the working-man' (118) of whom Colgan is obviously the particular example. This leads him on to mention 'a German monarch' who then becomes 'Edward Rex', 'a foreign king' (118) and then, later, 'King Eddie' (121), 'the King' (twice, 128), 'the King of England', 'this chap', 'the man' (three times), 'a man of the world', 'a jolly fine decent fellow', 'King Edward', 'an ordinary knockabout', 'a bit of a rake', 'a good sportsman', 'a man like that', 'Edward the Seventh' (129). Mr. Hynes retains his name for the most part, although he is 'Joe' first to Mr. O'Connor, then 'our friend', 'poor Joe', 'a man from the other camp', 'a spy of Colgan's', 'a decent skin', 'not nineteen carat', 'Joe Hynes' (121), 'a straight man', 'a clever chap', one of these 'hillsiders and fenians', one of those 'little jokers', 'castle hacks', is 'a stroke above that' (122), is 'one of them ... that didn't renege him' (130), is then, in counterpoint, 'Joe' (seven times) and 'Mr. Hynes' (four times, 130–1). Hynes is allowed to have had a father who 'was a decent and respectable man', 'Poor old Larry Hynes' (121), although this is merely a ploy on Henchy's part to throw the son's failings into relief, one he also uses against Tierney, by reminding his audience of how the 'little old father' (120) sold illegal liquor on Sunday mornings in his second-hand clothes shop in Mary's Lane. Father Keon appears first as 'a person resembling a poor clergyman or a poor actor' (122). Henchy names him and he remains as 'Father Keon' for three mentions before the inquiries begin. Then 'he's what you call a black sheep', 'an unfortunate man of some kind' (123), 'travelling on his own account' and was mistaken for 'the dozen of stout' (124). Parnell is initially 'this man' (119), 'a gentleman' (130), 'the only man', once he is 'the Chief', otherwise he is 'Parnell' (130), except for the title 'Our uncrowned King' in Hynes's poem (131).

The vicious and slithery Mr. Henchy is the most prolific name-caller. He is the one to accuse his fellows of betrayal, the chief apologist for the English king, the chief sponger who accuses others of sponging, the most anti-labour and anti-Fenian voice, the one to praise Hynes, whom he has condemned in his absence as a spy, for having remained loyal to Parnell and he is, above all, the chief mimic, the star performer in rendering other people's voices. Of course much of what Henchy says bears upon himself. He is the Pilate figure who is forever rubbing his hands 'as if he intended to produce a spark from them' (119), rubbing them over the fire 'at terrific speed' (120) and, on the arrival of the bottles of porter, beginning 'to rub his hands cheerfully' (125). His mimicry of others, like his naming of them, reminds us that this is a story that is, in a double sense, about imitation. With Henchy as master of ceremonies, everything will be brilliantly and degradingly represented and misrepresented. This is a pale imitation, a ghostly version, of the world of Parnell and yet it is also an accurate representation of that imitation. Insofar as representation in such a context can only be a misrepresentation, then betrayal is much more than a theme or preoccupation. Its status is ontological.

The namings are of two kinds – formal and demotic. Some stories sustain the chill of distance by exploiting formal titles and formal versions of names. In 'A Painful Case' the newspaper report is fastidious in its attribution of title – 'Deputy Coroner' (109), 'Captain Sinico', 'Police Sergeant Croly', 'Constable 57E', 'Dr. Halpin', 'Mr. H. B. Patterson Finlay' (110) – and the steady repetition of 'Mr. Duffy' throughout sustains this official formality, which is disturbingly internalized for a time when the train engine in its 'laborious drone' reiterates the syllables of Mrs. Sinico's name (113). 'A Mother' and 'Grace' also exploit the formal modes of naming and of address for the sake both of registering social chilliness and of ironizing the pomposity of the people involved. But in 'Ivy Day', the exchange between the different kinds of naming is much more intense.

Calling Tierney 'Tricky Dicky' is meant to demean him, not only by implying that he is dishonest and untrustworthy, but also by diminishing him to a junior level – Richard reduced to Dicky to provide the 'natural' rhyme with 'Tricky'. He is also 'a shoeboy', 'a little tinker', 'a hop o'my thumb'. Small in stature, low in status, dismissible, barely respectable, Tierney is also of low origins and therefore should not be allowed to forget these in his aspirations to high elective office. By the same token, virtue is grudgingly restored to Tierney after the porter arrives. Hynes is canvassing for Colgan, who is also 'a tinker', in the phrase of 'the old man', Jack the caretaker. Hynes's predictably angry and routine defence of 'the working-man', who is, unlike his class enemies, not looking for a job, but is honest, conscientious, the producer of the wealth that others enjoy, is not sufficient to impress Old Jack who, first, asserts that Hynes gets no 'warm welcome' (121) from him, and second, tells the story – culled from another in a lowly position, Keegan, the porter – about the working-class mayor who has demeaned his office by not entertaining on a grand scale, and then by sending out for a pound of chops for his dinner (125). Jack is a classic example of one of the gratefully oppressed; he admires authority when it is assumed by those who are of a higher class (and in Jack's world, only a 'tinker' could be of lower class). Any usurpation of authority, like that by his own son – refigured in the boy who delivers the porter and drinks a bottle of it at the invitation of Mr. Henchy – is to him a sign of the changing times, when natural authority is being challenged and all seems topsy-turvy. In short, the various name-callings indulged in by Jack and Henchy in particular, indicates a perverted class consciousness. Any one of their own class or family is demeaned and criticized for aspiring to either rebellion or leadership.

On the other hand, since King Edward is, in Henchy's view, a decent fellow, like himself, like one of us, he deserves to be received warmly; in his wake will come what Ireland needs – capital. Male camaraderie is offered here as an alternative to or as something that transcends class. It involves drinking, sport, and sexual dalliance (including adultery), although the sexual behaviour, which is critical in highlighting the 'analogy between the two cases' (129) as Lyons calls it – and which Henchy cannot see at all – is very delicately addressed by all concerned. No woman is mentioned, no woman is present. But gender is invoked to provide an ideology of the decent fellowship between men of the world, one that does not dwell on fine moral discriminations or indeed on any political discriminations, relying instead on practical business and capital development. King Edward has 'no damn nonsense about him' (129) and Mr. Tierney, in Henchy's reported canvass for him, is essentially a businessman who '*doesn't belong to any party, good, bad, or indifferent*' (128).

The Henchy view of King Edward and the imperial monarchy is very much based on the principle of making friends 'out of the mammon of iniquity' (173); it requires a reconciliation between spirituality and accountancy, Christianity and capitalism and, in Henchy's case, nationalism of the Parnellite era and Edwardian imperialism. But those who would resist such a manoeuvre – the hillsiders and Fenians and socialist-nationalists in particular – have to be renamed as traitors, Castle hacks, spies, spongers, people of low origin. Those who would wish to challenge or replace traditional English or unionist authority with self-government, democracy, Home Rule, or anything of that ilk are to be decried either as traitors interested only in money or as caricatures of what real authority is like. Hynes identified the type when he spoke of 'shoneens that are always hat in hand before any fellow with a handle to his name' (118) and Henchy later responded with his mock version of himself as Lord Mayor (qualified by virtue of being in debt to the City Fathers), Old

Jack as his footman, O'Connor as his private secretary and Father Keon as his private chaplain (124). Betrayal and caricature are the techniques adopted to defend the status quo against any kind of political or social advance or change. A modernizing democracy is the enemy of the plain-speaking decent fellows who are anxious for reconciliation with their imperial masters, these fellows who are ready to identify themselves in Mr. Henchy's words as members of 'these wild Irish', or as 'we Irish': 'Can't we Irish play fair?' (129). After all, this is not really, in the Henchy view, a carefully judged state visit and political act; it's just an impulse on the part of Eddie – 'He just says to himself . . .' (129).

But that begs, on this day of all days, and with this king of all kings, the question of Parnell. He cannot be recruited to the decent fellows' club; nor can his origins be impugned; nor can his career be caricatured as that of someone too diminutive in personal qualities to deserve respect. 'Respect' is the key word, first introduced by Mr. O'Connor and taken up by the conservative-unionist Crofton, who allows Parnell was a 'gentleman', a word that undergoes an immediate transformation by Henchy, who exclaims that Parnell 'was the only man that could keep that bag of cats in order. *Down, ye dogs! I Lie down, ye curs!* That's the way he treated them' (130).

This is the snarling Henchy imitation of Parnell's leadership of the members of the Irish Parliamentary Party who had met to betray him in that fateful committee room in Westminster in 1890. At that moment, Hynes, the faithful Parnellite and workingman's defendant, appears, to be called in by Henchy and congratulated for having 'stuck to the Chief', in Henchy's highest term of praise, 'like a man' (130). As preface to Hynes's poem, the idiom of class has reappeared, associated benignly now both with unionist and with nationalist politics and also with fidelity, the very element that is lacking in people of meaner status. But it has also made its necessary peace with the idiom of 'manliness' and 'decency', all the more important in relation to Hynes, the defender of the working-man, and *his* particular form of unmercenary decency. Hynes's formerly specific class allegiance is now blurring into the potent, depoliticized, and gender-based ideology that Henchy promotes. There remains only the political nationalist element to be blended into this moist fellowship, an effect nicely achieved by 'that thing' that Hynes wrote (122, 130), that 'splendid thing' (130) as Henchy calls it, 'O that thing is it . . . Sure, that's old now' (131), as Hynes pretends to strain to remember it. 'The Death of Parnell' is a wonderful display of kitsch that manages, more than anything previously, 'To befoul and smear th'exalted name' (132). Henchy appeals to Crofton and the conservative-unionist gives it his blessing by saying that 'it was a very fine piece of writing' (133).

It is not entirely to the point to say the poem is bad from an aesthetic point of view, although the aesthetic view is important here. For it is just that very 'fineness' of the writing and of the judgement of the audience that counts. By the time the poem is over, every class position, every political conviction, every version of 'decency' has been abandoned. Easy sentiment, greed, and amnesia, the features of the cultural world of capitalism, have taken over and the heroic world of Parnell has been incorporated into it, as a form of entertainment, a thing. We might at this moment remember the missing Father Keon, the priest who may have been silenced because he was a political 'extremist', an out-and-out supporter of Parnell, or who may have been and may still be an alcoholic, a hanger-on like so many of the men in the room (Joyce's father was both those things). It is the linkage between a political conviction that does not or cannot in these circumstances endure and the consequent and subsequent addictive consumerism which these marginalized canvassers crave to indulge, through alcohol, tobacco, political oblivion, and 'manly' sentiment, that Joyce dwells upon here, as he also does in several episodes of *Ulysses*. Like the priest, the linkage is silenced, although indubitably there.

In *Ulysses*, the contrast between the abstract and speculative Stephen and the physically immersed Bloom is one of the governing features of the opening episodes. Eating, drinking, urinating, defecating, burping and farting, bathing, luxuriating in sensations of warmth and taste, scent and odour, sexual fantasy and longing, Bloom is grounded to a comically extravagant degree in the world of the body, of the city-world and its streets, of the stereotype of *l'homme moyen sensuel*. With a comparable emphasis, Stephen belongs to the world of theorist-intellectual who longs for a world disembarrassed of the physical and the sexual, where the self can achieve a purity of origin that radically distinguishes it from the common or dominant forms of sociality. The effort to contrast these and to transform one into the other is already visible and even central in *Dubliners*. It is one of the signs of Joyce's conversion of realism into what seems like its opposite, an etherealized world that has been released from standard limitations and constraints. Such a world is often represented as final or ultimate – the snow at the end of 'The Dead', the ironic/not ironic boast at the end of *A Portrait*, the Molly soliloquy at the end of *Ulysses*, or that of Anna Livia Plurabelle at the close/beginning of *Finnegans Wake*. But these endings are ambiguous or at least indecisive in themselves, and all the more so when we remember that this is also a characteristic way of ending the stories in *Dubliners*. The unionist Crofton is a warning to all who applaud an ending that is 'a fine piece of writing'.

In effect, the Joycean drama whereby the world of the actual is processed into the world of consciousness is, of necessity, always incomplete, since the process is never-ending and it is never entirely persuasive. The place might dominate, producing paralysis; the consciousness might dominate, producing fantasy. What certainly dominates is the writer's capacity to represent both, either separately or in a series of complex ratios, one to the other. But I am suggesting here that Joyce's political critique of this condition as one that arose out of colonial conditions, involving derivativeness, economic backwardness, internalized submissiveness to established external authority, a *ressentiment* directed towards oneself and one's own culture, and various other modes of alienation, has the great virtue of pointing up how characteristic this also is of the condition of modernity, whether that be understood in Ibsenite, Arnoldian, Weberian, or Nietzschean versions. What the Dubliners suffer from is not the inability to enter into modernity; it is the inability to escape from it and from its emblematic place – their politically marginalized capital that is also on the margins of capital development.

Further, I want to suggest that this Joycean critique effectively comes to a close with 'Grace'. 'The Dead' inaugurates the second and more enduring phase of Joyce's work, wherein he surrenders critique for aesthetics and, in doing so, becomes a characteristically modernist writer. The triumph of form over content, of vocation over life are the catchcries of the new semi-subsidized bohemian for whom art is a religion and anything other than a select audience an embarrassment.[4] Thus, the famous endings of the fiction from 'The Dead' forward are examples of 'fine' writing that have, as a consequence of that fineness, the capacity to be understood either as moments of final liberation from routine and fate or as moments of final incarceration within these. Rather than say that this is an admirable and rich ambiguity, we should perhaps recognize that this is what happens when critique is aestheticized into a form of writing that has the ambition to be entirely autonomous and that, in pursuit of this ambition, will refine to an unprecedented degree Joyce's favoured technique of repetition – even to the point where the repetition merely becomes echoic lyricism. It is not surprising that these finales have so often been taken as celebrations of some essentialist position that is deemed to be 'universal' and transcendent of all the local positions that precede them. This is the toast to 'Humanity' that Ségouin offers in 'After the Race' and which international modernism, the cultural companion of transnational capitalism, has regularly drunk. Even the 'feminine' (but hardly feminist) closures, which parade the sovereignty of the fluid over the fixed, the candidly sexual over the prudishly discreet, are, in their politics, still repeating early Ibsen; but in their aesthetics they have become exemplary of the twentieth century's vision of humanism, in which the individual and the archetypal are related by a profoundly elegiac feeling for the future.

In 'The Dead', Dublin faces a West which is past and future, undergoing two revivals, one involving Michael Furey, the other Molly Ivors and Irish native culture. Two versions of the dead, locked away for years, now give promise of a rebirth. But there are other deaths – actual, impending, symbolic. The great opera singers of the past have gone (199–200), the grace and hospitality of the old generation is going (204), the monks sleeping in their coffins at Mount Melleray rehearse daily their symbolic death to redeem the world (202). Every item in the story accentuates the contrast between a deep past and a shallow present. But so too does the idea of revival. Gabriel knows that Gretta has lost her beauty, that her face is 'no longer the face for which Michel Furey had braved death' (223). His image has remained fixed while all else has changed. His devotion to Gretta is, perhaps, a deal more impressive than Gretta's devotion to him. Here is a centre of paralysis in the story, although it is usually read as an exemplary instance of the passion that other Dubliners are unable to feel.

Gretta has been devoted all her married life to the memory of a dead seventeen-year-old. What is buried in the past can only rearrive in the present in a spectral form – Furey, the Irish language, love, the idea of community. It is at the very least insinuated that the Gretta–Furey relationship, whatever its ostensible glamour might be, has another and less healthy aspect to it.

Then there is the other version of the West, the insulting 'West Briton' phrase with which Miss Ivors wounds Gabriel. This is the first revival Gabriel is faced with; Furey has yet to come. Both are potent and yet each has an ersatz quality, deriving perhaps from the immemorial nature of the claim the dead make upon the time-bound living. With his notions of literature's autonomy, his anxiously nursed cosmopolitanism, his refusal of his own nation and culture, Gabriel has many of the features of the colonial dependent. Still, although he is yet another Dubliner who lives a second-hand existence, he is, in that respect, very much like his wife, and like Miss Ivors, both of whom depend upon the reawakening of a buried life to give meaning to their own.

With this story, we have begun the journey out from Dublin to the West to all of Ireland and thence to the universe. The expansion of the final paragraphs of 'The Dead' is continued thereafter in all of Joyce's fiction. The key to the journey is repetition. The repetition may appear to be vicious when it brings the traveller or escapee back to the beginning, but it has many other forms. A revival is a repetition, as is an echo, or a memory, or an analogy, or a parallel. Joyce's prose incorporates all these variations, although it never entirely loses the love of monotony that he first discovered and exploited in *Dubliners*. However, repetition indicates the presence of a system of interrelated parts, of a destiny almost. It is this form of repetition that the close of 'The Dead' inaugurates. It is not the system of capital, or of the world-spirit; it is not a system that belongs to 'History' or to 'Humanity'. It belongs only to writing. Repetition, used in this fashion, aestheticizes the political. It provides a safety net of correspondences into which any apparently random element might fall and find its place in the universal scheme. In all the stories in *Dubliners* other than 'The Dead', repetition has a critical and disturbing function. It has analytic and polemical power. In this final story, all that is surrendered for lyricism.[5]

When the snow begins to tap upon the window pane, as Furey's gravel had danced years before upon Gretta's window, and as Gabriel had tapped his finger upon the window pane before his speech, Gabriel's identity and the 'solid world' are fading and dissolving. He tracks the snow westward, through the seven repetitions of the word 'falling', from the Dublin lamplight to Furey's grave and beyond that to its 'falling faintly through the universe' and, in the famous chiasmus, 'faintly falling, like the descent of their last end, upon all the living and the dead' (225). This is a marvellous instance of the universalizing impulse in Joyce, the conversion, through highly cadenced repetition, of something solid into something spectral. That has been an obsessive concern and technique throughout *Dubliners.* In this, its most self-consciously fine moment, everything is dissolved into writing, into an evocation of a world elsewhere, that of the aesthetic moment, in which conflict is annulled and the distinction between deathly paralysis and total liberation is designedly and with great virtuoso skill cancelled. It is one of Joyce's finest fine moments. There were at least three more to go between 1907 and 1939.

NOTES

1. The text used here is *Dubliners,* ed. T. Brown (Harmondsworth: Penguin, 1993).
2. This is suggested by Robert M. Adams, 'A Study in Weakness and Humiliation', in James R. Baker and Thomas F. Staley (eds.), *James Joyce's Dubliners: A Critical Handbook* (Belmont, CA.: Wadsworth, 1969), 101–4; see also Emer Nolan, *James Joyce and Nationalism,* (London: Routledge, 1995), 28–30 and Vincent J. Cheng, *Joyce, Race, and Empire,* (Cambridge: Cambridge University Press, 1995), 101–27.
3. There may be an echo of Kipling's story 'The Light that Failed' (1891) here, although there is no evidence that Joyce read it. But there is a similarity in the account of a rejection – in this case of a man by a woman – that leads to a tragic death and is much preoccupied with the demands of common life and high art.
4. For a sociological analysis of the new field of cultural production associated with figures like Flaubert and Joyce, see Pierre Bourdieu, *The Field of Cultural Production* (New York: Columbia University Press, 1993), 192–266.
5. In this regard, I am very far from the political optimism of Jacques Derrida's 'Ulysses Gramophone'. He finds affirmation in rhetorical instability. I do not.

See 'Ulysses Gramophone: Hear Say Yes in Joyce', in Bernard Benstock (ed.), *James Joyce: The Augmented Ninth. Proceedings of the Ninth International James Joyce Symposium* (Syracuse University Press, 1988), 27–75. But see Ewa Ziarek, *The Rhetoric of Failure: Deconstruction of Skepticism, Reinvention of Modernism* (Albany: State University of New York Press, 1996), 103–16.

CHAPTER 10

Elizabeth Bowen: Sentenced to Death

The House in Paris

THE HOUSE IN PARIS (1935), PRECEDED BY THE LAST SEPTEMBER (1929) and succeeded by *The Death of the Heart* (1938), is one of the three novels in which Elizabeth Bowen most memorably confronted the spectacle of the disintegration of nineteenth-century European civilization in the aftermath of World War I. A Big House in Ireland is the setting for the first; a pension in Paris for the second; a middle-class villa in London for the third. All three houses function as places, conditions, characters almost, and as stages for the enactment of a disaster from which there is only a tenuous chance of recovery. Getting out of these places offers their inhabitants a chance of redemption – but it is no more than that.[1]

In *The House in Paris*, one of the central protagonists, Karen Michaelis, we are told,

> had grown up in a world of grace and intelligence, in which the Boer War, the War and other fatigues and disasters had been so many opportunities to behave well . . . She saw this inherited world enough from the outside to see that it might not last, but, perhaps for this reason, obstinately stood by it. Her marriage to Ray would have that touch of inbreeding that makes a marriage so promising; he was a cousin's cousin; they had first met at her home . . . This was the world she sometimes wished to escape from but, through her marriage, meant to inhabit still. (II.i.71)[2]

The final placement of the word 'still' here is typical of Bowen's readiness to emphasize a word's strategic salience even at the expense of a smoother incorporation ('to still inhabit'). 'Still' here means to inhabit it, despite all; or simply to go on inhabiting it as by heredity. The implication that it might become *un*inhabitable remains, a knife in the sheath. These heavily pointed sentences are not, we learn, ever 'spoken'. They would have been spoken had Karen actually gone to see her abandoned seven-year-old son Leopold in the house in Paris, but she could not face him, and others – Naomi Fisher whose heart had been broken by the long-dead father of Leopold, nine years before, and Ray Forrestier, now married to Karen – have to deal with the non-meeting between Leopold and the mother he has never seen. All has been planned and arranged and does *not* take place. So this transition, narrated in Part II of the novel, is never realized by Karen, although we hear her 'tell' it; Leopold hears it, in oblique shapes, from others, particularly Ray and Naomi and Mme Fisher. The story as such migrates into another world, that of the Past, but never wholly makes it back into The Present, which has two modes. (The book is divided into three Parts – *The Present, The Past, The Present.*) This is a strange deferral or transposal, a characteristic mutation, I would suggest, in all Bowen's fiction at the levels of plot, grammar, and syntax. We learn, at regular intervals, in sometimes oddly magnified detail, of what did *not* happen and how that then became part of what did, the non-event becoming part of the truth. Part II of the novel, *The Past*, opens with this:

> Meetings that do not come off keep a character of their own. They stay as they were projected. So the mother who did not come to meet Leopold that afternoon, remained his creature, able to speak the truth. (II.i.66)

What does not happen, what Karen would ideally have told Leopold had they met, forms the whole of Part II, 'The Past'. The negative, the minus sign, governs everything we are told in this section, which is everything that Leopold has *not* been told. His own contribution is that his mother has written to say she will come and take him to England (which does not happen); his 'thought-reading' creates this out of the empty envelope of his mother's 'letter' to him. It is in this imagined, dislocating world that the rhythm from the preceding novel, *The Last September* (1929), is picked up when we learn in this later one that Karen is going to Ireland, to Rushbrooke, County Cork, to see her mother's sister Violet. Formerly widowed, Violet had once lived in Florence but now has chosen to live in Rushbrooke with her solicitous second husband Bill Brent who had been burned out of his Big House, Montebello, during the Irish Troubles. They now live in a more modest and manageable house, paid for in compensation by the government. Outside the bathroom of their smaller house still hang stark photos of the Montebello ruins after the attack. The English family is distressed that Violet had stayed in Ireland; 'it seemed insecure and pointless, as though she had chosen to settle on a raft' (II. i.76).

Worse, Violet is terminally ill, feels she has wasted her life, and the whole woebegone story greatly unsettles both Karen and her mother. Her stay in this house, Mount Idris, brings on her first epistemological migraine.

> It is a wary business, walking about a strange house *you know you* are to *know* well; . . . The *you* inside *you* gathers up defensively . . . virgin forests cannot be more entrapping than the inside of a house, which shows *you* what life is. To come in is as alarming as to be *born conscious* would be, *knowing you* are to feel; to look round is like *being*, still *conscious*, dead: you see a world without *yourself*. (II.ii.77, my italics)

The punctuation is relentless. Comma, semi-colon, colon, stop. There are half a dozen pronouns (you, yourself). The sequences – being born, becoming conscious, being at the same time dead – are later reproduced on an ampler scale in the house in Paris with Mme Fisher, Miss Fisher, Max, Ray, Leopold, Henrietta and her rag monkey doll. That house too lies under the evil spell of death.

It takes deceit to activate all this into a larger history, for everything is doubled, mirrored, reflective, and reflexive here. The first deceit: Karen did not tell her mother that her sister Violet was terminally ill, so the shock of her death is amplified and hastens that of Mrs Michaelis herself. Why Karen gave no warning – her uncle had indeed asked her to say nothing – has a touch of vengefulness about it that neither she nor her mother understand. That deceit pales beside the second one. Karen, engaged to Ray Forrestier, who is away in India on diplomatic service, has a sudden love affair with Max Ebhart, an English-French-Jew who is himself engaged to marry Naomi Fisher, Karen's friend, whose mother Mme Fisher owns the house in Paris which is the central arena for the whole story. Naomi also has an aunt recently dead and has inherited enough money to make her marriageable, a fact that is important in Max's offer of marriage to her and provokes hostile comment on his Jewishness. But although Naomi's inheritance makes marriage to her possible for Max, it is Karen, wealthier, of a better class and more beautiful than Naomi, for whom he has a complicated erotic attraction that makes marriage between them impossible, and not just because it is illicit and deceitful. Max offers a racial-psychological explanation that, like the financial one, is partly true but not sufficient.

> I am not English; you know I am nervous the whole time. (II.viii.155)

The racial idiom, which turns on a distinction, itself fluctuant – there are the Irish, for instance, to consider – between a masculinized native solidity and a feminized foreign instability, recurs frequently and had already had a long run in English fiction. But, like the idioms of wealth and class into which it is braided, it only helps to seduce us into believing that the 'races' involved are subjects of an inescapable destiny, a belief we are compelled to surrender as often as to confirm. For every explanation, there is a denial; there is always a 'something else' which may underlie everything – or it may not.

When does 'knowing' happen? From the moment Bill Brent meets Karen off the boat at Cork, the mood and tenses of the narrative verbs begin to slant into subjunctives and conditionals, future perfects, pluperfects, all the signs of belated, deferred knowing and imagined realities.

> When Karen came to know Uncle Bill's habits better she could guess how distractedly he must have paced the quay. She would know he would have been there an hour early, having driven in breakneck from Rushbrooke along the estuary, casting frantic backward glances for fear the boat should be overtaking him. He had never been late, ever. But dreams of unpunctuality woke him, sweating, quite often, Aunt Violet said: your poor Uncle Bill.

The gradient here from Karen coming to know all this and Aunt Violet having told her is only felt right at the end, where three commas, followed by the colon, steer the sentence round a hairpin turn. None of this comes from Bill, even his terrors about the ship being lost and how he would tell Violet, if it happened; he broods on the daily disasters of the newspaper (*The Times*) reports. 'Only towards the end of her stay at Rushbrooke did Karen begin to realise all Uncle Bill went through.' As ever, it's at the end that something about the past begins to be known. Further, there is the important generational perspective that identifies Karen's post-war awareness of Bill's pre-war attitudes. Bill's blushing awkwardness on meeting Karen at the quayside is explained:

> Ladies of his generation did not expect to travel well, they crushed like chrysanthemums and took days to revive. (II.ii.74)

Whose voice is this? Is this *style indirect libre* (voicing Bill's conventional beliefs), or Bowen's governing commentary about the period, or an amused observation or realization on Karen's part? Was it the 'ladies' who had this expectation or was this expectation had of them? Is it an either/or choice at all? Once the verbs begin to lean into the winds of possibility and subjunctivity, it is almost impossible to straighten them up again for simple statement.

As always, when the tension of deceit rises and the intimacy intensifies, a sort of historical generalization is proposed and withdrawn in almost the same breath. Karen has been caught out in a lie, but does not yet know this. She comes home; she does and yet does not know, except by an instinct – and is that knowledge? – that she is already pregnant with Leopold. Death is already edging in; the imminent death of Aunt Violet had earlier been associated with the fatalistic atmosphere of Rushbrooke. Light from the fanlight in the hallway falls on a letter from Ray, her future husband, and on a phone message her mother has taken and left written on a pad; this is the message that reveals Karen's deceit. At first, she reads neither and goes to meet her mother in the drawing-room; Mrs Michaelis is wearing a 'picture' dress 'that made her belong to no time'.

Then, like Bill, Mrs Michaelis is suddenly identified by her generation.

> She was not of the generation that fingers things on a mantelpiece, but Karen could see her eyes in the mirror, uncertainly moving from object to object in the reflected room. A yellow rose on the mantelpiece suddenly shed its petals, but did not make her start. (II.xi.181)

The lie, the pain, the not moving of the fingers, the moving of the eyes instead, the fall of the petal, her not moving in response, all mirrored and all watched by Karen and, above all, the mantelpiece – given how critical the mantelpiece becomes in the Fisher house in Paris – identify Mrs Michaelis as, in a sense, already dead, a member of the earlier generation of August 1914, of the time when the superior morale of the people won the war, of the time when fingers did not betray 'nervosity', did not disturb the world of objects and infuse them with a subjectivity foreign to them. Her dress, as we have been told, 'made her belong to no time', a strange function for a dress, a thing. But we are actually in a specific historical time, the time before people shifted items on the mantelpiece, but it is also a 'time' which claims to be now and always to have been and always to be the 'no time' or the 'all-time' of the 'natural', the universe of steady, ordinary human nature. That dimension existed, Mrs Michaelis believes, before technologies, like, for example, modern photography came to deform the relation between time and stillness, time and motion. In posing or staging human action and appearance, photography hinted at an 'over-great sense of mystery' that Mrs Michaelis dismisses:

> Nothing annoyed her more than to be told that the personality is mysterious; it made her think of Maeterlinck, people in green dresses winding through a blue wood. It is inexcusable not to be clear, she said. She preferred to think of people in terms of character. (II.vi.24)

The reference to the famous symbolist play, Maeterlinck's *Pelléas et Mélisande* (1893), is placed here to reinforce the general contrasting of home-grown, British ordinariness with exotic, usually French, foreignness, the former claiming universality, the latter condemned to fashionability. It is a worn contrast, but Bowen presses it home in this instance with subtlety. For the Maeterlinck play is also about betrayal in a love triangle, set in a strange country, Allemonde, that is under a spell and seeks release from it. Debussy's opera version of 1902 made the play even more famous and Bowen here reminds us of the haunting line, especially mesmerizing in the opera, in which Pelléas sings to Mélisande, 'Il ne faut pas s'inquiéter ainsi pour un bague' ('There is no need to be so upset about a ring'). But there is, both in the opera and here in the novel. For Karen has hidden her sapphire engagement ring – much admired earlier by the Irish girl, Yellow Hat, on the steamer crossing from Cork – given her by Ray, and has worn instead on her rendezvous with Max at Folkestone-Hythe a cheap wedding ring bought to make her and Max appear legitimately married. She had felt Max eye that engagement ring in the garden at Twickenham, 'as though her hand were exposed in a museum glass case or the ring itself had been dug up out of a tomb . . . ' (II.vi.119) She is still wearing a glove over the ring as she reaches home. So begins a week-long spell – a period of time and an enchantment – in which her mother holds her 'inside the lie till she makes me lose the power I felt I had' (II.xi.186). This prefiguring of Mme Fisher's spell over the house in Paris finally moves Karen to say that this week 'made me not feel I lived here' (II.xi.190). Then, the same night as release between Karen and her mother begins, a telegram from Paris arrives to announce Max's death. The spell intensifies again. Symbolist magic, elements of folk tale, instances of fortune-telling, as with the card game with Henrietta and Leopold (I.v.60–5), persist throughout.

Earlier still, Max had put his hand over Karen's as they sat on the grass in the garden at Twickenham (II.vi.126). They sit under a tree. 'Naomi's dead aunt had a flowering pink cherry at the foot of her garden at Twickenham' (II.v.108). Trees, in sunlight or in rain, the blurred tamarisks at Hythe, the boxed-in tree at Paris, stand sentinel on this relationship. And the way people stand (at a mantelpiece, in a train corridor) can indicate physical rigidity or awkwardness, moral uprightness, or a desire for release from these self-conscious tensions. At this Twickenham moment, Karen continues to stand before she and Max sit – 'she slid down too' – on the grass, some relief from 'Going on standing up in a rather rigid way, as though lashed to the tree-trunk' (II.v.115). There is a malign connection between intimacy and estrangement enacted here. When with her lover Max at Hythe, Karen probes for the source of Mme Fisher's malevolence towards Max, but is exhausted by her effort. As the rain falls more loudly than ever on the chestnut tree beyond their window, she wonders 'whether so much rain tires that tree'. Then 'she tried to imagine she was the tree' (II.ix.164–5). Henrietta standing beside Leopold had felt 'as if she had stood beside an unconscious strong little tree' (I.v.59). Her tacit connection with Mme Fisher is revealingly resumed when, years later, in her fatal illness, as Mme Fisher tells

Leopold the story of his abandonment by Karen, she pauses and we read: 'Her words showered slowly on to Leopold, like cold slow drops detached by their own weight from a tree standing passive, exhausted after rain' (III.ii.221). All the rain on this weekend cuts them off from everywhere; the town 'stayed like nowhere, near nowhere, cut off from everything else' (II.ix.157). This is a reprise of Twickenham:

> because today is hardly a day, is it? Here we are in a place that's hardly a place at all, in a house belonging to somebody dead. I'd never been to Twickenham till today, and I suppose I may never come again. (II. v.116)

Boulogne was much more like home; now, in her own country, the feeling of foreignness rises to one of utter isolation. Being close with Max has distanced her from the world she once knew, the 'ordinary', the 'nice' world she was born into: she 'felt more isolated with him, more cut off from her own country than if they had been in Peru. You feel most foreign when you no longer belong where you did' (II. ix.167). She realizes that he, for her family and for her family's wish to save her,

> would be disaster. They would not know where to turn to save me for themselves. They would have to see me as someone poisoned. Only poisons, they think, act on you. If a thing does act on you, it can only be poison, some foreign thing.

But also, in the next breath almost, 'The child would be disaster' (II. ix.163). So, father and child both; yet this is the child that must be rescued from a foreignness so utter that his very existence is in question. On the journey back, the catastrophe of her isolation is once again linked to the weather, and to other people. 'Rain *had* been a disaster; in the train you saw how hard it had come on them by the way they sat' (II.xi.178).

To stand, to take a stand, always to be upright, like the tree, implies effort. It can be, for instance, the habitual posture of a certain type such as Ray, pictured as the ideal Englishman at the late moment when Leopold's entry into the room made him 'conscious of his own height by the angle at which Leopold's eyes looked up'. Leopold sees Ray as an Englishman.

> It should be clear that Ray looked like any of these tall Englishmen who stand back in train corridors unobtrusively to let foreigners pass to meals or the lavatory . . . (III.iii.227)

As standing or sitting had been dramatized so pronouncedly at the garden in Twickenham when the affair between Max and Karen had begun, so too is it in the scene where Max proposes to Naomi in the salon of Mme Fisher's house. She is seated, knitting; drops her scissors, pricks her finger, sucks the bead of blood. He steps over, asks her to marry him, she looks up and 'I found it hard to remember', Max tells Karen, that

> I, in fact, stood above her, beside her chair and looking down at her face, and was not standing looking up from below at a more than life-sized figure, lit as far as the knee and then rising into the dark. I have never passed a figure like that unmoved; I am not rational: there is too much force in a figure of stone pity. (II.x.173)

This heroicizing of Naomi is also, characteristically for that room, a moment of petrifaction. Max's death scene later produces similar sculpting effects. Naomi recalls to him the three of them in the garden at Twickenham, then, feeling weak, 'sat down on that chair by the window where I sit to sew', where he had proposed to her, the sitting and standing repeated.[3] At that moment, Max flings open the door, finds the eaves-dropping Mme Fisher, who now knows everything; she enters and says with obvious sadism to Max, 'So with Karen you have already secured your position.' The 'position' is moral, social, psychological, physical. He tells Karen to go. 'He stood with his back to the mantelpiece; after that I saw that my presence martyrised him. So I went' (II.xii.195). When Max cuts his wrist, while standing there, Mme Fisher falls across the sofa, indicating wordlessly to the returning Naomi she should look at the mantelpiece where finally she sees 'his blood splashed on the marble, on the parquet where he had stood and in a trail to the door'. His penknife, like her scissors before, lies on the floor. Mme Fisher says 'He cut his wrist across, through the artery, to hurt me' (II.xiii.196). She never is able to stand again. Nor can people stand her. No more than Max could 'endure being always conscious of someone' (II.viii.155), of Naomi watching him, Mme

Fisher watching her, of people forever watching each other watching. The unflinching stare of the statue is kin to the gaze of devotion. Max cannot stand this from Naomi. 'I have never once felt her eyes leave my face. Imagine the statue's face on your own level' (II.x.174). Now she can forever bestow her gaze, not *as* a statue, but *on* the statue of her petrified, horizontal mother who seemed 'like someone cast, still alive, as an effigy for their own tomb' (I.iv.44).

The deaths of the Michaelis sisters, the dismissal of Bill and of Ireland, and the continued, near-mute presence of Mr Michaelis, Karen's father, who knows nothing and is a variation on the link between ignorance and innocence ('Look how he loved my mother. That is the love I wanted. *He* is the plain man', III.iii.234),[4] leave us with an appalling 'Present' into which a sinister and paralysing force has entered. Karen at one time had seen Ray in the light of her own father. She had said to Aunt Violet that, despite Ray's anxious letters to her, 'he really is a plain man; simply, it doesn't suit him to keep on asking questions' (II.ii.86). But the novel's sinuous manipulations of time make the contrast between 'plain' and 'natural' as against 'nervous' and 'complicated', as Max calls it, dissolve so far that it scarcely reforms again, certainly not as the antithesis it had once been imagined (by Karen) to be. In the late 'unspoken dialogue' of the married life of Karen and Ray, it is nevertheless recurrent. Karen says to him,

> You feed your complicated emotion on what happened to me. For God's sake, is there no plain man?
>
> HE. Was Max a plain man?
>
> SHE. No; that is just the point . . .

She does not want a mystic or a martyr. Without Ray's 'complicated emotion' or 'mystical ideas' she could have been 'natural again. I could be a natural mother.' No, he says,

> you would want him if I didn't?
>
> SHE. Yes, no, yes. The you I wanted wouldn't have wanted Leopold. (III. iii.232)

So it all swings back to Leopold. Not just who wants him, or does not; but who would have wanted him, earlier, when he was born. And who would those people have been? Have they been changed by history into something they had not previously been? Or is it an ethical question that abides historical change? Or are these aspects of the same spinning coin? Obviously only a clear choice can solve this: abandon Leopold completely once and for all to La Spezia and the dreadful American pseudo-parents, or save him from the house in Paris and bring him to England as their child. That would bring 'plain'and 'complicated' into a new harmony, but not as it was pre-war. Those days are gone. And look what has happened to Leopold, Karen's son, the Karen who in Mount Idris in Ireland had had the near-panic experience of '*being*, still *conscious*, dead: you see a world without *yourself* (II.ii.77). This has happened to her now nine-year-old child. At her age of thirty-nine, can she not rescue the child from a world that is without himself, a child who is conscious, not of being alive, but of being dead? He and Mme Fisher clarify his situation with an anguished logic; we have to remember he is, improbably, nine and she is over seventy, each virtually 'dead':

> 'People who knew me must not know I was born, and people who knew I was born must not know me?'
>
> 'Exactly,' she said, in the dry avid quick voice she kept for exact talk. (III.ii.213)

We owe part of the brutal decisiveness of Mme Fisher's reply here to the ambiguity of the word 'quick' (alive), to the double 'exact'.

Certainly now, in this first section of the novel, 'The Present', we are in a new generation, the anguished victims of the second section, 'The Past'. The reversed order is appropriate. The transposition of events, the switching of syntactical and semantic modifiers, the participial phrasings that are often mimicking the idea of foreignness and domesticity with their Latinate suspensions and word order, the alternation of voices from inner consciousness to external descriptions, all lend to the book's structure an ornate intricacy which is sometimes countered by the shocking brutality of the situations it engenders. All the central characters are entombed in time and space, in the years of their historical time and in the houses where they live, finally in the one house, the house in Paris, which inhales into it all those houses and rooms in Dorset, in London, in Cork, in Spezia, Mentone, in Germany and in Versailles and breathes them out again, contaminated. The entombment then becomes figurative; a cracked tomb in which a tree begins to grow and split and ramify, most specifically spoken of by Mme Fisher, even to provoke the pun on 'fissure'. In the course of telling Leopold she has been present but dead for ten years in that house and in that bed and that she does 'not feel and am not felt', she also exerts her terrible power over him to encourage him to believe that in his weirdly comparable but contrasting situation he can, 'by the exercise of a vulgar power', overcome the problem of, as he put it, 'People not knowing I am there'. Leopold is right. People must come to know of his existence. Then, overriding his anger at having been obliterated, as she claims she too has been, Mme Fisher provides the figure and the formula for survival, again in a typically Latinate sentence structure, simultaneously foreign and native:

> To find oneself like a young tree inside a tomb is to discover the power to crack the tomb and grow up to any height. (III.ii.215–16)

The figure, hereafter recurrent, retains its chill through its iterations, despite and because of its Christian topos of life from death and the broken tomb. Henrietta, interviewed by Mme Fisher, adds to it when she bridles to think that, here, on her first visit to Paris, she has 'seen this house only', longs to

> exchange these unseen streets, the Trocadéro, even Napoleon's tomb, for this air darkening her lungs with every breath she took, the built-in tree in the court . . . (I.iv.46)

Just as she never saw the outside of the house in daylight again after her arrival, so too she never sees Paris again, just mumbled images of it through a taxi window, as she comes and as she goes. She is later pleased by the thought she will see oranges growing on trees in Italy, even as she watches Leopold, with a demonic expression on his face, squeeze an orange and hears him ask, 'Have you seen a tree growing out of a crack in a grave?' When she says trees don't, and he insists they do, Henrietta's reply is: 'To begin with, no one would plant a tree in a grave' (III.iv.242). Yet that is precisely what has happened to begin with.

Thus it is a chilling 'Present' that opens the novel. Two children, Leopold, aged 9, and Henrietta, aged 11, have been sent by train to Paris, he from Italy, she from England, he with a dead father he never knew and who never knew him, she with a dead mother she scarcely remembers, she to spend the summer with her maternal grandmother, he to meet his own mother for the first time ever. The children are, in separate instances, exchanged under code and instruction at railway stations. The fairy-tale element is made more rather than less sinister by virtue of the high technology of the urban surroundings – trains, taxis, telegrams, phones, buses, cinemas, vast railway stations, crowds. This too mixes the modes of clock-time and of legendary time, even of timelessness. That mix remains chemically present in the minds of the children; they have a rhetoric of 'foreverness', like an accent or inflection of mind or manners. 'I *never* ask people things', says Henrietta primly. The Fishers' house 'looked miniature, like a doll's house'. The street is empty, so much so that 'it would not really have surprised Henrietta if no one *had ever* walked down that street again' (I.i.14–15; my italics). The placement of 'ever' here is characteristic of Bowen; would it add or detract a shade of meaning to put it more conventionally before 'again'? or to omit the 'had'? As often, the verb tenses are themselves tense, often stretched almost to breaking point. Henrietta enters, she 'took a last look at the outside of the house, which she never saw in daylight again' (I.i.16). The fairy-tale dimension darkens into actuality. This, after all, is a stolen child story, about child-trafficking, about Mme Fisher, 'a woman who sells girls, a witch' (II.ix165), about a double conspiracy over 'the theft of his own body' (III.iii.238) as Leopold calls it; the stealing is both tragic and redemptive, a fantasia and a social, political problem. At first, then, Henrietta enters a prison-house; no natural light:

> You saw no windows; the hall and stairs were undraughty, lit by electric light. The inside of the house – with its . . . stuffy red matt paper with stripes so artfully shadowed as to appear bars – was more than simply novel to Henrietta, it was antagonistic, as though it had been invented to put her out. She felt the house was acting . . . objects did not wait to be seen but came crowding in on her . . . Henrietta thought: If *this* is being abroad . . .

The idiom of 'put her out', when she is pressed in, is picked up nicely in the ironic 'abroad'; such little inversions speckle the prose throughout. As Miss Fisher and Henrietta, the latter sorely exercised by her wanting 'to be someone', eat breakfast, the furnishings of the room are surveyed. 'There were four green velvet chairs, like doll's-house furniture magnified' but most of all there is our first glimpse of 'a scrolled gray marble mantlepiece with an iron shutter pulled down inside'; the crimson sofa is also 'tight-scrolled' (I.i.18–19). The fabrics in the room and the hard surfaces are all wound-up, tense and solid. This is a petrified prison cell which needs to be softened, melted somehow by its human prisoners, Henrietta and Leopold; it is the past, challenging anyone to mollify the shape it has assumed. The adult world too has its own rhetoric of finality in relation to the abnormal house. 'One cannot afford to live in a house, in Paris', says Mme Fisher, 'But I prefer to die here.' And the house is anomalous, uncommon in being a house at all, is of a kind only found now in the provinces and will be sold immediately on Mme Fisher's death and it too will disappear (I.iv.47). Anyway, Mme Fisher typically includes and dismisses the fairy-tale aspect of the story in her conversation with Leopold:

> No doubt you do not care for fairy-tales, Leopold ... Fairy-tales always made me impatient also. But unfortunately there is no doubt that in life such things exist: we are all very much bound up in what happens. (III. ii.215)

The children meet in the Fisher house, under instruction not to speak to one another of anything personal, with Leopold particularly vulnerable to any knowledge since he has scarcely any and Henrietta curious, but in the dark, clinging to her toy cloth monkey Charlie, all her affection invested in this sad object. Naomi, Miss Fisher, is in charge of them both for the day. Upstairs lies Mme Fisher, stricken by a fatal illness for the last nine years, since the suicide in this room of Max, once Naomi's beloved, Leopold's father. Out in Versailles – 'where the king lived' (III. iii.238) notes Leopold – wait Ray Forrestier and his wife, Karen, Leopold's mother, who has up to now abandoned him but has decided, under pressure from Ray, finally to meet him. We have to remember that the prospect of her bringing him to England and rescuing him from the dreadful American substitute parents is imagined by Leopold. The particular ignorance shown by these parents – they, for instance, insist on forcing upon Leopold an artificial 'cultural' linkage with Shelley, the revolutionary English poet who drowned in the Bay of Spezia (I.ii.28, III. ii.218–19) – repeats that of his own parents. Leopold has indeed inherited his mother's epistemological/ontological migraine, first born in her in Cork but reborn in him in tragic mode, existence without being born; she foretells his fate: 'to look round is like *being*, still *conscious*, dead: you see a world without *yourself*' (II.ii.77).

Then, back to the mantelpiece. Years before, when she was eighteen, and staying in this house, Karen used to see Max, by whom she was already attracted, 'his weight shifting from foot to foot, as he leaned on the mantelpiece, talking to Mme Fisher' (II.v.111). But now, twenty-one years later, all postures change. Leopold enters, a quadruple action in a Latin absolute ablative construction:

> *Having shut* the door, Leopold *walked across to* the mantelpiece, *which* he *stood with* his back *to, looking at* Henrietta. (I.i.21, my italics)

The door first, Henrietta last, the mantelpiece centre. This at first reads like a bad translation into English from Latin or French. The pronouns 'which' and 'his' catch the mantelpiece and Leopold's back in a firm structural embrace. Bowen often uses such obliquities of syntax. At times, it can seem like pedantry. In this and other instances, the marble mantelpiece acts as a magnetic field on the syntactical surround, sending prepositions into single file at the tail of a phrase, like a comet streaming all it meets behind in its wake. This transposition, hypallage, needs delicate control, but its aim is always the same – the distribution and redistribution of weight without loss of momentum, so necessary in maintaining the tautness of a story that requires such close, incestuous repetitions, endless sleights of semantic and syntactical functions, the same words looking at one another in intricate conversations, like those of Max and Karen or of Karen and Ray. In the latter case we are given a formal dialogue, part of the point of which is to demonstrate its circularity and endlessness; in the former, the erotic and the instinctive gestures and feelings combine in exchanges of error and recognition, leading to a shock of knowledge that cannot be borne. The tense of the verbs rises step by step in Max's conversation and in Karen's consciousness before they make love and aferwards:

> 'I am supposing,' he said, 'that you know what you are doing. It will be too late when you ask yourself: What have I done?'
>
> She asked herself: What have I done? at about three o'clock. She only knew she had slept by finding an hour missing from her luminous watch ... The street-lamp still lit up the chestnut tree ... and cast the same inescapable barred squares over the bed. The mantelpiece with its mirror stood each side, darker than the dark walls. Having done as she knew she must she did not think there would be a child: all the same, the idea of you Leopold, began to be present with her ... The weight of being herself fell on her like a clock striking ... While it is still Before, Afterwards has no power, but afterwards it is the kingdom, the power and the glory. You do not ask yourself, what am I doing? You know. What you do ask yourself, what have I done? You will never know ... Naomi and my mother, who would die if they knew, will never know. What they never know will soon never have been. They will never know. I shall die like Aunt Violet wondering what else there was ... Max lies beside me, but Naomi sat on my bed in the dark; she was there first and will never go away. I have done what she does not know, so I have not done what I dread. (II.ix.160–1)

All the equipment, so to speak, is here. Narratively, we are in mid-stream; chronologically, we are at an early stage. Deceit, knowledge, secrecy, time, death, the child (along with that sudden second-person fracture of the address to 'the idea of you Leopold'); the tree, the mantelpiece, the mirror, the names, all that is later to be coordinated, has begun to cycle and be recycled through story and figure, into a legend, a fairy-tale, a historical novel. The bedroom at Hythe first melts into the salon, staircase, and bedroom in Paris and then, from this filmic dissolve the image of another world begins hesitantly to emerge, an altered civilization beginning to recover from the past it created and that created it. Yet it is not at all a world that, in becoming modern and mechanized, has thereby become alienated. After all, the two great mechanized bureaucratic systems that dominate this world – the magnificent postal-telegraphic and railway-shipping networks – exponentially increase intimacy and exchange, rhythmically, steadily, reliably. They are not alien powers, although they do exercise a measure of control over the human society they create and serve. Of course, these systems that have had such benign effects have also helped to destroy the European world in war. The so-called mask of civilization is also the face of civilization. One migrates, transfers, transposes into the other.[5] Bowen's pressure on these exchanges by which the individual and the impersonal merge, split, and come together again is inexorable. The train that brings Karen and Max together, 'as when they got jammed in the train corridor' (II.x.169), connects but also warns of death, as the car slows at a level-crossing and the driver looks at the skull-and-crossbones warning nailed to a post (II.x.168) or the rain-soaked crowd on the Folkestone train 'waited for the train to impale them on London' (II.x.179). But a crowd is not a class, a distinction made in train compartments.[6]

Ray's married sister Angela gives Karen her contorted account of the difference between a uniform mass society and a class society. In her world, a key term for being oneself and being like others at the same time is 'nice':

> 'We are all far too alike,' Angela said. 'But, after all, there *is* only one way to be nice. Nothing unlike oneself in people really is not a pity. It's better to inbreed than marry outside one's class. Even in talk, I think. Do let us be particular while we can.'
>
> Karen said coldly: 'I shall grow more like you, then?'
>
> 'Nonsense; you're so individual.'
>
> 'It costs money,' said Angela. 'But that's fair, I suppose.' She had two little girls; she went on: 'No doubt I shall live to see the poor children nationalised, or married in a laboratory. But while we *have* names, not numbers, I think it's nice to be like what one's like, don't you, even if everyone else is?' (II.vii.131)

Angela's view of modernity and her desire for a countering uniform niceness provide the comic rationale for the attempt by Ray and Karen to restore Leopold to precisely that nice world and name from which he has been torn. The terrible experiment of his life in Spezia, old European Italy perverted into a foreign, featureless contemporary America, is at once central to the novel's preoccupations and also a travesty of them. Bowen has a catalogue of trisyllabic words – e.g. *implacable, inexorable, imperturbable* – that loom fatally over the fugitive, individual self. Yet she exploits the histrionics of a self that opposes its autonomy to a foreign and malign mechanization. In her governing voice and grammar, the impersonal pronoun 'one' is at least as important as any of the personal pronouns; especially in the recurrent voice-overs of general wisdom (of which we can have too generous a supply), 'one' dominates – as one would expect in a novel in the English tradition. Class is also in England *the* system in which authority can be indicated by the use of the pronoun – the plural 'we' is rarely heard. Bowen generally has a tin ear for lower-class speech; her middle-class 'one' is in a decisive accent, but its tone can quaver. For 'one' is a collective singular that might not, for example, pass the test of marriage, whereby 'one' should, by convention, be transposed into a 'we'. We hear the echo of this in Karen's and Ray's marriage, previously offered as a light instance of interbreeding. Can 'one' be two? Can marriage be as supple as grammar, can social class be raised to a higher category, that of the human in general? But Angela's questions indicate that this can no longer be assumed. There is no easy answer, now that 'modernity' has arrived. Can a person or persons be both a noun and a pronoun together? Is that a marriage? Is that what it is to be 'nice'?[7]

But it is the children who make the final transposition. It happens in two phases. In the first phase, Henrietta, moved by Leopold's sudden announcement that he is going to England with his mother – this on foot of his having covertly read a letter from her to Miss Fisher – and seeing him as a heroic little figure, crosses the waxed and polished parquet floor of the salon (later to be stained by tobacco ash and a broken crock by his step-father, Ray, as it had been earlier by Max's blood and the knife he had used to kill himself, and earlier still by Naomi's dropped scissors in the proposal scene) and stands beside him at the mantelpiece. The figuring of the mantelpiece and the tree tightens; marble and wood are the inanimate textures that are yielding to the influence of the fleshly bodies as Henrietta tries to feel *through* the marble what Leopold feels:

> Still looking doubtfully at him, she came to stand by his side with her back to the mantelpiece, bracing her shoulders, also, against the marble, to feel as nearly as possible how he felt, and, as though in order to learn something, copying his attitude. She thought: I am taller, but ... He noted her nearness without noticing her. She studied the stiff blue folds

> of his sailor blouse-sleeve, and looked attentively at the lines round his collar. A scar from some operation showed on his neck; at her side, under the jaw. She looked at his ear and, unconvinced, touched her own, to assure herself he and she were even so much alike. She found herself for the first time no more asking for notice than if she had stood beside an unconscious strong little tree: moving her elbow his way she felt his arm as unknowing as wood. (I.v.59)

This passage is heavily pointed by the commas, the one semi-colon, the two colons, the suspension points and stops; eight commas in the first sentence alone. The pauses marked out by this musical notation indicate bodily movement, moments of internal consciousness (very different from 'notice', which is self-absorbed, unlike 'noted', which recognizes 'nearness' and leads to 'so much alike'). This inner line is then tracked against the touchings of the marble, the scar on the neck on the side nearest her, the jaw, the touching of her own ear, the arm, elbow, tracked in turn against the fabric folds and lines of collar and sleeve. No longer consumed in their childish egotism, they are now becoming friends in this legato passage from marble to wood, mantelpiece to tree. The taut bodies are beginning to show how they might grow together, ramify. 'Unconscious' and 'unknowing' are no longer negative terms here, although the minus prefix 'un-' reminds us of their deficit, which has still to be made up. Bowen's fondness for this prefix, of which there are many examples, some of them extreme – *unenmity, unresistance* (II.x.175), *unsalt* (II.ix.160), *unhumour* (II.v.115) – indicates how strenuously she searched for a vocabulary to represent or at least name interstitial conditions that outright contrast or antithesis would coarsen or deform.

By the second phase of the children's transposition, all has changed. Leopold's mother is not coming after all. He has been abandoned again, this time more thoroughly because he has renounced the substitute life in Spezia and, of course, because he has been exposed as an object of pity in Henrietta's eyes. She '*became* the fact that he could not escape or bear'. Having said the awful words, '*My mother is not here*', it is as though he now can read them, written all over Henrietta's face, dress, hair; he loses his self-possession, turns round as she, unable to speak, reaches for the doorknob as if to leave and he, now facing the mantelpiece,

> suddenly ground his forehead against the marble. One shoulder up dragged his sailor collar crooked; his arms were crushed between his chest and the mantelpiece. After a minute, one leg writhed round the other like ivy killing a tree. The clock ticked calmly away above his head.

Henrietta, appalled, watches him go into a convulsion of tears, as he sobs for everything that he has lost and, as it seems to her, for everything that has ever been denied by those who, like him, pretended to be stoic amidst utter ruin, weeping because he is not going to England, his mother is not coming,

> he has got nowhere to go. He is weeping because this is the end of imagination – imagination fails when there is no *now.* Disappointment tears the bearable film off life. (III.i.208–9)

Now, for the second time, she crosses the parquet floor. The first phase is now re-enacted, but at a much higher voltage:

> Leopold's solitary despair made Henrietta no more than the walls or table. This was not contempt for her presence: no one was there. Being not there disembodied her, so she fearlessly crossed the parquet to stand beside him. She watched his head, the back of his thin neck, the square blue collar shaken between his shoulders, wondering without diffidence where to put her hand. Finally, she leant her body against his, pressing her ribs to his elbow so that his sobs began to go through her too. Leopold rolled his face further away from her, so that one cheek and temple now pressed the marble, but did not withdraw his body from her touch. After a minute like this, his elbow undoubled itself against her and his left arm went round her with unfeeling tightness, as though he were gripping the bole of a tree. Held close like this to the mantelpiece he leant on, Henrietta let her forehead rest on the marble too: her face bent forward so that the tears she began shedding fell on the front of her dress. An angel stood up inside her with its hand to its lips, and Henrietta did not attempt to speak.
>
> Now that she cried, he could rest. His cheek no longer hurt itself on the marble. Reposing between two friends, the mantelpiece and her body, Leopold, she could feel, was looking out of the window, seeing the court-yard and the one bare tree swim into view again and patiently stand. His

> breathing steadied itself; each breath came sooner and was less painfully deep. (III.i.209–10)

The figurative intertwinings of mantelpiece and tree yield to the actual intertwinings of bodies. This is the release; the weeping has melted the stone, the wood, the material world into one of feeling and at last the quirky, damaged child Leopold is released via his friend Henrietta, then his step-father Ray (now we fully appreciate the associations of his name with light and with hope), out of the monomaniacal house to a miscellaneous and relaxed hotel and finally to a panoramic vision of the illuminated city. But it is by no means a smooth or inevitable transition. Leopold realizes Ray really has no idea how evil Mme Fisher is. He has not even met her. When he admits as much Leopold

> wheeled round on his heel to look at the mantelpiece, against which he had wept. He saw not the mantelpiece but a woman with long hair being propped up in bed to sign away Leopold, then his own head helplessly bobbing and rolling on that journey to Italy, like a kitten's or a puppy's. Nothing said undid that. (III.iii.236–7)

And Ray has only the merest glimpse of the possible retribution Leopold might later exact for his maltreatment.

> Behind the childish *méchanceté* Ray saw grown-up avengingness pick up what arms it could . . . saw for the moment what he was up against: the force of a cold, foreign personality.

This is one of several innuendos (and a neologism like 'avengingness' makes it hard not to notice) that make us briefly wonder about the power of innocence to corrupt as well as its vulnerability to being corrupted. 'A child knows what is fatal. The child at the back of the gun accident – is he always so ignorant?' (III.iii.236). It is more than thirty years later, in the final scene in Bowen's *Eva Trout* (1968), that this child figure – melodramatic, even absurd – emerges to kill his mother 'at the back of the gun accident'.[8]

Evil is patently present in *The House in Paris* but many cannot see it in themselves, hidden within their innocence and desire, to which it is foreign but where it is also at home. If vengeance were to be taken, by

Leopold, for instance, what form would it assume? And if it is taken by innocence, an innocence that has been betrayed – but by what? – will innocence itself not have become corrupt, since to avenge effectively it will have to match the evil that has sought to destroy it? Seán Ó'Faoláin catches a great deal of the presence in Bowen's work of the idea of fate, of the power of inertia, of 'the grammar of the style: the use of the passive voice, the impersonal pronoun, the impersonal verb'.[9] But surely we are not seeing just another example of young love and innocence being disabused by a corrupt, adult world. These three novels insist on a much more radical estrangement. The victims have been created outside the world they seek to re-enter. It is a world that survives on manners, protocols of taste, dress, class, behaviour – but all of this is evidently a remnant of what used to be, a world that once had stronger, larger beliefs, such as those of religion. Now that world is dying. What will become of it and of these people who are, wittingly or unwittingly, exposing or discovering the functions of class and manners, of syntax and of propriety as agencies of concealment? It is indeed a gothic trait in Bowen's work that there should be at the heart of all a secret. Maud Ellmann's extraordinary reading of *The House in Paris* sees the central erotic triangle, explored by René Girard, as one between the three females which has, as its concealed 'mimetic rivalry', the bond between Karen and Madame Fisher.[10] This is a more devastating insight than Ó'Faoláin's worldly wisdom could ever produce.

'THE GRIP OF OUR OWN PATHOS'

In *The Death of the Heart* we have a replay of the basic premise of the story of *The House in Paris*. Portia replaces Leopold as the central figure; like him, she is 'the child of an aberration' (III.ii.343),[11] in the words of Anna Quayne, wife of Portia's half-brother Thomas. Like Lois Farquar in *The Last September*, she is the one who feels herself to be different from the others and is so felt by them. The difference is satirically pronounced when it comes to a contrast with the English army wives – just before the news of the killing of Lesworth comes in, Lois, almost in depair, profiles them against the line in Dante's *Vita nuova*, 'donne ch'avere l'intelleto d'amore' (III.vii.270).[12] But, as with Leopold and Portia, her sense of isolation is that of a bereft child who has not been seen in the family for a long time. Mrs Montmorency, Francie, had met Laura, Lois's mother, in England – 'she was too Irish altogether for her own country' (I.ii.30) – but had never seen Lois until now, twelve years after Francie's first visit to Danielstown, when her eager glance senses something different – 'perhaps simply Lois's figure standing there on the steps' (I.ii.25). The question seems to be, how are these outsiders to be reintegrated into '*normal, cheerful* family life' (I.i.19), as Anna Quayne puts it?

Has it so changed that no such integration is possible? Certainly, the old family servant, Matchett, 'seemed ... to detect some lack of life in the house, some organic failure in its propriety' (I.iii. 57). To survive, the dislocated have to get out of these asphyxiating houses. But the chasm between them and others, especially the stupid, may be too wide to cross. In the final section of *The Last September,* Mr Montmorency – one of the stupid – asks Lois if she finds them all still much the same, but Lois

> could not try to explain the magnetism they all exercised by being static. Or how, after every return – or awakening, even, from sleep or preoccupation – she and these home surroundings penetrated each other mutually in the discovery of a lack. (III.iii.229)

Redolent of that, we catch a glimpse in *The House in Paris* of Karen, as she remembers Max's earlier remark, 'One cannot simply act' (II.viii.151), reinterpreting it: 'I thought he meant, must not, what it meant was cannot.' This seems to say that she initially believed Max had meant that the act of bluntly leaving Naomi was not tolerable, either to him or in itself. Now she sees the remark ('it') means that we ('one') are not able, do not have the opportunity or the capacity for originating *any* action. The placement of the word 'simply' in this sentence provides a characteristic top-spin. Perhaps we may say that 'it' denies the ethical dimension the remark first seemed to Karen to have. We do not make ethical choices, although we may imagine we do so; 'choices' are made for us by impersonal forces. Then she goes on:

> People must hope so much when they tear streets up and fight at barricades. But, whoever wins, the streets are laid again and the trams

> start running again. One hopes too much of destroying things. If revolutions do not fail, they fail you. (II.ix.162)

That final 'you' belongs to a world – possibly the inverse of utopian – where, whatever disintegrations take place, only a mute or almost muted private world remains, once autonomous or, now, finally damaged, traumatized, autistic.[13] There is another possibility: that Leopold, Lois, and Portia are three examples of new kinds of being, no longer inhabitants of the old world, not changelings in the old sense of the word but actual mutations, new beings who have discovered that ominous 'lack' Lois increasingly feels. They are aliens, in the sense that they have been virtually dead, missing for years. Revenants of an inverted sort, they belong, not to the past but to its product, the future.

The syntactical anomalies in Bowen's fiction often create an antagonistic effect; the transfer of agency to inanimate things seems often to imply a diffused blame at people for losing agency or an explanation for their unease: 'The sea not having been blue had made everyone meaner . . .' (II.xi.179), we read in *The House in Paris*; or in a later novel, the language twists into a baroque neo-Latin English:

> They played pat-ball on the old croquet lawn, or poked about looking for lost balls. Which were many, the lawn having no net round it, and hard to locate, age having turned them a dark green. Dead-seeming when hit, the balls could nevertheless bound away downhill with great velocity . . .
>
> More green balls being supplied, each games afternoon, had made it come to be held that Miss Ardingfay bought them in by the ton, third-hand. (II.iii.95)[14]

Awkwardness like this runs deep. We see it clearly in Bowen's constant use and counterintuitive placement of the word 'not'. It bespeaks the sense of lack that Lois had spoken of to Mr Montmorency in *The Last September*. In *The House in Paris*, Ray looks round from the window at Leopold who has been sitting tensely on the sofa and wonders, 'For how long has he *not* stopped gripping the sofa?' (III.iii.237, my italics). There are other instances; Anna, in *The Death of the Heart*, says of Portia's diary: 'At the time, it only made me superficially angry – but I've had time since then to think over it in' (I.i.13). Anna's fury has a comic pedantry.

The oddity of the final preposition's placement indicates an incisive pronunciation, a pitch of voice that the written word can't quite reach.

In her World War II fiction, Bowen sought to clarify the connection between a general traumatic dislocation and, during the Blitz, a kind of spiritual communion that paradoxically grew out of the first-hand experience of disintegration. 'Owing . . . to the thunder of those inordinate years, we were shaken out of the grip of our own pathos.' Her short stories of that period 'were true to the general life that was in me at that time'.[15] But the search for that connection was called off. It was succeeded by a lament for the loss of that deep, brief communal bonding and its replacement by a pallid bureaucratic enervation. A managed consensus replaced the harmony of feeling that had risen out of the experience of destruction. In her best work, a stereoscopic narrative method enables the historical dimension of what she calls a specific personal 'predicament'[16] to emerge via the hallucinatory effects it generates in 'The Happy Autumn Fields' (that especially) or, say, in a late, unstable compound such as *Eva Trout*.

Towards the end of *The House in Paris*, outside the Gare de Lyon, Leopold asks Ray no fewer than five times, 'Where are we going?' As Ray looks at him in the full light he realizes that Leopold 'had been someone drawing a first breath' (III.iv.256). Leopold is arriving in the world, almost as a new species, in a world of science fiction, gothic and dystopian, in the midst of World War II in London, in the 'rising tide of hallucination'[17] with its ghosts, flashbacks, tumbled houses, and stammering narratives. But it is the mechanization of the post-war world that Bowen seems to see as the most ominous threat. She has one truly inept story from the post-war period, 'Gone Away', set in a vicarage, which itself is set in a world of facades, 'the Reserve', separated from one another by 'high wire fencing, Whipsnade type'. This village, 'Brighterville', suddenly stops working, people flee in a suicidal frenzy – perhaps of utter boredom – and we are escorted into a kind of eternal nullity, the population suddenly passing from knowing nothing via administered boredom to extinction.[18] People, young and old, who are deeply imprisoned in the world of facades are regulars in Bowen's fiction. They mindlessly accept the status quo, ignore its fragility, cling to its rituals or, as a policy, close their eyes to what is happening, like Anna's father in *The Death of the Heart* who formed 'the habit of being self-protectively unobservant' (II.i.174).

Yet, even in the general disillusion that finally engulfs all in that novel, Bowen does not resist the urge to add a dab of colour – 'an intimation of summer coming' (III.vi.444). Even that urge seems to have left her in 1945, when the England of Churchill and of the War ended. The Blitz was over; the hallucination of heroic community, England's 'heroic To-day',[19] disappeared with it. The England of Attlee, socialism, and the 'mechanisation' of society appeared in its stead.[20]

NOTES

1. See Lauren Arrington, 'Irish Modernism and Its Legacies', in Richard Bourke and Ian McBride (eds.), *The Princeton History of Modern Ireland* (Princeton University Press and Oxford University Press, 2015), 236–54.
2. Elizabeth Bowen, *The House in Paris* (London: Jonathan Cape, 1949). Citations from Bowen's novels are identified in parentheses by Part, chapter, and page number.
3. The reference to the statue obliquely invokes Viola's famous lines in *Twelfth Night*, II.iv.112–13: 'Like Patience on a monument / Smiling at grief'. 'I Sit and Sew' was then a well-known poem by the black American writer, Alice Moore Dunbar-Nelson, voicing a woman's frustration and self-derision at her sealed domestic fate in a world of male heroism and war.
4. See Genesis 25:27: 'And the boys grew: and Esau was a cunning hunter, a man of the field; and Jacob was a plain man, dwelling in tents.'
5. On the effect of postal and railway systems and the establishment of Greenwich Mean Time on the general conception of time, see Sue Zemka, *Time and the Moment in Victorian Literature and Society* (Cambridge University Press, 2012). Conrad's *The Secret Agent* (1907) is the most famous novel about a terrorist attack on time, by the bombing of Greenwich Observatory. The most penetrating account of the organization and effects of the postal system is Patrick Joyce, *The State of Freedom: A Social History of the British State since 1800* (Cambridge University Press, 2013), 53–120.
6. See Maud Ellmann, *Elizabeth Bowen: The Shadow across the Page* (Edinburgh University Press, 2003), 111–12, on accidents and nervous illnesses on the railways.
7. The relationships between 'one' and the other personal pronouns are integral to Lacan's descriptions of the big Other. See *Écrits: A Selection*, trans. Bruce Fink (New York: W. W. Norton, 2002), 60–1.
8. See Victoria Glendinning, *Elizabeth Bowen: Portrait of a Writer* (London: Weidenfeld & Nicolson, 1977), 226: 'Yet the idea of the child with the gun – the supreme illustration of the lethal potential of innocence – had been there a long time.'
9. Seán Ó'Faoláin, 'Elizabeth Bowen or *Romance does not pay*', in *The Vanishing Hero: Studies in Novelists of the Twenties* (London: Eyre & Spottiswoode,1956), 169–90 (at 177). Ó'Faoláin's essay is mostly about *The Last September.*

10. Ellmann, *Elizabeth Bowen*, 124–5. Mimesis, as distinct from imitation, involves rivalry, desire for the same thing. See René Girard, *Deceit, Desire, and the Novel: Self and Other in Literary Structure* (Baltimore, MD: Johns Hopkins University Press, 1965).
11. Elizabeth Bowen, *The Death of the Heart* (London: Victor Gollancz, 1938).
12. Elizabeth Bowen, *The Last September* (London: Jonathan Cape, 1948).
13. See the powerful essay by Eluned Summers-Bremner, 'Dead Letters and Living Things: Historical Ethics in *The House in Paris* and *The Death of the Heart*', in Susan Osborn (ed.), *Elizabeth Bowen: New Critical Perspectives* (Cork University Press, 2009), 61–82. The mute and autistic conditions, implied in these three novels, obviously re-emerge in *Eva Trout*. Again, the reader is compelled to track the links in this quotation between 'people', 'one', and 'you', although not necessarily as a gradual intensification.
14. Elizabeth Bowen, *The Little Girls* (London: Jonathan Cape, 1964).
15. 'Postscript by the Author', in *The Demon Lover and Other Stories* (London: Jonathan Cape, 1945; 1952), 222–3.
16. Elizabeth Bowen, *English Novelists* (London: William Collins, 1942), 42. Writing of Henry James: 'He writes at once with the detachment of a spectator and the close-upness of someone under a spell. He might be called the analyst of civilization ... And predicament was his subject ... His sense of beauty is matched by his sense of evil: his villains do worse than oppress or threaten – they immeasurably corrupt.'
17. 'Postscript by the author', 218–24. This postscript, a key document in itself for the understanding of Bowen's war-time writings, describes with great power how in these stories, 'through the particular, in war-time, I felt the high-voltage current of the general pass'.
18. *The Collected Stories of Elizabeth Bowen*, intro. Angus Wilson (London: Jonathan Cape, 1980), 758–66. The story first appeared in 1946. Whipsnade is the name of a famous English zoo.
19. Bowen, *English Novelists*, 7.
20. See Glendinning, *Elizabeth Bowen*, 166.

CHAPTER 11

Elizabeth Bowen: Two Stories in One

> How to tell a story while another is being told? This question synthesizes the technical problems of the short story. Second thesis: the secret story is the form of the short story.
>
> Ricardo Piglia, 'Theses on the Short Story'[1]

THEMATICALLY BANAL, RATHER TIRESOMELY, EVEN CLUMSILY 'experimental', like so much modernist literature that laments and seeks formally to represent loss of contact with the past, and the ruin of the present, it is astonishing how exotic and heartbreaking Elizabeth Bowen's 'The Happy Autumn Fields' nevertheless is. Echoes of the traditional ghost story and of the new science fiction tale are audible to any reader, but the composite that Bowen creates in this instance has a texture and tonal complexity different to anything we find even in those novels, like *The Last September* (1929), that share common ground with it. It is not often that the story of the destruction of a building, of a way of life, and of a particular sensibility can achieve such momentum that we accede to the belief that we have also witnessed the destruction of a value system of which these things were only an historical, but now irreplaceable, expression. Can we really know what we claim to have lost the capacity to inherit? Or is the claim merely histrionic and/or contradictory? This is a region explored in some of Bowen's finest stories ('Ivy Gripped the Steps', 'In the Square', 'Mysterious Kôr', among them), although access to it had been gained by very few of her contemporaries.

In one quasi-doctrinal moment in 'The Happy Autumn Fields', the transitional figure 'Mary' asks,

> How are to live without natures? We only know inconvenience now, not sorrow . . . The source, the sap, must have dried up, or the pulse must have stopped, before you and I were conceived. So much flowed through people; so little flows through us. All we can do is imitate love or sorrow. (683–4)[2]

Her biological link with the story's central figure, Sarah, seems frail, is finally denied altogether, yet we are expected to accept that she *is*, in some sense, Sarah reincarnated. We are also told that Sarah and her beloved younger sister Henrietta died young, had no children, and that the key tragic moment from the distant pre-World War I time was the accidental death of her lover-to -be Eugene, killed when thrown by his horse which had inexplicably shied in the middle of the happy autumn fields as he returned home from a visit to the sisters' beautiful family home in the fading light of a day that has now dissolved into a summer day in London during World War II in a bombed and crumbling, once-grand terrace house. This is obviously a story that not very smoothly exploits a doubled structure at every point; Bowen herself had written that the short story was a modern genre, ideal for capturing the contemporary sense of disintegration.[3] Yet the surreal elements in the story do not draw all their force from the glaring contrast between the lush, many-coloured beauties of an earlier Irish landscape and house and the pulverized white plaster of the ravaged London terrace. What once was, now is no longer; soon it will be as though it had never been.

> There being nothing left, she wished he would come to take her to the hotel. The one way back to the fields was barred by Mary's surviving the fall of the ceiling. Sarah was right in doubting that there would be tomorrow: Eugene, Henrietta were lost in time to the woman weeping there on the bed, no longer reckoning who she was. (683)

Yet the story of the lost paradisal condition has itself an inner fold. For it was not Eugene's death that, by itself, changed everything. The change had already happened. It was his love for Sarah and her love for him, germinating in both, still unspoken except in the language or languages of looking, or of imagining. This is the love that has already destroyed the previously perfect relationship between the two sisters. Initially we see them bringing up the rear of a family party of ten, landowner father, brothers, cousin, and sisters, moving across a wide open landscape. Then Henrietta, the younger, sees her brother, Fitzgeorge, the eldest son and the inheritor of the property, and the neigbouring squire, Eugene, approaching on horseback. She waves her damson-stained handkerchief like a flag, encourages Sarah to join in; when she does not, '"I can see you are shy," she said in a dead voice, "So shy you won't even wave to *Fitzgeorge*?"' (674). By not speaking 'the *other* name', Eugene's, and not looking at Sarah's face, which she again refuses to do later in the drawing-room, where Eugene and Sarah look searchingly at one another, by connecting the word 'shy' with the word 'dead', she sets off the alarm that keeps sounding until the death of Eugene and the end of the story.

Thus begins the long dying fall into the last vision of the family, most achingly seen through Sarah's eyes as the sun begins to set, its rays opening wide a spectrum of reds and a dazzling of sight. The damson stain on the handkerchief first, then the changing of Fitzgeorge's 'flesh to coral', then Eugene dazzled as he dismounts, next Sarah 'enfolded, dizzied, blinded as though inside a wave' (we remember Henrietta's other kind of wave), as they walk back with Eugene's horse now between the sisters.

Henrietta begins to sing. 'At once her pain, like a scientific ray, passed through the horse and Eugene, to penetrate Sarah's heart' (675). The idea of a 'death ray' had appeared before in 1920s popular fiction. Here it links with the rays of the setting sun, which are increasingly bending towards darkness, and also with the notion of time passing through the bodies of the horse and the humans in a flash of pain that also pierces the figure of Mary some fifty years later. At that moment too, the angle of narration alters. 'We mount the skyline: the family come into our view, we into theirs.' The family, a 'handsome statufied group in strong yellow sunshine, aligned by Papa and crowned by Fitzgeorge', appears as a sculpture or painting, being seen for a moment while itself seeing, 'turning their judging eyes on the laggards'; this remains part of the story's subtle flexion between observing and being observed. These positions, physical and social, seem in that moment to be permanent. Yet, Sarah realizes, it is the turning point.

> 'One more moment and it will be too late: no further communication will be possible. Stop oh stop Henrietta's heartbreaking singing.' (675)

The premonitory signs and intimations gather as the sun sets. This has been a walk before the departure of the three boys next day for school. Education is no compensation for lack of inheritance; their body language hides 'a bodily grief. The repugnance of victims.' There is an old dying man on the estate whose crumbling cottage they do not visit. The rooks circle overhead, then 'planed one by one to the earth' (presaging the bombers over London); the boys rejoice 'at the imaginary fall of so many rooks'; these ominous birds cast their shadows on the sisters who 'in their turn cast one shadow'. Sarah 'recognized the colour of valediction, tasted sweet sadness'. Then, up ahead of them, 'a dislocation' when Emily, bending to tie a bootlace, causes others to trip up.

But it is the intensity of the relationship between the two sisters that in its brightness challenges – and provokes – threat. Henrietta says, 'You know we are always sad when the boys are going, but never sad when the boys have gone.' As often in Bowen's work, the habitual, what always happens, faces the unprecedented, what never happened before nor ever will again. The boys went off the year before; they'll be going off next year. 'But oh how should I feel, and how should you feel, if it were something that had not happened before?' This is where the tenses of the verbs begin to quiver in the changing light. The question of how each would feel about such a thing nudges open the space between never before and never again, asking for the appropriate feeling for such a time, even though it does not exist. Tuned to the habitual, can they imagine the unprecedented? And if the unprecedented happens, then are they in the world of never-again, of finality, not continuity? Sarah feels the fatality of this and thinks: 'Rather than they should cease to lie in the same bed she prayed they might lie in the same grave' (672). But Henrietta knows that the blow has fallen. Just as they spontaneously think of being left utterly alone forever with one another, Fitzgeorge and Eugene appear – 'In the glass of the distance, two horsemen came into view' (674) – and Henrietta starts semaphoring with her handkerchief. They can never be alone-together again.

As they pass indoors the mythic dimensions of the story begin to amplify. The declining sunlight again tints everything it touches with reds, golds, and purples. 'Now the sun was setting behind the trees, but its rays passed dazzling between the branches, into the beautiful warm red room.' Sarah, pressing a geranium leaf between her hands, sits apart from the others, outside the wreath-of-pomegranates pattern on the carpet; Henrietta, Arthur, their mother are all round the hearth – 'where they were grouped was a hearth' – where no fire has yet been lit, the ancient indication that no new life has yet been born in this darkening season.

> Against the white marble fireplace stood Eugene. The dark red shadows gathering in the drawing-room as the trees drowned more and more of the sun would reach him last, perhaps never: it seemed to Sarah that a lamp was lighted behind his face. (679)

Henrietta is posed beside her mother. 'This particular hour of subtle light . . . had always, for Sarah, been Henrietta's.' But precisely now, in refusing to look at Sarah, 'did she admit their eternal loss'. Eugene, on the other hand, takes every opportunity to look at Sarah.

> For her part, she looked at him, as though he, transfigured by the strange light, were indeed a picture, a picture who could not see her. The wallpaper now flamed scarlet behind his shoulder. (679)

Midst all these flames and reds sits the mother. She rules the room. Piano, harp, draperies, occasional tables, chairs, lustres, fringes, ferns, an alabaster Leaning Tower of Pisa, all

> had an equilibrium of their own. Nothing would fall or change. And everything in the drawing-room was muted, weighted, pivoted by Mama. (680)

Amid the references to the change of season and the oncoming darkness, the figure of the mother merges into that of Persephone, wife of Hades, in her underworld, surrounded by the ring of her red symbolic fruit, the pomegranates, the seeds of which she had eaten and been thereby doomed to her seasonal reign below. Their red is also in myth the colour of the blood of Dionysus/Adonis, or of Christ; the ring of purple fruit marks the line between the living and the dead. This is the moment at which Sarah claims, as she 'drew a light little gold chair into the middle of the wreath of the carpet, where no one ever sat, and sat down', that she thinks she must have been asleep and dreaming since she saw Eugene in the cornfield, the mythical moment of the earth and its fruit and flowers opening to the winter's sleep.

Henrietta mocks her with the old schoolbook sample on the importance of punctuation: 'Charles the First walked and talked half an hour after his head was cut off' (681). Yet this deepens the atmosphere of sudden death, trance, and deposition. Sarah is overcome by the 'feeling of dislocation' – that word now suddenly magnified from its earlier appearance; she can no longer speak of her swelling sense of loss, her sense of each second now being numbered. Would Henrietta or Eugene not reach out and touch her hand, she wonders as she throws out her hands (as Henrietta had done earlier in the cornfield as she exclaimed 'Forlorn!'), lets the shred of geranium fall, and Eugene goes down on one knee to retrieve it and enclose it in his handkerchief, as Henrietta had earlier disclosed the damson stain in hers when first she waved it. He returns it to his breast pocket in reverse of Henrietta's earlier gesture of disclaiming her own love for Sarah when she 'had locked the hour inside her breast'.

As Eugene stoops and Mama calls for Henretta to ring for the lamps, the sun sets, his head goes under the 'tide of dusk', the rooks stream over the house, the globed lights begin to appear in the hall, the others come into the room, led by Constance, the figure of the bride, and Henrietta tells her that Eugene is with them but 'on the point of asking if he may send for his horse' (682). The corn is in, the torches are called; these are ancient emblems of Persephone and her story. Yet again the conversation returns to the habitual world but its linear time now begins to tremble. Eugene says to Sarah he will be back tomorrow, Sarah, still in panic, cries for Henrietta. 'What could be sooner than tomorrow?' Henrietta replies; 'There cannot fail to be tomorrow', says Eugene who will of course never see it, Henrietta says she will see to it and then Henrietta's accusation explodes – 'Whatever tries to come between me and Sarah becomes nothing' (683).

In the World War II passage much in this sequence has found its slant rhyming event, especially as Mary tries to open the buttons of her dress to enclose the photograph of Henrietta and Sarah – her first sight of Sarah –

'but it offered no hospitality to the photograph' (678). This echoes Eugene's placing the geranium leaf in his breast pocket, Henrietta locking up the special hour in her breast. How, exclaims Mary, can that 'fragment torn out of a day' that she can't help but lay 'as a pattern against the poor stuff of everything else' mean anything? She 'had a sister called Henrietta'; she is not descended from Sarah; she cannot return to that vivid day in the past. Last thing to be heard of is the death of Eugene and of Fitzgeorge saying, in a letter, written long after, that he wonders and will always wonder 'what made the horse shy in those empty fields' (685).

In effect, 'Mary' is not a representation of a person, not a character in a story; she is presented as no more than a fictional device. Yet she is also no *less* than that. The music playing in the remains of the room below, the noise of a mob shattering a conservatory, and several other details, including the mute telephone beside her bed, form internal contrasts – like her black shoes and dress and the white plaster that has fallen on them – that operate as part of the larger design of the story's conversions that are grandly obvious. We witness the turning of a technicolor portrait into a black-and-white film strip, perfection into ruin, a complete love between two people who want to be one person into a story (more of an inference really) of barren disappointment, the failure of the intense personalities of Henrietta and Sarah to become anything more in time than this 'Mary'. This is really a kind of reversed ekphrasis, in which a detailed picture is described in rich detail and then shown after it has faded to dusty remnants. It is also a false valediction to fiction's supposed capacity to bestow upon society a timeless dimension. Who could not but grieve for the lost world here or for the ruin that followed it? But are the connections between those worlds only to be understood in a sequence in which realism gives way to myth which in turn gives way to a haunting which again gives way to realism? In the last phase of that sequence, the generic elements are confused; 'Mary' is actually neither Henrietta nor Sarah, nor their mythic counterpart, nothing but a name indicating their disappearance. They seem 'real', she merely instrumental. She has a function, is a sort of medium in an intermittent séance, no more. Travis is even more plainly a character in name only, only a name. He and Mary are pale versions of Henrietta and Sarah's passion to be fused together, two people who throw one shadow. We are aware primarily of what they, Travis and Mary, are not. Is the reason for or secret of the disappearance or ruin of the first world revealed in the second, or of the second in the first? The conceit is that one is a revelation of what is central to the other. But that is, rather, a deceit. Neither is revelatory of the other. It's a tale that seems to have set out to find in two stories a form in which they could become one story. It never does.

NOTES

1. *New Left Review*, 70 (July–August 2011), 63–6 (at 64).
2. Parenthetical references in this chapter are to *The Collected Stories of Elizabeth Bowen*, intro. Angus Wilson (London: Jonathan Cape, 1980).
3. Elizabeth Bowen, *People, Places, Things: Essays*, ed. Allan Hepburn (Edinburgh University Press, 2008), 314–15, cited in Neal Alexander, 'Metropolitan Modernity: Stories of London', in Dominic Head (ed.), *The Cambridge History of the English Short Story* (Cambridge University Press, 2016), 269–85.

CHAPTER 12

Mary Lavin: Celibates

Jésus annonçait la Royaume et c'est l'Église qui est venue (Jesus proclaimed the Kingdom, but what arrived was the Church).

Alfred Loisy, *L'évangile et l'Église,* 1902

MARY LAVIN TELLS THE SAME STORY OVER AND OVER. IT IS always a story of two lives, governed by love gained or lost. Love may be lost in or through a bad marriage; still, it commands lifelong fidelity, heightened by the socially enforced sexual abstinence that accompanies it. But even a happy marriage can lead to an enforced chastity, a version of celibacy (even though celibacy strictly means the state of being unmarried).[1] The early death of a husband can invoke this chastity/celibacy in the widow as a kind of loyalty to him, to their original marriage vows. Remarriage, or another sexual relationship, has to sometimes be figured as an almost defiant loyalty to oneself. There are many variations on these relationships. Yet the first happiness can never be relived or recaptured, not even in remarriage, although it remains as a ghostly presence, memory or fantasy, in any later state. An even worse fate awaits those whose initial 'true' love turns sour in marriage, or never culminates in marriage because of the beloved's death or for other myriad reasons.

Does celibacy-chastity help to retain love or does remarriage betray it? How many chances does one get? In this island – full of widows, widowers, priests, nuns, monks, Christian Brothers, spinsters, bachelors, virgins, missionaries – celibacy, however enforced it might be by accident or death, doctrine or social belief and structure, was treated as a synonym for chastity; this, in turn, could give to sexual solitude a measure of dignity.[2] Late marriage, emigration, and celibacy together cruelly exposed the failure of the state's autarkic, protectionist economic policies and its integration, in reverse gear (which emigration actually anticipates and hastens), into the system of global capital. Many also emigrated to Africa and Asia as Catholic missionaries, extending the ideology of the West and enhancing further the distinction between material and spiritual values which capitalism and fundamentalist Christianity expanded together, an apparent contradiction that fuelled a real alliance. Still, the specific Irish alliance between Church and state was exalted as a unique fusion of the two dimensions.[3]

In this Ireland, roughly of 1920–60, the ideologies of virginity, chastity, and celibacy provided the paradoxical justifications for large families, small incomes, sexual anguish, queues for confession, and for the emigrant boat. These had been apparently inescapable consequences of the Great Famine, but there had been, after all, a pivotal moment of potential radical change in 1916–22. But what arrived instead was a petit-bourgeois transvaluation of revolutionary values into an intellectually feeble, luxuriantly kitsch, unforgiving orthodoxy that belatedly realized that it was actually conspiring with the harsh economic conditions of the thirties, World War II, and its aftermath to produce a catastrophic decline. The Irish – fewer than three million left in 1961 – were vanishing faster than the bogus traditional values they mutilated themselves to retain.[4] It is from this world that Mary Lavin's short stories derive.[5]

Nonetheless, for all the 'grocer's republic' atmosphere, the internal, waspish discords, the setting, tone, even the slack garrulity and professional 'Oirish' idiom of so many of the stories ('The Green Grave and the Black Grave', 'A Likely Story', 'Bridal Sheets'), and the remarkable, implausible death rate, they usually do not fail to impart an abiding sense of security. This derives from the obsessional isolation of 'love', even in the most unlikely circumstances, as the counterweight to all that is gross and material. The nub of the matter is celibacy, a sexual abstinence akin to virginity willed by the exercise of fidelity.

VIRGIN LAND

What kind of condition is it? In many stories, it is a state of fidelity to the dead, keeping alive the flame of the love that once had been by remaining sexually chaste forever after. In the story 'In a Café', for instance, the reward for the faithful widow, after a near-violation of this code, is a vision of the dead husband in which, at last, she can again see his face as he walks, full-length, towards her. However, the sexual fast goes on – and on. In some cases, women 'steal' husbands-to-be from friends, leaving the victim stranded in a twilit, celibate loyalty to the love – often also to the lover – she has lost ('Heart of Gold', 'The Mouse', 'The Long Ago'). In Roman Catholic Christianity in particular, celibacy has had an intricate political and theological relationship with virginity, with the celibate Jesus (who founded no family) and his virgin mother, who founded *the* family. In early Christian Ireland, the role of women and the importance of virginity for them gave to the figure of Mary a peculiarly salient role that endured for centuries.[6] Sexual abstention had, from the early Christian period, been associated with salvation itself. Renunciation of the sexual was a renunciation of pagan beliefs and practices; chastity was regarded as a spiritual achievement, and was not particularly associated with beliefs about the Blessed Virgin. That connection is peculiarly modern and Roman Catholic.[7] The publication in 1843 of Louis de Montfort's seventeenth-century treatise *Traité de la vraie dévotion à la Vierge Marie* (translated by Father William Faber in 1863 as *True Devotion to the Blessed Virgin Mary*) ignited the Marian blaze, quickly intensified by the winds of fear blowing from an embattled papacy.[8]

The role of the Virgin Mary in Roman Catholicism's war on 'modernism' (or 'modernity'), and specifically on modernism's local version, Italian nationalism, was inaugurated by Pius IX's declaration on 8 December 1854 of her Immaculate Conception. As the territory of the Italian state grew and that of the Church shrank, the dramatic contest between Church and state, in which the Pope held for almost sixty years the eye-catching role of the Prisoner of the Vatican, was refigured if not quite resolved in the Lateran Treaties of 1929, when Vatican City became a unique version of a state, geographically tiny, globally huge.

It is still necessary to repeat that the new dogma of Mary's Immaculate Conception has, technically, nothing to do with her virginity. That had been declared dogma at the Lateran Council of 649. Her Divine Motherhood was pronounced at the Council of Ephesus in 431 (the year before St Patrick brought Christianity to Ireland). On 1 November 1950, Pope Pius XII, invoking the papal infallibility that had been declared dogma at the First Vatican Council, which was itself opened on the feast of the Immaculate Conception on 8 December 1869, stated as 'a divinely revealed dogma' that

> the Immaculate Mother of God, the ever Virgin Mary, having completed the course of her earthly life, was assumed body and soul into heavenly glory.

(Her 'dormition', as it was called, is a rare term, although Joyce used it in *Finnegans Wake* to describe the condition of the 'nightworld'.) The first ever Marian Year was declared by the same pope in 1954, the centennial year of the dogma of the Immaculate Conception. The second Marian year was declared by John Paul II in 1987; his encyclical, *Redemptoris Mater* (*On the Mother of the Redeemer*), subtitled *On the Blessed Virgin Mary in the Life of the Pilgrim Church*, is the longest ever devoted to the Virgin and is designed to give her undisputed primacy of intercession between Christ and humankind. The Polish John Paul II's apostolate is said to have contributed to the fall of communism in 1989, although ultimate credit for that has to be assigned, in this kind of discourse, to the Virgin. Modernism, however, had expanded beyond communism. The apparition at Fatima and the October Revolution, both of 1917, belonged to the first phase of the modernist struggle; this included the consecration, by Pope John Paul II, of Russia to the Immaculate Heart of Mary in 1987, supposedly the fulfilment of the Third Secret of Fatima. Soviet Russia, Fatima, and the ultimate fate of the world have always been spotlit together. On the centennial of the first apparition, in 2017, Pope Francis canonized two of the child visionaries.

Thus, from the nineteenth to the twenty-first centuries, in Western and Eastern rites, the Virgin Mary became a startling focus in the debates between religion and modernism, the principles of Good and Evil, a heretical Manichean division. The Four Marian Dogmas (two formulated between 1854 and 1950) show how an abstruse theology and dogmatic ferocity were combined to give an aureoled anti-modern image of sinlessness, purity, virginity, and motherhood. It is a twice-told narrative of son and mother, the son who ascends into heaven, the mother who is lifted up (assumed) into heaven, male and female, divine and human, interchangeable and integrated, flesh and spirit so unified that their separation is regarded as a victory for world, flesh, and devil. The triumph of a diabolic modernism, with sexual promiscuity as one of its defining characteristics, is the tragic inverse of the Assumption of the Virgin. The dogmatic definition and support commentary portray her as an anti-Eve who crushes the sibilant snake of the flesh. The music and iconography of the Western and Eastern churches, sentimentally fervent hymns, pie-faced statues, oratorios and Gregorian chant, miraculous apparitions (Lourdes, 1858; Knock, 1879; Fatima, 1917; Medjugorge, 1981, prominent among the European examples) expand the charismatic appeal.

The audience for that appeal was, in one sense, the poor, uneducated, often illiterate people living in remote areas. This was the Church's response to the liberal revolutions of 1848, an ingenious confiscation of the 'people' for a cause now purged of any connection with an intelligentsia. Such people, 'the faithful', were the counter-image to the degraded urban mob or crowd that, in Britain and France, in the face of social unrest, had been assiduously promoted by historians and sociologists to a demonic, leading role in the French Revolution.[9] This people was also immaculate, cleansed of any original stain of theories of historical process or progress. Eschatology was the new domain. The Virgin had come to warn of the approaching Last Days, the need to appease her angered Son, of the coming extinction of the cities of the plain. No imagined apocalypse matched the horrors of the World Wars and there was a notable surge in many forms of apparition, superstition, beliefs in protective charms, across all religions and classes.[10] Spiritualism was both a fraud and a solace in a world where so many of the young had died – most of them white Europeans, killed by other white Europeans. Once the idea of progress died, and the fear of general collapse spread, the secular world sought redemption, forgiveness for being so secular. The venerable champions of devotion to the Virgin, like St Bernard of Clairvaux (although he did not believe in the Immaculate Conception) whom Dante chose to lead his pilgrim into Paradise in *The Divine Comedy*, were extolled with renewed enthusiasm in Catholic teaching. The special mediating role of the beloved female, who is divine mother and daughter, guide and benefactress, the object of chivalric love, the apotheosis of sexual purity, is celebrated in the hierarchical chain of mediators in Dante's poem – the Virgin, Saint Lucy, Beatrice (the central role of Virgil, the pagan male, fades as Paradise comes closer). She is there the Queen of the White Rose, in whom all the blessed are contained; many of the great rose windows in gothic cathedrals were dedicated to the Virgin. But in the modern period, the Virgin's role gains a new eminence and is given dogmatic authority. Apparitions cease to be phantoms; appearances become events. Mary became a celebrity, permanently on tour, attracting vast audiences. It is said that after she visited a site in the north of Ireland, her return was awaited by such vast crowds that the stewards were obliged to plead with them to 'stand back an' give her room to land'.

Tellingly, Marie Antoinette, a martyred queen, a victim of modern revolution, the subject of Burke's great 1790 panegyric to European Catholicism, never appears either as rival to or emblem for the Virgin in the great surge of late nineteenth-century Marian pamphleteering. The king's wife had been beset by so much sexual scandal that she could hardly be recruited into the celestial company in which sexual purity and virginity played such central roles.[11] Her peculiar absence in papal celebrations and her steady political recurrence in French (and other) historical and literary works is in itself a potent image of the process by which the secular candidates for recruitment to sainthood were chosen or dismissed. Any hint of sexual delinquency in the CV was fatal.

Yet it was largely because of the translation of this mystery from theology to a predominantly visual cult of idolatrous celebrity – apparitions, visitations, solar spinnings – that it met with fierce resistance from the more text-bound, scriptural Protestant confessions.[12] There had been notable resistance too in both commentary and fiction to the Church's views on modernism for at least two decades before independence. Gerald O'Donovan's novel *Father Ralph* (1913) identifies the oppressive classes that threatened any form of emancipation – 'the priests, the land-hungry farmers, and the gombeen shopkeepers and publicans'. Finally for him, the syllabus of Pius X, *Lamentabili sane exitu* (1907), delivers the final stroke to what Father Ralph had taken to be true Christianity.[13] Just over a month later, on 8 September, the birthday of the Virgin, the encyclical *Pascendi dominici gregis,* the most strident of all the Vatican's attacks on modernism, was published. Evolution of doctrine, modern biblical exegetical methods, conspiratorial cabals to relativize the invariable truths and teachings of Scripture and Church, with much else, were condemned – as well as insinuations that priestly celibacy should be abandoned. Modernism was 'the synthesis of all heresies'. Catholic Ireland found a role in world history by being assigned an important part in this version of the Church's revival, begun in the French Restoration after 1815, continued by the papacy after 1848, accompanied by the new Catholic nations, Belgium and Poland, galvanized by O'Connell, Newman, Montalembert, Cardinal Cullen, and others.[14] The new state of 1922 had no other mildly comparable global career open to it. The new Church Militant was a spiritual enterprise that offered Ireland a leading role in the crusade against modernism. This it assumed, if not officially, with the founding of the Legion of Mary in 1921 by Frank Duff (1889–1980); the Legion was a remarkable instance of a militant lay apostolate (modelled on the structure of the Roman legion) which made the idea of the Virgin and of virginity central to its mission, much of which was devoted to the saving of women from prostitution. Pius XII sent a letter of encouragement to Duff in 1953 to commemorate the founding of the Legion 'on the fertile soil of Catholic Ireland'.[15] In the twentieth century, the Legion became a global phenomenon. Like much Irish literature, it needed modernism – understood as plague or as liberation – to project it on to a global screen, although the publication of *Ulysses* in 1922, the great Irish transnational novel, made the unique configuration of the new state and the old religion an exemplary instance of how political emancipation and cultural thralldom, in concert and in conflict, could simultaneously exist. Perhaps the Legion of Mary, Joyce's novel, and the new Free State can be taken as interlinked instances of the modernism the Vatican feared and that Fredric Jameson once famously described as 'the experience and result of *incomplete* modernization'. That was the 'new global' and Ireland was one of its centres, wonderfully complete in its varieties of incompletion, epic and small.[16]

Further, this updated pagan idolatry of the Virgin, of saints and apparitions, rosaries and miraculous medals, May altars, hospitals governed by new orders of nuns and by the 'Catholic ethos' surrounding childbirth and abortion, constituted a kind of second

Counter-Reformation that, since the days of the late nineteenth-century Devotional Revolution in Ireland, had been threatening that merger with Irish nationalism which finally produced the confessional Free State and the economically emaciated Irish republic. Since the Irish Civil War most radical elements had been effectively erased from Irish society; descendants of the old Irish Parliamentary Party returned to avenge their defeat in the 1918 election at the hands of Sinn Féin. The new, governing Cumann na nGaedheal party (1923–32), dominated by small businessmen and professional cadres, deferred entirely to the devotional Church and the papal versions of Christian corporatism espoused in Pius XI's encyclical *Quadragesimo anno* (1931). The most notable convergence between Roman Catholicism and communism came in the 1930s when, obviously for different reasons, they used comparably vitriolic terms ('degenerate', 'alien') to attack 'modernism', now become the enemy of both Marian mysticism and Socialist Realism.[17] This sexualized drama of Marian Catholicism against secular modernism is quietly, at times awkwardly, absorbed into the work of Lavin and many others, regularly staged as a conflict between provincialism and cosmopolitanism, an ideal one for magazines like *The New Yorker* which alchemized it for her stories and those of contemporaries like Frank O'Connor.[18]

Although the Irish Catholic bourgeoisie began in the 1960s to abandon Catholic anti-modernism for the joys and risks of late capitalism, as many of their forebears had abandoned the island for the joys and risks of employment abroad, the powerful idea of a miraculous fusion of body and spirit attainable through the ideology of the Virgin and associated practices of dedicated chastity, celibacy, purity, and an almost feudal fidelity to a feminized ideal, as in chivalric poetry, survived.[19] Although almost extinguished since by the revelations of rampant clerical sexual abuse, cover-up, and breathtaking hypocrisy, the devotional embers were fanned again and again by Vatican strategies of canonization, occasional admissions of its own inner corruption (one of the satanic triumphs of modernism), papal visits to Marian shrines, ratification of miraculous cures, and a whole repertoire of public relations projects which included the globalization of the papacy itself. In the *Lumen gentium* (*Light of the Peoples*), the *Dogmatic Constitution on the Church,* a key document of Vatican

II, promulgated by Paul VI in 1964, the new salience of the Virgin in the Church's doctrinal structure was confirmed in Chapter 8, despite the reservations of the Protestant Churches. 'It is the first time, in fact', said Paul VI,

> that an Ecumenical Council has presented such a vast synthesis of the Catholic doctrine regarding the place which the Blessed Virgin Mary occupies in the mystery of Christ and of the Church.

Ireland, like many other countries, joined the Catholic crusade (1854–1964) of the Virgin against modernism. It has now switched its devotion to the miracles of the media and consumer capitalism. Yet it is still marked by having been for so long detained in the spiritual-sexual Tower of Ivory. The litany of Loreto of the Blessed Virgin Mary, dating from the sixteenth century, contains titles that also belong to the Decadent vocabulary of the fin-de-siècle when Catholicism was the religion of choice among artists. Tower of Ivory reverses into the Ivory Tower but Mystic Rose belongs to both. Each has an erotic appeal but the Ivory Tower was the home of an esoteric ideology while Roman Catholicism had begun, since the 1848 revolutions, to transmute traditional belief into stark doctrine. The dialectic between them has a logic that is plainly visible but still hard to read.[20]

'EVEN SO'

For Lavin (and others), especially with the double structure of the short story as a genre, there was a representational dilemma. Celibacy was a theme and a preoccupation. Were her stories quietly to endorse or to query its importance in a state where a strange ideal of celibacy had become a governing doctrinal element in its social and political life? There were curious symptoms: late marriages, yet a high birth rate; endless emigration that showed how unattainable was any ideal of national integrity that sought to combine economic independence and sexual purity.[21] It was a dwindling society that lived at an ever-increasing level of tension. Virginity needed to be lost as a central value in a state in which weakening economic conditions remorselessly dictated the terms of survival. Hypocrisy flourished in the overlap between the prevailing systems, but so too did a specific anguish for those who felt that spiritual values had been commodified, that the idea of sexual chastity as a form of personal integrity had been – like themselves – pitilessly caricatured.

In Lavin's stories, widows form the subgroup that most acutely feels the hypocrisies and the anguish of a condition that brings the ideal of virginity to the test. Women who have been married and perhaps have had children are now confronted with the notion of fidelity to the dead husband as a noble fate. Are they to become 'virgins', so to say, for the rest of their lives? Even since Vatican II, the institution of Consecrated Virgins and Widowers has been revived; members of these bodies regard themselves as Brides of Christ. Thus, it is not a vanished world we encounter in Lavin's work; it is one that had begun rapidly to disappear in the 1960s but has never quite faded. Its increasingly spectral character seems to extend its durability. In Lavin's stories, for instance, a widow undergoes a second marriage with her dead husband. Do their worlds converge or run in parallel? One realm may be converted into the other, with love, the universal unit of exchange, as the mediator. The world of the senses is powerful but is not coincident with the world as such; the lovers keep reminding the solicitors and housewives of the limits of their material worlds. Water can be sacramental and asperged; it can also be boiled and drunk for comfort, as very material tea. A lot of tea is consumed in Lavin's stories.[22]

There is a further difficulty with the style of silent endorsement that makes the stories so placatory in their cumulative effect. It has to do with social prestige; it operates as a force at every level. Those women who do not or cannot have children are regarded as inferior to those who do have them. That is one of the paradoxes of the celibacy factor. Lay celibacy, to have its full value recognized, must be chosen. Priests and nuns have not simply chosen a career, they have followed a vocation; they constitute a kind of caste. But lay widows and widowers exercise a choice of a different kind. They are almost a caste, but never quite.

The laity of these stories usually have the prestige of class. The British military and political system was lifted away, to general relief, but the class system obdurately remained. The social historian Patrick Joyce, whose parents emigrated to London, wrote that the 'authority of the British state in Ireland had been succeeded by the petty authority of the local middle class, the priest and the doctor as well as that of the auctioneer and teacher'.[23] The middle classes in turn preside over a large subservient class who are treated, for the most part, with casual brutality – again, women are in the majority here as household slaves or waitresses of one kind or another, but there are also male farm labourers, shop assistants, gardeners, and so on. Below even them are the urban working classes, whose lives are ramshackle, dirty, and apparently without the moral scruple sometimes evinced by the more prosperous. Yet they all have 'the Faith'; only with the working classes is it hinted that their morals, like their accents, might be a little discordant. Less sexually strict, more given to drink and domestic violence, with more unwanted pregnancies, they are nevertheless heartwarmingly obedient, even servile, towards the Church and its ministers ('My Vocation'). To transgress the boundaries of class as, for instance, by having sex with a servant or being in love with a labourer, marrying beneath one's station, is a serious matter, punished by disinheritance, exclusion, a tremor of sexual revulsion, even murder ('A Gentle Soul', 'Sarah', 'A Single Lady', 'The Will').

Generally, the superiority of the privileged is taken as part of the natural order. It is a stable, hierarchic society: a celibate caste, family-centred petit-bourgeois class, steep gendered roles, obedient servants, apparently weak political consciousness, only the occasional frisson of sectarian hostility. Lay celibates, living, quite securely, between caste and class, disturb neither. Emigration is a difficult but conceivable escape, but there is little emigration from the general social consensus. Most internalize and reproduce their own oppression, always a great stabilizing deformation that keeps things steadily awry. Yet it is all in a slow free fall.

In Lavin's stories it seems inevitable, given the morbid fascination with the asexual and the sexual, that the figure of the lover, the 'true' lover, in whom these elements are differently conjugated, should so often occupy a central role. This figure is almost infallibly female and she seeks a fate neither vapidly asexual nor grossly materialistic. These alternatives take up almost all the space there is. Love, hypostasized as a condition that is not but should be central, drives these heroines to confront celibacy-chastity-virginity on one side, death on the other, claiming that the first is not as spiritual or eternal as it aspires to be nor the second as material and final as it is feared to be. The dogma of the Assumption of Mary into heaven did not, after all, concede that she actually died; not a death, then, more 'a departure'.[24]

Departure from this life into the world of dedicated chastity is a kind of death too. Mrs Latimer, of the story 'The Nun's Mother', speaks for both parents of a daughter who has chosen to become a nun at the age of eighteen. She and her husband Luke could accept two of the vows their daughter has just taken – of poverty, and obedience.

> But chastity? Ah, that was another thing altogether. About that Luke had nothing to say – not a word. Chastity floored him. To think that a daughter of his – the child of his own delight – should choose to live a celibate life – that was utterly beyond his capacity to understand. (II.52)[25]

The daughter's decision decides her mother's future also. To become a nun's mother alters her sexual relationship to her husband, her social relationship to her circle of acquaintance, even to the policing of any possible sexual behaviour. As their taxi draws up to their comfortable suburban house, Luke sees a man 'standing under a lamp-post ... not properly dressed, you know ... Not a pretty sight' (II.63). He must ring the police. No sexual threat is allowed any more, not in the bedroom, not in the neighbourhood. In fact, anything sexual is now a threat and anything threatening is now sexual. Mr and Mrs Latimer have become respectable – and celibate.

Death is the only rival as a theme to celibacy. The dead outnumber the celibates, who are usually lifelong loyalists to a condition their precociously dead spouses or children have laid on them.[26] Almost 70 per cent of Lavin's stories dwell on death, sudden deaths of the young, on deathbed scenes, funerals, graveyards, wills, the paraphernalia of mourning, and the memory of abandonments which are like deaths for the women involved.

Thus one dominant feature of these stories is a rhetoric of foreverness interwoven with that of the quotidian. The lover, like the young woman Liddy in 'Frail Vessel', is sometimes stylized into a near-idiocy in practical matters, while her sister, Bedelia, is assigned the role of the hopelessly materialistic person who, nevertheless, unconsciously wishes for and also wants to destroy the purity and happiness Liddy spontaneously embodies. Pregnant, abandoned by an embezzler husband, without any means of supporting herself, Liddy is finally forced to throw herself on the tender mercies of the dully secure, pregnant, and married Bedelia who demands to know for just how long she and her husband will have to support the upkeep of the coming 'brat', and shouts into Liddy's face that her husband has gone for good – she has 'seen the last of him'.

Liddy's reply is absolutely inexplicable. 'Even so', Liddy whispered, 'Even so.' (I.19) One can't help feeling for Bedelia.

Still, it's an effective way to end a story. A love thwarted by murder, again involving two sisters locked into a polarized enmity, more shockingly and abruptly provides the opening for 'A Gentle Soul':

> I have just come back from the graveside where the people of these parts performed their last neighbourly duties towards Agatha Darker. She was my sister. Since my father died two years ago, we lived alone in this house, we two, in silence and in bitterness. And there were times when I used to wish this day upon us when she would be lowered into the clay that could be no blacker, nor colder, no more close, no more silent, than her own black heart. (I.40)

The gothic note quickly fades: the bad (Darker!) sister has killed the labourer her timid sister has dared wordlessly, over many years, to love. The threat he posed appeared most obviously in the government-built house he was granted, right opposite the opening to the lane leading to their farmhouse. This was a mark of a big social change.

> Who ... could have thought when this country got its freedom, and they began to build ugly little concrete houses with hideous re-tiled roofs for the labourers and farm workers, that a day would come when they would be fitter for human habitation than our farmhouses that were such a source of pride to us. (I.41)

But this moment of social commentary throws a pale light on the contrast between the sisters. The good one was like her (inevitably) early dead and overborne mother; the bad one like her sullen and recently dead authoritarian father. Social or political history, marked by change, can aid and abet the feelings of love (and also, in this case, of hate), but it does not belong to the ultimate dimension they inhabit. In 'Lilacs', we are reminded that the family fortunes depend upon the dung heap outside;

the father and mother die, the elder sister gets married, and Stacy, the younger, now unmarried and alone, always the sensitive one who most wanted rid of the smell and their reputation for having such a source of income, tells the family solicitor she will finally get rid of the dung heap and plant lilac trees instead. 'But what will you live on, Miss Stacy?', he responds in the final line of the story (III.20). This states the obvious and traditional linkage between gold and shit. The crude contrast between that and the world of the true lovers is so frequently drawn that theirs has to be seen finally (and plausibly) to outface economic realities, political and social change, death itself, if it is to supervene. How can that be done?

It is a severe struggle, once the opposition is posed in these terms. They exclude any serious political hostility towards the class system, inheritance rights, or property, except as they extend male dominance. The figure of the lover, almost neurasthenically opposed to the bourgeois mentality, is a version of the artist. Part of being an artist is, in standard wisdom, to be without politics; this really means she is against society's failures of 'feeling', not of structure. In 'The Becker Wives' (1946), one of her best-known but punishingly long stories, Lavin introduces into the Dublin Becker family, almost concussed in its respectability, material comfort, and philistine dullness, an alien figure, Flora. The brothers of this family all have proper wives, furred, bejewelled, and fertile of children; this has told badly on the shape of their bodies. The 'odd' brother, Theodore, proudly presents an alternative to their buxom vacuity with his version of a trophy wife, Flora, thin and gossamery, vivid and stylish, whose great gift, it turns out, is brilliant mimicry of the other wives, especially of the most recent, Honoria. In the end, she tries so desperately to mimic Honoria's swelling, pregnant shape, that she comes to believe her anorexic self to *be* Honoria. Her eccentric individuality becomes mental breakdown; she cannot conceive that she cannot conceive. Theodore, her insubstantial husband, melts away; Flora is taken away for treatment. The husbands and the wives return to their normality. We as readers are reminded of the difference between actual reproduction and the mimicry of it, a writerly anxiety more than usually inflamed by such a society's anguish about sexual production and abstinence. The border between the material and the imagined world has a queasy element to it. Perhaps the pathological element ascribed to Flora belongs to those who believe in the border itself? Perish the thought. That is the point. Perish any thought in the face of extinction. Only love can engage in that combat.

While it is socially possible to be married and not have children, although not to have children and not be married, Flora's performance and fate show how pregnancy and celibacy are both totemic conditions for women in this tense and often brutal amalgam of sexual convention and religious belief. Yet Lavin's widows are confronted with an even more severe final demand. They face not only the husband's death after a happy marriage, but their own form of death-as-fidelity to that marriage. The widow feels the social, not the legal, weight of expectation to confirm the truth of the relationship by admitting no other. This is how fidelity survives in a phantasmal world. Like Flora in the material Becker world, she has to put on a performance. A widow must perform as a widow. The economic difficulties of the widowed world may be more challenging than those of the married world but so too are the social expectations of the other world of ethereal feeling to which this new celibate, the chaste post-marriage 'virgin', is assigned. It is much more of a problem for the middle-aged, since a young widow, especially one who has a child or children, has a general social warrant to find an appropriate father. But the older woman struggles even to admit in herself the existence of sexual desire, never mind managing the actual satisfaction of it. She does not consent to the communal disapproval that inhibits her, yet is oppressed enough to obey it.

This is painfully evident in *In the Middle of the Fields* (first published in *The New Yorker*, 1961) when Vera Traske, a recent widow, meets the former widower, Bartley Crossen, who has been able to marry again and has had several children by a woman formerly his servant. He has broken social taboos, as a man can; now, on meeting her in the lonesome conditions presented here, he makes an unwanted advance on her. This is far from rape – his clumsy attempt at a kiss fails, and he is immediately ashamed – but Vera's situation is in itself alarming because she recognizes that she, in one way like him, is haunted by a past to the spell and ordinances of which she has as yet neither given nor refused her consent. This condition makes her vulnerable; she finds she has to struggle against becoming a caricature of the widow. In an essay of 1942, Simone Weil wrote:

> Rape is a frightful caricature of love without consent. Next to rape oppression is the second horror of human existence. It is a frightful caricature of obedience. Consent is as essential to obedience as to love.[27]

This is both a plain and a subtle point. In this instance, the blame is quickly reversed by Vera:

> 'Oh, it was nothing,' she said.
> He shook his head. 'It wasn't as if I had cause for what I did.'
> 'But you did nothing,' she protested.
> 'It wasn't nothing to me,' he said dejectedly. (III.70)

What Vera does here is to switch the blame from herself or him to the dead woman to whom Crossen had been married long ago and who had died nearby. It has nothing, Vera cries, to do with any of the living trio, her, himself, his wife at home.

> 'It was the other one you should blame, that girl, your first wife, Bridie! Blame her!' ... 'You thought you could forget her', she cried, 'but see what she did to you when she got the chance.' (III.72)

Vera wants rid of him and, once he is out in the light, she can dismiss him, although it is more of an exorcism than a dismissal. She does it with a degree of derision, although that itself conceals the specious, even nefarious nature of the accusation. For the reader, Vera's insight rebounds on Vera herself. The retrospective power of this finale is drawn from the simplest contrast at its heart, that of a sinister surrounding darkness and of a central, flickering, unreliable light.

From the outset, Vera 'was islanded by fields'. Anxiety and fears 'were the stones across the mouth of the tomb'. She locked herself upstairs in the bedroom overlooking the moving sea of grass, a room which opened off where the children slept, praying 'devoutly' she would not have to come down again to answer the door. 'That was what in particular she dreaded: a knock on the door.' When Crossen belatedly comes to answer her summons to top the grass, she has switched off the light as she brushes her hair to see again the 'blue star' of static electricity appear in the darkness of the mirror as it did when she was a child, before electricity had been generally available. And as the star of the earlier time appears, the thunderous knock of the present on the door is heard. She goes down in her night attire, her hair pinned up, but it falls down again round her shoulders when Crossen is in the hallway; she is both bride and widow now. A faulty light keeps them in half-darkness for a time. This is an old damsel-in-distress tale, a rescue and a seduction, it takes place in the rich grasslands of County Meath and in a dimension of time infiltrated by sudden death. It is first the story of a revenant; second, in the climactic sleight of hand, really of two revenants – Crossen's former wife, Vera's former husband, the ghosts inhabiting these two people, he as her former husband, she as his former wife. Other stories, such as 'In A Café' (1960), 'The Cuckoo Spit' (1964), 'Happiness' (1972), interchange these elements too, seeking an integration of death and love that will yet allow the widow her autonomy as a person, haunted by the past and yet refusing to be defined by it. In that interval state, she remains celibate.

That's the widow story. The widower story is another matter, showing how fidelity to the dead wife can easily go along with emotional brutality to the living daughter through a sexual tension generated in and by the idea of fidelity. In 'One Summer' (1965), as her father dies, fearing the nullity of extinction, he is almost consoled by his daughter Vera, whose own love relationship he had helped destroy, the better to keep her enslaved to himself:

> 'Of course there is a hereafter,' she cried. 'Otherwise what would be the meaning of love?'
> Weak tears came into his eyes. 'Do you really believe that, Vera?' he said.
> Partly lying and, like himself, partly wanting to believe it, she nodded.

Then, having in her eyes almost betrayed his former wife and, doubly, Vera herself in responding so warmly to the nurse sent to help him in his last illness, he redeems himself and the 'pure' status of the widowed when, as his dying wish, he asks just to see 'her' again; when Vera asks who is this 'her', fearing the answer could be 'Rita', the nurse,

> 'Your mother,' he said, and looked surprised, 'Who else?' (III.155)

That's love and the pursuit of happiness; always pretending that the way out is the way back to the beloved. It's the celibate society's version of utopia, a theology of a carnal love that lasts forever through a celibacy that is maximized, in face of death, as virginity, the physical-material world vaporizing into the spiritual. Lavin's work, in presenting this, is 'partly lying ... and partly wanting to believe it', two stories in one.

NOTES

1. George Moore's pioneering collection of (three) short stories, *Celibates,* was published in 1895.
2. See Diarmaid Ferriter, *Occasions of Sin: Sex and Society in Modern Ireland* (London: Profile, 2010).
3. The most searching account of the linkages between control of sexuality, Irish Catholicism, and liberal capitalism is Michael G. Cronin, *Impure Thoughts: Sexuality, Catholicism and Literature in Twentieth-Century Ireland* (Manchester University Press, 2012). See especially Chapter 2, 'Growing Pains: Sexuality, Irish Moral Politics and Capitalist Crisis, 1920–40' (48–81); see also Michael G. Cronin, 'What We Talk About When We Talk About Sex: Modernization and Sexuality in Contemporary Irish Scholarship', *boundary 2*, 45/1 (2018), 231–52.
4. Mary E. Daly, *The Slow Failure: Population Decline and Independent Ireland* (Madison: University of Wisconsin Press, 2007).
5. See A. A. Kelly, *Mary Lavin: Quiet Rebel: A Study of her Short Stories* (Dublin: Wolfhound Press, 1980); Heather Ingman, 'The Short Story in Ireland since 1945: A Modernizing Tradition', in Dominic Head (ed.), *The Cambridge History of the English Short Story* (Cambridge University Press, 2016), 185–201; Anne Fogarty, 'Discontinuities: Tales from Bective Bridge and the Modernist Short Story', in Elke D'hoker (ed.), *Mary Lavin* (Dublin: Irish Academic Press, 2013), 30–48.
6. See Máirín Ní Dhonnchadha, 'Mary, Eve and the Church (c.600–1800)', in Angela Bourke et al. (eds.), *The Field Day Anthology of Irish Writing,* vol. IV: *Irish Women's Writing and Traditions* (Cork University Press, 2002), 45–250; Mary Clayton, *The Cult of the Virgin Mary In Anglo-Saxon England* (Cambridge University Press, 1990).
7. See Elaine Pagels, *Adam, Eve and the Serpent* (London: Weidenfeld, 1988); Peter Brown, *Men, Women and Sexual Renunciation in Early Christianity* (London: Faber and Faber, 1988).
8. Father de Montfort (1673–1706) was beatified by Pope Leo XIII in 1888 and canonized by Pius XII in 1947. See Owen Chadwick, *A History of the Popes, 1830–1914* (Oxford University Press, 1998).
9. See my *Strange Country: Modernity and Nationhood in Ireland since 1790* (Oxford: Clarendon Press, 1997), 117–22.

10. See Owen Davies, *A Supernatural War: Magic, Divination and Faith during the First World War* (Oxford University Press, 2018).
11. See Kalyn R. Baldridge, '"L'Auguste Autrichienne": Representations of Marie-Antoinette in Nineteenth-Century French Literature and History', unpublished PhD thesis, University of Missouri-Columbia (2016); Susan Dunn, *The Deaths of Louis XVI: Regicide and the French Political Imagination* (Princeton University Press, 1994).
12. See Régis Debray, 'Salve Regina', in *God: An Itinerary*, trans. Jeffrey Mehlman (London: Verso, 2004), 157–82.
13. See Emer Nolan, *Catholic Emancipations: Irish Fiction from Thomas Moore to James Joyce* (Syracuse University Press, 2007), 128–9. This is the only sustained study of Irish fiction in relation to Catholicism, notions of modernity, and of the national. Also groundbreaking in this regard for the nineteenth century is Terry Eagleton, *Heathcliff and the Great Hunger: Studies in Irish Culture* (London: Verso, 1995).
14. John Henry Newman (now canonized) in his sojourn as Rector of the new Catholic University of Dublin (1854–8), and the Comte de Montalembert, as political leader of French Catholicism, promoted both the role of the Marian devotion and of these countries in the global Catholic revival in the modern era. Yet even these were too 'liberal' for the Vatican. See my 'Newman: Converting the Empire', in *Foreign Affections: Essays on Edmund Burke* (Cork University Press, 2005), 147–670; and 'A Church Destroyed, the Church Restored: France's Irish Catholicism', *Field Day Review*, 7 (2011), 203–50; Thomas Docherty, 'Newman, Ireland and Universality', *boundary 2*, 31/1 (Spring 2004), 73–92.
15. Cited in *Legion of Mary Handbook*, rev. edn (Dublin: Concilium Legionis Mariae, 1993), Appendix I. See also Kieran A. Kennedy, '75 Years of the Legion of Mary', *Studies: An Irish Quarterly Review*, 86/343 (Autumn 1997), 268–75. Kennedy describes Duff, the first official Civil Service boss of the new state, as 'a great spiritual entrepreneur' who had contributed to building 'Ireland's greatest multi-national' (275).
16. Fredric Jameson, *Postmodernism and the Cultural Logic of Late Capitalism* (Durham, NC: Duke University Press, 1991), 362.
17. See John Willett, 'Art and Revolution', *New Left Review*, 112 (July–August 2018), 61–87.
18. See Gráinne Hurley, '"Trying to Get the Words Right": Mary Lavin and *The New Yorker*', in D'hoker (ed.), *Mary Lavin*, 81–99.
19. See also Tom Inglis, *Moral Monopoly: The Rise and Fall of the Catholic Church in Modern Ireland* (University College Dublin Press, 1998); Louise Fuller, *Irish Catholicism since 1950* (Dublin: Gill & Macmillan, 2002); Timothy J. White, 'The Impact of British Colonialism on Irish Catholicism and National Identity: Repression, Reemergence, and Divergence', *Études irlandaises*, 35/1 (2010), 21–37; Eamon Maher, 'Representations of Catholicism in the Twentieth-Century Irish Novel', in L. Fuller, J. Littleton, and E. Maher (eds.), *Irish and Catholic? Towards an Understanding of Identity* (Dublin: Columba Press, 2006); Oliver P. Rafferty (ed.), *Irish Catholic Identities* (Manchester University Press, 2013).

20. James Joyce was a leading member of the Sodality of the Blessed Virgin Mary when he was a student at University College, Dublin. In *Ulysses* the distinction between Spirit and Body is parodied and given a structural function via the contrast between the Trinity and the Holy Family, homosexuality (Greek) and heterosexuality (Roman), especially in episode 9, 'Scylla and Charybdis'. See my 'Joyce the Irishman', in Derek Attridge (ed.), *The Cambridge Companion to James Joyce* (Cambridge University Press, 1990), 31–54 (at 48). He has Molly Bloom sharing the birth date of the Virgin, 8 September. The prevalence of the cult within Ireland until the 1980s, and specifically within the Catholic minority in Northern Ireland during the Troubles, is unforgettably represented in Anna Burns's novel *Milkman* (London: Faber and Faber, 2018). The culminating transformations of Ireland's political and social culture are analysed in Emer Nolan, *Five Irish Women: The Second Republic, 1960–2018* (Manchester University Press, 2019).
21. This was not an ideal peculiar either to Catholicism or to Ireland. See again Cronin, *Impure Thoughts*, 1–21.
22. See Terence Brown, *Ireland: A Social and Cultural History 1922–79* (London: Fontana, 1981), esp. 155–61; Clair Wills, *That Neutral Island: A Cultural History of Ireland during the Second World War* (London: Faber and Faber, 2007), and 'The Aesthetics of Irish Neutrality during the Second World War', *boundary 2*, 31/1 (2004), 119–45; Anna Teekell, *Emergency Writing: Irish Literature, Neutrality and the Second World War* (Evanston, IL: Northwestern University Press, 2018).
23. Patrick Joyce, 'The Journey West', *Field Day Review*, 10 (2014), 61–92 (at 81). The life of the Irish itinerant labourer in Britain, part of the subject of Joyce's essay, had also within it the social world of the Ireland that had been left behind. See the novel by Timothy O'Grady (with photographs by Stephen Pyke), *I Could Touch the Sky* (London: Harvill Press, 1997), in which the journey described is from the west of Ireland to England.
24. See the remarks of Pope John Paul II, 25 June 1997, in a General Audience: 'In this regard, St Francis de Sales maintains that Mary's death was due to a transport of love. He speaks of a dying "in love, from love and through love", and of the Mother of God as having "died of love for her Son Jesus."'
25. *The Stories of Mary Lavin*, 3 vols. (London: Constable, 1964–85). Quotations are followed by a roman numeral for the volume and arabic number for the page.
26. See Ferriter, *Occasions of Sin*, 103, for the astonishing rates of celibacy in Ireland between the 1920s and 1950s.
27. Simone Weil, 'Are We Struggling for Justice?', trans. Marina Barabas, *Philosophical Investigations*, 53 (January 1987), 1–10 (at 3).

CHAPTER 13

Emergency Aesthetics

FLANN O'BRIEN WAS RIGHT. JAMES JOYCE WAS INVENTED BY Americans.[1]

He was part of their foreign policy, of the drive to make the USA a cultural presence and to recruit 'high' culture to its mission of world-domination. *Ulysses* became a seminal work because it showed how a broken European culture could be absorbed into 'modernity'. The reception of Joyce was a politically loaded issue in the Cold War; because of that Joycean studies became an industry, producing a cultural weaponry that remains effective, the Hiberno-Grecian gift that keeps on giving. Classical and Christian echoes sounded throughout the local Irish setting; American academics alerted us to them, annotated them for us. In addition, *Ulysses* implied the possibility of a structure in history; this was later replaced in the *Wake* by a history of structures. These turned out to be really one structure, of which Irish history was exemplary, the small world that was a microcosm of all. Ireland, its literature and its troubles, became part of a new global imaginary.

Yet, however Joyce was 'Americanized' or 'cosmopolitanized', something that had been a visible element in Irish fiction and political commentary, even in Joyce's lifetime, struggled to survive his remorseless achievement. That element was the future, a horizon for transformation or renewal which the cyclic pattern of recurrence, the *semper eadem*, the one story, disavowed. It was a brilliant disavowal; sameness was never so exhaustively catalogued. As in Ireland itself in the period between 1922 and 1939, history entered into a long paralysis – like that which we met in the first story of *Dubliners*, but deeper – as the Irish project for national freedom and the British project to resist it petrified into the two states (really one state, and a non-state) solution. The Free State and Northern Ireland were in bitter stalemate; the Union was a glacier that had only partly melted. The Catholic minority in the North was locked into the sectarian fortress of unionism. In both polities in the island, set to survive and outlast the other, the language of transformational change was confined to the religious arena because it was so effectively obliterated from the political; in the religious arena it was transmogrified into authoritarian abuse and evangelical hatred. In the aftermath of the Second War, the iterative patterns of the *Wake* seemed prophetic, especially in Ireland. It foretold the future; there would not be any, only the same, over and over. In the then prevailing exegetical light in which the book was read, the past was here to stay.

Few countries had known a 'state of emergency' more regularly than Ireland, especially in the period 1801–1922 when all of it was part of the United Kingdom. In Northern Ireland, in its first mutant phase (1922–72), emergency was indeed the rule, not the exception. Yet even in the melancholy catalogue of state violence in Ireland that unrolls under the various headings of Special Courts, Proscription, Emergency Legislation, Martial Law, Curfew, Coercion, Censorship, Insurrection Acts, Internment without Trial, and so on, Northern Ireland's Special Powers Act stands out in infamy. Its final clause merits a special mention. It decreed that anything not covered by the preceding (draconian) clauses was covered by it. On two hundred occasions, that clause was used by the unionist government and judiciary; by this squalid extension of the dread legal term 'special', a whole population was potentially in detention.[2]

In the light of the fourteen murders of Bloody Sunday in 1972 and the Hunger Strikes of 1980–1 in Northern Ireland, and the concerted propaganda campaigns against republicanism and for the 'state of exception' that has been used to legalize the crimes of the state, it is salutary to remember that in the UK in the nineteenth as in the twentieth century, it was habitually held to be crucial to suspend the law in order to sustain it. The special legislation could (had to) admit its abnormal status but those victimized by it could not be allowed special status. That would be to admit to the existence of political prisoners, which British governments from the nineteenth to the twentieth centuries refused to do, despite its varying brutal treatment of and Commissions on various groups in different decades – Chartists, Fenians, Suffragettes, Irish Republicans – and the amnesty campaigns that sometimes accompanied them.[3]

*

John Mitchel (1815–75) was the first victim of the Treason Felony Act of 1848: indeed he and his Young Ireland friends were its intended targets. The last people charged under it (so far), in January 1973, were Joseph Callinan, Louis Marcantonio, and Thomas Quinn, three Irish emigrants in London, who were accused of 'conspiring to fight against Her Majesty's forces' because they had called for resistance against the British soldiers who had carried out the mass murder in Derry a year earlier. Held in custody for almost a year, they were then deported. The Act is a lengthy piece of legislation that still stands, despite an effort by the *Guardian* newspaper in 2001 to have Section Three, which makes it a felony to advocate republican views, repealed. Between them, the courts and the House of Lords decided not to repeal the Act, although it was erroneously reported at first that they had in fact repealed Section Three. After much red-top tabloid screeching about the danger this posed to the Queen, it was affirmed that the legislation stood. It had been used, inevitably, in Ireland more than a dozen times before 1900 and, with equal inevitability, was used in Northern Ireland into the 1950s. As late as 2016, an English county councillor campaigned to have the act of supporting European Union membership declared a felony under an amendment to the Treason Felony Act.

Mitchel's *Jail Journal* (1854) was the first literary-political work that offered his countrymen a devastating account of the specific blend of imperial domination and liberal, if very limited, parliamentary democracy that had been developed within the constitutional monarchy of the UK. (There were predecessors, such as Thomas Moore's *Captain Rock*, 1824, but it was Mitchel who first identified the link between liberalism and imperialism.[4]) The UK ratified the European Convention on Human Rights in March 1951; it came into full effect in 1953. The Human Rights Act of 1998 incorporated the European Convention on Human Rights into domestic UK law where it came into force in October 2000. That legislation should have made prosecution under the Treason Felony Act impossible, but no challenge or plea for derogation from the ECHR was made. Anyway, the Northern Ireland (Emergency Provisions) Act of 1973 was already in place so that the state of emergency or exemption created by the Special Powers Act continued without a pause for breath.

In the first chapter of *Jail Journal*, Mitchel tells how, after he was sentenced to fourteen years' transportation, in May 1848, the jailer came into his cell in Newgate Prison in Dublin, carrying a suit of 'coarse gray clothes' in his hand and said he was to put them on 'directly'. He did. Then someone shouted from the foot of the stairs, 'Let him be removed in his own clothes.' He was ordered to change again and did so. Two days later, in Spike Island prison, Cork, waiting to board ship, the governor of the jail came into the cell, asked him to put on 'a suit of brown convict clothes' so that the governor of Smithfield prison in Dublin could report that Mitchel had been seen in convict clothes. Later he was told by the Cork governor that, on direction from Dublin Castle, he could wear his own clothes. 'Either I am or am not a felon', writes Mitchel. So began this long dispute over the clothes of the prisoner, his status as a criminal or political prisoner, and the attendant condition of Ireland as country, naked, without laws, or with only the appearance of them – which itself could be at any time cancelled.[5]

The initial indecision about what clothes Mitchel should wear during his transportation to Van Diemen's Land arose from the novelty of his status. Was he indeed a felon? Although clearly a political prisoner, for whom a parliamentary act had been framed and a jury notoriously packed, could this be officially acknowledged? Was it a felony to be a republican? The answer was yes, according to the letter of the law, but according to its application it could be a felony only to be an *Irish* republican in the United Kingdom. That law of 1848 still stands. Mitchel, like James Joyce and his work, has an American sequel, to which we can return later.

*

The richness of Irish gothic in the novel, short story, and drama is not surprising, given the long colonial history of invasion, dispossession, and crime. Unappeased ghosts, treacherous informers, vampires, prisons, scaffolds and barracks, decayed landowners and haunted houses, spells and curses, murder and revenge, are all familiar ingredients in those fictions in which ruin consistently returns to blight hopes of improvement or even of renovation.

But there are exceptions. One is Ernie O'Malley's memoir *On Another Man's Wound* (1936), 'an attempt', in his own words, 'to show the background of the Irish struggle from 1916 to 1921 between an Empire and an unarmed people'.[6] The dominant motif of the book, as in the opening section of Mitchel's *Jail Journal*, and of the various campaigns against political imprisonment policies, is clothing – hats, shirts, trousers, shoes, leggings, the insignia on collars and sleeves. The mixture of these has two combinations – that of the official uniform and that of the informal guerrilla outfit. Special Constables recruited into the Royal Irish Constabulary wore a hastily assembled police/army two-toned uniform, that gave them their name 'the Black-and-Tans' and revealed their dual role as official army and paramilitary terror group. Once, on board a train, O'Malley and some colleagues, travelling in plain sight in their own clothes, but under orders, encountered a group of Royal Irish Constabulary (RIC), frontline enemies of the IRA:

> They had a black swarthy complexion, the only colour there was came from a patch of claret cloth backing their cap badge, the crown above the harp, and the salted-butter yellow on the sergeants' V's. Their uniforms were blue-black with a touch of green ... The colour darkened their appearance.

O'Malley regularly uses the effect of a massed dark background in which bright dabs of colour – yellow, blue-black, claret, green – show against it; his descriptions of landscape have a similar overall effect in which, say, the blue strike of a kingfisher above a river, is like a gun-flash. Gradually we see in this painterly technique a stylistic analogy for the mobility and colour of the guerrilla against the dark massed background of the established system. The attitude of his own family and class towards the rather dilapidated uniforms of the Irish Volunteers is, like his own initial view, surly and prejudiced. The Volunteers can't march properly, their outfits are mix 'n match; at the scene of Pearse's speech over the grave of O'Donovan Rossa, he remains a hostile observer:

> Out of curiosity I passed by the glass coffin lid, objecting to the green-uniformed Fianna Boys who guided the long files ... I watched the funeral

> pass to Glasnevin cemetery, company after company of Irish Volunteers . . . some in uniform, some wearing uniform hats and bandoliers, others green ties only. I saw the ungainly side of the parade; irregular marching, faulty execution of the commands, strange slouch hats turned up at one side, uniform caps wobbling, long single-shot Howth Mauser rifles. They provided an amusing topic of conversation at dinner.[7]

This account is redolent of the world where, in Yeats's phrase from 'Easter 1916', 'motley is worn', the clothes of the harlequin or of the miscellaneous crowd. But in this case, the 'motley' clothes eventually become a military uniform, an achievement in organization. In the account of an ambush in 1920 a mix of colours, a chorus of birdsong, fleeting shadows in sunlight, transpose into hissing bullets, a flash of blood; or the act of cataloguing the names of different guns in an arms dump can alter a miscellaneous collection into an organized arsenal. These sheaves of particulars come to be owned collectively. The perceptual experiences become a conceptual shape, the effect of the book's republican, collective dynamic.

O'Malley echoes James Fintan Lalor (1807–49) and the Famine generation of writers in his recognition that an armed campaign against occupation had to confront, among many problems, the habituated condition of servility, hammered into the people by a long and cruel conquest. The sole source of their endurance lies in their relationship to the land, or more exactly, to the soil, since the land has become so denuded. That is the only material bond left of the complex culture that once existed. Out of that now rises the question – could a new consciousness be born? Lalor had the desolating evidence of the Famine, in which there was no resistance; O'Malley had 1916–21 as his contrasting example. A countering consciousness, a solid resistance, could emerge from this soil-land intimacy:

> There was a strange passionate love of the land amongst the people. Material possessions were low or gone, the arts were a broken tradition, the idea of beauty had gone into the soil and the physical body. Their eyes had long dwelt on the form, color and structure of the landscape . . . An old soil well loved had given much to them and they had put much into it. They clung to this last treasure and solace with imagination and with physical senses.[8]

Finally, the young man who left home with a stack of pressed shirts and linen comes into his inheritance in clothes that come from every part of the country:

> My clothes were now a composite collection from many counties. I had my coat from Donegal, my waistcoat from Dublin ... my shirts and socks generally belonged to the county I happened to be in at the time.[9]

But when he is wounded, or beaten remorselessly by the Auxiliaries in prison, when his blood or that of other victims stains the clothes he wears or when we hear that he was unrecognizable after the beating or of the savagery with which his friends were assaulted and killed in Dublin Castle, the subtle interplay between appearance, status, body, and spirit becomes an allegory of the mutual relationship between fleeting perception, glimpsed freedom, and a steely resolve to endure throughout all the threats and changes he undergoes. Bodily integrity and moral confidence are functions of one another. But clothing, the uniform and, eventually, nakedness become widely acknowledged as the mark of political identity and of the refusal to have it either withdrawn or granted. With that, inescapably, the physical body becomes the site of a brutal contest. The sovereign power and the naked body are embraced in a struggle neither can afford entirely to lose or to win. This is both a familiar image from the past and a proleptic image of what was to come in the Blanket Protest and the Dirty Protest, the precursors to the Hunger Strikes.

Mitchel and O'Malley, two of the more striking figures in nineteenth- and twentieth-century Irish republican writing, spent part of their later careers in the United States, each eventually returning to Ireland. Mitchel escaped Van Diemen's Land in 1853, settling in the United States where he edited the works of fellow Young Ireland associates, Thomas Davis and James Clarence Mangan. Infamously, there he also became an ardent defender of American slavery, arguing that the institution was a national institution of the United States (in some ways it was) and less detrimental to the welfare of the slaves than British imperialism and international capitalism were to Irish tenants or workers generally. Mitchel's passionately rational hatred of capitalism, anticipating in vehemence if not tenor that of

W. B. Yeats on 'the greasy till' and the burgher mentality, later to take its own dark directions, led him to a violent irrationality about race that still thrives globally amid latter-day slaveries. O'Malley would traffic in no such lunacies, but his visits to Taos, New Mexico, where he spent time with Mable Dodge Luhan's 'literary colony', and began work on *On Another Man's Wound*, and his stay in Mexico City, must have reminded him of how closely braided the histories of republicanisms and imperialisms, colonizations and extirpations, could be well beyond Ireland.

*

Since Swift and Burke in the eighteenth century, from *A Modest Proposal* (1729) to *Letters on A Regicide Peace* (1796), the collisions between state power and rebellion had been dominated by the imagery of an elaborately dressed British power and a contrastingly denuded Irish weakness. Such imageries have persisted into the present day, often so coherently and strenuously developed by powerful writers in their attempts to represent brutal realities that they seem overset, like the conspiracies of the paranoid in which nothing is believed to have been accidental. 'Nothing in the Revolution', Burke wrote, 'no, not a phrase or a gesture, not to the fashion of a hat or shoe, was left to accident.'[10] In Burke's view, like the Penal Laws in Ireland, the French Revolution aimed for the complete replacement (and debasement) of what once had been. Both, in his view, had been successful.

The most comprehensive contemporary attempt in Irish fiction to represent a society that is almost entirely in a state of emergency, is Anna Burns's novel *Milkman* (2018). There are two milkmen in *Milkman*, one bad, one good. The good one is the milkman, the bad one's actual name is Milkman. The good one emerges as a second virtual father to the protagonist and a second virtual husband to her mother. The occupying army eventually kills the bad one, having killed four others in error before that and also having shot and wounded the fatherly milkman in its penultimate display of lethal incompetence. A lot of people are shot dead, blown up, murdered, injured, wounded or, like the protagonist herself, poisoned; whole families are shattered. This happens in an enclave of a city not named either as Ardoyne or as

Belfast, a Catholic area although not formally identified as such, in the 1970s, when the Troubles were at their worst.

We are told all this in the narrator's voice, in a headlong, partly literary, partially demotic televisual voice-over style that seems to be a self-consciously adopted defence against the traumatic, surreal circumstances and events of a condition and a place for which the appropriate emblem is 'The Butcher's Apron', the community's name (in Belfast and elsewhere) for the hated Union Jack. This first-person voice is the register for all voices; everybody speaks in it, or is reported as having spoken in it, almost all improbably and polysyllabically articulate. They are both loquacious and eloquent, deploying the trusted ironic Irish device of counterpointing such speech with the actualities of their materially and culturally impoverished lives. The collision between archaic syntax and vocabulary, both beautifully controlled, and the conditions of cheap consumer surfeit capitalism and neocolonial civil war produces a series of grotesque detonations.

Even though it is narrated in the first person, the novel reads more like a case history than a personal tragedy. It has the faux-objectivity of sociology; but then, its elements of parody are so pervasive that it is ultimately hard to say whether these work to deflect or intensify the horrors of the account. There is a spectacular contrast between the concussed condition that prevails in this community and the consciousness of the protagonist. Yet while told in the past or pluperfect tense, it gives only a faint sense of any final release from its chosen place, period, or condition. 'In those early days, those darker of the dark days' (22) is the time of the action. The conventions that rule are those of war, colonial oppression, civil war, sectarian hatred, misogyny, intramural coercions, an asphyxiating conformity. This is Northern Ireland. The grotesque is the norm.

Middle sister, the narrator, is unique in that she reads books, does it while walking, books from the eighteenth or nineteenth centuries, since she does not like the twentieth. She is under continuous sinister sexual threat from the Milkman as her relationship with maybe-boyfriend slowly dissolves. Social change is undermining this gruesome world. Middle sister takes French classes with a 'mixed' group, she watches feminist groups form, feels coagulated beliefs and attitudes slowly beginning to melt. Political loyalties are embedded and their obverse – informing, betrayal – all risk death. Depression and psychic disturbance are widespread; sexual behaviour and identities are slowly uncoiling from the lairs in which they have for long been hidden or entrapped. All the food is junk food, fast food, the older ritual of meals abandoned. Children are forsaken; their parents, in the most spectacular instance, migrate to television. Running or jogging is the only healthy alternative offered to the endless smoking and drinking. Everybody has names that are generic – 'maybe-boyfriend, third sister, third brother-in-law', or they are renouncers or occupation forces or they live near or far from 'the red-light district' or 'the ten-minute area', the dead centre of all.

Burns's is perhaps a new form of gothic – Community Gothic – where the neighbourhood dogs are slaughtered en masse by the occupying forces, where a cat's head, the remnant of an afterminded explosion from a Luftwaffe bomb in 'the ten-minute' area, becomes the grisly connection between the protagonist and the good milkman. The general maltreatment of animals, cats and dogs, indicates the debasement of humans of themselves, of their own co-dependence (mirrored by the loyalty of the dog) and of their own autonomy (mirrored by the cat's self-sufficiency). The linkage between human and animal life is almost destroyed in this district. The very idea of a shared or ambiguous nature arouses hostility. Has the hyphen, which also operates as a minus sign, ever been worked so hard, ever before had an emotional range from the sinister to the welcoming? Only a single narrative voice, operating almost like an electronic recording device, could so fluently and impersonally achieve such en bloc concentration of everyday horror that the distinction between actuality and nightmare almost disappears.

Yet there is always a comic undertow, so extravagant is the violence, so absurd are the stylized exchanges between people and the almost deadpan commentary that surrounds them. The first name that we meet is 'Somebody McSomebody', the last phrase we read is 'I almost, nearly laughed'. Once the bad man called Milkman, the coercive male stalker and ultimately a species of succubus who has begun to absorb our protagonist into his realm, his 'subsoil' (343), is killed by 'that murder squad spawned by a terrorist state' (341), she finally can jog in freedom with third brother-in-law, who embodies a peculiarly outmoded yet genuine respect for women – but is that not 'almost nearly' the sinister-coercive other side of the coin? Are all those women who arrive at the hospital to see the real milkman part of 'a potential supergrass demographic' (319); is that phrase free of ridicule or full of it? Most of them have been subject to the form of spiritual and physical rape that is the paradigm for all the violence. If this is liberation from a warped world, the cost seems unbearably high. But it may be that we are hearing only a mocking version of the mind-set of the occupying forces. It is hard at times to keep one's footing on such glossy ground, with patches of black ice everywhere. We wonder if we are witnessing an overcoming of a gothic politics or only a near-release from it? *Milkman* has us in a vicious spin-cycle of recurrence, the same over and over again, with just a gleek, a glimpse of the moment it all ended or began to end. Does anyone ever really get out of jail or are we all caught 'in a slip of the time between a date and a ghostmark'?[11] Martin McDonagh's Leenane trilogy of plays (*The Beauty Queen of Leenane*, 1996; *A Skull in Connemara*, 1997; *The Lonesome West*, 1997) has a similar ensemble of violent and comic elements, as does Patrick McCabe's *Butcher Boy* (1992), itself indebted to Flann O'Brien's *The Third Policeman* (1967), the originating work of the whole genre (although it was written in 1939–40). This fusion of comedy with violence, found in cartoons, comic cuts, graphic novels, and computer games, is effective in both naturalizing violence, making it a glamorous commodity, and in showing how deeply violence saturates the social and political worlds of consumerism.

Part of the indecision generated by *Milkman* has to do with its mode of address. There are moments – some of the most appalling – when it passes from *roman noir* to cartoon, often just at the point where a connection is being made between local and global violence. Somebody McSomebody's 'calm and loving' sixteen-year-old brother is crossing the road one day to console his panicking fifteen-year-old brother, nuclear boy, who has a fixation about the America–Russia nuclear race, when his head is blown off by a bomb. Nuclear boy, mid the general panic, does not notice, remains locked within his obsession (62); later he commits suicide and leaves a note: 'Pills, drink, a plastic bag over his head and leaving a note which astounded everybody: "*It is because of Russia and because of America that I am doing this*"' (133). Is there an echo here of the character in Bergman's film *Winter Light* (1963), who is obsessed, in the isolation of his Arctic village, by the threat of the Yellow Peril, or of Francie Brady's preoccupation with the Cuban Missile Crisis in McCabe's *Butcher Boy* (1992)? Then later, at the pivotal, grotesque moment when redemption is beginning, middle sister and the good milkman are together in his lorry, the dead cat's head between them, and he tells her of the death that day of McSomebody's three-year-old brother. Imagining he was Superman or Batman, this child had thrown himself out of an upstairs back-bedroom window. But then maybe that was invented, because, the milkman continues:

> You couldn't just die here, couldn't have an ordinary death here, not anymore, not by natural causes, not by accident such as falling out a window, especially not after all the other violent deaths taking place in the district now. It had to be political, he said. Had to be about the border, meaning incomprehensible. Failing that, it had to be out-of-the-ordinary, dramatic, something startling, such as thinking oneself a super-hero and accidentally jumping to one's death. (146)

This is the inverse of politicizing everything. Middle sister's father, for instance, had been, according to her ma, not just depressed but depressing because he 'stole the right to suffer that belonged to somebody else' (86). He refused, when he was sixteen, to go to the bomb shelters during the Second World War blitz, that is during

> the big war, the world one, the one – ask any teenager – with nothing to do with up-to-date humanity and modern-society living; the one no-one my age could attend to which wasn't surprising since most of us could hardly attend to the current, more local one, we were in. (86)

Middle sister's father was insistent that there was no point to anything, as natural and man-made disasters (such as the Holocaust) proved. Everything, according to this community wisdom, has to be incomprehensible or exotically dramatic. The political is always incomprehensible and all-consuming; that infects all else and renders everyday life legible only as melodramatic extravagance, as something that belongs properly to a cartoon (in which a head can be blown off, a figure can fall from a window, to comic effect), or to a fantasy life, like McSomebody's vision of himself as a James Bond figure. Yet it is all actual; fantasy and actuality cross-pollinate, like the world of television, of the Debordian image, and of those who binge on it.

This is a dystopia, a 'district' in a time warp. Perhaps the only exit is provided by the locals who became television stars, the parents of maybe-boyfriend, who abandoned their children and became a dazzling dance-pair inspiring the little girls, 'the whole district of them' (341), to perform in the streets or, if dancing is too much, to jog. (Again, the echo here is from a play, in this case the climactic dance of the sisters in Brian Friel's *Dancing at Lughnasa* of 1990.) Dystopia is not too bad; it's a consumer choice as well as a political fate. Middle sister, her black eye still obvious, jogs with third brother-in-law towards the 'parks & reservoirs' (348), the ampersand perhaps indicative of normality at last, something usual, familiar, eased away from the clicking of the spy cameras of the ubiquitous army and the eyes of the forever-watchful district. In the case of McSomebody – the man who tried to step into the place of Milkman and who beat up middle sister, before being beaten up by the district's women, who are now the dominant force in this changed post-Milkman world – it is as well to get the facts right, separate the myth of violence from the facts of it. Brother-in-law gives his view:

> 'And what of principles? You're a woman. He's a man. You're a female. He's a male. You're my sister-in-law and I don't care how many of his family got murdered, he's a bastard even if they hadn't got murdered.' They hadn't got murdered. Only four had got murdered. The other two had been a suicide and an accidental death. (346)

Stick to the facts. In their light, a pulverized world can be represented and can perhaps be put together again. The occupying forces with their endless espionage, Milkman with his sanctioned coercion and rape of middle sister's autonomy, are suddenly gone. Is some version of a dawn beginning to break? If so, is it because the occupying forces finally killed the right Milkman? That would be a false dawn surely, for it would indicate a 'release' into their ruthless grasp. Yet, in a sense, it does not matter. The ethical/political issue is junior to the representational achievement. The aesthetic success outweighs all else. This is postmodernity, after all. Wear your jogging outfit in an emergency. The park becomes a gym, fitness is a condition of moral as well as physical health, better than the other obsessions – drink, sex, politics.

*

Sandra Smith, the translator of Irène Némirovsky's much-praised novel, *Suite française* (2006), says she left in a misquotation from Keats as it was; instead of 'A thing of beauty is a joy for ever', we have 'This thing of Beauty is a guilt for ever.'[12] Perhaps the misquotation is more appropriate now than it originally was, especially when we know of the author's murder at Auschwitz in 1942, and associate it in this novel with a character who is a selfish connoisseur and aesthete, fastened to his addiction in the midst of a general catastrophe, the fall of France. There has long been, perhaps since Baudelaire, an almost feral suspicion of the function of beauty in a work of art. Does it make atrocity or evil palatable, simply by the act of representation? This almost became an orthodoxy when Adorno famously declared that 'to write poetry after Auschwitz is barbaric'.[13]

The writers of the Irish Revival followed a long tradition in counterpointing self-conscious forms of colourful eloquence against materially harsh conditions, going so far as to suggest that there might be a causal, complex relation between the two – an action implied again in Burns's *Milkman.*[14] Nineteenth-century Irish novelists, such as the Banims, Gerald Griffin, and particularly William Carleton, stated time and again that conditions in Ireland were so unimaginably coercive and degrading that they could not be represented (to an English audience) in conventional language or forms. The radical experimentations of Joyce and Beckett memorably addressed the issue of representation that had so exercised some of their predecessors by making English ever stranger to itself. But no matter how many Houdini-acts Irish writing attempted in order to escape the double bind of representing the unrepresentable, the uneasy sense of asymmetry between actual conditions, especially when they involved violence, and their representation in art did not dissolve. *Waiting for Godot* (1953) shows this up more harshly than any later 'natural' Irish mimetic novel or play written in the English nineteenth-century manner and, as Adorno anticipated, atrocity lent itself more readily to aesthetic contemplation than to any serious attempt to politically overcome the conditions that spawned it. The suspicion that eloquence in literature and violence in politics produced a healing aesthetic was roused yet again in the north of Ireland in the 1970s, with another literary revival. The reception of Seamus Heaney's *North* (1975) was a key instance of this inflamed consciousness that atrocity could be and, in this case, had been aestheticized into a glamorizing ritual.[15] Structurally, the same anxiety or suspicion attends all rhetoric, whether it is (as, say, in Synge) parading its sumptuous qualities – even as a claim to authenticity – or, equally, (as, say, in Beckett or Brecht) parading its minimalist or stripped-down qualities.

This queasiness about the massaging effect of style and stylization is not confined to ethical and aesthetic discourse. Certainly in Ireland it is integral to any consideration of the linkages between law and politics, where emergency legislation, which of its nature must bring to the fore the foundational nature of violence for any political system, is so often deployed. In states of emergency a political association (the state) asserts its claim to a monopoly of the legitimate use of physical force within a given territory. While this claim is basic, its frequent exercise comes at a cost because it raises the question of legitimacy. The capacity to declare a state of emergency is hampered by its repeated deployment, although the invoked emergency's aim is to assert or reassert normality. So normality itself comes into question. The conversion of emergency into normality, and its converse, is analogous to the conversion of suffering into beauty, into appreciative reception. Sometimes, it would seem, the suspension, rather than the application of the law clarifies a confusion that cannot otherwise be dispelled and is welcomed on that account.

What had been standard European colonial practice beyond Europe suddenly became ominously authoritarian in the European sphere itself, first in Italy and then in Germany. In the latter, Carl Schmitt (and others) argued in the political debates of 1924–32 that Article 48 of the Weimar constitution for the state of exception allowed the President to become 'a commissarial dictator', no longer bound by legal norms but by the mass of the people (the *pouvoir constituant*) that elected him. This was exploited by Hitler's party to create a state of exception that legally became the norm. To claim the capacity to pluck from confusion a clarifying mode of rescue or exemption and then to say that such exemption is the true norm is to claim a decisiveness and clarity that only populism and authoritarianism can in tandem produce. It is an example of form rising out of formlessness or, in Schmittian terms, 'decisionism' out of endless debate.[16]

In Ireland, a standard and worn conception of the autonomous status of art, especially popular among artists themselves, is itself a reaction both to the various hallowed versions of that notion that were popular during the period of the Irish Revival, and to the anxieties that naturally arose from the island's bitterly contested political history in the twentieth century. The epithet 'ideological' in literary or aesthetic discussion is almost always used as an insult, a disqualifier from 'the realms of gold'. The inviolate status of art decries any challenge to its arcane nature. Seamus Heaney once told me that the question of literary criticism came up in a conversation he had with Bryan MacMahon, novelist and short-story writer from Kerry. 'Criticism?' said MacMahon, 'Sure, 'tis like shlitting the throat of a lark.' This is the logical conclusion of all discursive practice for those who genuflect before the Real Presence of Art and regularly deform the very idea of ideology (including their own), about which their hostile conviction is as firm as their intellectual grasp of it is faint.

Yet the elementary connection between the autonomy of art, as a form of exemption, and authoritarianism, as a form of exception, cannot be discounted in the histories of twentieth-century Europe, including Ireland. The fin-de-siècle decadence, *L'Art pour l'Art*, is the aesthetic that migrated most regularly (via, say, Ernst Jünger or the Italian Futurists) into the political territories of fascism. Benjamin's famous declaration that fascism aestheticizes politics and all the subsequent discussion and dispute have had little effect in Ireland on the accepted wisdom about the status and role of literature and of criticism or commentary about it. The issue here is the capacity of literature or of politics to redeem an original imperfection through the devices of 'autonomy' or 'exemption'.

Erich Auerbach's *Mimesis* (1946, English translation 1953) is the diagnostic companion to Joyce's work in the American recruitment of European culture, itself comparable to the Roman recruitment of classical Greek culture. In Auerbach's implied analogy, as Augustine saw the Roman Empire fall and Christianity replace it, we were in turn witnessing the end of that Christian era and the emergence of modernity – which then meant the hegemony of the USA. *Mimesis* is as bare of political reference as it is of footnotes. Edward Said's *Orientalism* (1978), in a sense, rewrote Auerbach, against the American hegemony, insisting (with footnotes) on the political dimension that had been so startlingly silenced by his German-Jewish predecessor and mentor.[17] *Mimesis,* written in the East (Istanbul), was the epic of how the old West was lost; *Orientalism,* written in the West (New York), became the epic of how the East was lost in the making of the new West. Like *Ulysses, Mimesis* and *Orientalism* were each works in which the idea and experience of individual exile stimulated a vision of global history.[18] Auerbach's conception of the West eventually became one of the powerful Cold War counter-Soviet images of the 'Free World'. Said's work, itself foundational in postcolonial studies, both contradicts and complements Auerbach's. The intimate and competitive relationship between those two is further complicated by the role in global commentary on the aesthetic/political dimension by the work of another German Jew, Walter Benjamin, although his lodestones are Marxism and the October Revolution of 1917.

Benjamin wrote *The Concept of History* in the aftermath of the Hitler-Stalin pact of November 1939, in the early months of 1940. One of its most famous formulations stated:

> The tradition of the oppressed teaches us that "the state of emergency" in which we live is not the exception but the rule.[19]

When Benjamin wrote these words, Irish neutrality in World War II, 'the big war, the world one, the one – ask any teenager – with nothing to do with up-to-date humanity and modern-society living' (86) as it is described in *Milkman,* was already almost a year old; the Emergency, as it was called in the South, created new difficulties, even in literature, for any version of autonomy that claimed the need to be apolitical. The semantic association of neutrality and impartiality is one of the obvious casualties of the discourse of that period, yet it still survives, politically convalescent after World War II, a ghost of its former self, dislodged from its central ethical location and compelled to live in the suburban aesthetic of mass-consumer society.

The reception of Joyce is only one example of the enormous absorptive power of the USA to inhale both the older imperialisms and the newer modernities. Yet, as in the New Criticism movement, or in the poetry of Wallace Stevens (*Harmonium*, 1923), the USA also created its own specific ideology of aesthetic autonomy as part of that absorptive process – e.g. in poetry, with Stevens absorbing and enriching the French decadence into an American hedonism. This is one instance of how an idea of autonomous freedom, a species of radical individualism, a correlative to ideas of political exception or judicial exemption could be incorporated into a political system as an attribute specific to that system but also universalizable as the most valuable of all human aspirations. John Rawls's *A Theory of Justice* (1971) would be a political-philosophical example, a parallel to Stevens's *Harmonium*. Constantly revamped and recycled, melded with versions of consumer freedom, to which it can lend both a retro and a utopian appeal, the protean idea of autonomy can claim that 'art' is the permanent free space in an increasingly crammed system to which violence no longer poses a threat. Violence can be presented as a prevailing regime in different genres, from westerns to serial killer, gangster, or sci-fi movies or novels, and also as spectacle, as cartoon, as robotic mutation, as fake apocalypse, gothic dystopia. In the American system, it has been co-opted as an integral feature of the aesthetic. The ethical dimension is usually a predictable add-on, almost an archaism in the regime(s)of violence. What was once the exception, in which law is suspended, can now safely be admired for having become the rule, perhaps even be rewritten as the rule of law. The most effective way to conceal violence, even foundational violence, is to aestheticize it. The Beast has become Beauty, Beauty the Beast. The process is still incomplete in Ireland. That's what makes it still visible. In the times of Mitchel and O'Malley, and, convulsively, into the 1980s, to be a political prisoner was an ethical choice. By 2018, with Anna Burns's work, no such space is available. The space of the political is fumigated of content where possible, but violence of all sorts, state-sanctioned, subversive, criminal, institutional, sexual and familial, technologically coordinated by computer and satellite, random and wanton on other levels, media-needed, media-glamorized and media-deplored in ritualized rhythms, has become omnipresent, regularized and routine, in few places more obviously so than in the United States, self-proclaimed guarantor of 'world order'. Everybody is in prison; the state of emergency is complete, although not perhaps permanent.

NOTES

1. Flann O'Brien, *The Hair of the Dogma* (London: Hart-Davis, MacGibbon, 1977), 107; see Ronald L. Dotterer, 'Flann O'Brien, James Joyce and the Dalkey Archive', *New Hibernian Review/Iris Eireannach Nua,* 8/2 (Summer 2004), 54–63; Lucas Harriman, 'Flann O'Brien's Creative Betrayal of Joyce', *New Hibernia Review/Iris Éireannach Nua,* 14/4 (Winter 2010), 90–109. The transformation of Henry James in critical commentary in the 1950s into the great American novelist, combining the drama of individual consciousness and the American encounter with the European world, is a companion piece to the assimilation of Joyce.
2. See Laura K. Donohue, *Counterterrorist Law and Emergency Law in the United Kingdom 1922–2000* (Dublin: Irish Academic Press, 2007); Ronan Keane, '"The Will of the General": Martial Law in Ireland, 1535–1924', *Irish Jurist,* New Series, 25–27 (1990–2),150–80.
3. See Leon Radzinowicz and Roger Hood, 'The Status of Political Prisoner in England: The Struggle for Recognition', *Virginia Law Review,* 65/8 (December 1979), 1421–81; Sean McConville, *Irish Political Prisoners 1848–1922: Theatre of War* (London: Routledge, 2003).
4. See Thomas Moore, *Memoirs of Captain Rock,* ed. Emer Nolan (Dublin: Field Day, 2005).
5. John Mitchel, *Jail Journal, with an Introductory Narrative of Transactions in Ireland* (1854; Dublin: M. H.Gill, 1913), 1–15; see also Christopher Morash, 'The Rhetoric of Right in Mitchel's *Jail Journal',* in Joep Leerssen, A. H. van der Weel, and Bart Westerweel (eds.), *Forging in the Smithy: National Identity and Representation in Anglo-Irish Literary History* (Amsterdam: Rodopi, 1995), 207–18; Niamh Lynch, 'Defining Irish Nationalist Anti-Imperialism: Thomas Davis and John Mitchel', *Éire-Ireland,* 42/1–2 (Earrach–Samhrad/Spring–Summer 2007), 82–107.
6. Ernie O'Malley, *On Another Man's Wound* (1936; Cork: Mercier Press, 2012), 9; see Luke Gibbons, 'On Another Man's Text: Ernie O'Malley, James Joyce and Irish Modernism', in Cormac O'Malley (ed.), *Modern Ireland and Revolution: Ernie O'Malley in Context* (Dublin: Irish Academic Press, 2016), 1–16.
7. O'Malley, *On Another Man's Wound,* 27.
8. Ibid., 182.
9. Ibid., 127.

10. 'First Letter on a Regicide Peace' (1796), in *The Writings and Speeches of Edmund Burke*, ed. Paul Langford et al., 9 vols. (Oxford: Clarendon Press, 1981–2015), vol. IX, 291. In general, see my *Foreign Affections: Essays on Edmund Burke* (Cork University Press, 2005), esp. 47–117.
11. James Joyce, *Finnegans Wake* (London: Faber and Faber, 1939), 473.
12. Sandra Smith, 'Translator's Note', in Irène Némirovsky, *Suite française* (London: Chatto & Windus, 2006); the Keats line is from *Endymion* (1818).
13. Theodor Adorno, *Prisms*, trans. Samuel and Sherry Weber (Cambridge, MA: MIT Press, 1981), 34.F.
14. See my 'Dumbness and Eloquence: A Note on English as We Write It in Ireland', in Clare Carroll and Patricia King (eds.), *Ireland and Postcolonial Theory* (University of Notre Dame Press, 2003), 109–28.
15. Ciaran Carson, 'Escaped from the Massacre?', *The Honest Ulsterman*, 50 (Winter 1975), 184–6.
16. See Carl Schmitt, *The Crisis of Parliamentary Democracy*, trans. Ellen Kennedy (1923; Cambridge, MA: MIT Press, 1988); Martin Jay '"The Aesthetic Ideology" as Ideology; Or, What Does It Mean to Aestheticize Politics?', *Cultural Critique*, 21 (Spring 1992), 41–61; George Schwab, *The Challenge of the Exception: An Introduction to the Political Ideas of Carl Schmitt between 1921 and 1936* (Berlin: Duncker & Humblot, 1970).
17. See Said's comments on Auerbach in 'Secular Criticism', the opening essay in *The World, The Text, and the Critic* (Cambridge MA: Harvard University Press, 1983), 5–9.
18. See Kader Konuk, *East West Mimesis: Auerbach in Turkey* (Stanford University Press, 2010).
19. Walter Benjamin, *Selected Writings*, gen. ed. Michael W. Jennings, 4 vols. (Cambridge, MA: Harvard University Press, 2003), vol. IV, 392.

CHAPTER 14

Wherever Green is Read

I

THE EASTER RISING OF 1916 HAS BEEN SO EFFECTIVELY revised that its seventy-fifth anniversary is a matter of official embarrassment. Nevertheless, the revisionists are now themselves more vulnerable to revision because their pseudo-scientific orthodoxy is so obviously tailored to match the prevailing political climate – especially in relation to the Northern crisis – that its claims to 'objectivity', to being 'value-free', have been abandoned as disguises no longer needed. Conor Cruise O'Brien has declared himself to be a unionist and, in that light, his writings can be understood as a polemic in favour of that position. A less strident example, free of any such declared *parti pris*, is provided by Roy Foster in his popular *Modern Ireland 1600–1972*, in which he writes about 1916 thus:

> Any theoretical contradictions present in the 1916 rising, however, were obscured by the fact that its rhetoric was poetic. Several poets took part, and the most famous reaction to it was a poem: Yeats's 'Easter 1916', written between May and September and strategically published during the Anglo-Irish war four years later. But an intrinsic component of the insurrection (for all the pluralist window-dressing of the Proclamation issued by Pearse) was the strain of mystic Catholicism identifying the Irish soul as Catholic and Gaelic. It could be argued that this was nothing new: literary Fenianism yet again. But the message would be read more clearly than ever in an Ulster heavily

> committed to the war effort, for whom 1916 would be marked not by the occupation of the GPO, but the terrible carnage on the Somme.[1]

All sorts of curious assumptions and shiftings reveal themselves here. Apparently, rhetoric is a bad thing, especially when it is poetic, because it obscures 'theoretical contradictions'. (This from Yeats's biographer!) It is the kind of approach one would expect from a nineteenth-century historian (for example, Lord Acton objecting to George Eliot's style on similar grounds), but its apparent intellectual naiveté serves a useful purpose. The Rising's 'rhetoric was poetic', poets participated in it, and the most famous reaction to it was a poem by Yeats. Even if we allow that stature to Yeats's long-delayed poem, what does it tell us about the Rising? That it was 'poetic' and *therefore* a bad thing, an absurdity? Clearly, insurrections should avoid poets and poems if they wish to be taken seriously. To be so taken, they should either be without 'theoretical contradictions' or, failing that, they should not obscure them.

However, poetry is not, after all, the real problem. It is 'the strain of mystic Catholicism identifying the Irish soul as Catholic and Gaelic' that is truly offensive. Some of the harm might be taken out of this if it is read as recycled 'literary Fenianism', and therefore 'incurably verbal'.[2] Irish revolutionaries all seem to suffer from this disease of discourse. Still, the antidote to their implacable writerliness is provided by a section of their readership – the Ulster unionists. Pearse's strain of mystic Catholicism 'would be read more clearly than ever' in an Ulster undergoing the much more acceptable, if terrible, 'carnage on the Somme'. For 'the strain' has now clarified into 'the message' that would be read in Ulster. It is surely of some importance to know *when* this reading took place. Did 1916 have to happen before the Ulster unionists perceived that Irish nationalists were Catholic and Gaelic? Or has Pearsean exclusivity been borne in upon the unionists only with the passage of time? Since it is going to be (or was) read 'more clearly than ever', it is fair to assume that it had been read before, albeit less clearly. Perhaps it is the poetic rhetoric that previously made it obscure. The poetry of the Rising has to be separated from its 'message'.

This is achieved by a single connective. *But* it is an 'intrinsic component' of mystic Catholicism that would be read as the message of 1916 in Ulster and not the 'pluralist window-dressing' of the Proclamation. It is hard to know if that *but* is entirely meant to separate the poetry from the Catholicism or to conjoin them, although it does seem that the poetry is not as intrinsic a component as the Catholicism. Perhaps the real bridge word here is 'mystic', since it links the two entities by allowing that they share the same obfuscating and irrational function. Ulster cannot read the poetry but it can read the Catholic strain. They may be distinct, they may be conjoined, *but* it is the latter that counts.

The paragraph is itself an exercise in rhetoric and its central trope is that of 'reading' clearly what has been obscured. First theory is obscured by rhetoric (but read nonetheless); then an 'intrinsic' element, 'mystic Catholicism', emerges as 'the message' that would be read in Ulster behind all the 'pluralist window-dressing'. Clear reading is an Ulster prerogative and is associated with the Somme; obscure (and, by implication, obscurantist) writing is a Southern characteristic and is associated with the GPO. The trope is not local, of course; it extends to the whole treatment of the 1912–16 period, in which the South consistently misreads the North (for example, the Howth gun-running as a bad reading of the Larne gun-running) while the North accurately reads the true intentions that lie behind the Gaelic-Catholic-revivalist jargon of the South.[3] This has a very familiar ring. The perceptive Ulster readers have been displaying their interpretive skills on deceitful Southern texts up to the present day. Maybe they have classes on the hermeneutics of suspicion in Glengall Street or at the Bob Jones University. Certainly, whatever the South writes, the North will read and Ulster will be right.

That 'pluralist window-dressing' of the Proclamation, we may take it, is the residue of Connolly's contribution to the Rising. In the preceding pages, Foster wonders what persuaded Connolly to give up his 'hard-headed Marxian socialism' for the vaporous mysticism of Pearse. The relationship between a soft-focused Irish nationalism and socialism is, in this view, necessarily contradictory and – for present purposes – Marxian socialism may be allowed to be 'hard-headed', a figurative compliment of the most strategic kind. Still, theory has taken a fair hammering. It is bedevilled by contradictions, it is obscured by rhetoric, it secretes within itself a mystic strain and yet, for all its shyness, theory can be exposed and read as a message. But it has even more blows to take. In the next paragraph it appears in another of its stereotyped adversarial roles – against practice.

'Theory apart, what about the practicalities *of* insurrection?' Theory always seems to be apart from, not *of* the Rising. The other stock opposite to theory – instinct – is also invoked. The IRB reacted to World War I in a fashion that was 'almost Pavlovian in its dogmatism'.[4] I find it difficult to remember what Pavlov's experiments have to do with dogmatism, although they did indeed have a lot to do with dogs. Anyway, the verbal associationism of the sentence is almost rescued by its 'almost'.

The whole point of Foster's representation is that the Easter Rising was an exercise in irrationalism, a word entirely congruent with nationalism (of the Irish, not the British, kind) and that it was read as such in Ulster. The legacy of the Rising is the Northern crisis. The North can read the South; the South cannot read the North. Writing is the characteristic practice of the 'incurably verbal' South and it is always, explicitly or implicitly, separate from pragmatic considerations and infused with demonic, atavistic, and chaotically 'spiritual' energies. Reading is what the North is good at, the extrapolation from verbiage of the real message, a capacity that is characteristically pragmatic, hard-headed, rational. Thus the North and the South are constituted as both politically and culturally distinct entities: one authorial, the other readerly; one obscure, the other clear; one poetic, the other prosaic. Foster's own writing is itself a reading, dependent on the congealed stereotype of the partitionist mentality that is subsequent to the process he affects to describe. Perhaps it is now time for the stereotype to invert, so that the South can start reading the jargon of the North's newly acquired writerly status, complete with its 'myths' of the 'Cruithin' (Ian Adamson's redaction of the Gaelic story of dispossession, much favoured by the UDA and, increasingly, by Glengall Street[5]), its evangelical religion and, of course, its poetic rhetoric.

But, incurably verbal, 'history' legitimates its version of the present by its interpretations of the past. It has become almost a solecism to rehearse the well-known similarities between British imperial and Irish nationalist practices in the first decades of this century. Blood-sacrifice, a lot of bad and some good poetry, racist ideology, a glorification of violence, belief in the destiny of the nation, the recreation of a glorious past in fancy-dress charades (for instance, the reinvention of the British monarchy), health and strength movements (sports and bodybuilding as a new form of morality, the

Boy Scouts, predecessors of the Pearsean Fianna) – these and much else of the same kind were carefully nurtured cultural activities in Britain and in Europe between 1880 and 1914.[6] Further, the tide of irrationalism continued to run, despite the bloodshed of 1914–18, until 1939–45.

But it would, in the current vocabulary, be 'Anglophobic' or 'atavistic' to pursue such an inquiry, especially since among its consequences might be a recognition that it was 1912, not 1916, that created the ghastly circumstances of the Northern statelet and that made religious bigotry the central organizing principle of its political life. It is, in present circumstances, an inadmissible notion. For the reaction to Easter 1916 is part of the reaction to the Provisional IRA. The lamentations about that organization's use of violence in the furtherance of political ends come most loudly from those who have a well-established notoriety for that practice themselves – the British and the unionists. They are not opposed to violence as such; they are opposed to violence directed against them. But they are perfectly happy to direct violence against their opponents and even, if need be, against one another. Yet it is the violence of Easter 1916 that is regarded as originary and therefore legitimizing.

Easter 1916 was a sorry reproduction, in its forms and its practice, of the ideology of imperialism. It was not only the immense military disadvantage that made it so. Culturally, it was armed with primitive weapons. It could not compete with the British Army's regimental tradition of glorified violence; it had no evangelical fervour that could match Victorian Protestantism's euphoria; it had no war poets to compare in ferocity with Kipling or Sir Henry Newbolt; it had no theory of racial degeneration, regression, and atavism to compare with those of Edwin Ray Lankester or Thomas Huxley, and those in Ireland who did promote such theories – like Standish O'Grady and Yeats – were not among the insurrection's most notable participants or supporters.[7] At least it can be said for Easter 1916 that it tried; but as a response to its imperial mentor's example (on the Somme and elsewhere) it was a grievous failure. Only the Ulster unionists managed to approximate the imperial example, possibly because they regarded themselves (rightly) as the representatives in Ireland of the imperialist system. Their 'rebellion' in 1912 was a reminder to Westminster that any attempt to modify that status would bring the whole system into question.

Still, Irish historians and commentators are anxious to assign Easter 1916 to a curious double fate. On the one hand, it is a point of origin that should be erased as much as possible. Had it not happened, it is argued, we would be better off – without partition (possibly) and without all the bloodshed of the years 1916–22. On the other hand, it is to be remembered as a point of origin for all our ills – clientism in politics, economic illiteracy, nationalist vapourings and, above all, the Northern crisis and the IRA. Nationalism, we are told, is not compatible with democracy, nor with socialism. It is provincial and provincializing. Until 1989, it was even possible to argue that it was a nineteenth-century phenomenon, an anachronism in the modern world. Similarly, imperialism or colonialism were myths generated by nationalists, unless, that is, they are spoken of by heroic little republics struggling to free themselves from the Soviet embrace. That is reality, not myth. But British imperialism? In Ireland? Even the Workers' Party has ditched that fantasy, exchanging it for the other fantasy of the multinational system of late capitalism. The hostility to the idea that there might be a system – apart from nationalism, of course – whether it is called capitalism (a system that prides itself on not being one), imperialism, or colonialism, is itself a symptom of revisionism's desire to deny the validity or the possibility of any totalizing concept, and to replace this with a series of monographic, empiricist studies that disintegrate the established history of 'Ireland' into a set of specific and discrete problems or issues that have at best only a weak continuity to link them.[8]

II

To theorize a total system is, perhaps, a contradiction in terms, since no system that is truly total would leave any space for anyone to stand outside it and theorize it. Empiricists often manage this dilemma best by implying that if there is a system, then it can be modified, improved, or altered in such-and-such a particular way so that a discernible goal or purpose can be realized. Empiricists make good liberals; that is to say, all good liberals are empiricists, but not all empiricists are good liberals. The kindest view of liberalism in present-day Ireland would credit it with the wish to improve the existing political-economic system in such a manner that people would be as economically secure and as free as possible from all the demonic influences of 'ideologies', religious and political. Its buzz word is ' pluralism'; its idea of the best of all possible worlds is based on the hope of depoliticizing the society to the point where it is essentially a consumerist organism, absorbing the whole array of goods that can be produced within the free market. No doubt there is a suspicion that the market is, in some sense of the word, a system and that consumption is allied in particular ways to production and distribution. But the emphasis is on the idea of the individual and his/her liberty within a system that is junior to the individual self. Systems change, but individuals – as an idea, not, thank heaven, as individuals – go on forever. The full realization of the individual self is regarded as an ambition that institutions exist to serve. Those that do not – religion, education, the 1937 Constitution, for example – are to be liberalized, gentrified, or abolished.

Self-fulfilment is not an aim that threatens any system that produces it. Rather the reverse: it is one of the achievements of capitalism to have created it. Its ultimate political expression is pluralism, the Pearsean-Connolly 'window-dressing' in the Proclamation. Its desire is for variety and accessibility. Its pride is to be modern, its dread to be out of step with what is deemed to be modernity, or Europe – commonly assumed to be the same thing. Its general attitude to what it does not like is that it is out-of-date, out-of-place in this wonderful world of the late twentieth century. Pluralism has only one time – the present; everything else is, literally, anachronistic. It has the egregious tolerance of the indifferent to anything or anyone else who is willing to live in a hermetically sealed micro-climate of individual or group privacy. Alas, it is also very expensive. The economic system must be functioning at a high level to sustain it and it can do that only in specific places at specific times. Ireland cannot afford to live in such presentness. It must perforce live with its past. That is a matter of some resentment to this sort of liberal mind.

I do not think it is answer enough to say that, even if it could afford it, Ireland would not have pluralism. The abortion, contraception, and divorce issues seem to point that way, but if Ireland could afford pluralism, it would not be the Ireland we know. What we have instead is a dilapidated version of pluralism, media-led, centred in Dublin 4, a mini-metropolis that regards the rest of Ireland as the hinterland of its benighted past. Still, in so far as it can, Ireland now treats the past as a kind of supermarket for tourists, a place well-provided with 'interpretive centres' that will allow Newgrange and Joyce, the flora and fauna of the Burren, the execution cells at Kilmainham, the Derrynaflan hoard, and the Blarney stone to be viewed as the exotic debris thrown up by the convulsions of a history from which we have now escaped into a genial depthlessness. Easter 1916 or Ulster in 1912 – not to mention Ulster in 1991 – are altogether too present in their pastness to be commodified in this manner. It is perfectly in tune with this blandness that people in the South wonder what the killing in the North is all about. 'Why can't they live in peace together and forget the Boyne and 1916?' They are irrational creatures, those Northerners, because they are caught in the past and still have to catch up with the present. It is all the more irrational because they belong to an economic world that would allow for pluralism.

But then, on top of all that, there is the question of democracy and the need to preserve it, North and South. Any unionist will tell you now that there is no democracy left in the North. The British took it away and replaced it with a system of Orders-in-Council, issued through the Northern Ireland Office and the Secretary of State, all appointed, not elected, officials. Any nationalist or republican (or Lord Devlin) will tell you that there never was democracy in Northern Ireland, even before the proroguing of Stormont that succeeded the massacre of Bloody Sunday in 1972. (This is a well-tried tactic – a massacre of the enemies of those whom you are going to betray politically in order to make the betrayal palatable.) Still, the democracy that ain't and the democracy that never was have to be preserved from the men of violence who threaten it. That is, in case there might be doubt, not the British Army or the RUC or the UDR or the UDA, but the other men of violence, the IRA. This is, in fact, a delusion. It is the Union that is to be preserved, not democracy. The mass of the Irish people did not want the Union, but they got it with the help of the corrupt Irish parliament in which those same people were regularly referred to as 'the common enemy'. The unionists of the North did not want the modifications of the Union Treaty that came in 1922, 1972, and then again in 1985, but they got them and were outraged at this treatment of the majority. But that's how democracy works in what is now a neocolonial system. No matter how often it is abolished, the phantasm of its presence remains. If democracy is abolished legally by a parliament, then it cannot really be abolished – it is just in a state of suspended animation and will resume its life-giving contact with the people once all the objections to its suspension have been overcome.

Nevertheless, the biggest threat to democracy is that outlandishly retarded form of nationalist violence that Easter 1916 spawned and the IRA inherited. The only fully democratic system that Ireland has ever known is that developed since independence. Yet nationalism is not compatible with democracy. Maybe it could be suggested that, in colonial conditions, nationalism is often the preconditioning climate for democracy. But then, of course, colonialism probably does not exist, is merely a figment of the nationalist imagination – as phantasmal as democracy in Northern Ireland or as pluralism in the Republic. But it is precisely such 'window-dressing' that a consumerist society wants. If pluralism or democracy is too expensive to buy, then at least we can window-shop, gazing fondly at their simulacra on the TV, along with the other glamorous advertisements. In the end, it may be the 'window-dressing' that has survived best from the Proclamation. It was unreal then, we may feel, but now we have transformed it into the real unreal.

It would indeed be ironic if, in our anxiety to liberate ourselves from 1916 and its presumed legacy, we fell into such a psychosis. For one of the characteristic ways of discrediting the Rising has been to intimate that its leaders were an odd lot, psychologically unstable, given to Anglophobia and dread homoerotic tendencies. Pearse has been the favourite target of this kind of psycho-history but it is a dangerous precedent.[9] If the same kind of attention were to be directed at, say, Carson, Asquith, Lloyd George, Churchill, who should 'scape whipping' – if the phrase may be allowed in such a context. Anyway, it is just an inverse form of the 'great man' school of history, in which the agency of the individual, however disturbed (maybe because disturbed), is given priority over all the other determinant and impersonal forces of which we might otherwise believe the ostensibly free individual to be the instrument. The problem with 'forces' is that they extend over long periods of time and are readable only when they constitute patterns – or when they are constituted as patterns. Individuals whose intervention warps or alters these patterns are often seen as eccentric and freakish. But to pursue that line of polemical investigation is to go down a cul-de-sac with a mirror at the end.

So, no system, no metanarrative, just discrete issues discreetly interlinked now and then. Irish history, like any history, has to represent the past for the present. The anxieties of the present determine what elements of the past are most in need of signification. Easter 1916 was an action predicated on a version of Irish history that has now been rewritten so that its force may be denied, particularly the force that came from the rebels' conception of themselves as the culmination of a long, single narrative that had been submerged by deceit and oppression. Revisionism attacks the notion of a single narrative and pretends to supplant it with a plurality of narratives. It downplays the oppression the Rising sought to overthrow and upgrades the oppression the Rising itself inaugurated in the name of freedom. The rewriting of modern history has, as its terminus, the Northern problem and thus explains its present intransigence by criticizing those who did not anticipate or recognize its inevitability and its depth. It is a retrospective vision – as all history must be – but its pretensions to objectivity are as much a part of its rhetoric as are the internal characteristic strategies of the discourses of its various practitioners. Its most interesting achievement has been to place the problem of historical writing as such on the agenda. Inescapably a fiction, history, of whatever kind, owes its allegiance to fact, however selective, however organized. (This does not mean that historians do not tell lies; they do. But let us say that a writer who tells lies is not, in virtue of that, being at that moment an historian. Froude was, on that count, infrequently an historian. Sir John Temple never was.) But history is discourse; events and conditions are not. They are outside discourse, but can only be reached through it – to paraphrase Barthes.[10] It is a slippery discipline that has the additional merit or demerit of itself being an integral part of the object it addresses. We do not know the past except through the interpretations of it. Historians do not write about the past; they create the past in writing about it. And, when they do that, they are also writing in and of and for the present. It says a good deal about historians that so many of them still believe in their capacity to be 'objective'.

III

One of the outstanding features of historical revisionism is its philosophical innocence, perhaps the basic requirement for its peculiar brand of political incrimination that pretends to be a rational form of 'detachment'. This might help to explain the paradox whereby it actually collaborates – unconsciously – with the very mentality it wishes to defeat. There is indeed a brand of Irish nationalism that is willing to deny to 'Ulster' the independent tradition that it claims for itself and to swallow it up in the fond embrace of all-Ireland nationalism proper. (This is not a brand that can, on any reading of the evidence, be legitimately associated with people as diverse as Thomas MacDonagh, George Sigerson, Frederick Ryan, W. P. Ryan, James Connolly, and many others, although they have all been huddled together under the sign of nationalist messianism.) But what the revisionists do is to deny to the 'South' the tradition that they then, perforce, accede to the 'North'. The 'two-nations' theory is an anomaly in historical revisionism, because it is conceding that idea of continuity and tradition that is the bedrock of all nationalist thinking, of whatever variety. But it is, of course, a *necessary* anomaly. To legitimize partition, Northern Ireland must be allowed its separate 'identity', 'tradition', 'essence', while nationalist Ireland must have those qualities denied it. Alas, you cannot have one without the other. If Ulster is 'different', its difference can be described only in contrast with the 'sameness' of the rest of the island. Abandon the sameness and you abandon the difference. The only grounds on which partition can be legitimized are the same as those on which it can be refused. What is 'Protestant' in Christianity is defined in relation to what is 'Catholic'; both are still within the one embrace. The more one argues for two nations, the more one fuels the argument for one nation. Allow the concept of nation, nationality, tradition, and all the rest of those continuities that make metanarratives possible, then the rest is history – or history of the present-day Irish kind. Revisionists are nationalists despite themselves; by refusing to be Irish nationalists, they simply become defenders of Ulster or British nationalism, thereby switching sides in the dispute while believing themselves to be switching the terms of it.

It is only the inverted nationalism of historical revisionism that makes Easter 1916 a date so central that it has to be so assiduously ignored. Roy Foster mentioned the strategically delayed publication of Yeats's poem 'Easter 1916', perhaps to point out that it had a deeper repercussion during the War of Independence (or the 'Anglo-Irish war', as he, with comparable strategy, calls it) than it would have had earlier. But 1916 saw the equally delayed publication in New York of Joyce's *A Portrait of the Artist as a Young Man*. With the benefit of hindsight, it could be pointed out that the McCann of *A Portrait* is modelled on Francis Sheehy-Skeffington, who was to be murdered by a British officer in 1916, and that the Davin of the same novel is a partial portrait of George Clancy, murdered in 1921 by the Black and Tans. Do these later facts add 'significance' to *A Portrait*? Perhaps it is safer and saner to say that Joyce's attack in this novel on the servility of the Irish in the face of the Roman Catholic and British imperia is of much greater historical import, although the attack is ventriloquized through Stephen Dedalus and he may not be too readily taken as a reliable narrator of Joyce's own views or of the existing state of things.

Literary discourse[11] has its own specific problems, although they differ from those that attend historical discourse. But does retrospect not lend (dis)enchantment to the view we take either of historical or literary texts? A novel finished in 1910, but not published until 1916, a poem written in 1916 but not published until 1920, are both subject to the pressure of retrospect even before they appear in print. Even if we take their 'origin' as the moment they were completed (or begun), they produce another 'origin' at the moment they are published and yet another at the moment they are interpreted or reinterpreted according to the prevailing literary or historical paradigm inside which they are read. History would like to disembarrass itself of this 'literary' burden. Conversely, literature, in its 'humanist' mode, takes that weight gladly upon itself and dissolves the problem of time and retrospect that historians have to face, by chattering gaily about 'timeless' works of art, 'the autonomy of the artefact', and so on.

A Portrait is an artefact, the Rising is a fact. The production, transmission, and consumption of a text is a process that is obviously part of its meaning, but in literary studies the endlessness of the meaning has conventionally been terminated by conferring upon the text the destiny of form. Everything else may be mobile, but form abides.[12]

Historians would draw the bottom line elsewhere. Events took place. There is an undeniable zone that no manipulation can alter. But historical facts or events are artefacts. Once an event is characterized as 'historical', it has entered into the world of historical discourse. Even discourse itself is an event, but it is often the case – in recent historical writing in Ireland at any rate – that the written word, when treated as historical evidence, has a very peculiar relation to action, especially action of the revolutionary kind. In the Fosterian view of the 'South', there are many examples of the process by which people like the Fenians or the Parnellites produced writing that led unwittingly to action, when 'literary rhetoric would threaten to take on a mobilizing force all its own'.[13] The oddity of the phrasing does make the linkage between language and action a little obscure. Did revolutionary language produce revolution? Can that be shown by someone who is himself using language? Is 'rhetoric' the word for the kind of language that 'produces' actions of which the historian disapproves?[14]

Similarly, it seems that actions can be tailor-made to suit a pre-existent language, as when the British foolishly commit atrocities and thereby make a 'propaganda gift' to the IRA.[15] The propaganda is, so to say, prior to the atrocities; it is a language trap into which the British stupidly fall by killing people. It is not killing people that turns the populace against the Black and Tans; it is IRA propaganda. No doubt the British propaganda machine, notoriously efficient then and since, lay in wait for the IRA to kill people too. This is, perhaps, a posteriori 'rhetoric', where the action is inscribed beforehand and the falsity of the language is, oddly, cancelled by the performance of the kind of action imputed to be characteristic of the British. It is difficult, in such a context, to know where language begins and action ends, what is an event and what is rhetoric. The only security the reader has is that the philosophical problems that are raised by historical writing can be ignored because the writing is so heavily coded. There is no doubt about the distribution of approval and disapproval. But such writing, while very effective, is highly polemical. Its pretence to detachment, if it has any such pretence, is part of its polemical strategy. It too is 'rhetoric'.

So, discourse validates itself in many ways. It claims either to be self-referential (literature) or to refer to facts outside itself which it nevertheless includes within itself (history). This is the South and North of writing, the partitional 'rhetoric' that confirms the partition between literature and history.

It used to be said, and is still in some quarters felt, that Irish nationalism had managed to produce a nation-state just at the moment when the 'time' for nation-states had passed. Now we are seeing the nation-state, and the theories of discourse that accompanied it, defended by those who fancy they are questioning the assumptions that underlay their formation. The sponsorship of pluralism and diversity is merely an addition to nation-state politics and the language of 'individual' discourse, not a replacement for it. Seventy-five years after the Rising, the revising of it has led to the revision of the revisionists, who, for all the pluralist window-dressing of their proclamations, are victims of a strain of mystic rhetoric of the kind that we should now read all the more clearly, precisely because of the differences between the Somme and the GPO. We do not only read and write history; history also reads and writes us, most especially when we persuade ourselves that we are escaping from its thrall into the never-never land of 'objectivity'.

NOTES

1. R. F. Foster, *Modern Ireland 1600–1972* (London: Allen Lane, 1988), 479.
2. Ibid., 393.
3. See John Hutchinson, *The Dynamics of Cultural Nationalism: The Gaelic Revival and the Creation of the Irish National State* (London: Allen & Unwin, 1987).
4. Ibid., 461.
5. Ian Adamson, *Cruithin: The Ancient Kindred* (Newtownards: Nosmada, 1974).
6. See Mark Girouard, *The Return to Camelot: Chivalry and the English Gentleman* (New Haven, CT: Yale University Press, 1981).
7. See Daniel Peck, *Faces of Degeneration: A European Disorder, c.1848–c.1918* (Cambridge University Press, 1989).
8. Benedict Anderson, *Imagined Communities: Reflections on the Origin and Spread of Nationalism* (London: Routledge & Kegan Paul, 1983).
9. See Ruth Dudley Edwards, *Patrick Pearse: The Triumph of Failure* (London: Gollancz, 1977).
10. See Roland Barthes, 'Le discours de l'histoire', *Poetique*, 49 (1982), 13–21.

11. See Robert H. Canary and Henry Kozicki (eds.), *The Writing of History: Literary Form and Historical Understanding* (Madison: University of Wisconsin Press, 1978).
12. See Hayden White, *Metahistory: The Historical Imagination in Nineteenth-Century Europe* (Baltimore, MD: Johns Hopkins University Press, 1973); *The Content of the Form: Narrative Discourse and Historical Representation* (Baltimore, MD: Johns Hopkins University Press, 1987).
13. Foster, *Modern Ireland*, 428.
14. See Ann Rigney, *The Rhetoric of Historical Representation* (Cambridge University Press, 1990).
15. Ibid., 498.

CHAPTER 15

The Famous Seamus

JOURNALIST TO FAMOUS AND TIRED-OF-BEING-ASKED-IT comedian: 'Tell me, sir, what is the secret of' – Comedian, impatiently: 'Timing, timing.'

That's one of Seamus Heaney's jokes. Once he had become famous, he told jokes, with a nice smirk of irony, about famous people being pestered. He began to be famous in 1966, after the publication of his first volume of poems, *Death of a Naturalist.* I've now known the famous Seamus, 'Seamus Heaney', longer than I knew him before the fame, when he was just Seamus Heaney or Seamus Justin Heaney, or Heaney, S. J., as his name appeared on examination lists at schools and universities that we attended together for eleven years. If you were named Seamus, you needed another initial, to distinguish you from the throng of Seamuses that emerged in Northern Ireland in the thirties and forties and have continued to emerge ever since. The name Seamus was the Irish version of James and a signal that the Northern Irish Catholic community was loyal to the Gaelic, and not to the British, account of things. I remember my distress on being told that Seamus was not a real Gaelic name at all. Legend had it that it derived from James, indeed, but from the English James: King James II, the one who, by losing to the Dutch King William of Orange, in 1690, ensured the Protestant succession in England and a version of it in Ireland – whence all our woe. And, because that King James had been such a wimp, he was called Seamus a'Chaca, meaning Shitty Seamus. Not a noble lineage.

> Christ, it's near time that some small leak was sprung
> In the great dykes the Dutchman made
> To dam the dangerous tide that followed Seamus.

That poem, 'Whatever You Say Say Nothing', was published in 1975 in a volume called *North*. The first poem of the final sequence in that volume, 'Singing School', was dedicated to me and remembered the local Protestant militia, the B-Specials, a thuggish lot who patrolled the roads at night during and after the campaign the IRA launched at the end of 1956. To be called Seamus then was a giveaway, and identified you as a Catholic, or a Fenian, or a Teague:

> 'What's your name driver?'
> 'Seamus . . .'
> Seamus?

It was a name that always seemed to need a qualifier of some kind, even if only a raised eyebrow, until Heaney made it rhyme with 'famous'. Then the name Seamus was his in a special way. I became Seamus eile – Irish for 'the other Seamus'. Otherhood via brotherhood.

Seamus Heaney and I met at St Columb's College, in 1950, when he was eleven years old and I was ten. St Columb's College is a diocesan grammar school for boys in the city of Derry (as we called it), or Londonderry (as the official title had it). Derry is only a few miles from the border that separates Northern Ireland from the Republic of Ireland. It has a historical resonance for Protestants, because they endured a famous siege there in 1689 by the Catholic armies of King James II, and also for Catholics, because between 1922 and 1972 the city was notorious for discriminating against the local Catholic majority. The Protestants remained in power by openly gerrymandering the elections.

Although some of the teachers at St Columb's were laymen, the president in those days was always a priest, and the school, like all Catholic schools in Northern Ireland, was controlled by the Catholic hierarchy and, specifically and beadily, by the local bishop, His Lordship Neil Farren, who was a small round man with a piping voice and an air of implacable authority.

The school was divided between boarders and day-boys. I was a day-boy; I came from the city. Boarders came from the city's hinterland – in County Derry and County Donegal. The countryside that the boarders came from seemed to the day-boys strange, and indicated a wildness. Beyond the city, all civility ceased. Heaney was a boarder from Bellaghy, which was near Swatragh and Maghera and Magherafelt, on the far side of the mountain range. The names of those places, with all their 'gh's squatting on wide vowels, seemed designed for the boarders' accents. Boarders talked so slowly that sometimes you thought a sentence had been spoken when in fact only a place-name had been. The names seemed to be divided equally between liquid, or open-vowelled, and frozen, or consonantal, combinations. This, for instance, was how Heaney later described the local river, the Moyola:

> The tawny, guttural water
> spells itself: Moyola
> is its own score and consort,
>
> bedding the locale
> in the utterance,
> reed music, an old chanter
>
> breathing its mists
> through vowels and history.
> *('Gifts of Rain', Wintering Out, 1972)*

This was in contrast with another local name, Broagh:

> its low tattoo
> among the windy boor-trees
> and rhubarb-blades
>
> ended almost
> suddenly, like that last
> *gh* the strangers found
> difficult to manage.
> *('Broagh', Wintering Out, 1972)*

The fate of boarders seemed to us day-boys a dismal one. They lodged in the college, ate the lousy food, and had to attend regular supervised homework sessions before and after dinner; their sole recreation seemed to be walking around the looped driveways that encircled the wide, sloping lawn in front of the college buildings. Years later, when I read Heaney on Wordsworth, I smiled at how he concentrated on Wordsworth's habit of composing 'somehow aided by the automatic, monotonous turns and returns of the walk'. This was Wordsworth as boarder, Heaneyfied into that forever ambling monotony that seemed to me typical of the boarders' existence when class was over.

Day-boys escaped at 3:30 pm, or later if we stayed to play soccer on the bumpy, grassless, stone-studded pitches that were officially used for Gaelic football. Gaelic football, a cross between soccer and rugby, was for the country boys, the boarders; day-boys played soccer – although some teachers jeered at our lack of national spirit or at our sly evasiveness when we were faced with the uncompromising physical confrontation that Gaelic football involved.

Heaney didn't play football, either soccer or Gaelic, except when required. He would smile from the sidelines. He had boarder friends – Hugh Bredin (now a philosopher), Tom Mullarkey (now an architect), Desmond Kavanagh (now an orthodontist) – and they spoke a strange language among themselves, switching from jokes to bog Latin and on to composite phrasings that included French and Irish, English and Latin, and maybe some Greek. They had crystal sets in the dorms, on which they listened to – what? Radio Athlone, the national station of the Free State? The BBC? I imagined that they had a splintered, ethereal vision of the world beyond as it came hissing through those clever and pathetic sets. Whereas we, the day-boys, went home and listened to the loud popular-music world of Radio Luxembourg on our regular valve radios.

That distinction between boarders and day-boys became for Heaney and me a convention within which we described our differences. Each of us could caricature himself happily: Heaney slow, calm, solid, country-cunning; Deane quick, volatile, city-smart. Heaney had bulk; I was a wisp. Musically, he was hopeless: he liked comic ballads and knew all the words, and he did ceili dancing – a kind of traditional crossroads dancing – whereas I liked anything from Peggy Lee to the jazz of Django Reinhardt and Cannonball Adderley and the arias of Caruso, Björling, and Tagliavini. I knew the opera music from 78 rpm records belonging to one of my father's brothers. Both Heaney and I were satisfied that such a shorthand was available to us. Each could be the other's Other, the other Seamus.

Once we almost starred together, in *The Merchant of Venice.* But we got only as far as an audition on the school stage, where a pile of cushions formed the set. The class was watching. A love scene. Heaney was Lorenzo, I was Jessica. Shirt-sleeved, I lay back on the cushions and put my left hand behind my head, the elbow crooked. In my right hand I held a purple rose. Heaney's face, crowned by a tricornered hat with fraying gold stitching, leaned over me. He was controlling himself, just. I closed my eyes.

'Nearer,' shouted a voice. 'Get closer.'

I could feel his breath on my cheek. He made a noise. Swallowing his spittle.

'Sit, Jess – '

His voice broke and he half fell on me. We were both helpless for a moment. 'Stop that at once. Start again. Both of you. Stop giggling like schoolgirls.'

The voice came from below the stage. Rusty Gallagher, the teacher who always produced the Christmas play, was there, his neck twitching inside his tight, striped collar, as usual.

'Right, Jessica, recline. Recline!'

I reclined. I tried to imagine I was being kissed by a girl I knew. It almost worked for a moment. Then I felt and heard Heaney's voice again.

'Sit, Jessica. Look how the floor of heaven . . . '

He moved his hand, and his weight fell on my leg for a moment.

'Jesus, you gom.'

We rolled about laughing. Rusty was really angry now, standing above us on the stage, his crinkled reddish hair showing little beads of sweat at the roots. We had been rehearsing all morning and he was past it.

'Get up, the two of you. You're out. Maybe you can make it as stagehands – that'd be the height of your powers. Heaney, I'm disappointed in you.

> I thought you had more sense. And a nice little Jessica you'd have been, too,' he said, pulling my ear. 'If only you could speak two consecutive words.'

It was in our last two years in St Columb's, 1956 and 1957, that we really began to know each other. We both won university scholarships but delayed taking them up, and stayed on for an extra, transitional year. In an English class we took together, there were only four of us – Michael Cassoni, Paddy Mullarkey, Heaney, and me. Cassoni and I were the day-boys. Cassoni was socially smooth, fond of poker and girls. He wasn't really interested in school. Mullarkey was almost shyly pragmatic. For him, literature was a bit airy-fairy. That left Heaney and me and our teacher, Sean B. O'Kelly, who was a man of such sweetness and enthusiasm that even at sixteen or seventeen years of age we appreciated how fortunate we were to have him. He took us through Chaucer's 'General Prologue' to the *Canterbury Tales*, *Hamlet*, *Paradise Lost*, Wordsworth and Keats, Lamb and Hazlitt, Hardy, Hopkins, Shelley, Tennyson, and Arnold. Since our scholarships had already been won, all we needed to aim for was a State Exhibition, a sort of super-scholarship, which provided an additional financial boon. It was a perfect year. Heaney and I became fast friends.

I remember reading Hazlitt, and his recognition that the memory of the sun coming through the window of the blue room where he first read Rousseau was forever afterward part of his understanding of Rousseau's work. It seemed so obviously true to us then, reading his essays in the red octavo edition we used, with its close-printed pages, Sean B. half leaning out the window into the incoming sunlight with a haze of motes dancing over his suit, Heaney crouched slightly over the book beside me, the town spread out below the hill where the school stood. We absorbed those texts deeply, drank them like hot tea and then felt the faint sweat of pleasure come out on our skin as they reacted within us. Even when we giggled at the occasional sentence ('Those are the Irishman's balls' was one: Hazlitt's description of Cavanagh, the fives player), or at an error in reading *Hamlet* aloud ('And in the cup an onion shall he throw' – 'onion' instead of 'union'), the glee then became part of the text thereafter. Heaney misremembered this in his poem 'Granite Chip' (*Station Island*, 1984):

> In reading these authors, with their heavily impregnated allusions and references, we gazed as through a lattice at the mysterious world of writing,

> where people with names like Sir Thomas Browne, George Herbert, Beaumont and Fletcher, John Dryden, moved dimly among their titles and citations.

Now and then, a chill came off the page. In Hardy's *The Woodlanders*, an early sequence of words rolled out like a premonition. To move from the Hintock plantation to the deserted highway, Hardy wrote, was to 'exchange by the act of a single stride the simple absence of human companionship for an incubus of the forlorn'. Sean B. O'Kelly read that out; I remember looking sidewise at Heaney and found that he was looking sidewise at me. The air between us was cold. Sean B. asked us if we liked it. We shook our heads. We didn't like it, but we were impressed by the force with which we didn't. So small and tight was our knowledge that we heard in Hardy's words echoes of our other authors: Keats's 'forlorn' in his 'Ode to a Nightingale', Wordsworth's large therapies of recovery in 'Tintern Abbey' – a poem we knew by heart. I think it was the first time a literary work made me feel miserable and isolated, and I saw Heaney resisting the misery and isolation, then accepting them, then overriding them. I recognized then – also for the first time – why Heaney responded so fully, with such timbre, to Wordsworth. Like Wordsworth, Heaney was of the healing school of readers and writers.

Despite the fact that we were environed by examinations, I remember those last years at school as leisurely, literary, almost excessively privileged. It was not a matter of ignoring the outside world; that would have been difficult, even for adolescents. In 1957, an IRA campaign had just begun, and the local police were more aggressively sectarian than ever before, especially at night; unemployment in our area was running at nearly 50 per cent; housing was appalling; discrimination, with a Sten gun behind it, was what we knew of British democracy – with one glorious exception. That was the introduction of the welfare state, the great socialist experiment of the post-war years in Britain, which guaranteed secondary schooling for every British subject up to the age of fifteen, provided unemployment insurance, and dispensed free medicine under the auspices of the National Health Service. The unionists who ran Northern Ireland opposed and delayed this legislation as long as they could, for it struck at their sectarian system of inequality. But it had to be implemented. When it came to the crunch, it was London, not Belfast, that ruled Northern Ireland. Quite appropriately, it was education that delivered the first serious injury to the unionists' blind bigotry: advancement was now to be achieved on the basis of merit, not on sectarian affiliation. As a consequence, school became vital to us. Learning had an extra dimension to it, an extra pleasure; it now carried a political implication, a sense of promise.

In the autumn of 1957, Heaney and I started university together – Queen's University, in Belfast. Even here, we were in the same English class. The outstanding teacher was Laurence Lerner, a poet and critic from South Africa, who appeared to recognize as familiar much in the Northern Irish political landscape. He opened a lecture on Shakespeare, in a downtown Presbyterian hall, with the remark that Shakespeare was very probably a Roman Catholic. This lost him half his audience straightaway. In a tutorial group, he asked his students if they really believed that they could distinguish between Catholics and Protestants by any feature other than their names or the schools they had attended. Usually, everybody said yes: Prods were better dressed (because they had jobs, because they were Prods), and had thin mouths, blue noses, pinched, disapproving faces with starched expressions; Teagues had dirty shoes, curly hair, and nervous eyes, and didn't wear suits. Lerner did not teach us anything that was in itself new, but, being South African he reordered the local tyranny in our minds, by showing us how deeply introjected the sour hegemony of our sectarianism had become.

In retrospect, I think that his lessons were silently meant to teach us how to read literary texts in a living way – reminding us that our lives, too, were embroiled with these books. I remember the oddness of seeing Protestant working-class Belfast for the first time: I would cross its most notorious street, Sandy Row, and hear the Saturday night evangelicals screaming and raving through loudspeakers about Popery and repentance, and pass by the clamorous shops, and smell the sweet aromas from the Erinmore tobacco factory, above the railway bridge, and then return to my rented room in a nearby Catholic neighbourhood, to read Milton and Dickens – whose seventeenth- and nineteenth-century worlds were suddenly coexistent with my own. I knew the bitterness of Protestantism, and its philistine pride, but for the first time I began to sense its magnificence. Lerner brought the streets of Belfast and the poems and novels we read into contact with one another. It was a salutary lesson.

In our second year, Heaney and I lived in the same digs – in Mrs Clifford's house, in Park Road. One of the other residents was also from our secondary school and was a boarder from Heaney's part of the country. He hated Heaney, though, and took every opportunity to rile him. Why? Heaney had been head prefect at school, a residual grouse. But it was surely because Heaney was Heaney: calm and sly, recognizably a south-county Derry boarder and recognizably something other, unforgivably foreign. One night, the animosity climaxed in a fight. Hearing the commotion, I opened the door to find the two of them rolling in a furious, wrestling embrace on the floor. It was comic, but it was also serious. It was an early instance of a peculiar kind of hostility that Heaney could provoke. Heaney was always 'well in' with those in power – teachers, professors, and the like. At the same time, he was conspiratorially against them, holding them at arm's length by his humour, his gift for parody. To many people, this seemed merely to be an exercise in cunning, and it was. But it was also Heaney's way of dealing with his own contradictory sense of himself: his authority and his uncertainty. The balance between these is not delicate. The authority usually wins out, but it needs the self-doubt to keep it from hardening, to keep vulnerabilities open.

As undergraduates, we began to write poems and, especially in the long summer vacation, to exchange them. Then, in our second year, we started publishing our work in student magazines. At this stage, almost all Heaney's poems were pastiches, poems moulded around the contours of poems by the writers he favoured – Hopkins, Frost, and Dylan Thomas being the ones I recall most from then. Even in poetry, we seemed to keep the boarder and day-boy contrast alive. Heaney went in for sturdy, muscular 'nature' types; I went in for the 'metropolitans' – Wallace Stevens, Rimbaud, John Crowe Ransom, Allen Tate. Also, I was drinking quite a lot and generally played the delinquent; Heaney did not drink, became an official of the university Catholic Students' Society, attended lectures, went to the library, wrote his essays.

I remember (with some embarrassment) an issue of the English Department student magazine, *Gorgon*, in which I published a long, shapeless poem, full of vacuous profundities, based on Allen Tate's

'Ode to the Confederate Dead', and in which Heaney had a short, shapely poem entitled 'Aran': it was as modest as mine was pretentious, as precise as mine was vague. Laurence Lerner asked me if I had noticed Heaney's poem. I had, but I wanted to hear what Lerner had to say about mine. Of course, that was what he had to say about mine, but I was too dumb to realize it then. Lerner did encourage me to write poetry, but I recall a letter from him in which he told me that these days a poet was still young at forty. That made me snort in derision. I told Heaney. He smiled and handed me a book of poems, *Domestic Interior,* by Lerner. He had been reading Lerner's poems; I had been reading Lerner's letters. The contrast was typical. Heaney was serving an apprenticeship. I was just being an undergraduate. Lerner put it nicely. Heaney, he said, was trying to write poems, and I was trying to write poetry.

We graduated in 1961. I went back to Derry briefly, to teach in a secondary school there, and then went on to Cambridge University to do doctoral research on the European Enlightenment.

Heaney stayed in Belfast, teaching in a secondary school. In the next five years, Belfast, and Queen's University in particular, became the site of a new literary energy. An English poet, Philip Hobsbaum, arrived to start a series of workshops. Heaney, Michael Longley, and other Belfast poets participated in them. A Belfast festival was inaugurated; it published several pamphlets of poems by these two, their friend Derek Mahon, and others. Heaney wrote to me in Cambridge and inveigled a sequence of poems from me which, unfortunately, was also published in that series. An exchange of letters on these poems was the first intimation I had that there was a new sense of excitement in the literary world of Belfast. It was also the first solid indication to me that Heaney was turning to a career as a poet. We lost contact after that for about two years. The Northern Revival, effectively the literary predecessor of, and then companion to, the Northern Troubles, initially passed me by – and then I had a surprise visit from Heaney in Cambridge. He had just been married, and he arrived with his wife, Marie, bearing a copy of his first book, *Death of a Naturalist,* news of a prize that went with it, and, wonder of wonders, a bottle of whiskey. Heaney the teetotaller had gone. Heaney the poet had arrived.

Within a few months, I left Cambridge to teach in America, where I stayed for two years. I came back from Berkeley and its storms and riots in 1968, just in time for the civil rights marches in Northern Ireland. By then, Heaney was a central figure in the Irish literary world, which had altered so much that I scarcely knew anyone in it. In the spring of 1969, he published his second volume, *Door Into the Dark*; in the next few years, with *Wintering Out* (1972) and, above all, with *North* (1975), he won widespread recognition both at home and abroad.

The early poems are like an acoustic autobiography. Heaney dwells on the names of places and people, their formal and official titles, their informal and demotic variants. Like any Irish countryman, Heaney has to lock a personal name into a place-name so that he can get a fix on the whole history and geography with which each is freighted. Names, titles, accents, nicknames, pronunciations are like a syrup in which a complex politics is suspended; they indicate class, sectarian divisions, family lineage, belongingness, even degrees of intelligence.

Throughout the first four volumes, he remained formally conservative. His poetry was concerned with retrieval, rediscovery, re-enactment. But it was clear, too, that every disinterred memory, every recaptured sensation, came in a nimbus of radiant light and feeling that made it seem new. After these early volumes, he began to expand the territory he was exploring. With *North*, he got out of Irish bogs and into Viking ones. All the Viking corpses and artefacts so beautifully Brailled onto the page were also relics of tribal revenge and violence. The poems are both repressing atrocity and acknowledging it. Their bearing upon the Northern Irish landscape was sadly vivid, vividly sad, for they mutate suddenly into an image of a living girl, tarred and feathered and tied to railings outside a church, to punish her for consorting with British soldiers:

> I who have stood dumb
> when your betraying sisters,
> cauled in tar,
> wept by the railings
>
> who would connive
> in civilized outrage

yet understood the exact
and tribal, intimate revenge.
('Punishment', North, 1975)

During those early years of the Troubles, Heaney was teaching in Queen's University, in the department where we had been students together. In Belfast, Heaney, increasingly well known as a voice from the nationalist community, received the occasional threatening phone call, and was eventually singled out for attention by Ian Paisley's newspaper, the *Protestant Telegraph.* In 1972, he left his university position to live in County Wicklow, twenty-five miles south of Dublin, and to concentrate on his writing. I was married by then and was teaching at University College, Dublin. A couple of years later, while house-hunting in Dublin, my wife, Marion, and I saw, and considered bidding for, a house that she said the Heaneys would love; the next day, they saw it and bought it. Now we were once again in the same city.

In those years, it was easy to meet often. Sometimes we talked in pubs, or in one another's houses; more often, it seemed, we talked while driving the winding road down to Wicklow through Shanganagh, Shankill, Newtownmountkennedy, under the hill of the Sugar Loaf above Kilmacanogue and the Glen of the Downs, into Ashford, then a right turn towards the Devil's Glen, below which his gate-lodge hideaway stood. It seemed to rain a lot, specifically on us. I now recall half a dozen conversations as a hypnotized drone dominated by the metronomic dunk-dunk of the windscreen wipers clearing their half-moon snapshots of gleaming road and dripping trees.

One night in October, 1976, after I had given a talk at Heaney's invitation, at Carysfort Training College, in Blackrock, County Dublin, where he was teaching in the English Department, and had taken a lot of tea and buns, we agreed to go back to my house in our separate cars for a redemptive whiskey. I was driving ahead of him. A motorcyclist swerved in front of me, and, when I turned my car to avoid him, it began to ascend a lamppost, which blazed whitely through my window while one of the wheels erupted through the floor. I managed, somehow, to lift my legs away from being crushed just as the car gave up its attempt to travel vertically and slammed despondently to the ground. I tried to open the door, but it had jammed, and there was Heaney's face at the window, frantic, and Heaney dragging on the door handle, beating the glass. I finally emerged, to be met by one very upset poet. After the police had done their business, Heaney drove me home. I was totally unhurt. As we sat – Marion, Seamus, and I – in the living-room, drinking strong tea and talking about the accident, he seemed to go into sudden shock, and began talking in the slow, drawly way of the boarder. 'Och aye', 'Man, dear', 'Them's the boys', and other phrases from the rural dialect emerged, with much head shaking and rattling of the teacup. He came out of it soon enough to tell me that he had thought I was a goner, 'you fucker, you'. We agreed that driving and drinking tea was not a combination to be recommended or repeated. But it had been a close call. Such a boarder he was, and, when I saw his shock and distress again, such a friend. It almost made me shy to think of it.

Robert Lowell had become one of Heaney's better-known friends after they met in London, in the early seventies. In 1977, at Heaney's request, Lowell gave a reading in Kilkenny, about seventy-five miles southwest of Dublin. I wanted to attend, but I was delayed. By the time I got there, the dinner afterward was well under way and a massacre of literary Ireland appeared to have taken place. Various figures were lying about in chairs or slumped over tables as though they had been shot. In the midst of it all sat Lowell, drinking whiskey and milk alternately. He summoned me over to talk to him, since I seemed to be the only person still conscious. A long monologue ensued, in which Lowell wondered about poetry and power, the relative status in world history of Shakespeare, Virgil, and Dante, on the one hand, and of Napoleon, Stalin, and Hitler, on the other. He was talking very fast, his eyes darting like fish, and he grabbed my arm every so often and then apologized for having done so. 'Should we take poetry – all of that – seriously at all? Tell me yes, give me reasons.' But he wouldn't have listened if I had replied. Still, in his distress, he managed to look very senatorial and upright amid that scene of magnificent debauch.

Heaney revered Lowell's patrician authority, his Daedalus–Icarus combination of the classical and the Romantic, repeatedly driving itself to the point of breakdown. I guess Heaney showed too much respect for people who took risks, because he disliked in himself a characteristic that he felt was a failure. He was, indeed, as cautious as a cat, and instinctively played safe, was nice to everyone, entertained (in every sense of the word) multitudes of people at his home, among whom the percentage of hangers-on must have been considerable. But, as usual, Heaney was also fomenting a little rebellion in his more recondite provinces of feeling. Heaney, the man who writes poems, can sometimes rail at Heaney the Poet, the public persona. The authority of reputation is not identical with the authority of the writer's voice; it may undermine it. What Heaney observed and admired in Lowell was his way of dealing with this conflict.

In the 1980s, Heaney became a more pronounced and profiled figure; he was appointed the Boylston Professor of Rhetoric and Oratory at Harvard and the Professor of Poetry at Oxford. Like Robert Lowell, he began to have the appearance not so much of someone who writes poetry as of someone who embodies an idea of poetry, the stamped-on-a-coin look of impersonal gravity. But the poetry itself, especially after the publication of *The Haw Lantern*, in 1987, was becoming lighter, moving off the sucking, dragging ground and into the air. Miłosz, Brodsky, and Walcott would eventually become his new mentors and friends, new exemplars for the complicated passages he was tracking from conditions of oppression to those of freedom, from dispute, clamour, and violence to serenity, oracularity, and wisdom, from the transformation of memory into the condition of reverie, a Yeatsian manoeuvre.

This process continued into *The Spirit Level*, the winner of the 1996 Whitbread Book of the Year and the first volume of poetry he published after he was awarded the Nobel Prize in Literature, in 1995. But it was his third Whitbread winner, his translation of the Old English poem *Beowulf* (1999), that reminded readers of the battle that lies at the heart of his work. The deadly combat between the dragon and Beowulf is not only a story of a fight with a monstrous and evil force. It is also an emblem of the struggle between civilization and its opposite. If freedom has the air as its natural habitat, violence clings to the ground. Yet, like the dragon, it can rise from its buried lair and infect the air: the 'ground-burner' is also the 'sky-roamer'. Since his undergraduate days, Heaney has been fascinated by this poem. His translation is one further act of retrieval, taking an Old English poem into the ambit of Northern Ireland, where the ancient combat between monstrous violence and the search for peace is even now being refought at a political level.

In Heaney's work, peace needs a space that is not emptiness: it needs to be a rich space, brimming with light. In one of his essays, Heaney remembers a chestnut tree that was planted in front of his house the year he was born. Later, when his family moved, the tree was cut down. In his early forties, he 'began to think of the space where the tree had been' and 'to identify with that space'. It is remarkable how fond Heaney becomes of empty spaces that only light can fill; how within them there remains in the memory the trace of a physical object that defines the emptiness. It is a parable of what happens in his poetry, how all the *quidditas, haecceitas* – the thinghood of things – is transmuted into an air that remains alive and actual. I remember meeting his parents at their home; his parents meeting mine at our graduation from university; the ready sympathy between them; then their deaths. The sense of the space that they vacated and created for both of us was like a resource, for which Heaney found the appropriately confident words:

> Do not waver
> Into language. Do not waver in it.
> *('Squarings', Seeing Things, 1991)*

*

Stockholm, December, 1995. The tall, brooding houses, the candles and braziers that everywhere rebuked the early dark and the glittering cold; the sheen from Lake Malaren beyond the windows of the Grand Hotel. There was a smile in the air that emanated from the Irish guests, including old friends of Heaney's, among them Ann Friel and David Hammond; from friends and publishers like Matthew Evans, Caroline Michel, Peter Fallon, Helen Vendler. Faber and Faber, someone suggested, should get a Nobel Prize for winning Nobel Prizes. In the glare of a prize like this, a sense of unreality emerges. That was readily heightened by the staggering bill for drinks that David Hammond, a singer and filmmaker from Belfast, received after he had sat in the bar for the first evening, on 8 December, like a master of ceremonies, inviting all and sundry whom he knew, and many whom he did not, to join him. We pored over the bill together, converting kronur into pounds and then looking at each other in wild surmise. 'Can't be', he said, and we did it again. But it was. He had spent the price of his air ticket twice over.

So, too, with the prize. 'It can't be' was one reaction that ran in me. But it was so. After a false alarm, a couple of years earlier, when a rumour swept Dublin that he had won, here it was. Heaney, when I finally met him coming out of the elevator, was exhausted, burdened by a heavy cold. Burdened, too, by this immensity. At a reception later that evening in his suite, and at another the next day, at the Irish Embassy, he seemed to have become more dignified and at the same time more shy. The shyness reminded me of a pen name he had used when he first started to publish poems in the university magazine – 'Incertus'. Yet with this shyness there was a leonine air.

The next evening, as I watched him receive the Nobel Prize in Literature, sitting there on the stage of the concert hall, to the left of the King and Queen of Sweden, shifting the boxed medal in his hands, I began to feel a certain emptiness. That feeling was still there in the great banquet room of Stockholm's Town Hall, when he spoke to more than a thousand guests seated at tables and announced that he found it hard to believe but knew it was true that he had won the Nobel Prize in Literature. The celebrations were a mixture of solemnity and exuberance. In the middle of the meal, the musical accompaniments that had been supplied by various choirs and musicians in a gallery above gave way to a moment straight out of the Eurovision song contest. A group of men and women, in Nordic folk outfits, began to descend the stairs, singing; halfway down, their leader suddenly leaped on the wide balustrade, straddled it, and began to slide down it backward, yodelling over his shoulder. That capped the sense of unreality.

What was the emptiness? I felt that I was witnessing two things: the real celebration, the real prize, the real achievement, and a simulacrum of that. The difference between them was like the difference between the moment of winning the prize and the moment of having won it. I remembered that I had once addressed a letter to Heaney with his name in quotation marks on the envelope – 'Seamus Heaney'. He liked that. But Heaney was aware, too, of the chemistry that alters a writer who has gained fame and transforms him from what he is to what his reputation is. I felt as though I were seeing him recede into an abstraction, another one of the Irish Nobel winners, up there with Shaw and Yeats and Beckett, an object of national pride, a writer reified into a prize.

Yes, that was the emptiness.

Would we ever be as we had been? Would his fame now leave me, and others, feeling that we, I, had nothing left to say except that we had remained ordinary, whereas he had become extraordinary? It was a powerful, spurious emotion. I recalled a phrase he had used in an essay about dramatizing the strains between 'collective historical experience' and 'the emerging self'. He hoped that he could do so 'by meeting shades from my own dream-life who had also been inhabitants of the actual Irish world'.

And I could already hear the jealous murmurings that were to come, especially in Ireland: 'He got it too early. That's him finished now.' On that evening in Stockholm, no one could have predicted that, over the next four years, with *The Spirit Level* and *Beowulf*, Heaney would intensify the earlier conflict in his work between a serene freedom and a haunting violence. Reading his version of *Beowulf* now, I find it strange that the Swedes of old should return again in the aftermath of Beowulf's death:

> Nor do I expect peace or pact-keeping
> Of any sort from the Swedes.
>
> *(Beowulf, 1999)*

Today, these lines rise menacingly and ironically above my memory of the Swedish King and Queen as they rose at the end of the celebrations, and we with them, to lead the Nobel laureates out of the hall.

As I watched Heaney move with the others at a steady pace, I thought, Here it is, December, 1995, and, whatever is said hereafter, the moment has not only chosen Heaney but Heaney has also chosen the moment. I imagined shouting across the tables and above the applause, 'Tell me, Seamus, what is the secret of –' And him turning, smiling, without breaking stride, and answering, 'Timing, timing.'

CHAPTER 16

The End of the World

HELGA

THE STEAMSHIP *Helga* TOOK PART IN THE FIRST *Clare Island* Survey OF 1909–11; THEN, REFITTED AS A GUNBOAT, SHE shelled the centre of Dublin during the 1916 Rising. She later became a troopship and transported some of the notorious Black and Tans to different ports in Ireland when the roads were blocked. Eventually, the new Free State bought the ship while the Black and Tans and RIC men, hardened by their Irish experience, left to continue their rampages among the unfortunate villagers of Iraq in 1922. The *Helga* thus passed out of the history of world domination and into the quiet desuetude of the Irish Free State naval service.

LUSITANIA

The son of Lady Gregory's sister Adelaide, Sir Hugh Lane, the art dealer, once Director of the Irish National Gallery, Gregory's favourite nephew and a friend of Yeats, left for the United States on 12 February 1915 from Liverpool on board the *Lusitania*. It was then, just before the journey out, that he decided to change his will for a second time and to bequeath his important collection of Impressionist paintings to the Dublin Municipal Gallery, as he had initially done. But the codicil he added was never witnessed. The collection was claimed by the National Gallery in London, to whom Lane, in disgust at the failure of the Dublin municipal authorities to build a gallery for the paintings, had, in his second will, assigned the collection. Lane took the *Lusitania* on its return journey to Liverpool and perished, with 1,200 others, off the coast of County Cork on the afternoon of 7 May 1915, when the liner was struck by a torpedo fired from a German U-boat. A long dispute over the will, in which Lady Gregory was prominent, followed; but her persuasive *Case for the Return of Sir Hugh Lane's Pictures to Dublin* of 1926, although it did contribute to the eventual settlement of the dispute, was not successful at the time.

The Lane pictures controversy was no more than a sideshow to the controversy which followed the sinking. It was a powerful exercise in propaganda, carefully aimed at an American audience. The strike was presented as a uniquely barbaric act; a ship with no military purpose or capacity attacked without warning in an extension of war to innocent civilians, a fearful harbinger of what was to come. Centrally, since some of the dead were Americans, it was taken as an act of war by Germany on the USA. The initial statement by President Woodrow Wilson in 1914 of the American position on the war, 'to be neutral in fact as well as in name', allowed him to be re-elected in November 1916 as the man who 'kept us out of the war'. But Wilson's increasingly aggressive diplomatic notes to Germany about the *Lusitania* attack made war inevitable. His Secretary of State William Jennings Bryan resigned over the issue, claiming that it was British policy to use US passengers on civilian liners to disguise the shipment of military contraband. By 1917, Wilson abandoned his earlier position, declared the era and time of neutrality had passed, that the causes of world peace and the freedom of peoples made America's intervention in the war necessary.

The impetus for this turn also came from internal American politics. In Wilson's bitter struggle against the unions, especially against the International Workers of the World, the famous IWW, he had made the legal justification of 'Emergency Powers' for either the President or Congress a strategic goal. Joe Hill, the IWW leader, was 'the author of a cartoon in *Class War News* figuring an IWW submarine firing on the ship of "Capitalism"'.[1] (The first animated cartoon made for propaganda purposes was of the sinking of the *Lusitania*.)

Certainly, the distinction between making 'the world safe for democracy' and making it safe for Americans became so slight that it quickly became a widespread belief that most or all of those who perished on the *Lusitania* were American. Meyers points up the similarities between this event and September 11, and how emergency powers for internal purposes and for war abroad were fused in both cases in the atmosphere of 'civic war'[2] that obtained between the sinking of the *Lusitania* and the American declaration of war on 6 April 1917. The fact that the German embassy in the USA had warned on 1 May 1915, when the *Lusitania* was leaving New York, that civilian ships were being used by the Allies to transport munitions and that they would be on that account regarded as legitimate targets was dismissed as in any way excusing the sinking.

Even at the time, there were suspicions. The liner exploded with a force that seemed remarkable for one torpedo hit. It sank just eighteen minutes after being struck. It had sailed so close to the Irish coast, against specific instructions for liners in this stretch of dangerous water, it had no armed escort, it pursued a straight rather than the usual zigzag course advised for large ships, and the regular armed escort for that area had been ordered away some hours before by Churchill. Was the ship deliberately sacrificed to bring America into the war? Seven hundred and sixty-one passengers were saved, but the newspapers concentrated on those who died, particularly on Alfred of the famous Vanderbilt family, much more than on Hugh Lane and the collection of famous paintings in lead-lined tubes that he reputedly had on board – Impressionist paintings, maybe even a Rembrandt, a Rubens, a Titian? One wealthy passenger, Welsh mining magnate D. A. Thomas, survived; a newspaper printed the headline: 'Terrible Disaster: D. A. Thomas Saved'.[3] One who did not survive, Thomas Atkinson, from London, was not wealthy. With three sixpences in his jacket pocket, he was brought ashore behind a small currach, his body attached to a buoy, floating vertically in the water, at the Blasket Islands off the coast of Kerry to where he and sections of the ship's structure and cargo were swept by the tides over the next few days. The bodies of two passengers were swept up on the beach of Aran Island and buried in the corner of the communal graveyard. And there was another echoic return to this area of the sea off Kerry. The torpedo officer who pressed the button that sank the *Lusitania* was Raimund Weisbach who, six months later, was the captain of the U-19 that brought Roger Casement to Banna Strand on Good Friday 1916. U-20 was in fact the submarine on which Casement set out; but it developed engine trouble, so the Irish party was transferred to U-19.

The Irish novelist Violet Martin (of Somerville and Ross fame) while out for a walk had seen the *Lusitania* pass half an hour before its sinking. In the sixth volume, *Le temps retrouvé*, of *À la recherche du temps perdu*, published in 1927, the ghastly Mme Verdurin is presented as reading of the sinking the day after in the newspaper. In this passage, Proust is – among other things – satirizing and relishing the sumptuous selfishness of those who live comfortably and ignorantly in the midst of disaster. Charlus, the novel's chief grotesque, pursues his sexual pleasures 'never dreaming that the Germans – albeit immobilized by a bloody yet constantly replenished barrier – were an hour by car from Paris'. The Verdurins have a political salon every week, so they

> must have thought about it ... And they did, it is true, think about the hecatombs of regiments annihilated and passengers swallowed by the sea ... but a reciprocal process so far multiplies whatever concerns our own well-being, and divides by such a formidable number whatever does not concern us, that the death of millions of unknown people hardly troubles us, and we find it scarcely as disagreeable as a cold draught. Mme Verdurin, suffering from migraines again now that there were no croissants to dip in her coffee, had finally obtained an order ... allowing her to have them made for her ... She received the first of these croissants on the morning when the newspapers reported the wreck of the *Lusitania*. As she dipped it in her coffee, and flicked her newspaper with one hand so that it would stay open without her having to remove her other hand from the croissant she was soaking, she said, 'How awful! It's worse than the most horrific tragedy'. But ... even while she uttered, through a mouthful of croissant, these distressing thoughts, the look which lingered on her face, probably induced by the taste of the croissant, so valuable in preventing migraine, was more like one of quiet satisfaction.[4]

Medically speaking, eating her precious croissant should have made Mme Verdurin's migraine worse, not better, but, when combined with her reading of the news of the *Lusitania*, it felt to her like the perfect cure. She consumes the news that the newspaper provides. The Viennese journalist Karl Kraus, always alert to the mass media's inexhaustible capacity to turn 'the most horrific tragedy' into cliché, to reduce disaster into the sheer materiality of printer's ink, the 'covering' of the page becoming the 'covering' of the event, believed that the miracles of technological advance catastrophically reduced the ethical capacity of the audiences they created. This is the abiding preoccupation of his epic collage-play of 1918, *The Last Days of Mankind*, in which the voices of the drowned children of the *Lusitania* are heard singing in the general uproar. Elias Canetti wrote that Kraus had a capacity for 'acoustic quotation' which allowed him to read the 'newspapers as though he were hearing them. The black, printed dead words were audible to him. When he quoted them, he seemed to be letting voices speak acoustic quotations.'[5] In Kraus's view, anyone who speaks a language of congealed cliché and stock phrases, whose consciousness is dominated by the newspaper, advertising, and bureaucratic officialese, is equipped to accept massacre in a placid, robotic spirit. It's on the surface of society, where the media dominate, that the roots of society's problems lie – specifically the capacity to endorse, even enjoy, the mass killing of others, preferably with a croissant in hand.

Kraus was speaking of Europe in general but of Austria, and especially Vienna, in particular. In Germany and in Austria the news of the *Lusitania* was received with delight as a proof that submarine warfare was working against the British attempt to impose mass starvation by naval blockade. (Thomas Mann rejoiced at the news in his *Reflections of an Unpolitical Man*.) Still, the image of the doomed *Lusitania* was a gift for British recruiting posters; since they controlled the transatlantic cable, British newspaper owners influenced American news. This was a propaganda feast. There were riots in Liverpool, Manchester, and London after news of the sinking was broadcast. Most of the coal trimmers and stokers on the liner were Liverpool Irish from the north end of the city; the first riots began there with attacks on shops (particularly pork butchers) owned by long-settled German families. Crowds in other English cities followed suit as the wave of outrage rose. The government finally intervened by introducing internment for 'enemy aliens' and repatriating large numbers of ethnic Germans.[6] The Hun, the barbarian, in France the Boche – this was the common enemy of humankind. In the final volume of his great novel, Proust predicted that the name 'Boche', like that of 'Dreyfusard', would become almost meaningless within a few years – hard as that was to believe for those who had lived through the storms of the Dreyfus affair.[7] He overstated the case. The 'sale Boche' survived intact for some decades.[8] Still, having barbarians as enemies had its advantages. Cavafy's famous poem of 1904, 'Waiting for the Barbarians', concludes, 'In a way, those people were a solution.'

*

Some years later, one of Freud's patients, an American, who claimed he loved his wife very much, invited her to take the *Lusitania* and join him in Europe. He had meant to say the name of the sister-ship, the *Mauretania,* on which he himself had come over. But, Freud told him, this showed that he really wanted to kill his wife. Such a diagnosis, based on this example of what Freud called 'parapraxis', really irritated the Italian Marxist Sebastiano Timpanaro whose book *The Freudian Slip: Psychoanalysis and Textual Criticism* (1974; trans. 1976) attacked Freud's 'mania for psychologising':

> The transatlantic steamer, *Lusitania,* which was sunk in the war by a German submarine and thus became the subject of much emotion and hostility, was much better known than her sister-ship the *Mauretania* – all the more so in the case of the 'slip' cited by Freud, whose author was an American, since it was for the most part Americans who had perished in the disaster of the *Lusitania.*[9]

Just over 10 per cent of the dead were Americans. Timpanaro here makes the political slip, a mark of the incident's reputation for having directly brought the USA into the War. Freud's 'slip', as Timpanaro called it, provoked Timpanaro's.

Writing in the 1970s, Timpanaro felt it important to affirm materialism in the face of so many sophistries that claimed to be in alliance with Marxism. 'Psychoanalysis', he wrote, 'is neither a natural nor a human science, but a self-confession by the bourgeoisie of its own misery and perfidy, which blends the bitter insight and ideological blindness of a class in decline'.[10] Moreover, Timpanaro accuses Freud of relying on intuition, or at least of not revealing the code of his system.[11] Perhaps now, in retrospect, Timpanaro's objection to this kind of detective work on Freud's part seems justified, although his general description of psychoanalysis is more troubling. Certainly, when we reread Freud and

Proust together, the death of the European bourgeoisie is more evidently than ever a shared theme. In the gap between the physical taste of Mme Verdurin's croissant and her sense of gratification at having it, we can sense the decay that surrounds the story of the Verdurins and the disintegration of the society that once despised them. As with the analysis of Freud's middle-class Viennese, it is civilization, not just a class, that is being exposed.

So Timpanaro's charge survives his own slip. It has been often said that psychoanalysis (or psychology, with which it is frequently conflated) is an ideal pseudo-science for and of the bourgeoisie in the last phase of its historical domination of Europe – and, by extension, of much of the world. With that bite of the croissant, as Mme Verdurin reads the newspaper account of the sinking and exclaims how dreadful it all is, and as a European public reads the novel in 1927 twelve years after the event (and in English in 1931), the *Lusitania* sinks again, definitively, into the density of literature. Watched for those last eighteen minutes from the Old Head of Kinsale by a picnic party and from underwater through a periscope glass, as it toppled into the waves, it reappeared the next day in photographs, and then again and again, in poster images, paintings, sculpted memorials, year on year. Whatever the sinking was – a diabolic act, engineered by the British to bring in the Americans, a barbarous act by the U-boat commander, its 'meaning' was quickly captured by the media and deeply imprinted in public opinion thereafter as an image of the threat sliding under the surface of civilized life. The sinking of the *Titanic* three years earlier was a blow to technological pride by an impersonal Nature, but here there was a villain. A great ethical divide had opened into which the old world suddenly vanished as the passengers and lifeboats were tilted into the now-distant sea. In Paris, wrote Proust, 'one of the most fashionable ideas was the claim that the pre-war period was separated from the war by something as deep, something seemingly as long-lasting, as a geological period'.[12] This 'fashionable idea' became almost proverbial in modernism. Adorno ended his essay of 1941, 'Schoenberg and Progress', on the fate of modern music which

> has taken upon itself all the darkness and guilt of the world . . . music which has not been heard falls into empty time like an impotent bullet . . .

> Modern music sees absolute oblivion as its goal. It is the surviving message of despair from the shipwrecked.[13]

*

The Irish-American Fenian Brotherhood financed the first submarine, 'Holland Boat Number 1', launched on the Passaic River, New Jersey on 22 May 1878. The vessel was named after John Holland from Liscannor in Co. Clare, the inventor and designer of the new submersible. The Fenians hoped that the new invention would be a threat to British naval supremacy; once their financing of the project became known, the New York newspapers named the underwater craft the *Fenian Ram.* But it was the US Navy, not the Fenians, who eventually bought USS *Holland VI,* its first submarine, from Holland's firm, by then owned by a German-born businessman. The successful trial runs Holland conducted off Staten Island on St Patrick's Day 1898, convinced the American authorities, including Theodore Roosevelt, of its potential usefulness against the Spanish fleet in Cuba in the Spanish-American war of that year. The *Holland* was never used against the Spanish but its successors were used against Germany in the First World War, which broke out two weeks before Holland's death on 12 August 1914. Submarine Day in the US Fleet, 11 April 1900, is the day of the submarine's (USS-1) purchase.

Could the submarine be anything but a machine of war? It was a vexed question. Were the *Bremen* or the *Deutschland* merchant vessels, 'commercial submarines' when they travelled unarmed with cargo to New York?[14] So too with a ship that was torpedoed, especially during a blockade. If it was named as a legitimate target, did that make it so? If it was, like the *Lusitania,* both a civilian liner and a warship, what was its status in international law? The character of the war at sea was drastically altered by the submarine, not only in its legal aspects but also in popular perception. The menace from below, the silent intent shadow pursuing an unsuspecting, vulnerable prey on the surface, intensified the nightmare of industrialized war more than the tank did on land, only exceeded in menace later by the scream of the dive bomber and the continuous thunder of approaching mass attacks from the air. In the case of the

Lusitania, it was the nomination of the victims that became crucial in the propaganda war. Most of the dead were Europeans but were 'remembered' as Americans. Dead Americans were the political point; the 'ethical' issue was subordinate. The survival of the dead in popular memory as Americans indicated an abrupt shift in world power to the USA.

Moreover, with the arrival of the submarine, the sea had become a theatre of war in a new sense. Submarines did not, could not take ships or crews prisoner as 'prize'. The emergence of a new international legal order at the expense of the European Public Law (*Jus Publicum Europaeum*) was almost as sudden as the American reversal of foreign policy. 'The purely maritime character of an important component of the conduct of sea war ... had been changed fundamentally and conclusively by the introduction of submarines.' So wrote Carl Schmitt, caustic, envious, and clear-sighted, the fascist jurist who recognized that the US had gained the power, by its dexterity in the quarrel over the use of the submarine, that Germany had believed was necessary for its own survival – to rewrite the law of the sea. The Great War had been a European affair; it became a World War with the American intervention. In 1928, the Kellogg Pact in effect made the US the arbiter of the international system. The old balance of powers had given way to a new hegemony. Universality, Globalization, and the World became the key terms of the vocabulary that began to rival, then replace, the legal idioms of the nation-state and the European balance of power. 'The praxis of the *Jus Publicum Europaeum* had sought to encompass conflicts within the framework of a system of equilibrium. Now they were universalized in the name of world unity.'[15]

The USA, in justifying its intervention in the First World War on the basis of what it claimed were international human rights – a repeated 'justification' for many future wars and, according to Hedley Bull and others, 'a direct offshoot of the missionary and colonizing tradition of the West, with its roots in the early nineteenth century, the period of US intervention in Cuba and the European intervention in the Ottoman Empire'[16] – criminalized war. Was Walther Schweiger, the U-boat commander, a war criminal? Was the declaration of unrestricted submarine warfare by Germany in 1917 outside the law? And what of all those submarine commanders, German, British, and American, who sank ships without warning in the Atlantic, the North Sea, and the Baltic in both World Wars and in the Pacific in the Second? Not to mention Captain Alexander Marinesko, of the Soviet S-13, whose three torpedoes brought down the German ship *Wilhelm Gustloff* in the Baltic off Danzig in 1945; it was crammed with refugees; 9,500 died, 4,000 of them children. Günter Grass's novel *Im Krebsgang* (*Crabwalk*) of 2002 not only commemorated that event but tried (by his own account) to deny the opportunistic charge by right-wing parties in Germany that this was a war crime. Grass claimed this was 'war', and *therefore* not a crime. Did this reasoning also apply in the case of the Argentine destroyer *Belgrano* which, as the US *Phoenix*, had survived Pearl Harbour, only to be sunk, without warning but after consultation with prime minister Thatcher, by the British nuclear submarine *Conqueror*, outside a declared war zone, with the loss of 323 lives, in May 1982? The *Lusitania* had a desolate and bloody heritage.

THE BLASKETS

> Ourselves, our souls alone. At the site of salvocean ... Based on traumscrapt from Maston, Boss.
>
> *Finnegans Wake*, 623

[An Blascaod Mór, the Great Blasket, is the largest of an archipelago of seven islands, just less than 2 kilometres off the coast of Kerry in southwest Ireland. It is one kilometre wide, 5 kilometres long. Its profile is perhaps 300 metres high, stretching southwesterly between the Blasket Sound and the Great Sound that separates it from the mainland at Dunquin and one of its smaller companion islands, Inis na Bró. The population never exceeded 200; in the early twentieth century this seems to have fallen to just over 100, but since 1953 the island has been uninhabited. In 1933, Fiche Bliain ag Fás (Twenty Years A-Growing*), by Muiris Ó Súilleabháin (Maurice O'Sullivan, 1904–50), was published in Irish in Dublin and in English translation (with a couple of passages omitted) in London. E. M. Forster contributed an Introductory Note to the English translation and the translators themselves, Moya Llewelyn Davies and George Thomson, added a Preface. Pádraig O Fiannachta and George Thomson co-edited the second edition of Fiche Bliain in 1976; Oxford University Press published*

a revised translation in 1953. The book is a memoir in which the author gives an account of his first twenty years on the Great Blasket. Dylan Thomas wrote a filmscript, published in 1964, but no movie of the book was ever made.]

We read in the memoir that shortly after the news reached the island that England and Germany were 'hurled against each other'[17] in war, came the harvest of the marine battle. German submarines (two of which were sunk near the Blaskets by Q-boats between 1915 and 1917) took a heavy toll of shipping off the Irish coast. Cargoes were often completely lost – coal, munitions, chemicals – but others regularly washed up on the beaches. The first great haul was timber. Almost the entire population of the island, over a hundred people, came down to the shore one day to collect a great forest of wooden planking that had filled the bay quite suddenly and that a storm tide then heaped upon the sand, some of the beams sixty feet long. This was wealth untold for the islanders. It was a day later that they learned it was fragments of the *Lusitania* that were dangerously overloading their currachs in their repeated plunges to the shore.

> 'By God,' one man would say, 'war is good.'
>
> 'Arra, man,' said another, 'if it continues, this island will be the Land of The Young.'[18]

That evening the 'King' of the Island announced that 'the end of the world is coming ... and England is going to send out conscription through the whole of Ireland'. But such news was beside the point for those listening. Impatiently a listener asked, 'did you hear of any ship being sunk in any place since?' It is then the 'King' tells them of the

> *Lusitania,* the finest ship the Americans ever had. They say there were millionaires in plenty on board and isn't it a terrible thing that not a sinner of them came ashore alive. If this breeze lasts from, the south tonight, the coast of the island will be full of drowned men tomorrow.' And everyone that night and next morning was out 'in search of the millionaires.[19]

But only one body came in after the wreckage of the liner. O'Sullivan's father pulled the corpse of Thomas Atkinson of London, identified by his pocket book as 'First-class Officer, S.S. *Lusitania*', from the sea, 'the eyes plucked out by the gulls, the face swollen, and the clothes ready to burst with the swelling of the body'; he had three sixpences in his pocket, which the islander who had drawn the pocket book from the foul-smelling corpse was allowed to keep by the police who came to collect the body. Thereafter, on at least two occasions, shipwrecked sailors made it to shore on lifeboats. Their survival perhaps indicated that the Germans were now giving warning before firing on merchant ships, as they had agreed to do in response to President Woodrow Wilson's protest over the sinking of the *Lusitania*. For several weeks, cargo washed ashore – boxed chocolates, barrels of apples, flour, wine, bacon, castor oil, pocket watches, clothes, leather strips and cowhides, cotton bales, wooden planks; 'there was plenty and abundance in the Island – food of all sorts, clothes from head to heel ... not a penny leaving home; everything a mouth could ask for coming in with the tide from day to day – all except the sugar, which melted as soon as it touched water'. One rescued sailor, telling how he had jumped from his doomed ship and gained land, says

> 'We thought then that it was some backward country with no one alive in it. But, upon my word,' said he, glancing around, 'you are here – fine, well-favoured people, mannerly, intelligent, generous, and hospitable.'[20]

The search of the islanders for millionaires was unsuccessful, but it was an American millionaire who eventually gained possession of the sunken liner and carried out a thorough and expensive investigation of the wreck. Gregg Bemis, a Texan millionaire, was granted a five-year licence by a Heritage Order of 2007, issued under the National Monuments Act of 1995, which had declared the site and the wreck of the liner a national monument, to undertake this task. The long search culminated in a two-hour television programme, *Dark Secrets of the Lusitania*, first aired on 14 July 2012 by National Geographic Broadcasters. (The Discovery Channel had aired an American-German production, *The Sinking of the Lusitania: Terror at Sea*, in 2007.) The 'secrets' had long been available. The *Lusitania* was both a civilian liner and a warship. In this dual role she was used to sustain the supply of war material and goods to Britain, which itself was blockading all supplies to Germany, particularly in the North Sea and the Baltic Sea. Some artefacts from the ship's bridge were recovered and donated to the Irish state and were accepted as memorials of 'a key moment' in that series of 'historic events that shaped the course of Irish history between 1912 and 1922',[21] which have now entered upon their centenary commemorations. The difficulties of underwater survey and retrieval had been enormously increased by the bombing of the site with depth charges by the British Navy in the 1950s; some of these hedgehog mines have been clearly seen on the monitor screens of the diving operation. In 2008, divers found a huge quantity of rusted weapons. The ship was indeed a warship. Yet, with all the evidence that has piled up against the accusation that the torpedoing was an unprecedented act of barbarism, outside the limits of international law, the *Lusitania* has remained an emblem of the pitiful consequences of war for humankind. (The evidence of a conspiracy or of opportunism makes it an even darker portent.) The names and numbers of the dead and of the survivors are known, but the numbers of those seduced by the unceasing propaganda about it into armed service are unknowable – one key constituency targeted in the recruitment drive that followed, especially given the Irish resistance to conscription, were Irishmen who were exhorted to 'AVENGE THE LUSITANIA / JOIN AN IRISH REGIMENT'.

'MAR NÁ BEIDH ÁR LEITHÉIDÍ ARÍS ANN . . .'

The literature of the Blasket Islands and indeed of all the western islands of Ireland (from Gola in Donegal to Aran in Galway) in the twentieth century is woven, sometimes exquisitely, around a belief by and about the islanders themselves:

> I have written minutely of much that we did, for it was my wish that somewhere there should be a memorial of it all, and I have done my best to set down the character of the people around me so that some record of us might live after us, for the like of us will never be again.[22]

Tomás Ó Criomhthain's *An t-Oileánach* (1929), translated by Robin Flower as *The Islandman* (1937), is the abiding classic of this elusive genre which is a memorial to the island people, to the Irish language, and to the European idea of an 'organic' community. The moment of extinction, when the elements of wind and sea will prevail over an abandoned island, is mobilized from the beginning of the narrative to render the sense of the personal life or of the habitual life of the community more precious. Against the natural, the human is as helpless as a body in a vast, running sea. Only these final images, we are told, will be left to us of a heroic, eloquent, and lovable people; we gaze at them now and they gaze at us like Easter Island statues across the ocean that walled them in throughout history. The communal time stretches from beyond the Christian era to the earliest stages of human existence. The lure of these writings is increased, not only by their extraordinary idiomatic eloquence but also by the implication of a natural equality, that this gift is a 'natural' acquisition, perhaps even an instinct (not that the word 'instinct' explains anything, but has the merit of claiming there is no longer any need for explanation). Here we have a living language in the most enhanced sense of the term, especially as it is Irish, a language that had been almost exterminated and was still in the 1930s trying to sustain, as a political as well as a cultural project, the revival that had begun in the 1890s. Some of the islanders could remember how they had once been despised by the people of Dunquin on the mainland because they had Irish only and no English. But since the first language revival and especially since the publication and warm reception of *The Islandman*, the islanders had become respected and celebrated, not least because of the increased tourist trade they had begun to attract. In February 2009, the Irish government purchased the Great Blasket from a private company (Blascaod Mór Teoranta) for €2 million and it became a National Historic Park under the aegis of the Office of Public Works, which has now completed the restoration of the deserted village. Dunquin opened a Heritage Centre devoted to the abandoned island facing it.

The life realized in these writings is the more enchanting because it has been 'discovered', has always been there and yet has only now arrived in the modern consciousness. This is as unexpected and more troubling than a geographic/anthropological discovery. 'Only in the middle of the twentieth century CE did two Australian prospectors stumble, to mutual astonishment, on the hitherto unknown societies of the New Guinea Highlands.'[23] Synge had of course 'discovered' the Aran islands in the last years of the nineteenth century; *The Aran Islands, The Playboy of the Western World*, and *North Kerry* all belong to 1907, and all enact that thrill of discovery that was supposed to belong only to the anthropologist and was equally supposed, in the highly globalized late nineteenth or early twentieth century, not to be any longer possible, since the world was so comprehensively known, mapped, invaded, dominated, and recognizable. And yet in Europe, in the first quarter of the twentieth century, two such 'places' had been discovered, both of them part of the geography, history, and ideology of the old and the new Ireland.

It could be argued that for painters, writers, and patriots – especially of the counter-revolutionary family – Brittany, as a 'Romantic' territory, had anticipated these discovered Irish islands. Yet because it was part of a or of *the* continent (or Continent, *le Vieux Continent*), because it had figured prominently in French history since the Revolutionary era, it was 'known' and so lacked the surprise element of the Blaskets. It was indeed as 'Celtic' as anyone in search for an enchantment to counter-modernity could wish for. But it had been too long embroiled in the crises of modernity, however faithful it was to its ancient religious and pagan traditions. It was in thrall to the sea, but not surrounded by it; it had had, since the middle of the nineteenth century, the staged symbolism of Chateaubriand's grave alternately appearing above and disappearing under the waves. And Frédéric Mistral's campaign for the recovery of Occitan in Provence and the idea of that language and territory as the enchanted realm of the ancient and Graeco-Roman-French spirit of the premodern world had ensnared many in 'the false brilliance of a bogus history'[24] peddled by the French Right of Barrès and Maurras.[25] And another image of perfection, as in Alain Fournier's *Le Grand Meaulnes* (1913), appearing just before the war in which its creator died, was heartbreakingly unreachable, a realm not a place, a flash photograph of what had never existed until it was, in that moment of capture, as war began, revealed as lost.

The Blaskets were different. They were a place that became an image, an actuality that became an ideal type. This micro-archipelago looked to its largest island, the Great Blasket; in turn it looked to a yet larger island, Ireland; and Ireland to a continent that it could belong to or that could belong to it. As this serial synecdoche was pursued, Ireland once more in the twentieth century offered to modernity an opportunity for re-enchantment. Yeats and Synge in their generation had already seized it in the image of the Aran islands and the Irish West. That was before political independence; now here it was to be seized again, after political independence. Although both seizures belong in a continuum, they are nevertheless distinct phases. They have the same structure. A part (an island) that stands in for the whole (Ireland); that is then repeated, as Ireland (an island) stands in for the whole (Europe); and within this structure of replication and enlargement in geography, there is the accompanying transition in historical time, from the present moment to the most distant past (ancient or medieval Ireland or ancient Greece); then the dimension of the historical itself dissolves into the prehistorical or eternal (where the human and the natural become fused in an originary human nature). In this latter case, whereby the Blaskets become the site of a national project, closely allied to that of the Revival, the process of memorializing – dependent throughout on the *acknowledgement* of extinction that is itself a creative act, a cultural stimulant to which the Irish had developed a necessary addiction – is intricate, hidden within the fiction of its spontaneity.

Ireland had two revivals in the first fifty years of the twentieth century. They are structurally so similar that in them the same thing appears to happen twice; or, as has been said of the two acts in *Waiting for Godot*, 'nothing happens – twice'. But this 'nothing' is the feeble word we use for the pressure that builds within to disintegrate the meaning of 'happens'. The key Blasket island memoirs conflate the period they recall with the process of remembering it. That period is historical, in that it has datable moments and even more in the sense that for the narrators everything swings on the pivot of time, 'that time when' (*fadó* in Irish, *olim* in Latin), and yet it is the dimension of time that melts, like a frozen sea in a climbing temperature, into a sempiternity that, only when it has successfully replaced historical time, reveals and performs its historical function. That, in short, is the function of legitimizing the newly formed Irish state (which of course only reaches its specific gravity in 1932 with the accession of De Valera to power) as the domain of the ancient European civilization, which had elsewhere collapsed – and had Europe but known, it was, in 1929–33, finally to fall away, as in a geological disaster, from the continent that it had created and that had created it.

Twice, versions of the West and of the immemorial had become in Ireland new sites for the creative act by which 'a people is a people'.[26] In each case, the immemorial was a code for the utopian. But in the second case, the 1930s, the centrality of the memoir secured the notion of the generic individual as the inhabitant of this condition and had, as its stated aim, the commemoration of a community that was about to disappear and the (unstated) aim of thereby creating in it a heightened consciousness of itself. It produces a utopian political community by lamenting the disappearance of an historic one. Its goal was the collective, not any version of the realization of the 'self'. In a sense, the genre of the 'memoir', which is highly problematic (ethnographic, auto-ethnographic?), reveals the function of the form more readily than any specifiable protocols. The generic mode, although it certainly allows for and even promotes the idea of the heroic, also promotes the concept of equality. This is not heroic individuality, not Christy Mahon becoming a playboy as the community reverts to nullity. This is an heroic community that is being created, an island people becoming, for Ireland, *le peuple*; what is set down here is not an 'I' but 'the character of the people around me', in Ó Criomthain's phrase.

*

A MINOR LITERATURE, A MAJOR LANGUAGE

Ever since 'general theory' gave way to cultural studies, there has been by the latter an occasional attempt to smuggle in by the back door what had been expelled by the front. This has been peculiarly the case in relation to the Deleuze/Guattari idea of a 'minor' literature, which has had an irresistible appeal for postcolonial studies, since it seems to reformulate the relationship between a dominant major literature and the literature of an oppressed group. This misreading would be particularly unfortunate in the present case, although Irish or Irish-English seems ready-made for the occasion, because the central issues are so easily coarsened into banality by dividing them into a set of binary oppositions. For the idea of a minor literature, when more amply understood, has a bearing on the phenomenon of the Blaskets literature. Deleuze turns to Proust for support.

> We can see more clearly the effect of literature on language: as Proust says, it opens a kind of foreign language within language, which is neither another language nor a rediscovered patois, but a becoming-other of language, a 'minorization' of this major language, a delirium that carries it off, a witch's line that escapes the dominant system.[27]

Two of Deleuze's examples are from American literature – Thomas Wolfe and Herman Melville – since they demonstrate 'health as literature', which 'consists in inventing a people that is missing. It is the task of the fabulating function to invent a people.' Another example is T. E. Lawrence in *The Seven Pillars of Wisdom.* Drawing on E. M. Forster's distinction between 'granular' and 'fluid' writing, Deleuze shows how, out of the blazing light and emptiness of the desert, Lawrence invents a revolutionary people – in this case, the Arabs. Kafka is of course his central example. He and Melville, for Central Europe and America, respectively, 'present literature as the collective enunciation of a minor people, or of all minor people, who find their expression only in and through the writer'. It's a struggle for Deleuze to sustain the notion that a people so enunciated is always 'minor'. Writing at high intensity ('delirium') loses its force and becomes 'the disease par excellence, whenever it erects a race it claims is pure and dominant'. This is domination, racism. But the measure of writing's 'health' is taken when 'this oppressed bastard race that ceaselessly stirs beneath dominations' appears instead. This is 'a race that is outlined in relief in literature as process'. It is often the case that one kind of delirium, of domination, 'will be mixed with a bastard delirium', and in that mix, the racial can become racism, literature is pushed 'towards a larval fascism'.[28] (This is perhaps the outcome of reflection on Rousseau's *Du contrat social,* 1762.) Deleuze certainly makes the association of a 'major' literature with domination seem inescapable at times; and a 'minor' literature aspires to subversion, to refusal or at least sporadically realizes its ambition not to be canonized or even canonizable.

The pertinence of this to Irish writing is that translation, mostly between Irish and English but also, in Beckett's case, between French and English, is such a central activity, that it regularly raises questions of major and minor writings, of colonial and native, of original and copy, themselves regular victims of ambush in the guerrilla wars between the folkloric and the historical over the legitimacy of the the oral or the written. Do all of these form a set, a series, a hierarchy, an echelon, a double helix? Translation provides a theoretical basis for Pascale Casanova's work on the *Republic of Letters* in which the distinction between minor and major has to be worked hard and Ireland's prestigious place in that Republic illuminated.[29] Deleuze's work also leaves its mark in his student Anne Querrien's 'The Metropolis and the Capital' (1986) in which the metropolis is receptive to migration and multiversity while the capital dominates in the name of a single or consolidated set of interests. Inevitably, an island literature like that of the Blaskets will be claimed both by capital and by metropole, national and global readings. It will be weighed in relation to the 'minor' Irish language and 'major' English language traditions, although the demonstration that there is a major tradition of writing in the Irish language, preceding any such in English, or that there are more than enough Oedipal figures in Irish writing in English, makes everything more fissile and can lead readers to cry halt and settle for a plain and gross binary division that keeps life simple and literature simpler.

By the thirties, the Revival's claims for a natural (primitive, originary) eloquence had lost some of the power they had won in the early century. At least, the claims had changed and once more the emphasis moved from the achievement of an individuality through eloquence to the realization of a community's self-consciousness in language. The latent political function of the claim to eloquence was realized by a system of mediated writing, by which the question of individual authorship is raised not to weaken but rather to extend the text's communal authority. Language is a cultural wealth that is in inverse proportion to economic prosperity, the riches-in-rags story that had so many nuanced versions in the tramps of Synge and Yeats (and, again in the thirties, Beckett), and that had for over a century been an embedded feature of commentators on Irish-language speakers – 'natives', 'peasants'. Even in the late eighteenth and early nineteenth century, the impoverished Irish peasant had had a reputation for eloquence – in Latin – usually the only other language he/she shared with an English-speaking observer. This eloquence and learning were explained by the enormous impact of the ruined and learned Gaelic poets on the populace into whose weak and welcoming arms they fell after the final destruction of their courtly civilization in the seventeenth century. By keeping Ireland economically poor, the Union could advance the claim to be keeping it culturally rich – at least until the deadly and classic colonial use of famine as a weapon against a threateningly disobedient population, much used by the British in India also. That finally destroyed any notion that there was a near-mystical correlation between eloquence and poverty. The consequences for the Irish people and their language were almost fatal. Whatever was to be salvaged of the old civilization had to be 'collected' as quickly as possible – folklore, stories, curious turns of speech (*cora cainte*), customs, rituals. These memoirs stand within that tradition of collection which, as far as folk stories are concerned, goes back to the 1820s, again in the shadow of famine (and of Malthus), although its first impulse, belonging to the Enlightenment and not to Romanticism, comes from the Royal Irish Academy (1786). Eventually, the catastrophic economic relationship segued, attended by an anxious scholarship, from an imperial into a national stride in the Revival and then again, into its second wind, in the thirties.

*

Eloquence in Irish in the colonial mode had unexpected consequences. Since the language Revival, most notably in and since An t-athair Peadar Ó Laoghaire's *Mo Sgéal Féin* (*My Story*, 1915), much admired for its idiomatic richness, the quality of writing in Irish has been judged by its closeness to the spoken word. Writing here is secondary to speaking, in part because the speaking of the language had been since the Famine such a contested issue and because the superiority of the native as opposed to the school speaker was plainly audible in its ease, richness, and power, unmediated by enforced compromises with English or by any of the painful social embarrassments or self-consciousness that attended the choice of speaking a minority language that was supposedly outmoded. Therefore, the more isolated the area the more likely was the

Irish spoken there to be the real thing. And, since the Celtic languages had become of such strategic importance in the great Indo-European language tree largely created by German scholarship in the nineteenth century, a 'pure' example of this Celtic language, a surviving remnant, was a philological treasure. In the case of the Blaskets, the philological 'find' also became a civilizational find, a lost world discovered – with its enormous inner richness audible in its speech rather than in written texts. So even when the written texts appear, as with these memoirs of Peig Sayers, Ó Súilleabháin, or Ó Criomthain, they enact for the reader a contest for priority between the spoken and written. Some adaptation of Karl Kraus's acoustic gift would help, so that we could read them as though we were hearing them. But the usual difficulties of translation are, in such instances, so magnified that the act seems pointless. How can we 'hear' in English a language which has been compelled, for its survival, to proclaim a kind of acoustic autarky? All the translators of these texts are acutely aware of the near-impossibility of their position. Robin Flower, who translated *An t-Oileánach*, claims in his Foreword that 'Irish and English are so widely separated in their mode of expression that nothing like a literal rendering from the one language to the other is possible.' Although translation had of course been central to the Revival, Flower – important and emphatic in the making of this distinction – rejects the 'literary dialect', 'the mixture of Irish and English idioms' that had formerly been used 'for translation from the Irish or for the purpose of giving the effect of Irish speech'. No Synge song for this work. 'This literary dialect could not be used to render the forthright, colloquial simplicity of the original of this book.'[30] In fact, all the most obvious features of the earlier Irish English, its rich, slow obesity above all, needed to be replaced by an idiom that was sharp and fit, moulded by the harsh necessities of its social world.

Thus in these works, Irish has a mythical presence – something between a god of language and the language of God. Like any such presence it is knowable to the subordinate world through privileged or chosen speakers only. The language can be learned by members of a caste or elite, but it can only be mediated to the world at large in another language and another medium (print). The act of mediation or translation carries with it the inescapable whiff of betrayal; an oral culture is no longer so when recorded in writing – or later, on tape recorder or radio. Or at least what we have in these media is either the trace of the oral culture or another kind of culture that is born out of the contest between mediacy and immediacy. The choice is to lose it or record it but, in recording it, to change it. The contest between the oral culture and a recorded or collected version of it is thereby claimed to be fought on the demarcation line between nature and culture, with twentieth-century Irish uniquely bearing in itself the sound of that battle. Thus the scholars and antiquarians who have learned Irish and have come to recognize it as having a special place and role in the history, not just of linguistics but of civilization itself, are witnesses to and participants in a moment of birth. They are coaxing Ó Criomthain and Ó Súilleabháin to bear witness indeed but in doing so to re-enact the process by which culture ratifies itself – by revealing its source and spirit in nature.

The Blasket writings are not autobiographies or ethnographies, neither folklore nor legends. (*The Islandman* was originally a series of letters.) They are, so to speak, before genre. But they have something else – their newness, which is also something ancient, already-known. This language, like its speakers, is about to go into exile; for its recorders the emigration, which they cannot prevent, is to the world of culture. Irish is the world of nature and the Blaskets are the place in which the passage from one to the other is, incredibly but actually, happening – and they are watching, even enabling it. The mediation of such writing by people drawn to the islands from beyond magnifies the strong maieutic effect of the works. The spark of cognition is attended by the light of re-cognition. In this dappled linguistic weather, Irish and English lights are interwoven, often beautifully. But the overall action is one of modulation from one system to another, analogue to digital. Irish turns into English, a community becomes a set of emigrants, Dunquin becomes Springfield, Massachusetts. The rate of emigration quickened in the thirties; by 1942, what mackerel remained were being vacuumed up by Spanish fishing trawlers; the destitution of the islanders was radical. The death rate was as alarming as the emigration rate. One woman, Eibhlís Ní Súilleabháin, whose English was rudimentary, described their condition on 5 February 1942: cataloguing is now effective eloquence. There was

> No sugar . . . no soap, no tea, no tobacco and the worst of all no flour nor bread nor biscuits nor paraffin oil for light nor a candle.[31]

'Here', wrote Seán Ó Coileáin in 1978, 'the struggle is not for the luxury of meaning in existence, but for existence itself'.[32] Instead of visitors, from Synge in 1905 to Carl Marstrander in 1907 to Flower (1910) and Thomson (1923), whose love for the place had transformed it, the islands now have tourists, what Ní Súilleabháin calls the 'Lá breághs' – that is, those who had learned to say 'Fine day' in Irish and no more. The brutal hardship and poverty which was for a time one of the conditions for the exaltation of the island's 'spiritual' status, lost that function in the late thirties and brought what earlier had been the dramatic prospect of extinction to the numb reality of it.

PEIG

In all the writing about the Blaskets, this contrast between actual conditions and some 'idealized' version of them drones on, as is also the case for 'De Valera's Ireland', an inexhaustible cliché of the commentariat. The linkage between the two is common knowledge. Certainly, De Valera, his colleagues, and many of his notable contemporaries made it clear that there was a traditional Ireland, of which only traces remained, but which it was the (noble) ideology of the state to incarnate and preserve as far as possible. Thus the Irish Folklore Commission was founded in 1935 with Dev's approval. Under its chairman James Delargy (Séamus Ó Duilearga), it embarked on the task of recovering as much as possible of the old rural culture of the country; Delargy was also the editor of the important folklore journal *Béaloideas,* founded in 1927, for its first forty-six years. Its motto, from John 6:12, could have been that of the Irish Free State, 'Colligite quae superaverunt fragmenta ne pereant' ('Gather up what fragments remain that none may be lost'). Douglas Hyde, who had relinquished his leadership of the Gaelic League in 1915 after it decided to support military measures to achieve national independence, returned to the political arena at Dev's instigation to become President in 1938, a dexterous manoeuvre on Dev's part. But his most ingenious recruit was folklore, or the memoir as the innovative form of folklore. It was accompanied by a hesitant, half-fearful recognition of film which was, anyway, too expensive and for which there was not any comparable body of expertise. The most famous of all storytellers chosen by the state as part of its ideological appeal, was Peig Sayers.

Sayers (1873–1958) was encouraged by Flower and another linguist and folklorist, Kenneth Jackson, to dictate her three autobiographical narratives, two to her son Mícheál Ó Gaoithín – *Peig* (1936) and *Beatha Pheig Sayers* (*The Life of Peig Sayers*, 1970) – and the third, *Machtnamh Seanamhná* (*Reflections of an Old Woman*, 1939), to Máire Ní Chinnéide. The first, *Peig*, was chosen as a text for the Leaving Certificate state examination and remained on the syllabus for almost sixty years. As a consequence, almost all the disputes about the language, its compulsory status in schools and for entrance to university, polarized around this book. In addition, the implicit endorsement by the state of the form of patriarchal society the memoir revealed aroused increasing protest, so much so that the Irish language became for many an emblem of coercion and regression. No book in Irish ever damaged the cause of the language revival so effectively as this one. Yet Peig was one of the finest of all storytellers, blessed with a greater repertoire of stories than any other individual, a signal contributor to the wealth of the National Folklore Archives. Her book had been under the spell of the state for so long that only when it was lifted in 1995, when it was taken off the syllabus, did the impact of her (written) work as a whole begin to be felt. Yet since she dictated and did not write her account of her own life, she is not in an important sense its author. Nor are those who recorded it. As a work on the national syllabus, we may say that its silent author was the state, its influence pervasive and deadly.[33]

As a consequence, the stoicism of the narrators of these memoirs, for which the state acted as the currency converter, did not translate effectively in the case of Peig. Yet it did, with some qualification, for Ó Criomthain and Ó Súilleabháin. The stoic resignation to God's will, in the Christian idiom, or national endurance in the political, or even – in George Thomson's case – as its historical version in ancient Greece, had the appeal of a noble confrontation with a universal fate. That dimension, salient in *Peig*, is what in her case became most derided. It was 'translated' by her captive student audience into a purblind peasant ignorance. Thus, annexed by the state as exemplary, *Peig* was polemically read for decades as an instance of the regression and boredom the state had unwittingly exposed as its presiding ethos. Flann O'Brien's *An Béal Bocht* (1941) / *The Poor Mouth* (1964) is a savage satire of the whole genre and of the mode of relentless lamentation indicated in its title. Its immediate target is *An t-Oileánach*; its recurrent theme of 'we'll never see the like again' became a deadly and scornful refrain. It made fun of the state policy of reviving Irish and suffocating almost everything else, including the language's real capacities. O'Brien's humour and satire cast a long shadow over the whole genre of the memoir and the mannerisms of proverbial wisdom that are common in oral traditions. Thus a telling source of amusement to him and his audience was the love affair between public discourse and the cliché, the decanted wisdom of the intellectually impoverished – and the drunk. Precisely because much of his work was journalism, the cliché's residence of choice, the medium was the message for O'Brien, as for Karl Kraus. The usual antidote to the cliché is the aphorism, but in O'Brien's case it was another cliché – and then another, nested within the first. The vulnerability of these memoirs to parody of this sort indicates how risky the whole venture was; getting to print from an oral tradition and becoming an ideal to counter modernity was a hazardous process of which *Peig* was a prominent victim. For all that, the ethical dimension, taken to include the courage and the dignity of a stoical outlook, was worth reaching for. The capture of the idea of universality is a key moment in any ideological formation, especially when it can be presented, simultaneously, as a fresh discovery and an ancient lore, the composite which the new state, as the embodiment of an ancient nation, wanted to claim as the blend of the historical and the timeless which was specific to it.

THERAPEUTIC REALISM

It would have been impossible for most people outside his own Parisian cénacle, in the period between the publication of *Ulysses* and Joyce's death, to believe that he, of all people, would ever become a singular example of literary and ethical heroism. Dispute and disrepute dominated the reception of his work; it now seems odd that *Ulysses* appeared in the same decade as *An t-Oileánach* and that both these Irish works have been taken to be – amidst much else – 'classic' instances of realism. For the outraged, it was not only the appalling sexual candour of Joyce that shocked but also his multiple violations of literary and social propriety, ominously related in their jolting way to photography and cinema. (Fritz Lang's *Metropolis* appeared in 1927, the same year as the final volume of Proust.) This sort of realism was seen as a relentless inventory, an encyclopaedic debauch. Early cinema was not criticized on similar grounds. It was a different matter when a more traditional art adapted new techniques, especially when they emphasized the crass or inhuman aspects of urban life. The animus against literary realism was not confined to newspapers. It retained political and cultural prestige within modernist and anti-modernist circles. The modernist epic *Ulysses* was taken to be a scandalous perversion of what epic had been and a demonstration of what modernism was – bereft of serenity or wisdom, stricken by incontinence in language and form. In Ireland, the modernist epic met its antithesis, the folk memoir. The dissonances of modernity were confronted with a formidable opponent, 'the concept of true or original or uncorrupted absolute human nature as opposed to history'.[34] Mikhail Bakhtin declares 'The world of the epic is the national heroic past, it is a world of "beginnings" and of "peak times" in the national history, a world of fathers and founders of families, a world of "firsts" and "bests".'[35]

In 1934, Dev and his cabinet attended the premiere of Robert Flaherty's *Man of Aran* in which the new medium of modernity commemorated the immemorial world of Ireland in the brilliant genre christened 'fictional documentary', a title which could plausibly include the Blasket memoirs as well. Flaherty was quite candid about the effects he wished to produce, whether these involved him in anachronisms or not. Therefore, it is not entirely to the point to say that shark hunting had long died out as a practice in the Aran islands.[36] That only tells us that the film, like all of Flaherty's 'documentaries', is very carefully staged to embody a struggle between the human person and the elemental, indifferent forces of nature. The immense seas that pound the cliffs and shores from the opening shot and the tiny currach with its human figures lifted by this moving wall of noise and energy need only the most basic story line to imprint their 'meaning'. However, Flaherty's film performs an additional function. It is about a heroic dying community indeed; but the world of Tiger King and his family is not entering upon a meaningless dissolution. Their world has an end (telos), not just an ending. The harpooning of the basking shark, the endless collection of seaweed to create a bed for a crop of potatoes, the sheer effort of daily existence all enhance that element of documentary realism that translates or converts into an epic register. Oddly, the realism is the the source of the therapeutic element in such works. It is when the quotidian is convertible into the immemorial that its curative, religious element is mobilized. All action, especially repeated action, is meaningful; the art of both this film and the Blasket memoirs is to slow down the regular pace of the day-to-day to the point where it becomes a ritual. The ritual, in its repetitive sameness, has become sacred, an appeasement of the Gods. Monotonous labour provides the basis for a sacred rite – the monotony remains but for the listener or reader, especially, the ritual element begins to predominate. This cinematic feature, especially its ritual-dramatic-mythic element, the musical signature that regularly identifies it, had already been noticed by George Thomson and became central to his 'Hellenization' of the Blaskets.

A THERAPEUTIC LANGUAGE

What might be the capacity of either English or Irish, or of a middle, interstitial language which is neither and both at the same time, to register the specific historical experience of the Irish people is a question almost as difficult to formulate as to answer. The critical works that addressed it most memorably are Thomas MacDonagh's *Literature in Ireland: Studies Irish and Anglo-Irish* (1916), Robin Flower's *The Irish Tradition* (1947), and Daniel Corkery's *Synge and Anglo-Irish Literature* (1931). The publication date of *The Irish Tradition* is a little misleading. Flower's work was in fact, as the Preface tells us, 'a selection he had put together of what he had already said or written on the subject on various occasions over a long period of years'. The central essay, Chapter V of the book, 'Ireland and Medieval Europe', had been given in 1927 as the John Rhys Memorial Lecture at the British Academy and published the following year. Ill health dogged Flower from 1930, delayed his translation of *An t-Oileánach* until 1937, and made him despair of ever writing a long-planned history of Irish literature. Much of the remaining chapters of the book were given as the Donnellan Lectures, delivered at Trinity College in 1938. So this book properly belongs to the period 1927–38.

THOMAS MACDONAGH

MacDonagh was dead within four months of his book's publication, shot by the British as a rebel leader. His political status has almost entirely obliterated the memory of his academic career as a teacher of English at University College, Dublin and his pursuit of what he called 'The Irish Mode' – a literature in two languages, Gaelic and Anglo-Irish. He wrote these studies before the summer of 1914.

> The present European wars have altered our outlook on many things, but as they have not altered the truth or the probability of what I have written here, I have not altered my words. As will be seen, I anticipated turbulence and change in the arts. These wars and their sequel may turn literature definitely into ways towards which I looked, confirming the promise of our high destiny here.[37]

MacDonagh regards the Irish language as having suffered a 'temporary abandonment' after the Famine. Although the Gaelic League had now brought the people back to it, he clearly regarded this revived Irish as somewhat artificial or mechanical. It was not from its committees and organization that he expected the new creative work in Irish to come. Here, as is inevitably the case with any discussion about revival, the condition to be revived is always beyond the reach of the revivers. They can only achieve an approximation. In the modern history of the Irish language this creates that characteristic structure of dissatisfaction with the present and more than usually intense apotheosis of the original, of the past, of the authentic which has an ultimately disheartening effect on all the serial efforts to sustain the process of revival or even the hope of survival. But MacDonagh's view in 1914–16 is sanguine.

> But above all we are fresh in language, which the most city-hating English lover of nature cannot be. We are the children of a race that, through need or choice, turned from Irish to English. We have now so well mastered this language of our adoption that we use it with a freshness and power that the English of these days rarely have. But now also we have begun to turn back to the old language, not old to us. The future poets of the country will probably be the sons and daughters of a generation that learned Irish as a strange tongue; the words and phrases of Irish will have a new wonder for them; the figures of speech will have all their first poetry.[38]

MacDonagh sees as a preliminary the need to distinguish the Irish Mode in both languages, especially in Anglo-Irish, which has a different acoustic from English and requires in its poetry a different metrical system, perhaps with the line rather than the foot as the basic unit. He explored the possibility of defining the metrical effect of a number of chosen poems to give substance to his notion of an Irish Mode (a composite inheritance of the intricate sound patterns of Gaelic metres, Anglo-Irish speech patterns, and folk songs) and thereby to replace the notorious vagueness of the 'Celtic Note', introduced by Matthew Arnold in his essay 'On the Study of Celtic Literature' (1867), which MacDonagh describes as 'largely a work of fiction'.[39] Flower makes a much more emphatic and sustained repudiation of the Arnoldian 'Celtic' and he, unlike MacDonagh, lived long enough to see in the Blaskets memoirs, as he believed, the modern incarnation of the genuine tradition of Irish letters in which 'the figures of speech will have all their first poetry'.[40] Flower's own position is as ambiguous as it is important. He is remembered best as a scholar, translator, collector, of refined judgement and of an indisputably English tradition which was itself undergoing a contemporary Christian (and antimodernist) revival. The Blaskets writings initially (that is, in the period *c.*1930–50) belong to that as much as to any Irish tradition.

DANIEL CORKERY

Corkery is the ideal ideologue; his search is for the essential and, for all that he owes to MacDonagh, his stance is that of the pioneer who, because he is the first, is ready to say that therefore he is a traveller in the realms of gold where no individual has gone before but where the community of race awaits him. The question is – even though he is writing in English – can any other Irish writer in English be admitted to that territory and be greeted as a native? The answer, tortuous in its reasoning, but blunt in its finality, is no. The ideology is in his style and syntax in which a laborious archaism passes itself off as profundity. For all the similarity of theme between him, MacDonagh, and Flower, he is far from them because of the ultimate dishonesty of the reasoning by which he justifies exclusion.

Corkery's book on Synge has one anxious question to ask. Why is Synge, for all his virtues, not a 'classic' writer? The answer is wrapped in a vocabulary and syntax that Dev might have envied but never emulated. Synge's defect, we learn, is that he was not fully a member of the community of the Aran Islands because he, like his class, has 'always been reared on an alien porridge'.[41] Yet his allegiance to Aran has made his work much more enduring than the rootless achievements of 'the Internationalists'. It is indeed 'almost as old-fashioned as that of Periclean Greece'. Synge is compared favourably with Shaw who is the quintessence of the shallow cosmopolite (like Yeats also). Terence MacSwiney, the Lord Mayor of Cork, who died on hunger strike, an exemplary nationalist, although 'not enamoured of certain of Synge's plays . . . saw that his work was rich in those qualities that literature cannot do without'. We find that these qualities 'give us respite from the vexing criss-cross of daily life'[42] – they offer therapy. Synge may not have the full serenity of the ancient Greeks, but he does provide a version of it. Moreover, through him, Corkery is enabled to distinguish weak from strong books. In 'weak books' the common idiom is replaced by bookish words. The more bookish writing is, the more easily is it translated, 'the more easily also will it shame-facedly slip away after a short time into the eternal silence'. Therefore, the fake ideal of a universal language that would do away with all the thorny problems of translation, is the very antithesis of the universal appeal of the 'common idiom' which is rooted in the local and stubbornly remains there.

> To have nationalism ruling the world is to have the natural . . . organised to stand in the way of International literature, just as languages do, languages themselves also being natural pieties.

As for Synge's work, 'wrought out in the ancient and natural way', it 'may be destined', he says, 'to exert on the world's literature such influence as a work of a classical nature cannot help doing'. But no further than that. Corkery's phrasing and syntax become more and more contorted, affecting to bear the weight of an argument while averring banalities and producing grand abstractions such as 'natural pieties' like rabbits out of a hat. A negative is being insinuated into the body of the prose but, to be effective, it has to have the same generic valency as all the positives about language, Greeks, 'classical nature', and the like. 'If universality be felt as wanting to his creations, therein is the cause.' For Synge's

> people, except those in *Riders to the Sea,* are inclined to be naturalistic rather than human, for it is human to practice inhibitions for the sake of ideas, to curb appetite by traditions, dreams, faiths well or ill-founded (if so we may put the matter under its most general aspect).[43]

Such sentences should be extracted and kept as specimens in a jar, 'if so we may put the matter'. What Corkery is saying, but trying not to appear to be saying, is that Synge does not quite make it into the classical pantheon because he does not recognize the need for censorship. Thus the censorship of the Free State finds its justification in classical Greece, human nature, etc. The abrupt appearance of 'naturalistic' as the antonym of 'human' is a reminder of earlier debates about the immorality of 'naturalism' (documentary realism) as a genre, when the names of Zola and George Moore, his scandalous Irish disciple, dominated the tirades of the 1890s on 'the modern novel'.

ROBIN FLOWER

In *The Irish Tradition,* Robin Flower tells the legend of Cenn Faelad son of Ailill and Betan, who suffered a head wound in battle and had the organ of forgetting struck out of him. He was carried to an abbot's house and compulsively began to write everything he knew down on slates. The legend is taken to be an account of how the recording of vernacular knowledge began – a heroic warrior in effect becoming a cleric, pagan becoming Christian.[44] Flower was intrigued by the passage from oral to written culture, especially as the first was pagan and the latter Christian.

Not everything historical is Christian but everything Christian is historical.

> The 7th century monks had oral pagan traditions, and Church material from Israel, Greece and Rome; they sought to blend both in the new writing, since it was imperative to give a validity to the oral tradition upon which they depended for the Irish events of their chronicle. How was this to be done? It has often been imagined ... if only an appropriate machinery could be devised and the wave-lengths of the innumerable periods of the past be established, we might listen in to history and eavesdrop upon all that part of action which is committed to the living voice ... Our Irish historians improved upon this idea: they brought the saints who were their warrants for history into a personal relation with those who had figured in past events, and fabled that their accounts were authenticated by the actual testimony and eye-witnesses and participants of the great deeds of the past ... Either the informant might be recalled from the dead, or by God's grace his life might be miraculously prolonged until the time of the saints and the coming of the written record.

Flower gives as one example of the recall from the dead the story of how Pope Gregory, Gregory Goldenmouth, brought the Emperor Trajan out of hell and baptised and blessed him. This is one variant of the story of the skull with a tongue (adapted by Yeats and in the talking head motif in Beckett); it is found in the Glossary of Cormac of the ninth century, in early commentary on Dante;[45] at either end of Aran island, Gríor Béal an Óir (Gregory Goldenmouth) is commemorated (his supposed tomb overlooking Gregory's Sound at one end, and at the other, a valley, hillock, and a terrace sloping into the sea called An Gríor, the Gregory). This hermit saint was said in the chronicles to have 'gnawed off his lower lip in a spasm of anguish over the sins of his early life ... or simply because he was hungry ... and a golden lip grew in its place'.[46] The conceit of the golden mouth or lip is a perfect image too, like the speaking skull, of the oral tradition being preserved in or replaced by the written. The shape-changers that engage in the heroic battles are also images of the person of knowledge in all its changeable forms; the dead are called in various shapes to bear witness to the truth of the heroic past and of its congruence with the Christian present. This is the full and copious world of epic deed and record. The secular and the religious dimensions are interfused, making the chronicles resonate with the sound of past and present, the goal of the 'principle of divarication, typical of medieval art between classical themes reproduced anachronistically and ancient images Christianized'.[47] Dialogues with the Dead was renewed as a literary genre with Fontenelle (*Nouveaux dialogues des morts*, 1683, dedicated to his Roman predecessor Lucian); Flower's image of the labyrinth of radio voices typically emphasizes the range of oral history – obviously by far the greater part of the past – 'that part of action which is committed to the living voice'. The act of listening to the storyteller is in part always an eavesdropping. So, on the Great Blasket, when an old man digging potatoes calls him over for conversation and then flawlessly recites to him Ossianic lays, Flower both hears and overhears the dead speak again in the voice of the living at this world's end which is also the end of a world:

> I listened spellbound and, as I listened, it came to me suddenly that there on the last inhabited piece of European land, looking out to the Atlantic horizon, I was hearing the oldest living tradition in the British Isles ... Tomorrow this too will be dead, and the world will be the poorer when this last shade of that which once was great has passed away. The voice ceased, and I awoke out of reverie as the old man said: 'I have kept you from your dinner with my tales of the *fianna*.' 'You have done well,' I said, 'for a tale is better than food,' and thanked him before we went our several ways.[48]

Flower, more than MacDonagh or Corkery, is at pains to distinguish his idea of the Irish Tradition from everything that 'Celtic' has meant in literary criticism since the days of Macpherson's *Ossian* and the later solecisms of Renan and Arnold, 'neither of whom, I believe, knew any Celtic language'.

> The concrete cast of language, the epigrammatic concision of speech, the pleasure in sharp, bright colour which we find everywhere in the best of the literature, is confused in the worst periods and examples by strange pedantries of rhetorical expansion ... But these [characteristics] ... are inherent in the very being of the language as a spoken tongue and cannot be carried over into translation. They are the extreme antithesis of the

> twilight vagueness which in popular criticism is often associated with the word 'Celtic'.[49]

This is the product of Flower's fascination with the transition from oral to written. No matter how it is done, the most basic characteristics, 'inherent in the very being of the language as a spoken tongue ... cannot be carried over into translation'. That loyalty to the spoken, as I have indicated, remains alive in Irish writing today, really a potent and paradoxical disclaimer of any kind of translation at all, not into any specific foreign language but into any *written* language at all. For there is no written language that does not have a spoken predecessor, even if the predecessor is 'created' by the act of writing. Flower, conscious of the contradictions in his own roles as translator and recorder, nevertheless presents these as inescapable, perhaps even constitutive features of the acts of memory which have created European culture in the ongoing exchanges between speaking, listening, recording. In Ireland's case the noise of the vulgarizing 'Celtic note', itself an example of the modern world's arrival, blurred the reception of Irish and, globally, all kinds of static polluted the atmosphere as the dread dawn of modernism broke. In his book of 1944, *The Western Island, or, The Great Blasket,* given initially by Flower in 1935 as the Lowell lectures in Boston, in a typical moment, a storyteller, filled with the ancient lore, complains that the traditional stories are being driven out of his head because his son is forever reading to him out of the newspaper; this jabbering of the ephemeral news drives tradition into forgetfulness. In Ireland, there is the double threat of the newspapers on one hand and on the other, the 'Celtic'-influenced ignoramuses who regard themselves as guardians of the language.

These are the ultimate target of Flann O'Brien's wrath in *The Poor Mouth.* To reduce the freshness of the original to the stale cliché of the contemporary is the standard and unavoidable sin in the Irish language world. Patrick Power, who translated *An Béal Bocht* into English, catches in his 'Translator's Preface' some of the impossible ironies that bedevil the translator: 'It is time that this book, which should have acted as a cauterization of the wounds inflicted on Gaelic Ireland by its official friends, might do its work in the second official language of Ireland. That it may do so is the translator's wish and hope.' O'Brien, in the guise of the

'Editor', closes the foreword to the 1964 edition, dated like the Foreword of the 1941 original, 'The Day of Doom', with these words: 'I recommend that this book be in every habitation and mansion where love for our country's traditions lives at this hour when, as Standish Hayes O'Grady says, "the day is drawing to a close and the sweet wee maternal tongue has almost ebbed".'[50]

Flower, as keeper of manuscripts in the British Museum, had continued Standish Hayes O'Grady's work on the catalogue of Irish manuscripts there. As product of his life's work, the vision of the monastic Ireland of the seventh to ninth centuries as the prelude to the European Middle Ages was created as a key element of the ancient nation's heritage and its rediscovery one of the cultural achievements of the new state, further enriched by the poetry of Austin Clarke in which that Ireland became the dynamic of his poetry, including the fierce reaction to the sexual oppressions of the time which Clarke contrasted with the candour of the early Irish sources. Flann O'Brien shared this view of the emancipated values implicit in the old language. Flower's scholarship, and his translations of Irish poems, *Love's Bitter-Sweet,* are of a piece with this; more, he is the source of this vision of Ireland. In scholarship, it culminates in Ludwig Bieler's *Ireland: Harbinger of the Middle Ages* of 1961. Yet, at the heart of his scholarly and imaginative venture, lay the Blaskets, already doomed by the time he died in 1946; as he had asked, his ashes were scattered on the Great Blasket.

Still, the 'medievalism' of the twenties and thirties was an English as well as an Irish phenomenon and Flower contributed to both. The rechristianizing of the genre of epic, the inclusion within it of myth and allegory as types of a 'human' and 'Christian' thinking, had as its base a belief in language as in itself a mode of creation, radical to any religious sense of the world, now under threat from the diabolic agencies of a culture that had, as a deliberate aim or policy, the impoverishment of language. 'All language proceeds from mythology and an "ancient unity" of meanings', declared Owen Barfield in *Poetic Diction,* his influential book of 1927. In the Preface to the second edition of the following year, he wrote:

> Of all the devices for dragooning the human spirit, the least clumsy is to procure its abortion in the womb of language; and we should recognise . . .

> that those ... who are driven by an impulse to reduce the specifically human to a mechanical or animal regularity, will continue to be increasingly irritated by the nature of the mother tongue and make it their point of attack.

The paranoid tone and front-loaded vocabulary (spirit, abortion, womb, animal, nature, mother) remain features of the English 'medievalism'. Flower's rhetoric never aspires to such aggression. Barfield's friendship with C. S. Lewis and J. R. R. Tolkien is well known; he was a member of the Inklings, the Oxford group that successfully, in literary criticism and in children's books, popularized the relationship between the 'modern world' and the past as a clash between the forces of Evil and the Good, an epic re-enactment of the ancient story. Flower's work belongs in this context; so too does the 'Blasket moment' in Irish writing.

GEORGE THOMSON

Two kinds of extinction throw their shadows across the Blaskets as a human habitation. One is the Great Famine (not to mention the periodic famines which were a feature of British rule in Ireland). The Blaskets re-enact the story of the nation's extinction, in hunger, emigration, and gradual abandonment of the language for the language of England and America. The other is the World Wars and the growing consciousness, to be confirmed in the Cold War, that the extinction of civilization itself had become a real possibility – not only in the cultural sense (for many that had already happened), but in the sheerly physical sense. Thus as an individual death is absorbed into the death of a small community, that of the community itself seems to merge with the imminent death of the 'Big World' beyond. From there had come a brief flare of prosperity to the island, with the rich debris of the *Lusitania* catastrophe and others. The re-enactment of the experiences of the Famine in the Blaskets, the loss of people and of language, actually operates as part of a vivifying ideology for the new state, the synecdoche of what it must overcome, the replacement of a policy of immiseration by one of preservation, the stoic endurance in the face of adversity, the teleological confidence of national and Christian convictions. It is a demonstration of the state's failure that the policy of preservation with respect to people and language was eventually replaced – as a substitute – by one of pious (if sporadic) conservation of parts of the built environment and of the natural habitat. It is also evident that, at least since the late sixties, the idea of preservation as a political policy has passed from right-wing to left-wing parties, emerging more and more from the latter as ecological warnings and demands, softened usually for easy mass consumption into the pulp of 'heritage'.

When George Thomson, a classicist from the University of Birmingham, came to the Blaskets in 1923 he turned the idea of an imminent extinction inside out and claimed to have found there, not the Free State, but a pre-state civilization of the kind Homer had known. His translation of *Fiche Bliain ag Fás* carried an Introductory Note by E. M. Forster (who must have known of this kind of 'discovery' before in India in Sir Henry Maine's apotheosis of the Indian village as the cradle of all civilization) in which Forster warns the reader of

> what a very odd document he [sic] has got hold of. He is about to read an account of neolithic civilisation from the inside. Synge and others have described it from the outside, and very sympathetically, but I know of no other instance where it has itself become vocal, and addressed modernity.[51]

Maine's thesis about the 'immemorial' Indian village community, introduced in 1871, wilted somewhat under a combined Indian and Irish readiness to attack imperial versions of property law precisely in the name of an immemorial communal ownership.[52]

Immemoriality could be taken too far. But not in Thomson's case. He was a classicist and a Marxist. He saw the poverty of the Blaskets (and Ireland) as an example of capitalist underdevelopment. The Blaskets had remained so wholly an archaic community that the typically capitalist-liberal notion of self-autonomy had never been known there. This lost communal world, he claimed in *An Blascaod a bhí* (1977; expanded version *The Blasket that Was*, 1982), immured in poverty by industrial capitalism, was in some respects 'medieval' and yet, because of its history, was even more like the 'pre-capitalist' world of Homer's ancient Greece than any other. In the Preface to the first edition of *Aeschylus and Athens*, Thomson acknowledges his debt

> to my friends the peasant-fishermen of the Blasket Island in West Kerry, who taught me . . . what it is like to live in a pre-capitalist society . . . and in general their traditions, especially their poetry, date from a time when social relations were profoundly different from those in which I have been brought up.[53]

Marx's sixth thesis on Feuerbach, a utopian vision when written in 1845 (and unknown to Thomson, since it was not published until 1924), expressed Marxism's rejection of liberal individualism: 'The human essence is no abstraction inherent in each individual. It is the *ensemble* of human relations.' The Blaskets were, at one and the same time, an image for the future as well as an image from the past. The cherishing of the communal life and the repudiation of individuality was both a conservative and nationalist, as well as a radical and collectivist political position. (The 'Conclusion' to Corkery's *The Hidden Ireland*, 1924, opens with an account of the absence of 'individuality' in ancient Greek sculpture.[54]) Thomson thought the 'idea' of the Blaskets could survive, but that the immiseration of the people should be ended. In the dialectic between 'the growing individuation of society' and the division of labour, 'the emotional and intellectual life of the people' in a modern society has been so deepened and enriched that, faced with the theatrical spectacle of a tragedy, for instance, the 'higher level of sublimation' they can achieve secures the endorsement of the established order. 'The emotional stresses set up by the class struggle are relieved by a spectacle in which they are sublimated as a conflict between man and God, or Fate, or Necessity.' When the behaviour of an Athenian audience is compared to that of a London theatre, the atmosphere of the latter is greatly subdued; 'but in the cinemas of the west of Ireland, where the spectators are peasants, the atmosphere is far more intense. At the critical moments of the plot, almost every face wears a terrified look and continuous sobbing may be heard. In this respect, an Athenian would undoubtedly have felt more at home in the west of Ireland than in the West End of London.'[55] Thomson's analysis of tragedy in Greece and of storytelling in Ireland is in each case an account of the social function of catharsis or purging by which the performance of the actor or storyteller revealed a patterned variation between solo virtuosity and communal, choric consensus that produced a therapeutic sense of relief in the audience.

He, like all visitors to the island in those decades, was fascinated by the speech, or perhaps more exactly, the conversational protocols of the islanders. He did not regard their flourishes, invocations of the deity, appeals to human experience, as routine additions that had become traditional and could even be regarded as immemorial in the sense of being proverbial or simply well-worn. Instead he heard these flourishes and the conduct of conversation in general as a participation in a ritual. The storyteller, a key figure in the shared life, is not the holder of a hidden, inscrutable essence; she is not conjugating as story a paraphrasable 'world view'; the role of memorization and of dramatic adaptation does not have the function of conveying this or any other comparable type of information. Pascal Boyer pointed out that 'if traditions were about world views, the study of traditional discourse should have no difficulty in uncovering them. It turns out that ... traditions ... cannot be linked to underlying conceptions without systematically distorting the data.'[56] Thus, formal and ritual features are primary, not secondary. Rites are repeated exactly so that their specific meaning is both expressed and preserved in the repetition. There is no target language into which to translate them. It is difficult to say how much of this Thomson drew from the researches and writings of the 'Cambridge school' of anthropology, founded by Jane Harrison. Richard Seaford regards his work as its 'culmination'.[57] Certainly, Harrison's *Ancient Art and Ritual* (1913) helped create the ethnographic modernism that began seriously to undermine the accepted romantic conception of popular or epic poetry as a product of folk genius.[58] Thomson's disavowal of that distinguishes his notion of 'community' from most writings on the Blaskets. But the notion that myth is founded on ritual – Harrison's central point – enabled Thomson's concentration on the poetry and speech and, of course, on the Irish language of the Blaskets people. The purity of the genre of storytelling (in particular that of Peig Sayers) depended on the enforced backwardness of the conditions of the islanders; but it was also for him a revelation of the origins of European civilization, being re-enacted here at its ending.

He was consistent in urging that this form of 'backwardness' be preserved while a form of economic development compatible with it be discovered or achieved by the new Irish state. And it became part of his life's work to canvass for the economic help that they needed (and didn't get) and the cultural help the language needed to survive.

Yet there is inevitably a sense in which he reified this community as an object to be understood; this outsider gained through it what he considered to be an insider's view of the ancient Greek community and this in part enabled his powerful study of ancient Greece in which he reproduces the idea of an enormous rift between a 'medieval' and a 'renaissance' Greece. Perhaps more to the point, the vision of the tragedies of Aeschylus as marking the point of final transition in the evolutionary process from a tribal to a state culture is clearly indebted to Thomson's understanding of the Blaskets. They are integrated into Thomson's own philosophy of history which pivots (as do many modernist accounts of the emergence of modernism itself) on the notion of a break, usually catastrophic, in which one ancient civilization ends and another, barbaric in its energy, appears. That 'break' or moment of transition for him began with his first visit to the islands. But the ethnographic riddle, insider or outsider, was not solved by his becoming more of an insider than almost any outsider could be. It seems proper that E. M. Forster wrote the Introductory Note to his translation of *Twenty Years A-Growing*. His *A Passage to India* was as problematical as Thomson's passage to the Blaskets. The telling sense of slight anomaly, Ireland as Greece, touchingly appears in Thomson's act of dedicating his great edition of the *Oresteia* (1938) of Aeschylus to his friend Maurice O'Sullivan. He learned modern Greek as he learned modern Irish so that he could know the continuities of both cultures; it was 'in the cultural unconscious of peasants and fishermen that he discovered the survival of ancient cults and practices'.[59] In both cases, however, and more particularly in the Irish case, his belief in continuity was provoked by the simultaneous and unavoidable sense of an ending. He could hardly have imagined the disappearance of that community into Springfield, Massachusetts, the world, not of the Greek Homer, but of Homer Simpson.

NOTES

1. Peter Alexander Meyers, *Civic War and the Corruption of the Citizen* (University of Chicago Press, 2008), 10.
2. Ibid., 107.
3. For a review of books on the *Lusitania*, see David Reynolds, 'Too Proud to Fight', *London Review of Books*, 24 (23 November 2002), 29–31; Philippe Masson, *Les Naufrageurs du Lusitania et la guerre de l'ombre* (Paris: Albin Michel, 2000); Raymond Hitchcock, *Attack the Lusitania* (London: St Martin's Press, 1980), a novel in which Churchill and naval intelligence decide to sink the ship and say the Germans did it.
4. Marcel Proust, *In Search of Lost Time*, vol. VI: *Finding Time Again*, trans. Ian Patterson (London: Penguin, 2002), 80–1.
5. Elias Canetti, *The Conscience of Words* (New York: Seabury Press, 1979), 32.
6. Nicolette Gullace, 'Friendly Aliens and Enemies: Fictive Communities and the *Lusitania* Riots of 1915', *Journal of Social History*, 39/2 (Winter 2005), 345–67.
7. Proust, *Finding Time Again*, 35.
8. Unsurprisingly, it was much used by Charles Maurras; see *La vie et l'œuvre de Charles Maurras*, 'L'Allemagne et nous', http://maurras.net/texts/169.html.
9. Sebastiano Timpanaro, *The Freudian Slip: Psychoanalysis and Textual Criticism* (London: Verso, 1976), 144, 146.
10. Ibid., 224.
11. Ibid., 222.
12. Proust, *Finding Time Again*, 16.
13. Theodor Adorno, *Philosophy of Modern Music* (1948), trans. Anne G. Mitchell and Wesley V. Blomster (London: Sheed and Ward, 1987), 133.
14. See Carl Schmitt, *The Nomos of the Earth in the International Law of the Jus publicum Europaeum* (1950), trans. G. L. Ulmen (New York: Telos Press, 2005), 314.
15. Ibid., 315, 307.
16. Quoted in Danilo Zolo, *Invoking Humanity: War, Law and Global Order* (London: Continuum, 2002), 87.
17. Muiris Ó Súilleabháin, *Twenty Years A-Growing*, trans. Moya Llewelyn Davies and George Thomson (1933; London: Oxford University Press, 1953), 140.
18. Ibid., 142.
19. Ibid.,143.
20. Ibid., 146, 145.
21. Jimmy Deenihan, minister for arts, heritage and the gaeltacht, on 26 April 2012, welcomed the gift to the state by Mr Greg Bemis, owner of the wreck of the *Lusitania*, of a number of important artefacts recovered from the ship.
22. Tomás Ó Crohan, *The Islandman* (1929), trans. Robin Flower (Oxford University Press, 1937), 244.
23. W. G. Runciman, *The Theory of Cultural and Social Selection* (Cambridge University Press, 2009), 191.

24. Marc Bloch, *The Historian's Craft*, trans. Peter Putnam (1949; Manchester University Press, 2012), 72.
25. See for example, Charles Maurras, 'Vingt-cinq ans de monarchisme', in *Œuvres capitales: essais politiques* (1924; Paris: Flammarion, 1954), 456, 506.
26. Jean-Jacques Rousseau, *Du contrat social*, Book I (1762), Chapter V, par. 2; 'Of the Social Contract', in *The Political Writings of Jean-Jacques Rousseau*, ed. C. E. Vaughan, 2 vols. (Oxford: Basil Blackwell, 1962), vol. II, 31: 'l'acte par lequel un peuple est un peuple; car cet acte . . . est le vrai fondement de société'.
27. Gilles Deleuze, 'Literature and Life', trans. Daniel W. Smith and Michael A. Greco, *Critical Inquiry*, 23/2 (Winter 1997), 225–30 (at 229). For the present purpose, I am taking this essay rather than the book he co-authored with Félix Guattari, *Kafka: Towards a Minor Literature*, trans. Dana Pollen (1975; Minneapolis: University of Minnesota Press, 1992), as the best account of his thinking on these matters.
28. Deleuze, 'Literature and Life', 228, 229. See also, Ronald Bogue 'Minor Writing and Minor Literature', *symploké*, 5/1–2 (1997), 99–118.
29. See Christopher Prendergast, 'Negotiating World Literature', *New Left Review*, 8 (March/April 2001), 100–21; Stanley Corngold, 'Kafka and the Dialect of Minor Literatures', *College Literature*, 21/10 (February 1994), 89–101.
30. Flower, 'Foreword', *The Islandman*, x.
31. Eibhlis Ní Shuilleabháin, *Letters from the Great Blasket* (Dublin and Cork: Mercier Press, 1978), 83.
32. Seán Ó Coileáin, Introduction to *Letters from the Great Blasket*, 12.
33. *Peig: The Autobiography of Peig Sayers of the Great Blasket Island*, trans. Bryan MacMahon (Dublin: Talbot Press, 1974); John Eastlake, 'The (Original) Islandman? Examining the Origin in Blasket Autobiography', in Nessa Cronin, Seán Crosson, and John Eastlake (eds.), *Anáil an Bhéil Beo: Orality and Modern Irish Culture* (Newcastle-upon-Tyne: Cambridge Scholars, 2009), 241–9; Angela Bourke et al. (eds.), *The Field Day Anthology of Irish Writing*, vol. IV: *Irish Women's Writing and Traditions* (Cork University Press, 2002): Angela Bourke, 'Oral Traditions', 1191–8; 'Life Stories', 1198; Éilís Ní Dhuibhne, 'International Folktales', 1214–18; Patricia Lysaght, 'Tá an seana-shaol imithe go maith: The Changing Folk Narrative Environment in Ireland', *Proceedings of the International Society for Folk Narrative Research* (Mysore, India, 1999), 19–37; Patricia Coughlan, 'Rereading Peig Sayers: Women's Autobiography, Social History and Narrative Art', in Patricia Boyle Haberstroh and Christine St Peter (eds.), *Opening the Field: Irish Women: Texts and Contexts* (Cork University Press, 2007), 58–73; Lillis Ó Laoire, 'Augmenting Memory, Dispelling Amnesia', *Dublin Review of Books*, 17 (Spring 2011).
34. Erich Auerbach, 'Vico and Aesthetic Historism', in *Scenes from the Drama of European Literature* (1959; Minneapolis: University of Minnesota Press, 1984), 184.
35. Mikhail Bakhtin, 'Epic and Novel', in *The Dialogic Imagination: Four Essays*, ed. Michael Holquist, trans. Caryl Emerson and Michael Holquist (Austin: University of Texas Press, 1981), 13.

36. Among the first to say this was R. Lloyd Praeger, *The Way that I Went* (1937; Dublin: Figgis, 1997), 153: 'Before the days of petroleum, the islanders of the west coast hunted them [basking sharks] for the sake of the oil contained in the liver, which furnished many a house with its only source of light – a practice resurrected by Robert Flaherty to add picturesqueness to his film *Man of Aran* a few years ago, but belonging in fact to a bygone time.' For commentary on the film, see Luke Gibbons, 'Romanticism, Realism and Irish Cinema', in Kevin Rockett, Luke Gibbons, and John Hill (eds.), *Cinema and Ireland* (London: Routledge, 1987), 200–3.
37. Thomas MacDonagh, *Literature in Ireland: Studies Irish and Anglo-Irish* (Dublin: Talbot Press, 1916), ix.
38. Ibid., 169.
39. Ibid., 55.
40. Ibid., 169.
41. Daniel Corkery, *Synge and Anglo-Irish Literature* (1931; Cork University Press, 1966), 240.
42. Ibid., 235.
43. Ibid., 237–9.
44. Robin Flower, *The Irish Tradition* (Oxford University Press, 1947), 10–11.
45. Ibid., 6–7.
46. Tim Robinson, *Stones of Aran: Pilgrimage* (Harmondsworth: Penguin, 1990), 22.
47. Carlo Ginzburg, *Threads and Traces: True, False, Fictive*, trans. Anne C. Tedeschi and John Tedeschi (Berkeley: University of California Press, 2012), 186, 152–3.
48. Flower, *Irish Tradition*, 105–6.
49. Ibid., 110–11.
50. Flann O'Brien, *An Béal Bocht/The Poor Mouth*, trans. Patrick Power (1941; London: Paladin Press, 1988), 6, 9.
51. Ó Súilleabháin, *Twenty Years A-Growing*, 5.
52. See Henry Maine, *Village Communities in East and West* (London: John Murray, 1871); *The Effects of Observation on India in Modern European Thought* (London: John Murray, 1875); Thomas R. Metcalf, *Ideologies of the Raj* (Cambridge University Press, 1995), 66–159; Mahmood Mamdani, 'What is a Tribe?', *London Review of Books*, 34/17 (September 2012), 20–2.
53. George Thomson, *Aeschylus and Athens: A Study in the Social Origins of Drama* (London: Lawrence & Wishart, 1941), vii. The Preface is dated 'September, 1940'.
54. Daniel Corkery, *The Hidden Ireland* (Dublin: Gill, 1925), 302–4.
55. Thomson, *Aeschylus and Athens*, 380–3.
56. Pascal Boyer, *Tradition, Truth and Communication* (Cambridge University Press, 1992), 107. Boyer's title is Henry Luce Professor of Individual and Collective Memory.
57. Richard Seaford, 'George Thomson and Ancient Greece', *Classics Ireland*, 4 (1997), 121–33 (at 131); on Thomson, Greece, and Ireland, see also J. V. Luce, 'Homeric Qualities in the Life and Literature of the Great

Blasket Island', *Greece and Rome,* Second Series, 16/2 (1969), 151–68; Seán Ó Lúing, 'George Thomson', *Classics Ireland,* 3 (1996), 141–62.

58. See Carey J. Snyder, *British Fiction and Cross-Cultural Encounters: Ethnographic Modernism from Wells to Woolf* (New York: Palgrave Macmillan, 2008). See also Diarmuid Ó Giolláin, *Locating Irish Folklore: Tradition, Modernity, Identity* (Cork University Press, 2000).
59. Dimitris Tziovas, 'George Thomson and the Dialectics of Hellenism', *Byzantine and Modern Greek Studies,* 13 (1989), 296–305 (at 303).

Index